YEAR B   1994

workbook
FOR LECTORS AND GOSPEL READERS

Aelred Rosser

LITURGY TRAINING PUBLICATIONS

WORKBOOK FOR LECTORS AND GOSPEL READERS 1994. Copyright ©1993, Archdiocese of Chicago. All rights reserved.

Liturgy Training Publications
1800 North Hermitage Avenue
Chicago IL 60622-1101
Order phone: 1-800-933-1800
FAX: 1-800-933-7094

Editor: Elizabeth Hoffman
Editorial assistance: Jerry Reedy
Interior art: Steve Erspamer
Cover art: Barbara Simcoe
Cover design: Ana M. Aguilar-Islas
Book design: Jane Kremsreiter
Layout: Jill Smith
Typesetting: James Mellody-Pizzato

Printed in the United States of America.

ISBN 0-929650-96-4
CL94

CONTENTS

The Author

Aelred Rosser has been teaching communication arts for 25 years, including courses in public speaking, theater and writing. He has conducted lector workshops at parishes nationwide. He also is a lyricist whose religious and scriptural verse has been published by GIA Publications and The Liturgical Press. He received his liturgical and theological formation at Conception Abbey, Conception, Missouri, and holds a PhD in rhetoric from the University of Southern California.

Dedication

To Liturgy Training Publications, whose commitment to efficacious worship speaks for itself; and to the monks of Conception Abbey, whose loving support of the author of this book has given it birth.
—Aelred Rosser

Acknowledgments

Many thanks to Barbara E. Bowe, RSCJ, and Mark R. Francis, CSV, both of Catholic Theological Union in Chicago, for their constructive comments on the 1993 edition of the *Workbook*. Their suggestions have been incorporated in this edition.

PREFACE

As ministers of the word we are John the Baptist, proclaiming again and again, "Prepare the way of the Lord!" We are the herald's voice in the desert crying, "Make for the Lord a straight path in your heart." Our ministry—performed well—fills in the valleys and lowers the hills so that the word can make its way more easily into the lives of all who have ears to hear. Isaiah the prophet says of us as he said of John, "I am sending my messenger." And, as did John, we say of ourselves, "I must decrease; Christ must increase." In other words, an important part of our ministry, while we are *preparing the way,* is to *get out of the way.*

All good ministry is humble ministry—but certainly not timid or lukewarm. Imagine describing John the Baptist as "timid"! No, we approach our service boldly. The purpose of the book you hold in your hands is to help you become a good servant, a good prophet ("one who speaks on behalf of God"), another John the Baptist.

Blessings on your ministry!
Aelred Rosser

The Word of God Is Alive with Power

There are Christian communities "of the word" and Christian communities "of the sacrament" (meaning the meal of the eucharist). But many Christian communities are regaining a sense of themselves as communities "of word *and* sacrament." The Catholic community began to regain this balance when Vatican II resolved to "open the riches of sacred scripture more fully" (*Constitution on the Sacred Liturgy* [CSL], #51). The result is that we are realizing again the power of God's word, a sacramental power: It effects what it signifies; it does what it says!

Those who proclaim the word of God in the assembly will determine, in large part, how soon we regain a truly profound love for the Bible and its power to sanctify us. We really do believe that when the word of God is proclaimed in the liturgy, far more than a history lesson is involved. The loving and healing movement of God through history is reenacted, made present *now*. God's promises to us are fulfilled in our hearing.

Those are daunting words! The church is teaching several things:

1 ▪ *The lector's function is genuinely liturgical.* This means that we are more than "priests' helpers" when we serve as lectors. We are ministers who determine, in large part, whether or not the liturgy builds up faith among the People of God.

2 ▪ *We have a responsibility to discharge with sincere piety and decorum.* We have more than a "duty," even more than a "privilege," and the People of God rightly expect much of us.

3 ▪ *Training and formation are necessary for those who proclaim the scriptures at the liturgy.* Reading at the liturgy requires a very special kind of expertise, different in many ways from what is required for other kinds of public speaking. Even (and perhaps especially) those who are effective public communicators in other arenas need training and formation to absorb the spirit of the liturgy and to be able to express that spirit well.

4 ▪ And most daunting of all: *It is Christ himself who speaks when the holy scriptures are read in the church.* This bold assertion is more than a pretty thought, and it requires of us nothing less than conversion. To *be* Christ at the lectern or in the pulpit is to proclaim the word with universal appeal. A difficult challenge, but none more noble!

The Ministry of the Reader

Of readers at the liturgy, Vatican II had this to say: *"[They] exercise a genuine liturgical function. They ought, therefore, to discharge their office with the sincere piety and decorum demanded by so exalted a ministry and rightly expected of them by God's people. Consequently they must all be imbued with the spirit of the liturgy . . . and they must be trained to perform their functions in a correct and orderly manner"* (CSL, #29).

And again: *"Christ is present in his word since it is he himself who speaks when the holy scriptures are read in the church"* (CSL, #7).

Elements of Liturgical Proclamation of the Word: *Who, What, When, Where, Why, How.*

We recognize the above words as questions—questions used by news reporters to cover a story thoroughly. They can be used by anyone to look closely at any act or situation. For our purposes, the *Who* is you, the reader.

The *What* is the act of reading the word itself, the printed text that you communicate through the miracle of human speech.

The *When* reminds us not only that liturgies are celebrated at different times of the day, but on different kinds of occasions: Sunday Masses, weddings, funerals, communion services, and so forth.

The *Where* question concerns itself with the liturgical environment—a very important consideration. Your bearing and attitude as a reader help to determine whether a suitable environment for your hearers is created. And just as important: The physical environment in which you read can enhance or inhibit the proclamation.

The *Why* may seem obvious, but ask yourself seriously why the church reads the scriptures aloud in the assembly. The *General Instruction of the Roman Missal*, a document that discusses how and why we celebrate Mass, gives an answer: "In the readings, God speaks to his people of the mystery of salvation and nourishes their spirit; Christ is present through his word" (#33). Proclaiming the word in the assembly gives God's love a voice. It provides food for the hungry spirit. It makes the risen Christ present. What better reasons for celebration?

Finally, the question most readers want answered first: *How?* How do I proclaim the word effectively? The entire range of human communication skills comes into play, as well as those considerations that make the liturgical reader's goal unique.

The news reporter's questions reveal the essential elements of the situation in which you exercise your ministry as reader:

Who?	Reader
What?	Proclaiming Sacred Scripture
When?	Time and Occasion
Where?	Liturgical Environment
Why?	To Give God's Love a Voice
How?	Communication Skills

Who Are You, the Minister of the Word?

As a public reader of scripture you are truly a minister—in every sense of the word. You comfort, you challenge, you encourage, you rebuke, you rejoice with those who rejoice, and you weep with those who weep. Your ministry is a sign of God's presence in the world. As a minister, then, your task is very different from that of other public speakers. Yes, there are similarities and they are fairly obvious. You can profit from a study of the techniques of effective public communicators. The differences may not be so obvious. The setting, the subject matter and the purpose of liturgical proclamation are of such profound and universal significance that other arenas of public

on. But none of these seems as appropriate as "proclaiming" when God's word is the text. After all, a proclamation is a text of special importance that deserves special treatment and attention.

OPENINGS AND CLOSINGS. Every reading from the Bible at liturgy begins with a ritual address to the assembly, "A reading from . . . ," and ends with a ritual dialogue, "The word [gospel] of the Lord," and "Thanks be to God" or "Praise to you, Lord Jesus Christ." This, in itself, gives us a clue that something is happening that is different from a newscast, a storytelling session or a theater piece. We realize immediately that a different situation prevails. That's why the opening and closing words should not be altered or elaborated on. To do so is to distract the assembly and inhibit their ability to respond enthusiastically. For example, to end with something like, "And this, my brothers and sisters, is the word of the Lord," is

...ord

..."Lord."

...anguage we

...t from everyday

...t from everyday activ-

...else, something we do, not

...And the kind of language we use in

...often language that *does something*, not

...that *tells something*.

...language specialists know well that language has more than one purpose. We can use it to convey information ("The opening hymn is on page 364") or to accomplish an action (" I forgive you all your sins"). Sometimes the words we use have little to do with the meaning we want to convey. When we are being introduced, for instance, and we say "How do you do?" we don't expect our new acquaintances to answer the question! If they respond with "How do I do *what?*", we might wonder whether the meeting is a happy one! "How do you do?" is an accepted ritual expression that doesn't mean literally "How do you do?" It is simply courteous behavior.

So what's the difference between "This is the word of the Lord" and "The word of the Lord"? A great deal! From a grammatical point of view, "This" (a demonstrative pronoun) and "is" (a verb) make the sentence more like the language we use to tell something rather than to do something. At this point in the liturgy we are doing something—celebrating the word of God as it still rings in our ears. "The word of the Lord" is more like a trumpet blast than a piece of information. It is the kind of language we use when we want our words to mean more than meets the ear. Our response is an exalted piece of ritual language too: "Thanks be to God."

There are other examples of such language in the liturgy. The closest parallel to "The word of the Lord" is what we hear when we receive holy communion: "The body of Christ." The communion minister is not simply telling us what we are receiving; the words are not "This is the body of Christ." No, the minister is doing something—celebrating the faith you have in this sacrament. And so are you when you reply, "Amen." So, this little change in the liturgy is not so little after all. It reminds us that liturgy is not a classroom. It is not a gathering where people tell each other things they already know. It is a community that does something very special together. The language we use echoes our purpose for being there.

BE INVOLVED WITH THE TEXT. Remember that a certain degree of formality and restraint must characterize your ministry as a reader. You need not sound cold or distant, of course. And your energy level should be high. The challenge, however, is to communicate a degree of humility that places the assembly's attention on the text and not on yourself. The best way to ensure the assembly's involvement in the text is to become genuinely involved in the text yourself.

All of sacred scripture is written in exalted language. Yes, there are a few contemporary translations that lean toward "folksy," almost "cutesy," diction. These invariably trivialize the message—as well as the assembly. Avoid them. Likewise, there are some readers (especially priests, I'm afraid) who feel obliged to recast the biblical texts in a more contemporary idiom. The intention, of course, is to make the Bible warmer, more intimate, more accessible. The effect, however, is to trivialize both text and hearer—and, inevitably, to draw attention to the reader.

THE BIBLE IS LITERATURE. The Bible is a collection of many different kinds of literature: narratives (stories), poetry, sermons, parables, allegories, hymns and so on. Your instincts will tell you that different kinds of literature require different treatments. Trust your instincts, but avoid stereotypes. There is no reason to imitate bad Shakespearean actors when reading poetry, or Mother Goose when reading a story.

There is a very important reason for recognizing and respecting the different literary styles in the Bible: The writer's message is told in a particular way (literary form) because the writer is making a particular point. The choice of style is not arbitrary. A classic example, of course, is the poetry of Genesis and the accounts of creation. If we forget that the writer's purpose is to show that God is the origin and the sustaining power of all that

exists, we could repeat the mistake of trying to understand the poetic text literally. Knowing that there are two accounts of creation in Genesis—which do not agree—should be enough to convince us that the authors were not concerned with scientific data. Poetry is usually not the style of choice for scientists.

Jesus' parables are concerned with spiritual or moral lessons. If we get lost in the details of a parable, we will surely miss its larger purpose. Events that are described in miraculous terms (such as the feeding of the multitude with five loaves and two fishes) may or may not be interpreted as "breaking the laws of nature." But the author's larger point must not be missed: God's provident love will not be thwarted—by natural or supernatural agents.

In addition to literary styles, there are many literary devices employed in the Bible—parallelism, alliteration, onomatopoeia. The careful and attentive reader will exploit these devices effectively without calling undue attention to them. Literary devices, after all, like choices of literary form, are simply ways to make an idea or message more memorable. If they draw attention to themselves, and away from the message, they are ineffective.

Those who use this workbook carefully will find that the margin notes point out literary styles or devices when attention to them is particularly important. Lectors who take their ministry seriously will soon find themselves developing a sixth sense regarding literary form. There can be no better guarantee that the text will be treated with respect and proclaimed effectively.

INCLUSIVE LANGUAGE. There is one contemporary issue with biblical texts that deserves very special attention: inclusive language. Translations of the Bible still lag behind our sensitivity to language that implies the exclusion of women or a prejudice against certain peoples. Progress is being made in this regard. And we must further it. The New Revised Standard Version of the Bible (NRSV) has been approved by the United States bishops for liturgical use, but does not yet exist in a lectionary form approved by them. It carefully addresses inclusive language for human beings. In the margin notes throughout this workbook, there are recommendations for substituting words or phrases from the NRSV for words or phrases that are exclusive in the current lectionary translation (based on the *New American Bible.*) These will be helpful in settings where the scripture is proclaimed apart from the liturgy. Changing the language will require special effort on your part. Strive for a balance between drawing too much attention to the issue itself (and therefore away from the message of the text) and offending the assembly with language that excludes many of them.

To keep our wits about us in the midst of the inclusive language issue, there are several things to remember. First, the English language is biased toward the masculine form. Second, both testaments of the Bible were

composed in cultures that were strongly patriarchal. This explains, in part at least, why the masculine form is almost always used in reference to God. Third, most existing English translations, themselves being culture-bound, reflect the bias of the language—often to the point of actually distorting the original language. The classic example is the Greek word *anthropoi.* Greek dictionaries define this word as "human beings," yet it is often rendered "men."

As a lector, you may find that using inclusive language may not sit well with some who hear it. You may be approached by a member of the assembly and dressed down for changing the text. If this should happen, assume that the person is expressing a genuine concern about something he or she perceives as frivolous or disrespectful treatment of the sacred texts. It is a valid concern. But it must be balanced by an equally valid concern on your part that many in the assembly feel disenfranchised by language that excludes them. Though you may not wish to defend yourself with the observations in the preceding paragraphs, you can at least assure the concerned worshiper that you have every respect for the Bible text and that the inclusive form you chose comes from the NRSV—a translation that has been approved by the bishops.

When? The Day, the Hour, the Occasion
Different times of the day and the year, as well as different occasions, require adjustments for an effective proclamation of the word. Readers at Masses with children perform their ministry differently from readers at large Sunday assemblies composed mostly of adults. And readers in a tiny chapel do not read quite the same as those who perform their ministry in cavernous cathedrals.

Obviously, we are speaking here of sensitivity to time, place and occasion. Assess each situation carefully, and adjust your manner of reading so that it respects those particular circumstances.

Where? The Environment for the Ministry of the Word

Consider the special environment in which our ministry takes place. And consider how much our ministry depends on its environment to be effective. We minister in the midst of the assembly—that particular group of God's people who have come together to celebrate and renew the gift of faith. What a wonderful mixture of lives comes together at the liturgy—and for the purpose of worshiping God and demonstrating mutual love and unity of faith!

In such gatherings, everything depends on everything else if the purpose of the gathering is to be fulfilled. That's why ministers of the word must see themselves as part of a team: assembly, servers, presider, readers, maintenance engineers, communion ministers, ushers, song leaders, musicians, sacristans, decorators—and the list goes on. All of these serve one common goal: to provide a setting in which to worship God and where faith and love can be celebrated and grow.

The practical considerations are legion: arrangement of the space and the furnishings, the public address system, lighting, liturgical books, missalettes/worship aids, seating of latecomers, liturgical "pace," and so on. These will differ from assembly to assembly and according to the local situation. The point here is to take these considerations seriously, for they do affect the celebration of the Word—for good or ill.

The issue of missalettes deserves special mention. Ideally, there should be no need or desire on the part of the assembly to use a printed text of the readings. (The obvious exception being persons who are hearing impaired.) The sacramental nature of the act of proclamation (bringing the printed word to life through the human voice) is completed by the act of hearing the word proclaimed. Those who say they get more out of the text by reading along with the lector probably have not experienced effective lectors! In assemblies served by excellent lectors, the use of missalettes declines sharply. Whatever needs to be done to enhance the experience of "hearing the word proclaimed well" (lector formation, public address system, building acoustics) should be attended to vigorously.

Why? To Be God's Voice

The word will achieve its purpose when we hear God speaking the good news, when our faith is nourished, and when we are led into the celebration of Christ's presence. Yes, the word of God *does* something: it teaches us, it nourishes us, and it makes the transforming presence of Christ real to us. Hearing the scriptures actually transforms us, makes us holy, just as receiving the sacrament of the eucharist does. Recall the well-known saying of Jesus: "Happy are those who hear the word of God and keep it." The very act of "hearing" the word is part of the sanctifying process. "Hearing" the word is the prelude to

"keeping it" well. The reader's ultimate purpose is to enable people to "hear the word of God and keep it."

The *purpose* of reading aloud at the liturgy is to present to the assembly a sacred text in its *intellectual*, *emotional* and *aesthetic* entirety. This definition is adapted from a writer (Charlotte Lee), whose works on oral interpretation are widely used in public speaking classes. It has been adapted because of the special nature of liturgical proclamation.

Presentation, not *interpretation*. The point here is that the word "interpretation" has connotations for us more proper to the homily or sermon than to Bible texts that are read aloud. Our task as readers is to *present* what is written rather than to *interpret* it. More about this later; for now we simply remind ourselves that "universal appeal" requires as much objectivity in our ministry as humanly possible. For the liturgical reader, anything like reenactment or idiosyncratic interpretation is inappropriate. It anchors the word to particular notions—instead of allowing the word to work its "universal appeal."

Intellectual entirety: the *meaning* of the text. The meaning of Bible texts is often subtle and elusive. Remember that old saying, "East is East and West is West and ne'er the twain shall meet"? Well, the Bible is the word of God—as recorded by people of the East (the Middle East, to be exact). For us Westerners, this presents a real challenge. We tend to be more rational, less intuitive, more literal and less poetic. An example: When Jesus says, "offer no resistance to injury," or "turn the other cheek," he is employing very dramatic language to describe what is required of his followers. A literal interpretation of this advice would not be conceivable to the Eastern mind. Nor would they think Jesus is talking crazy. They would see in Jesus' words the challenge to change—to be radically different—but would not for a moment think they were being asked to tolerate deliberate physical abuse. Discovering and communicating the *meaning* of sacred scripture is not easy; we need to rely on more than the words themselves. Those who devote their lives to the study of the Bible are our greatest helpers toward this part of our goal. Thus the work of scripture scholars is offered in this book, in the form of the commentary that accompanies each reading.

Emotional entirety: the *feeling* of the text. Bible readings are filled with emotion. In fact, that may be why so many readings cause us discomfort as we imagine ourselves proclaiming them aloud. If this is the case, we need to relax a bit and realize that our ministry does not involve "acting out" or "imitating" the emotional voices in the Bible. That must be done in the hearts of the hearers.

This is not to say that our reading must be cold or lifeless. Far from it! We must communicate the feeling of

the text with sensitivity, warmth—and restraint. The liturgy is a symbolic and universally appealing celebration of our faith, not a staged reenactment of salvation history. As ministers of the word, we are readers, not actors. And we must not usurp the experience of the assembly by forcing upon them a limited and personal rendering of the text.

Aesthetic entirety: a difficult term, but we can understand it as the "beauty" of the text. The minister of the word encounters readings of many different kinds: poems, stories, parables, hymns, letters, arguments, scoldings, visions, and so on. But in each case, there is beauty—the beauty of "truth" (even if it's the "painful truth"), the beauty of "reason," the beauty of "goodness," or simply the beauty of the words themselves. Our task is to become sensitive to the beauty of a particular text and communicate it as a gift welcomed by the assembly.

When the sacred texts are proclaimed in their intellectual, emotional, and aesthetic entirety, they will be fulfilled in the hearing of the assembly. They will celebrate the covenant between heaven and earth, even as they sanctify the recipients of that covenant.

How? Communication Skills for Public Ministry

And now for the part you've been waiting for—especially if you are new to the ministry of lector. Space prevents a thorough course in effective oral communication skills, but the basics are reviewed here.

The best way to become a good lector is to have a good coach who is able to address your weaknesses and build on your strengths. The parish without an ongoing lector formation program is a parish that is not realizing how powerful the word of God is when proclaimed effectively at the liturgy.

STAGEFRIGHT. Whether you are experienced or new at this ministry, you are probably dealing with the number one phobia of nearly every human being: public communication anxiety—or, in more popular terms, "stagefright." If you do not experience this anxiety at all, chances are you are not taking your ministry seriously enough—or you have settled for safe methods that render your reading lifeless and ineffective.

And that rather stern remark brings us to the first step in dealing with stagefright: It has a positive side. Remind yourself that such anxiety (fear of speaking publicly) is the fear of not doing a good job—or the fear of looking ridiculous. The positive side is that your fear is really the energetic desire to do well. Thank God for that!

Thus we have no wish to "cure" public speaking anxiety. Rather, the constructive approach is to "control" it—to use the energy it reveals. And the best way to use that energy is to *prepare well*. All experts in the field of communication agree that thorough preparation is the best way to bring stagefright under control.

In addition, you can control the physical evidence of stagefright by breathing deeply and slowly, by paying special attention to the liturgical environment (a suitable lectern, a beautiful lectionary that is worthy of its function, an adequate public address system, and so forth). Seek every opportunity for public speaking experience—so that your success rate is elevated. Finally, remind yourself that you share the challenge of stagefright with every dedicated performer, preacher and lector.

The most basic communication skills are these: complementary nonverbal communication, vocal variety, effective volume and pitch, and effective pacing and pauses. A word about each.

NONVERBAL COMMUNICATION. Actions speak louder than words. If your actions (nonverbal communication), including posture, gesture, facial expression, do not complement your words, people will pay more attention to the actions. Even the most well-meaning and generous listener will miss the message (the text) if the medium (the lector) is slouching, jiggling pocket change, shifting from one foot to the other, or in any other way distracting the assembly from the words being read.

Though you may think that "eye contact" is a primary consideration, be assured that effective eye contact is the result of experience and sensitivity. For *lectors* (not public speakers) eye contact is most important (required) during the opening and closing dialogues with the assembly. You must look at the assembly when you announce "A [pronounced "uh," not "aye"] reading from . . ." and "The word of the Lord."

VOCAL VARIETY. Vocal inflection (the opposite of monotone) is the most important kind of nonverbal language. Communication experts have demonstrated that "vocal variety" does more to ensure effective communication than any other feature of the communicator's art. Conversely, the lack of vocal variety will cancel every other positive aspect of a speaker's presentation—including the message itself. So how do you develop or refine vocal variety? Primarily by becoming involved with the text and all the nuances of expression that lie within it. And then by experimenting with your voice to discover its wonderfully wide range of potential. Nothing like artificial exaggeration is being advised here. A tape recorder will instantly reveal to you whether the variation of your voice is sufficient to maintain interest and present any given text effectively.

RATE AND PAUSES. Finally a word about rate (speed) and pauses. These are very flexible concepts. But generally, beginning readers go too fast and are fearful of pauses. The scripture texts in this workbook have been marked to suggest effective pausing. But these marks can probably do no more than encourage you to slow down and read with more deliberateness—which does not imply less energy.

A TEACHER. Let it be said again, and often, that the most effective way to learn communication skills is with a teacher. Nothing is more reassuring and formative than a sensitive coach when it comes to developing oral communication skills. Every parish that buys this workbook for their lectors should realize that it will be most useful in the context of a lector formation program headed by an effective communicator who is clear about the unique requirements of liturgical proclamation.

variety of readers just how a text should be rendered. In any case, it seemed best to address potential problem spots rather than give the appearance of legislating in a discipline where there is a wide range of equally effective choices.

• To summarize the above: The design of the book is aimed at assisting you as you strive to communicate the readings in their intellectual, emotional and aesthetic entirety.

• The lectionary assigns a number to each set of readings throughout the liturgical seasons. Those numbers appear in this workbook, too, to help you find the corresponding readings in the lectionary. The workbook is not designed for use at the liturgy. It is important that your ministry of the word is performed with a beautifully bound lectionary—one worthy of the exalted purpose it serves.

• The workbook does not include the responsorial psalms that follow the first reading in the liturgy. Why? Because the responsorial psalms belong to the cantor (singer), not the lector. Granted, in many parishes the reader is expected to read the responsorial psalm, thus betraying a misunderstanding of its purpose. A realistic compromise (if the psalm is not sung) is to have it read by another reader.

• The readings for Mary, Mother of God (January 1), and the Assumption (August 15) are not included because these days are not holy days of obligation in 1994.

Features of the Workbook

• Printed beside the lectionary readings in this book are commentaries designed to help you communicate the meaning of each scripture selection.

• The margin notes deal with the more immediate matters of inclusive language, pronunciation of proper names, and the emotional or aesthetic aspects of the texts.

• Each reading has some words singled out (in italics) for emphasis—especially in cases where the text is complex or where the best emphasis may be difficult to determine. Likewise, pauses that are not dictated by punctuation or the sense of the text are indicated by the insertion of one or two small squares. (The pause marks in this book are based on the work of the previous authors, Graziano Marcheschi and Nancy Seitz Marcheschi.) Readers who are familiar with earlier editions of this book will see at once that indications for emphasis and pauses have been somewhat reduced. This editorial choice was made in the conviction that "less is more" when it comes to telling a

Bibliography of Recommended Works

Guides for the Public Reader
Any good textbook in the discipline of public speaking or oral interpretation can be of help to the lector. I recommend the following merely as examples of the best:

Charlotte I. Lee and Frank Galati. *Oral Interpretation* (7th Edition) Boston: Houghton Mifflin Company, 1986.

Michael Osborn and Susan Osborn. *Public Speaking* (Second Edition). Boston: Houghton Mifflin Company, 1991.

Staudacher, Joseph M. *Lector's Guide to Biblical Pronunciations*. Huntington IN: Our Sunday Visitor, Inc., 1979.

General Introductions to the Bible

Raymond E. Brown, *The Critical Meaning of the Bible: How a Modern Reading of the Bible Challenges Christians, the Church, and the Churches.* New York/Ramsey: Paulist Press, 1981. A clear, readable introduction to modern tools of biblical interpretation and the importance of the critical approach for today's church.

Etienne Charpentier, *How to Read the Old Testament.* London: SCM Press, 1982. *How to Read the New Testament.* London: SCM Press, 1982. These two volumes provide a basic introduction to all of the major themes and traditions of the Bible. Using selected texts from the Old and New Testaments, Charpentier introduces students to key passages and principles of interpretation in biblical study. Very helpful for lectors.

The Gospel of Mark

Paul Achtemeier, *Invitation to Mark: A Commentary on the Gospel of Mark with Complete Text from the Jerusalem Bible.* Garden City NY: Image, 1978. The volumes in this *Invitation* series are designed for contemporary study of the Bible by laypersons. They combine the best of modern biblical scholarship with attention to pastoral issues.

William Barclay, *The Gospel of Mark.* Daily Study Bible Series, revised edition. Philadelphia: Westminster, 1975. A brief and pastorally oriented commentary on the gospel designed for laypersons to use in their personal Bible study and reflection. Helpful in situating the gospel in its historical context and in drawing out its meaning for today.

Wilfred Harrington, *Mark.* New Testament Message 4. Wilmington DE: Michael Glazier, 1979. The volumes in this series present a clear and concise commentary on each of the New Testament books. Harrington's commentary on Mark gives brief comments on each section of Mark, helping the reader to understand the theology, historical situation, and literary dimensions of the gospel.

Augustine Stock, *The Method and Message of Mark.* Wilmington DE: Michael Glazier, 1989. Another helpful and readable commentary on the gospel of Mark for laypersons. Readers will find this text an invaluable resource for understanding the challenge of this gospel in its own time, as well as in ours.

The Liturgical Use of the Bible

John Baldovin, "The Bible and the Liturgy." In *City, Church and Renewal,* 209–25. Washington: The Pastoral Press, 1991. Published previously in two parts in *Catechumenate* 11 (September and November 1989). This easy-to-read essay addresses fundamental questions: why we bother to read the Bible in the Liturgy, the relationship between the Bible and God's revelation to us in Jesus Christ, how the liturgy interprets the Bible, and how the Bible interprets the liturgy.

Gerard Sloyan, "Overview of the Lectionary for Mass." In *The Liturgy Documents: A Parish Resource,* edited by Elizabeth Hoffman, 118–23. Chicago: Liturgy Training Publications, 1991. This concise and informative article presents the official document on the lectionary, "Lectionary for Mass: Introduction." It not only discusses the rationale behind the organization of the lectionary, but also offers a pastoral critique of that organization. After reading this essay, the lector will be inspired to expore the official document that follows.

Pierre Jounel, "Sunday and the Week," and "The Year." In *The Church at Prayer IV: The Liturgy and Time,* edited by A. G. Martimort, 9–130. Collegeville: The Liturgical Press, 1986. These two essays trace the history of the liturgical year and describe the theology of time presupposed in every liturgical celebration. A helpful guide.

James Wilde, ed., *At That Time: Cycles and Seasons in the Life of a Christian.* Chicago: Liturgy Training Publications, 1989. This book is a collection of engaging, nontechnical articles that address the liturgical year fom various angles; for example, "The Christian Day" (Andrew Ciferni), "Fast Days" (Barbara O'Dea), "The Christian Year" (John Baldovin), and "Initiation in the Church Year" (Mark Searle). A wonderful resource for introducing a spirituality of time found in the liturgical year.

The Word becomes flesh and dwells among us when the reader removes it from the printed page and enables it to live anew.

READING I The hopeful green of Ordinary Time is laid aside for the urgent purple of Advent. The change is dramatic, but we have seen it coming. For the past several weeks the scripture readings have been concerned with the "end time," the return of the Lord of glory, rising toward a climax in last Sunday's celebration of Christ the King.

The urgency of change is vivid in today's first reading. Isaiah cries out, "Return, Lord!" We can look at our world and lament its wretched state; our first recourse is to plead for God to act on our behalf. Try to communicate the intensity of the lament by your attention to the strong verbs: harden, return, rend, come down, withered, hidden, delivered.

Advent celebrates the hope we foster for that day when all that separates us from God will be torn away forever, when all our wretchedness will be changed into perfect peace.

READING II This reading is the beginning of a letter. The first line is a standard greeting, and what follows is a thanksgiving. This order is typical of Paul's letters.

Our situation as Christians places us between two worlds—the old world of corruption and death and that perfect world to come at the end of time. It is a situation that some have described as "already, but not yet." Paul voices this paradox when he reminds the Corinthians "you lack no spiritual gift as you wait for the revelation of our Lord Jesus." It would seem, logically, that if we're waiting for something, then we must lack something. But no. Salvation has come to us, yet we await its fulfillment "on the day of our Lord"—the return of Jesus at the end of time. The Corinthians tended to focus on the present, so Paul reminds them that there is more to come.

In a sense, Paul defines hope. The Christian virtue of hope is not simply a wish or desire or longing. It is far more profound than that. Hope is the great comfort of knowing that God will keep the promises made to us in Jesus. It is a virtue because it enables us to live in expectant joy; this joy is meant to be our Advent attitude. The hopeful Christian's life is very different from the lives of those who have no such joyful expectations. It is also very different from the lives of those whose giddiness

FIRST SUNDAY OF ADVENT

LECTIONARY #2

READING I   Isaiah 63:16–17, 19; 64:2–7

A reading from the book of the prophet *Isaiah* ▪ ▪

The poetry begins with a strong assertion of God's paternity. The entire reading is in direct address; you are speaking to God on behalf of the assembly. Be big!

You, Lord, are our *father*, ▪
  our *redeemer* you are named forever. ▪
Why do you let us wander, O Lord,
    from your ways, ▪
  and harden our hearts so that we
    fear you not? ▪ ▪
Return for the sake of your servants,
  the tribes of your heritage. ▪

The "Oh" should not be singled out, so ignore the comma: "Oh that you would. . . ."

Oh, that you would *rend* the heavens
    and come down,
  with the mountains quaking before you, ▪
While you wrought awesome deeds we could not
    hope for,
  such as they had not heard of from of old. ▪
No ear has ever heard, no eye ever seen,
  any God but you
    doing such deeds for those who *wait*
    for him. ▪

Pause slightly before this section and lower your voice a bit. There is a clear feeling of remorse here, an admission of guilt in quiet humility.

Would that you might *meet* us doing right, ▪
  that we were *mindful* of you in our ways! ▪ ▪
Behold, *you* are angry, and *we* are sinful; ▪
  all of us have become unclean men,
  all our good deeds are like polluted rags; ▪
We have all withered like leaves,
  and our guilt carries us away like the wind. ▪

"There are none who call . . . who rouse themselves."

There is none who calls upon your name,
  who rouses himself to cling to you; ▪
For you have hidden your face from us
  and have delivered us up to our guilt. ▪ ▪

Another slight pause, then raise your voice to proclaim this final act of faith and confidence. Despite our sinfulness, the Lord claims us.

Yet, O Lord, ▪ you are our *father*; ▪
  we are the *clay* and you are the *potter*: ▪
  we are *all* the work of your hands. ▪ ▪

**A reading from the first letter of *Paul*
to the *Corinthians* ▪▪**

You are getting the assembly's attention. Let "grace" and "peace" sound like brand new ideas.

Grace and *peace* from God our *Father* and the Lord Jesus *Christ.* ▪▪

I continually *thank* my God for you because of the favor he has *bestowed* on you in Christ Jesus, in whom you have been richly endowed with *every* gift of *speech* and *knowledge.* ▪ Likewise, the witness I bore to Christ has been so confirmed among you that you lack *no* spiritual gift as you wait for the revelation of our Lord Jesus [Christ.] ▪ He will strengthen you to the end, so that you will be blameless on the day of our Lord Jesus Christ. ▪ God is *faithful*, and it was *he* who called you to fellowship with his Son, Jesus Christ our Lord. ▪▪

Two very long sentences here, but this need not be a problem. Read each phrase; the text will carry itself.

There is a clear sense of closure in the pronouncement of "Jesus Christ our Lord." Then a significant pause.

GOSPEL   Mark 13:33–37

A reading from the holy *gospel* according to *Mark* ▪▪

Pause after "Be constantly on the watch," and again after "Stay awake." These two imperatives sum up the reading.

The word "watch" has become the theme. Emphasize it.

Jesus said to his disciples: ▪ "Be constantly on the *watch!* ▪ Stay awake! ▪ You do *not know* when the appointed time will come. ▪ It is like a man traveling abroad. ▪ He leaves home and places his servants in charge, each with his own task; ▪ and he orders the man at the gate to *watch* with a sharp eye. ▪ Look around you! ▪ You *do not* know when the master of the house is coming, ▪ whether at dusk, at midnight, when the cock crows, or at early dawn. ▪ Do not let him come suddenly and catch you asleep. ▪▪ What I say to *you*, I say to *all:* ▪ Be on guard!" ▪▪

The final sentence is beautifully constructed to get the point across in a new way. "Be on guard" should ring in the assembly's ears.

makes them forget that complete fulfillment is yet to come. Hopeful Christians "will be blameless"—not fearful or startled or presumptuous—"on the day of our Lord Jesus Christ."

GOSPEL   Notice how much this gospel reading is like those of the last three Sundays. The theme is preparedness, being ready, living like a vigilant guard. Thus the season of Ordinary Time eases us into the season of Advent, concentrating on that all-important Christian theme: "The Lord Jesus will return and we must be ready when he comes."

Scripture scholars point out that Mark's treatment of this theme emphasizes the watchfulness of those in charge. Notice that the gatekeeper is most responsible for vigilance as the other servants go about their normal everyday tasks. It is possible that Mark presents church leaders with a special challenge to keep an eye out for signs of the Lord's return. It is their particular duty to help others maintain a state of readiness.

In any case, the "Advent Christian" prepares best for the Lord's coming by remembering that the ultimate Advent (the word means "coming") is the hope and expectation of every waking moment.

READING I The poetic text from Isaiah today has captured the hearts of poets and musicians for generations. Anyone who has heard the Christmas section of Handel's *Messiah* will read (and listen to) these words with special affection and with the melodies echoing in their minds.

Isaiah's poems celebrate the return of the Israelites from Babylonian exile 700 years before Christ. Isaiah himself is the voice crying in the wilderness, and the heart of his message is that the "word of God" accomplishes what it speaks.

When we hear part of this reading quoted in the gospel passage for today, we realize that Isaiah's poetry is being applied to the coming of Jesus as Messiah. Now John the Baptist is the voice in the wilderness, and his good news is that we can look at Jesus and say, "Here is your God!"

A Christian interpretation of this passage takes nothing away from its historical significance. In fact, when the return of Israel is seen as a foreshadowing of the event we celebrate at Christmas, our appreciation for our spiritual heritage in Israel's history is heightened. The point may well be made that we Christians need to remind ourselves that our record of God's movement in love toward humankind begins with the Jews. And it is through the Jews that, as Isaiah so beautifully writes, "the glory of the Lord shall be revealed."

READING II From the poetry of the first reading we move to argumentation. Faced with those who were denying that Christ will come a second time, this writer is at pains to show that this is not true. The author appeals to logic. Because the world as we know it is going to come to an end, and because we don't know when this will happen, isn't it obvious that we should live in readiness and with devout attention?

Are you growing impatient for the new heavens and the new earth? The writer tells us we can hasten the coming of this glorious event by leading holy lives. Our impatience should be with ourselves, not with God. God is not delaying the "day of the Lord"; rather, God is patient with us and with all, so that all will have time to come to repentance and thus to holy lives.

This reading finds a home in Advent for several reasons: its focus on the end of time, its insistence on our leading holy lives now to prepare for the "day of God,"

SECOND SUNDAY OF ADVENT

LECTIONARY #5

READING I   Isaiah 40:1–5, 9–11

A reading from the book of the prophet *Isaiah* ▪ ▪

There are three sections here, each a bit more animated than the last. The word "comfort" makes for an abrupt beginning. You may wish to soften it by starting with "Give": "Give comfort, give comfort. . . ."

Comfort, give *comfort* to my people,
    says your God. ▪
Speak tenderly to Jerusalem, and proclaim
        to her
    that her service is at an end,
    her guilt is expiated; ▪

"Indeed" and "double" receive parallel emphasis.

Indeed, she has received from the hand
        of the Lord
    double for all her sins. ▪ ▪

    A voice cries out: ▪

Precede this section with a pause, then let your voice take on a note of urgency—slightly faster, slightly louder.

In the *desert* prepare the way of the *Lord!* ▪
    Make straight in the *wasteland* a highway
        for our *God!* ▪
Every valley shall be *filled in*,
    every mountain and hill shall be *made low*; ▪
The rugged land shall be made a plain,
    the rough country, a broad valley. ▪
Then the glory of the Lord shall be revealed,

NRSV: "all people."

    and all mankind shall see it *together*; ▪
    for the mouth of the Lord has spoken. ▪ ▪

Another pause here, then even more animation. The reading must continue to build. Notice the three uses of the word "here." Each one should be bigger than the last.

Go up onto a high mountain,
    Zion, herald of glad tidings; ▪
Cry out at the top of your voice,
    Jerusalem, herald of good news! ▪
Fear not to cry out
    and say to the cities of Judah: ▪
    Here is your God! ▪
Here comes with power
    the Lord God,
    who rules by his strong arm; ▪
Here is his *reward* with him,
    his *recompense* before him. ▪

Now the resolution begins. From the peak of exaltation, your voice begins to fall naturally into the warmth and intimacy with which the reading ends.

Like a shepherd he *feeds* his flock; ▪
    in his arms he *gathers* the lambs, ▪
Carrying them in his bosom,
    and leading the ewes with care. ▪ ▪

A reading from the second letter of *Peter* ▪▪

A very strong beginning: "This point. . . ." Emphasize "must not."

This point must *not* be overlooked, dear friends. ▪ In the *Lord's* eyes, one day is as a thousand years and a thousand years are as a day. ▪ The Lord does *not* delay in keeping his promise—though *some* consider it "delay." ▪ Rather, he shows you generous patience, since he wants *none* to perish but *all* to come to repentance. ▪ The day of the Lord *will* come like a thief, and on that day the heavens *will* vanish with a roar; ▪ the elements *will* be destroyed by fire, and the earth and all its deeds *will* be made manifest. ▪▪

You are patiently explaining why the Lord has not yet returned. It is for the good of the people.

An abrupt change with "will." The feeling is "Oh yes, the day will come!"

A new section. Pause slightly. Then ask a question with the line, "What sort of men [people] must you not be!" even though no question mark appears in the text. Then go on to answer the question. The NRSV puts the question positively and is inclusive: "What sort of persons ought you to be!"

"So" clearly signals a conclusion. Your voice must signal the imminent closure.

Since everything is to be destroyed in this way, what sort of men must you not *be!* ▪ How holy in your conduct and devotion, *looking* for the coming of the day of God and trying to *hasten* it! ▪ Because of it, the heavens will be destroyed in flames and the elements will melt away in a blaze. ▪ What we await are *new* heavens and a *new* earth where, according to his promise, the justice of God will reside. ▪ *So*, beloved, while waiting for this, make every effort to be found without stain or defilement, ▪ and at peace in his sight. ▪▪

The *beginning* of the holy *gospel* according to *Mark* ▪▪

Let your voice indicate that what follows is a quotation.

Here begins the gospel of *Jesus Christ*, the Son of God. ▪ In Isaiah the prophet, it is written: ▪
"I send my messenger before you
to prepare your way: ▪
a herald's voice in the desert, crying, ▪
'Make ready the way of the *Lord*,
clear him a straight path.'" ▪▪

Be sure to make it clear that the quotation has ended and the narrative resumes here.

Thus it was that *John the Baptizer* appeared in the desert proclaiming a baptism of repentance which led to the forgiveness of sins. ▪ All the Judean countryside and the people of Jerusalem went out to him in great numbers. ▪ They were being baptized by him in the Jordan River as they confessed their sins. ▪ John was *clothed* in camel's hair, and wore a leather belt around his waist. ▪ His *food* was grasshoppers and wild honey. ▪ The theme of his *preaching* was: ▪ "One more powerful than I is to come after me. ▪ I am not fit to stoop and untie his sandal straps. ▪ *I* have baptized you in *water:* ▪ *he* will baptize you in the *Holy Spirit.*" ▪▪

The description of John is almost an aside. The narrative continues with "The theme of his preaching was," so your voice should signal the change.

and its classic images of "new heavens and a new earth . . . where the justice of God will reside."

GOSPEL   With this passage we turn our attention toward the historical coming of Jesus, to the mystery of the incarnation (the word becoming flesh). Consequently, our attention is diverted from that time in the future when Jesus will return in glory. However, Advent celebrates both, and we need to remind ourselves that the two events are inseparable. The first two readings in today's liturgy provide that reminder.

The beginning of the gospel according to Mark is a bold assertion that Isaiah's words of prophecy (see the first reading) were fulfilled when John the Baptist appeared. He is now the herald of the good news that "one more powerful" than himself is on the way.

The Second Sunday of Advent features John the Baptist in all three years of the liturgical cycle. He is the great precursor (one who runs before and heralds the arrival of another). John's rather bizarre lifestyle and appearance make him memorable, but it is his message that makes him great. He preaches repentance and judgment. He is in for some surprises when Jesus' message turns out to be more concerned with mercy and love. We cannot help but be reminded that all Christians share in the mission of John, for all proclaim the good news of Christ's coming in the way they live. Nor can we help thinking that many who concentrate on judgment will likewise be surprised when the fullness of God's love and mercy are revealed at the end of time.

READING I You have a story to tell today—a familiar and important one. It has the quality of an ancient legend. Revered by all, it demands a faithful rendering so that every detail can be heard again. The familiarity of it all will be a comfort to your listeners.

Avoid the mistake of thinking that unless you "act it out," this well-known tale will be boring. Favorite stories are revered precisely because they communicate on their own merits and need no innovations to make them fresh.

The adventures of Adam and Eve and the serpent are our way of understanding the origin of sin. The "moral" is that evil exists because we are not faithful to God's plan to save us—and we keep repeating our infidelity. However, the evil is somehow greater than the sum of individual human sins; thus the character of the serpent. But there is always a happy ending. In the verse that begins, "I will put enmity," the good news of redemption is already hinted at. And that is why this story is told on today's feast.

READING II Perhaps the most effective rendering of this joyful passage is to read it as a lengthy gospel acclamation—for that is what it is. Paul is trumpeting the triumph of God's purpose in our regard: "God chose us in [Christ] before the world began. . . ."

Among those who are "the first to hope in Christ," Mary occupies a privileged place. She was the first to receive the good news and, puzzling though it was to her, she cancelled Adam and Eve's disobedience when she uttered the purest act of faith ever recorded: "Let it be done to me as you say."

The unsuppressed joy of this brief reading requires a combination of intensity and peace that can best be achieved by savoring each well-constructed phrase. The passage is a fanfare, and you are the silver trumpet that gives it voice.

IMMACULATE CONCEPTION

LECTIONARY #689

READING I   Genesis 3:9–15, 20

As reader of this revered tale, your task is not to convey new information, but to tell the story with an energy that bespeaks its significance and timelessness. This energy will be characterized by the seriousness appropriate to the liturgical setting.

A reading from the book of *Genesis* ··

After Adam had eaten of the tree the Lord *God* called to the man and *asked* him, · "Where are you?" · He answered, · "I heard you in the garden; but I was *afraid,* because I was *naked,* so I hid myself." · Then he asked, · "Who *told* you that you were *naked?* · You have eaten, then, from the tree of which I had *forbidden* you to eat!" · The man replied, · "The *woman* whom you put here with me—*she* gave me fruit from the tree, and so I *ate* it." · The Lord God then asked the *woman,* · "Why did you *do* such a thing?" · The woman answered, · "The serpent *tricked* me into it, so I ate it." ··

This is a decree (notice the poetic structure). Avoid sounding harsh or angry. A more appropriate tone would be solemnity, with a touch of sadness.

Then the Lord God said to the *serpent:* ·
"Because you have done this, you shall
     be banned
   from *all* the *animals*
   and from *all* the wild *creatures;* ·
On your *belly* shall you crawl,
   and *dirt* shall you eat
   all the days of your *life.* ·
I will put *enmity* between you and the *woman,* ·
   and between *your* offspring and *hers:* ·
He will strike at your *head,*
   while *you* strike at his *heel.*" ··

A solemn ending—reminding us that we are all children of Adam and Eve.

The man called his wife *Eve,* because she became the mother of *all* the *living.* ··

READING II   Ephesians 1:3–6, 11–12

A reading from the letter of *Paul* to the *Ephesians* ··

Paul is exultant here. Raise your voice in joy.

Praised be the God and Father of our Lord Jesus *Christ,* who has bestowed on us in Christ every spiritual *blessing* in the *heavens!* · God chose us in him before the world *began,* to be *holy* and *blameless* in his sight, ▪ to be full of *love;* ▪ ▪ likewise he predestined us through Christ *Jesus* to be his adopted sons—such was his *will* and *pleasure*—that *all* might praise the divine favor he has bestowed on us in his beloved. ▪ ▪

In him we were chosen; for in the decree of *God,* who administers everything according to his will and counsel, we were *predestined* to praise his glory by being the *first* to hope in *Christ.* ▪ ▪

GOSPEL   Luke 1:26–38

A reading from the holy *gospel* according to *Luke* ▪ ▪

The angel *Gabriel* was sent from God to a town of Galilee named *Nazareth,* to a *virgin* betrothed to a man named *Joseph,* of the house of *David.* ▪ The virgin's name was *Mary.* ▪ Upon arriving, the angel said to her: ▪ *"Rejoice,* O highly favored daughter! ▪ The Lord is with you. *Blessed* are you among *women."* ▪ ▪ She was deeply *troubled* by his words, and wondered what his greeting *meant.* ▪ The angel went on to say to her: ▪ "Do not *fear,* Mary. You have found favor with *God.* You shall *conceive* and bear a *son* and give him the name *Jesus.* ▪ *Great* will be his *dignity* and he will be called *Son* of the Most *High.* ▪ The Lord God will give him the throne of *David* his *father.* ▪ He will *rule* over the house of *Jacob forever* and his reign will be without *end."* ▪ ▪

Mary said to the angel, "How can this *be* since I do not know man?" ▪ The angel answered her: ▪ "The Holy *Spirit* will come upon you and the power of the Most *High* will over*shadow* you; ▪ hence, the holy offspring to be born will be called Son of *God.* ▪ Know that *Elizabeth* your kinswoman has conceived a son in her old age; she who was thought to be *sterile* is now in her sixth *month,* ▪ for *nothing* is impossible with *God."* ▪ ▪

Mary said: "I am the *maidservant* of the Lord. Let it be *done* to me as you *say."* ▪ With that ▪ the angel *left* her. ▪ ▪

GOSPEL   The problems that arise in the Genesis story (the first reading) are addressed in the gospel story. The predestination spoken of in the second reading is acted out here.

Again, we have one of the most familiar and treasured stories of our tradition. Thus, it deserves a reverential and highly energetic treatment that will enable the assembly to hear it afresh—and rejoice in the familiarity of its profound message.

Very often the mistake made by readers of this story is to attempt to make it sound too conversational. True, there is a conversation here, but it is between a highly favored daughter and a mysterious messenger of the Most High. To diminish the special nature of this story by striving for an air of informality will inevitably trivialize the event and its significance.

An elevated tone that communicates the awe and wonder of the text is best. Mary's question, for example, must not sound casual or excessively puzzled. It is a formal question that receives a formal response. Remember, of course, that "formality" is not a synonym for "coldness," just as "informality" does not necessarily lead to "warmth."

You are reading the first of a series of events that usher in the era of Christianity. Strive to communicate the significance of the event, so that your listeners will be renewed in their gratefulness to the Most High God who has intervened in human history on their behalf.

READING I Every lector should take great delight in reading this lovely poem from Isaiah. It might be called the lector's theme song, since it certainly describes the lector's mission: "to bring glad tidings to the lowly, to heal the brokenhearted." The original meaning of the text is that the Lord's servant has a noble and exalted task: to proclaim God's favor and vindication. Any servant entrusted with such a message cannot but "rejoice heartily."

Remember that poetry draws its power from its meticulous attention to word choice, rhythm and images—be careful to speak slowly so the images have a chance to paint their pictures in the hearers' imaginations. Note especially all the clothing images in the second stanza: clothed, robe, wrapped, mantle, adorned, bedecked.

The last four lines of the poem are filled with hope and trust. They are, in effect, a demonstration of how much we can depend on God to keep the promises made through the centuries: As sure as the earth brings forth life, all nations will experience God's divine justice.

READING II Although our progression through the Advent season becomes more and more concerned with the historical birth of Jesus, we are never very far away from the thought of his second coming at the end of time. The apostle Paul presents us with something of a list of good works that will keep us ready for that second coming.

The first thing we must do is "rejoice always." We are not being counseled "giddiness" here. Far from it. The realistic Christian knows full well that honest striving for holiness involves suffering. And suffering threatens to take away our happiness. Paul speaks of the kind of joy that endures (perhaps is even increased) in the face of suffering. It is the kind of joy that comes with Advent hope, the sure belief that God's promises to us will be fulfilled.

Joseph Campbell, a brilliant man who spent a lifetime studying the world's mythologies and religions, summarized the primary goal of all of them in these words: "to participate joyfully in the sorrows of the world." It sounds contradictory, until we realize the kind of joy he is speaking of—the expectant kind that rests firmly on faith in our inexorable and inevitable progress toward the divine. We have it on

THIRD SUNDAY OF ADVENT

LECTIONARY #8

READING I   Isaiah 61:1–2, 10–11

A reading from the book of the prophet *Isaiah* ··

This lovely poetic passage employs the most common feature of Hebrew verse: parallelism. Every line is echoed in the line that follows; the sense of the first line is expanded upon in the second.

The spirit of the *Lord God* is upon me,
  because the Lord has *anointed* me; ·
He has sent me to bring glad *tidings*
    to the lowly,
  to *heal* the brokenhearted, ·
To proclaim liberty to the captives
  and release to the prisoners, ·
To *announce* a year of *favor* from the Lord
  and a day of vindication by our God. ··

A new feeling appears here. The speaker has moved from a proclamation of mission to a song of personal exultation.

I rejoice heartily in the Lord,
  in my God is the *joy* of my soul; ·
For he has *clothed* me with a robe of salvation,
  and *wrapped* me in a mantle of justice, ·
Like a bridegroom *adorned* with a diadem,
  like a bride *bedecked* with her jewels. ·

The final four lines proclaim the ultimate fulfillment of God's plan. Speak them with confidence.

As the earth brings forth its plants,
  and a garden makes its *growth* spring up, ·
So will the Lord God make justice and praise
  spring up before all the nations. ··

READING II   1 Thessalonians 5:16–24

A reading from the first letter of *Paul* to the *Thessalonians* ··

The reading begins with three imperatives. Single out each one for emphasis.

Rejoice *always*, · *never* cease praying, · render *constant* thanks; · such is God's will for you in Christ Jesus. ··

Pause here; a list of more imperatives begins. Be sure each element gets equal emphasis.

Do not stifle the *spirit*. · Do not despise prophecies. · Test everything; · retain what is good. · Avoid any *semblance* of evil. ··

The reading ends with a blessing and a promise.

May the God of peace make you perfect in *holiness*. · May you be preserved whole and entire, · spirit, soul, *and* body, irreproachable at the coming of our Lord Jesus Christ. · He who calls us is *trustworthy*, · therefore he will *do* it. ··

A reading from the holy *gospel* according to *John* ▪ ▪

This first paragraph is a preface, introducing us to the character of John. Drop "men" to be inclusive.

There was a man named John sent by God, who came as a witness to *testify* to the light, so that through him all men might believe— ▪ but only to *testify* to the light, for he himself was *not* the light. ▪ ▪

Now the narrative begins. Use plenty of vocal variety to make the story sound fresh and new. This long sentence builds to a climax. Take a deep breath and sustain the flow until you get to the point: "I am not the Messiah."

The testimony John gave when the Jews sent priests and Levites from Jerusalem to ask ▪ "Who are you?" ▪ was the *absolute* statement, ▪ "I am *not* the Messiah." ▪ They questioned him further, ▪ "Who, then? Elijah?" ▪ "I am *not* Elijah," he answered. ▪ "Are you the prophet?" ▪ *"No,"* he replied. ▪ ▪

Finally they said to him: ▪ "Tell us who you *are*, so that we can give some answer to those who sent us. ▪ What do you have to say for yourself?" ▪ He said, quoting the prophet Isaiah, ▪ "I am
    'a voice in the desert, crying out: ▪
    Make straight the way of the *Lord!*'" ▪ ▪

A new section begins here. Precede it with a pause.

Those whom the Pharisees had sent proceeded to question him further: ▪ "If you are *not* the Messiah, *nor* Elijah, *nor* the prophet, ▪ why do you baptize?" ▪ John answered them: ▪ "I baptize with *water*. ▪ There is one among you whom you do not recognize—the one who is to come after me— ▪ the strap of whose sandal I am not worthy to unfasten." ▪ ▪ This happened in Bethany, across the Jordan, where John was baptizing. ▪ ▪

The narrative closes with this final comment. Let your tone indicate a clear sense of closure.

the best authority: "The God who calls us is trustworthy."

GOSPEL   Last Sunday we read Mark's account of John the Baptist's appearance. Today we read John's. What is most obvious in John's account is that the Baptist is absolutely determined to deny any role greater than that of a "voice in the desert, crying out: 'Make straight the way of the Lord.'" This quotation from the prophet Isaiah makes the direct claim, of course, that the Messianic time spoken of for centuries is about to arrive.

In a series of denials, John makes several assertions about himself and about "the one who is to come after." The religious authorities who questioned him were doing so in the best interests of his followers. They needed some credentials from John to be assured that he was not leading the people astray. Thus their persistence and John's readiness to explain himself. He was, after all, baptizing, so there was good reason to examine his motives. Ritual ablution (cleansing) was not uncommon, but it clearly had spiritual implications and, most disturbing for the religious leaders of the time, John had apparently attracted quite a large number of followers.

We know more than the priests and Levites do from the very first words of the reading: "There was a man *sent by God*." The evangelist John makes it clear to us that the Baptist's mission was an authentic one. He also makes it clear what that mission was: to prepare the way for the one who would baptize with more than water; indeed, with the very life of God.

READING I We all must continually remind ourselves that the connections we see so clearly between prophecies such as this one and the coming of Jesus are the result of centuries of interpretation and hindsight. Looking back from our perspective, it is easy to see Nathan's prophecy fulfilled in Jesus, a descendant of David. But to see only this is to rewrite history and indeed, to rob the Hebrew Scriptures of their power. Nathan the prophet speaks for God and reveals God's fidelity and undying love for Israel, the Chosen People.

Having said that, here is the clearest and surest promise of a messiah in the Hebrew Scriptures. And God's promise to David comes about as the result of an alteration in David's plans. The scene takes place in a time of peace, when David can turn his attention to a more fitting place for the ark of the covenant than the portable tent it now resides in. The king's noble intention receives the approval of his faithful prophet Nathan. But the Lord uses the occasion for a far more important and lasting plan.

The entire reading turns on the word "house," which of course has a double meaning. Though David wants to build a house (temple) for God, God's intention is to build a house (dynasty) for David. It's as though God is saying, "If there's any house building going on here, I'll be the architect and builder—and I'll show you what 'house' really means." There is no sense of reprimand here on God's part. David is in need of instruction regarding priorities, and he is the beloved of God, worthy of the promise of an everlasting kingdom.

The promise extends even beyond David's death and includes the assurance of an heir who fits Israel's hope for a messiah— a good and mighty king whose reign will be firm and whose loyalty to God will be unquestionable. The Lord paints a picture that is immediately recognizable to every Jew who hopes for the final restoration of Israel. It is a beautiful promise. It reminds us that the promises of God far outshine even our wildest hopes.

READING II This is a very difficult reading—not difficult to understand, but difficult to proclaim effectively. The grammatical structure contains so much subordination (so many levels) that it's hard to remember the simple base clause: "To

---

DECEMBER 19, 1993

FOURTH SUNDAY OF ADVENT

LECTIONARY #11

READING I   2 Samuel 7:1–5, 8–11, 16

A reading from the second book of *Samuel* ▪▪

This is a story that contains a "reversal of expectations." Set the scene calmly.

When King David was settled in his palace, and the Lord had given him rest from his enemies on every side, he said to Nathan the prophet, ▪ "Here *I* am living in a house of *cedar*, while the ark of *God* dwells in a *tent!*" ▪ Nathan answered the king, ▪ "Go, do whatever you have in mind, for the *Lord* is with you." ▪ But that night the Lord spoke to Nathan and said: ▪ "Go, tell my servant David, ▪ '*Thus* says the Lord: ▪ Should *you* build *me* a house to dwell in?' ▪▪

"But!" The reversal has come. The Lord is almost incredulous in the question, "Should you *build* ME *a house to dwell in!" Let us clearly hear that the tables are about to be turned.*

" 'It was I who took you from the pasture and from the care of the flock to be commander of my people Israel. ▪ I have *been* with you wherever you went, and I have destroyed all your enemies before you. ▪ And I will make you famous like the great ones of the earth. ▪ I will fix a place for my people Israel; ▪ I will plant them so that they may dwell in their place without further disturbance. ▪ Neither shall the wicked *continue* to afflict them as they did of old, since the time I first appointed judges over my people Israel. ▪ I will give you *rest* from all your enemies. ▪ The Lord also reveals to you that *he* will establish a house for *you*. ▪ Your house and your kingdom shall endure forever before me; ▪ your throne shall stand firm forever.' " ▪▪

After a long preface, here is the point: "HE will establish a house for YOU!" And the meaning of "house" has completely changed from "temple" or "dwelling place" to "dynasty" or "kingdom."

READING II   Romans 16:25–27

A reading from the letter of *Paul* to the *Romans* • ▪

The abruptness of the opening is quite effective if you make sure you have the assembly's attention before you begin. Treat the text like the multi-layered shout of praise it is.

To him who is able to strengthen you in the *gospel* which I proclaim when I preach *Jesus Christ,* the gospel which reveals the mystery *hidden* for many ages but now *manifested* through the writings of the prophets, and, at the command of the eternal God, *made known* to all the Gentiles that they may believe and obey— ▪ to *him,* the God who alone is *wise,* may *glory* be given through Jesus Christ unto endless ages. ▪ Amen. • ▪

GOSPEL   Luke 1:26–38

A reading from the holy *gospel* according to *Luke* • ▪

The scene you are setting here is not in a humble Palestinian hut. It is in the brilliant and spacious corridors of Luke's theology. Begin with solemnity.

The angel Gabriel was sent from God to a town of Galilee named Nazareth, to a virgin betrothed to a man named Joseph, of the house of David. ▪ The virgin's *name* was *Mary.* ▪ Upon arriving, the angel said to her: ▪ "Rejoice, O highly favored daughter! ▪ The *Lord* is with you. Blessed are you among women." • ▪ She was deeply *troubled* by his words, and wondered what his greeting meant. ▪ The angel went on to say to her: ▪ "Do not fear, Mary. You have found favor with *God.* You shall conceive and bear a son and give him the name Jesus. ▪ Great will be his *dignity* and he will be called *Son* of the Most High. ▪ The Lord God will give him the throne of David his father. ▪ *He* will rule over the house of Jacob forever and *his* reign will be without end." • ▪

Mary's perplexity provides the opportunity for Gabriel to reveal God's plan. It is a formal, almost ritual, moment.

Mary's second question paves the way for the astounding news that the child she is to bear comes from above. Read the question with great calm and solidity, almost rhetorically.

Mary said to the angel, "*How* can this be since I do not know *man?*" ▪ The angel answered her: ▪ "The Holy Spirit will come upon you and the power of the Most High will overshadow you; ▪ hence, the holy offspring to be born will be called Son of *God.* ▪ Know that Elizabeth your kinswoman has conceived a son in her *old age;* she who was thought to be sterile is now in her sixth month, ▪ for *nothing* is impossible with *God.*" • ▪

This is the "yes" that ushered in our salvation. Proclaim it with all the solemnity and dignity it deserves.

Mary said: "I am the maidservant of the Lord. Let it be done to me as you say." ▪ With that ▪ the angel left her. • ▪

God . . . be glory for ever and ever." The secret to an effective reading is to treat the text like a poem—in which attribute is stacked upon attribute to create a multi-layered and theologically rich summation of God's plan to save the world. Dwell carefully on each level and treat the text rather like poetry. Let the images build to a climax.

There is no indication in Paul's meaning here that God intentionally kept his plan secret until the coming of Jesus. God's intervention in human history is a constant throughout Israel's history. Paul implies simply that we didn't fully understand God's plan until it was revealed in Christ's coming. This doxology, then, is an ideal selection of "Advent" literature.

GOSPEL   The Fourth Sunday of Advent has brought us to the moment of God's coming into the world. In this reading the Word becomes flesh. The drama of this text (indeed, this event!) has captured the imagination of so many great painters throughout history. "The Annunciation" has all the elements of a short story or play: a situation into which conflict is introduced, a crisis appears, a solution is given and a resolution achieved that leaves the original situation completely altered.

It is not difficult to analyze the movement of the reading in such a way that it can unfold for the audience, moving from question to response, from puzzle to solution, from agitation to calm, from doubt to assurance. However, there is one element in this story that must dominate all others and sear its way into the souls of the hearers: This promised Jesus comes not from the earth, but from heaven, not from the normal union of husband with wife, but from the union of God with humanity. This is Luke's point: "The child to be born will be called holy, the Son of God."

When the shattering news hits us, any sweet and tender notions we have about this gospel event are burned away by the sheer magnitude of such a cosmic upheaval. The best of the painters who have been brave enough to depict this scene have always given us a stylized and formal picture—as if to indicate that no representation can capture the profundity of it, and anything like sentimental realism would completely miss the point.

READING I Few, if any, scripture passages surpass this one in sheer exultation. The historical situation explains why. The Israelites had been in exile for years, and God seemed silent. Now Zion (Jerusalem) is to be restored as the dwelling place of the Most High and the glory of the world. Returning exiles see that the temple is being rebuilt, restored to its former splendor. (Worship in the temple was an important aspect of their religion.) The prophet is ecstatic.

And the relationship between God and Israel is likened to that of lover and beloved—bride and bridegroom—the most intimate of human experiences. No other comparison seems to do justice to the degree of closeness God wants with us. Marriage henceforth becomes a powerful metaphor to describe what happens at the Incarnation (when God takes flesh in Jesus). The Holy Spirit becomes the spouse of Mary. Heaven and earth are wed as the divine and human become one.

The combination of ecstasy and tenderness in this reading indicates how it should be proclaimed: with great energy, care and sensitivity. Take extra time with each image, being aware that we stand on the eve of the great feast that inaugurates a bright new era in salvation history.

READING II This reading is made up of selections from a sermon by Paul, delivered in the midst of a synagogue assembly. More specifically, it is a sermon in the form of an argument—a recitation of historical events that Paul wants us to see as evidence that God's plan for our salvation has been fulfilled.

In a masterful short summary, Paul covers such essentials as "election" (Israel is the chosen people), "exile," "deliverance" and the "royal descent" of Jesus through King David's descendants. With a special kind of logic, Paul seeks to prove to his hearers that Jesus is the fulfillment of God's promises and the culmination of the divine plan.

The delivery of this kind of argument should be strong and straightforward, communicating something of this attitude: "Here's the evidence; how can you doubt that Jesus is indeed the promised Messiah?" From our modern point of view, the kind of "proof" offered here is far from

CHRISTMAS VIGIL

LECTIONARY #13

READING I   Isaiah 62:1–5

A reading from the book of the prophet *Isaiah* ▪ ▪

Notice the parallelism. Almost every line is echoed in the line that follows it. This poetic structure should be heard in your delivery.

For *Zion's* sake I will not be *silent*, ▪
   for *Jerusalem's* sake I will not be *quiet*,
Until her vindication shines forth like the *dawn*
   and her *victory* like a burning *torch*. ▪

Nations shall *behold* your vindication,
   and all *kings* your glory; ▪
You shall be called by a *new* name
   pronounced by the mouth of the *Lord*. ▪
You shall be a glorious *crown* in the hand
     of the *Lord*,
   a royal *diadem* held by your *God*. ▪

NRSV: "You shall no more be termed 'Forsaken.'"

No more shall men call you *"Forsaken,"* ▪
   or your land *"Desolate,"* ▪
But you shall be called *"My Delight,"* ▪
   and your *land "Espoused."* ▪
For the Lord *delights* in you,
   and makes your land his *spouse*. ▪

The final images (virgin, marriage, bridegroom, bride) are tender and intimate.

As a young man marries a *virgin*,
   your Builder shall marry *you*; ▪
And as a bridegroom rejoices in his *bride*
   so shall your *God* rejoice in *you*. ▪ ▪

READING II   Acts 13:16–17, 22–25

A reading from the *Acts* of the *Apostles* ▪ ▪

Antioch Pisidia = AN-tih-ahk pih-SIH-dih-uh

[When Paul came to Antioch Pisidia, he entered the *synagogue* there] and motioning to them for *silence*, he began: ▪ "Fellow Israelites and you *others* who reverence our God, *listen* to what I have to *say!* ▪ The God of the people *Israel* once chose our fathers. ▪ He made this people *great* during their sojourn in the land of *Egypt*, and 'with an outstretched *arm*' he led them *out* of it. ▪ God raised up *David* as their *king*; ▪ on his behalf he *testified*, ▪ 'I have found *David* son of *Jesse* to be a man after my own *heart* who will fulfill my every *wish*.' ▪ ▪

NRSV: "ancestors" instead of "fathers."

"According to his *promise*, God has brought forth from this man's *descendants Jesus*, a savior for *Israel*. ▪ *John* heralded the *coming* of Jesus by proclaiming a baptism of *repentance* to all the people of Israel. ▪ As John's career was coming to an *end*, he would say, ▪ 'What you *suppose* me to be I am *not*. ▪ Rather, look for the one who comes *after* me. ▪ I am not worthy to unfasten the sandals on his feet.'" ▪ ▪

scientific, and therefore not quite so compelling, perhaps, as it might have been to Paul's contemporaries—though it won many converts. It is an argument offered to the ear of faith rather than the mind of logic.

The last section, which may seem anti-climactic, hints clearly at the notion that John is the last of the prophets who heralded the coming of Christ—who is, of course, the fulfillment of the law and the prophets.

GOSPEL   Matthew 1:1–25

The beginning of the holy *gospel* according to *Matthew* ▪ ▪

A family *record* of Jesus *Christ*, son of *David*, son of *Abraham*. ▪ Abraham was the father of Isaac, Isaac the father of Jacob, Jacob the father of Judah and his brothers. ▪

Judah was the father of Perez and Zerah,
 whose mother was Tamar. ▪
Perez was the father of Hezron,
Hezron the father of Ram. ▪
Ram was the father of Amminadab,
Amminadab the father of Nahshon,
Nahshon the father of Salmon. ▪
Salmon was the father of Boaz,
 whose mother was Rahab, ▪
Boaz was the father of Obed,
 whose mother was Ruth. ▪
Obed was the father of Jesse,
Jesse the father of King David. ▪
David was the father of Solomon,
 whose mother had been the wife of Uriah. ▪
Solomon was the father of Rehoboam,
Rehoboam the father of Abijah,
Abijah the father of Asa. ▪
Asa was the father of Jehoshaphat,
Jehoshaphat the father of Joram,
Joram the father of Uzziah. ▪
Uzziah was the father of Jotham,
Jotham the father of Ahaz,
Ahaz the father of Hezekiah. ▪
Hezekiah was the father of Manasseh,
Manasseh the father of Amos,
Amos the father of Josiah. ▪ ▪
Josiah became the father of Jechoniah and his
 brothers at the time of the
 Babylonian *exile*. ▪

GOSPEL   More often than not, only the last eight verses of this reading are proclaimed. Many gospel readers are put off by the long list of names—and presume that the assembly will find it boring. The genealogy is certainly intimidating; thus, the lectionary provides the option of omitting it.

But let's consider what it can teach us—with a little help from the homilist. First of all, it says, "If you want to know this Jesus, read the entire Bible, which is a record of his origins." Second, it makes specific mention of several women who played important roles in salvation history—something we can hear with great profit, given our male-dominated notions about God and church. Finally, it demonstrates, with a special kind of logic, that God's good will on our behalf is documented clear back to Abraham (our father in faith) and that God's plan has not, and will not, be thwarted.

The genealogy is also a neatly constructed word game. There are three sets of 14 generations (before, during and after the Exile). The number 14 in Hebrew (which uses its alphabet as numbers) spells "David." D = 4, V = 6, D = 4. And a major point of the list is to demonstrate that Jesus has been born, as prophesied, in the royal line of David.

It seems a shame that this lovely litany is so easily tossed aside. It can be proclaimed in a variety of ways (sung or chanted, with two or more readers, perhaps interspersed with commentary) to ease the fear of boredom. Complete mastery of the pronunciation of the proper names is necessary, and not difficult. In any case, this passage deserves more consideration than it usually gets.

The story of how the birth of Jesus Christ came about is a classic literary form: situation (engaged couple), conflict (presumed illicit pregnancy), climax (threat of scandal and separation) and resolution (divine revelation). The challenge is twofold: Read the passage as the short *story* that it is, and make it so fresh that the assembly will "hear it again for the first time."

Shealtiel = shee-AL-tih-ehl

Zerubbabel = zeh-RUH-buh-behl

Abiud = uh-BAI-uhd

Eliakim = ee-LAI-uh-kihm

Azor = AY-zawr

Zadok = ZAY-dahk

Achim = AY-kihm

Eliud = ee-LAI-uhd

Eleazar = ehl-ee-AY-zer

Matthan = MAT-than

An obvious break. Make it very obvious—with a new and fresh intonation: "Now! This is how. . . ."

The point is that Jesus has a divine origin. The last paragraph is calm and peaceful.

After the Babylonian exile
Jechoniah was the father of Shealtiel,
Shealtiel the father of Zerubbabel. ▪
Zerubbabel was the father of Abiud,
Abiud the father of Eliakim,
Eliakim the father of Azor. ▪
Azor was the father of Zadok,
Zadok the father of Achim,
Achim the father of Eliud. ▪
Eliud was the father of Eleazar,
Eleazar the father of Matthan,
Matthan the father of Jacob. ▪
Jacob was the father of Joseph
    the husband of Mary. ▪
It was of *her* that Jesus who is called the
    Messiah was born. ▪ ▪
Thus the total number of *generations* is: ▪
  from Abraham to David, *fourteen*
    generations; ▪
  from David to the Babylonian captivity,
    fourteen generations; ▪
  from the Babylonian captivity to the Messiah,
    fourteen generations. ▪ ▪

Now *this* is how the *birth* of Jesus *Christ* came about. ▪ When his mother *Mary* was engaged to *Joseph*, but before they *lived* together, she was found with *child* ▪ through the power of the Holy *Spirit*. ▪ Joseph her husband, an *upright* man unwilling to expose her to the *law*, decided to *divorce* her *quietly*. ▪ Such was his *intention* when suddenly the angel of the *Lord* appeared in a *dream* and said to him: ▪ "Joseph, son of David, have no *fear* about taking Mary as your *wife*. ▪ It is by the Holy *Spirit* that she has conceived this child. She is to have a *son* and you are to name him *Jesus* because he will save his people from their *sins*." ▪ ▪ All this happened to fulfill what the Lord had said through the *prophet*: ▪
  "The *virgin* shall be with *child*
    and give *birth* to a *son*, ▪
    and they shall call him *Emmanuel*,"
a name which means "God is *with* us." ▪ ▪

When Joseph *awoke* he did as the angel of the Lord had *directed* him and received her into his home as his *wife*. ▪ He had no *relations* with her at any time before she bore a *son*, whom he named *Jesus*. ▪ ▪

[Shorter: Matthew 1:18–25]

CHRISTMAS MIDNIGHT

LECTIONARY #14

READING I   Isaiah 9:1–6

A reading from the book of the prophet
Isaiah ▪ ▪

The people who walked in _darkness_
    have seen a great _light;_ ▪
Upon those who dwelt in the land of _gloom_
    a _light_ has shone. ▪
You have brought them abundant _joy_
    and great _rejoicing,_
As they rejoice before you as at the _harvest,_
    as men make _merry_ when dividing _spoils._ ▪

NRSV: "as people exult when dividing plunder."

For the yoke that _burdened_ them,
    the _pole_ on their _shoulder,_
And the rod of their _taskmaster_
    you have _smashed,_ as on the day of _Midian._ ▪
For every _boot_ that tramped in _battle,_
    every _cloak_ rolled in _blood,_
    will be burned as fuel for _flames._ ▪ ▪

Here are the words the assembly is waiting to hear. Read them with all the joy you can muster.

For a _child_ is _born_ to us, a _son_ is _given_ us;
    upon his shoulder _dominion_ rests. ▪
They name him Wonder-_Counselor,_
    God-_Hero,_
    Father-_Forever,_ Prince of _Peace._ ▪
His dominion is _vast_
    and forever _peaceful,_
From _David's_ throne, and over his _kingdom,_
    which he _confirms_ and _sustains_
By _judgment_ and _justice,_
    both _now_ and _forever._ ▪
The zeal of the _Lord of hosts_ will _do_ this! ▪ ▪

The NRSV rendering of this sentence is easier to understand: "His authority shall grow continually, and there shall be endless peace for the throne of David and his kingdom. He will establish and uphold it with justice and with righteousness from this time onward and forevermore."

READING II   Titus 2:11–14

A reading from the letter of _Paul_ to _Titus_ ▪ ▪

NRSV: "offering salvation to all."

The grace of God has _appeared,_ offering salvation to
all men. ▪ It trains us to reject _godless_ ways and

READING I   You are probably reading to a packed house, and to an assembly that is especially receptive. It is also likely that distractions are abundant. In any case, the moment of preparation before this reading is crucial. The announcement ("A reading from . . .") should be proclaimed with great authority and strength and followed by a momentary silence—often the best attention-grabber. Then launch into this familiar and beautiful text with all the energy with which it is imbued in Handel's _Messiah._

Isaiah writes of liberation from oppression through the ascendancy of a human king (Hezekiah). The yoke, pole and rod of the oppressor (the nation of Assyria) will be smashed, and the holy war (because God sides with Israel) will end in triumph. Further, this mighty king will possess that greatest of human virtues that make for good leadership: justice.

Hezekiah didn't live up to this prophecy, so Isaiah will have to look further ahead. We, of course, look back—and forward—hearing these words as the description of the new messianic age ushered in by the birth of Jesus. This reading alone should enable us to avoid the sentimental notion that the Christmas festival concentrates only on the birth of a child. Indeed, it is primarily a celebration of the kingdom to come—which has been long in coming, has now arrived, but still strains toward perfect fulfillment.

All the confidence of Christian belief is sounded in the words, "The zeal of the Lord of hosts will do this." Let this final sentence ring throughout the assembly as a clarion call to renewed hope.

READING II   For all the exaltation of this passage, there is a quiet strength that is striking. It is almost as if the writer is shrugging his shoulders as he muses: "Considering the powerful effect that the grace of God has upon us, is it any wonder that we reject whatever is evil and embrace in peace a new life of goodness?" The presumption is that, once we recognize God's redeeming love, our inclination to live devoutly in this age will come naturally.

Let that same degree of quiet strength motivate you as you proclaim this short reading. Beware, however, lest the brevity of the passage cause you to breeze through it. Even a glance reveals that the text is packed with important images and ideas. Each phrase is a kernel of truth and deserves to be lingered over—especially tonight.

The newborn babe does not appear in this reading. Here we have, in capsule form, the deeper meaning of Christmas. The birth of the Messiah is proof of God's limitless love—which makes us long for the perfect kingdom to come, and to live our lives as a grateful response to that love.

GOSPEL What is so difficult about reading and hearing very well-known scripture passages is that we stop listening intently. The words roll over us with the warmth of familiarity, and we rejoice in hearing them again—almost through a haze of expectation and fulfillment. And that is a perfectly valid worship experience.

An especially effective proclamation, however, can enhance the gratifying experience of familiarity with new discovery. As the reader, strive to provide your hearers with that enrichment.

There is not one historical fact in this passage without its deeper theological meaning. Indeed, some of the facts are disputed. But this does not alter the meaning one bit. For example, Caesar Augustus may, or may not, have ordered a census (there is no evidence apart from this passage). The point is that Caesar Augustus had a solid reputation as the "bringer of peace." Luke wants to show that the bringer of *real* peace is Jesus. Or consider this: Whether or not Jesus was laid in a manger, Luke's point is that Jesus will become food for the world. Whether or not shepherds saw angels, they certainly were the lowliest of the low—the very kind for whom this Messiah will demonstrate a special love. This all happened in Bethlehem because it is the "city of David," and Jesus is born from that royal line, as the prophets foretold.

It is up to the homilist to make explicit the lessons implied here. But the point being made for you, the reader, is crucial: Every detail of this beautiful passage has profound significance. It must be read with exquisite care, despite the fact that it seems so straightforward and simple—and familiar. Neglect nothing.

This reading is only three sentences. The first is brief. The second and third are long series of phrases. The secret is not to rush, and to give each phrase its due.

worldly desires, and live *temperately, justly,* and *devoutly* in this age as we await our blessed *hope,* the appearing of the glory of the great *God* and of our Savior Christ *Jesus.* ▪ It was he who *sacrificed* himself for us, to *redeem* us from all *unrighteousness* and to *cleanse* for himself a people of his *own,* eager to do what is *right.* ▪▪

GOSPEL   Luke 2:1–14

A reading from the holy *gospel* according to *Luke* ▪▪

Quirinius = kwai-RIHN-ih-uhs
NRSV: "All went to their own towns to be registered."

In those days Caesar *Augustus* published a *decree* ordering a census of the whole *world.* ▪ This first census took place while *Quirinius* was governor of *Syria.* ▪ *Everyone* went to register, each to his own *town.* ▪ And so *Joseph* went from the town of Nazareth in *Galilee* to *Judea,* to *David's* town of *Bethlehem*—because he was of the *house* and *lineage* of David—to register with *Mary,* his espoused *wife,* who was with *child.* ▪▪

The scene has been set; now for the event! Let your voice indicate the change.

While they were *there* the days of her *confinement* were completed. ▪ She gave birth to her first-born *son* and wrapped him in *swaddling* clothes and laid him in a *manger,* because there was no *room* for them in the place where *travelers* lodged. ▪▪

And now for immediate reactions to the event. A new section begins here.

There were *shepherds* in the locality, living in the *fields* and keeping night watch by turns over their *flock.* ▪ The angel of the *Lord* appeared to them, as the *glory* of the Lord shone around them, and they were very much *afraid.* ▪ The angel *said* to them: ▪ "You have nothing to *fear!* I come to proclaim *good news* to you—tidings of great *joy* to be shared by the whole *people.* ▪ This day in *David's* city a *savior* has been born to you, the *Messiah* and *Lord.* ▪ Let this be a *sign* to you: ▪ in a *manger* you will find an *infant* wrapped in *swaddling clothes."* ▪ *Suddenly,* there was with the angel a multitude of the heavenly *host,* praising *God* and saying, ▪

With great joy and peace!

"*Glory* to God in high *heaven,*
 peace on *earth* to those on whom his
  favor rests." ▪▪

CHRISTMAS DAWN

LECTIONARY #15

READING I   Isaiah 62:11–12

A reading from the book of the prophet Isaiah ▪▪

"Behold" would be stronger than "See."

See, the Lord proclaims
    to the ends of the *earth:* ▪
Say to daughter *Zion,*
    your *savior* comes! ▪

Stress the nouns "reward" and "recompense," not the prepositions "with" and "before."

Here is his *reward* with him,
    his *recompense* before him. ▪
They shall be called the *holy* people,
    the *redeemed* of the Lord,

"Frequented" is an odd word. If you use it, put the accent on the second syllable. Consider the slightly better choice in the NRSV: "Sought Out."

and you shall be called *"Frequented,"*
    a city that is *not forsaken.* ▪▪

READING II   Titus 3:4–7

A reading from the letter of *Paul* to *Titus* ▪▪

A summary of the "good news." Read slowly.

When the kindness and love of God our *Savior* appeared, he *saved* us, not because of any righteous deeds *we* had done, but because of *his mercy.* ▪

"Saved" and "lavished" are the power words here. The final sentence is a series of phrases that must be read very deliberately.

He saved us through the *baptism* of new *birth* and *renewal* by the Holy *Spirit.* ▪ This Spirit he *lavished* on us through Jesus *Christ* our *Savior,* that we might be justified by *his grace* and become *heirs,* in *hope,* of eternal *life.* ▪▪

READING I   All three readings assigned for the Christmas morning liturgy are exceptionally brief. It's as though we are being told how simple and clear the good news is. Isaiah says, "Your savior comes." Paul says, "The love of God saved us." Luke says, "The shepherds saw Mary and Joseph and the baby."

Notice that the first reading is taken from the same section of Isaiah as the first reading on Christmas Eve. The ancient Feast of Tabernacles (a feast of lights!) is the historical context here—and unbounded joy at the evidence of God's presence among the people is the theme. Christmas is a feast of light, too—the dawn of a new age. At this early morning celebration, communicate the brightness of the Christmas good news.

The briefer the reading, the more sensitive and painstaking the reader must be! Consider this first reading as a series of acclamations, each containing one or more kernels of joyous discovery or realization. The last sentence is a list of titles for God's holy people—the people to whom you are reading!

READING II   Here it is . . . the central truth. This tiny reading is the essence of the good news at its most distilled. Not one word is superfluous or unimportant. The text deserves exhaustive meditation, and a thoroughly nuanced proclamation.

I did a little experiment with this reading. My findings may help: If it takes you less than one full minute (60 seconds) to proclaim this reading (with its announcement and "The Word of the Lord" at the end), then you are not reading it slowly or carefully enough. There should be no disproportionate pauses, either. If each phrase is given its due, and natural (varied) inflection is employed, this reading cannot be done effectively in less than 60 seconds. Try it.

This selection from Luke's gospel picks up where the Midnight Mass gospel reading left off. Please see the comments there.

The narrative (story) is treasured and familiar, thus deserving special attention and an attempt to have it heard again as though for the first time. It will be heard this way if you proclaim it with the feeling that it is, indeed, news.

This text contains a trap—into which many an unwary reader has fallen: "They went in haste and found Mary and Joseph, and the baby lying in the manger." Practice this out loud until it is no longer even remotely possible for the assembly to hear you imply that all three (mother, father and baby) are in the manger! The solution is just the right inflection of "Joseph," and just the right pause afterward.

There are two special items here to consider. First of all, a translation problem. Instead of "once they [the shepherds] saw, they *understood* what had been told them," the NRSV reads, "When they saw this, they *made known* what had been told them." (Emphasis mine.) The difference is critical, and the second translation is the more accurate one. Consider substituting it. In the next sentence, "All who heard of it [what the angels made known] . . ." includes Mary and Joseph—which makes more clear what things Mary treasured and reflected on. She now has two angelic encounters to ponder, which brings us to a second important item.

Mary is always the perfect exemplar. Here she is presented to us as the model for anyone who believes. Belief is different from knowledge. The significance of these mysterious messages and events is not at all clear to Mary. She must reflect on them. We must do the same. Believing, not knowing or understanding fully, is the natural state of the prayerful believer. We need to be content with that.

Clearly, the final paragraph of this reading is important for us—containing two wonderful responses to the good news of Christmas. Mary's response is love-filled reflection; the shepherds glorify and praise God with grateful joy. Try to elicit such responses from your hearers.

A reading from the holy *gospel* according to *Luke* ▪▪

When the *angels* had returned to *heaven*, the *shepherds* said to one another: ▪ "Let us go over to *Bethlehem* and *see* this event which the Lord has made *known* to us." ▪ They went in *haste* and found *Mary* and *Joseph*, ▪ and the *baby* lying in the *manger*; ▪ once they *saw*, they *understood* what had been told them concerning this child. ▪ All who *heard* of it were *astonished* at the report given them by the *shepherds*. ▪▪

Mary treasured *all* these things ▪ and *reflected* on them in her *heart*. ▪ The shepherds *returned*, glorifying and praising *God* for all they had *heard* and *seen*, in accord with what had been *told* them. ▪▪

Be careful to phrase this so that you avoid making it sound like all three (Mary, Joseph, baby) were in the manger. Pause after "Joseph," and do not pause after "baby."

A new section. Pause, then proceed with new emphasis.

LITURGY GUIDES FOR 1994 YEAR B

1994 Sourcebook for Sundays and Seasons

is an almanac for parish liturgy containing season by season and Sunday by Sunday notes on the celebration of Mass with practical suggestions for keeping the seasons. A wealth of useful texts, notes on the order of Mass, and suggestions for music and worship decor make this a unique resource.

Single copies: **$10** each
2 or more copies: **$7.50** each

THREE CONVENIENT WAYS TO ORDER:

PHONE
1•800•933•1800
(7:30 am to 7:00 pm CST)

FAX
1•800•933•7094
(anytime day or night)

MAIL
Send this card ▶
(To inquire about orders or payments call 1•800•933•4779.)

USE THIS CARD TO ORDER ADDITIONAL 1994 BOOKS ONLY!

To order 1995 books early use the card placed further on in this book.

1994 Year of Grace Liturgical Calendar

has striking, full-color art by Rhonda Krum of Kansas City, Missouri. The seasons have distinctive colors and the Sundays, feasts and holy days are clearly indicated. Great as a gift, as a teaching aid, and for anyone working with the liturgy. Quantity prices make it affordable for all parish families. Order extras for each classroom and the sacristy.

Poster size (26 x 26 inches, paper)
Single copies: **$7** each
2 – 24 copies: **$4** each
25 or more copies: **$3** each

Poster Size (26 x 26 inches, laminated)
$15

Notebook Size (17 x 11 inches, paper)
Pack of 25: **$10** per pack
(Sorry, we cannot ship less than a full pack.)

Notebook Size (17 x 11 inches, laminated)
$3 each

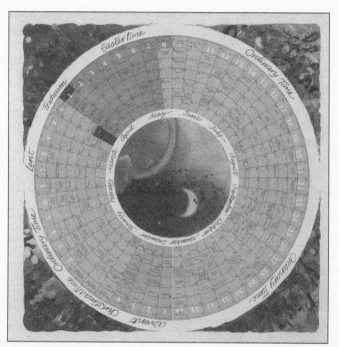

Reorder Department
Liturgy Training Publications
 1800 North Hermitage Avenue
Chicago IL 60622-1101

Place postage here

1994 AT HOME WITH THE WORD

A wonderful, inexpensive gift from the parish to each household!

How can we prepare to listen well to the scriptures each Sunday? How can those readings be present in the homes of parishioners to be read and discussed during the week?

At Home with the Word has the three readings for each Sunday of 1994 (Year B). The Bible translation is taken from the *Lectionary for the Christian People*, based on the Revised Standard Version. The readings are followed by short, thought-provoking and discussion-starting comments and questions. Each week a special set of lively notes suggests all sorts of ways to accept the challenge of the gospel and act on it at home, in the parish and in our world.

At Home with the Word includes beautifully illustrated seasonal psalms, daily home prayers, as well as the prayers of the Mass. The size of the book is 8 x 10 inches.

Single copies: **$6** each
2 – 99 copies: **$4** each
100 or more copies: **$2.50** each

Sample Page

AT HOME WITH THE WORD—1994

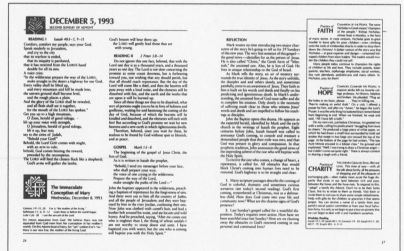

This book is for:

- individuals and families
- small study groups
- high school or college catechesis
- liturgy planners, homilists, catechumenate teams
- those confined to their homes who wish to read the scriptures each week with the church
- ministers of communion to the sick
- teachers and catechists

Get the best deal!

Check with the parish staff and organizations and other parishes. Order together to receive the best discount.

1994 ORDER FORM

Please send the number of copies indicated below:

_____ 1994 *At Home with the Word* = _____

_____ 1994 *Workbook for Lectors and Gospel Readers* = _____

_____ 1994 *Manual para proclamadores de la palabra* = _____

_____ 1994 *Sourcebook for Sundays and Seasons* = _____

1994 *Liturgical Calendars*

_____ Poster Size, *paper* = _____

_____ Poster Size, *laminated* = _____

_____ Notebook Size *(Pack of 25)* = _____

_____ Notebook Size, *laminated* = _____

Total = _____

See above for shipping and handling charges.

Read carefully and select your method of payment.

$_____ Full payment enclosed. IF sending full payment with order add 5% for shipping and handling in the U.S. **Minimum $3.00.** (10% for Canada. 15% for all other countries.) U.S. funds only.

$_____ Bill me. 10% shipping and handling will be added to the bill. (15% for Canada. 20% for all other countries.)

Bill to _____

Account # _____

Address _____

City, State, ZIP _____

Phone _____ / _____

Send to/Attention _____

Street address _____
(We ship UPS. Give only street address please. No PO Boxes.)

City, State, ZIP _____

Date ordered: ___/___/___ . To avoid duplication of orders, please keep a copy for your records.

Thank you for your order! 313

USE THIS CARD TO ORDER 1994 (YEAR B) BOOKS AND CALENDARS ONLY!

To order 1995 (Year C) books early, use the card placed further on in this book. To order 1995 books early use the card placed further on in this book.

CHRISTMAS DAY

LECTIONARY #16

READING I   Isaiah 52:7–10

A reading from the book of the prophet *Isaiah* ▪ ▪

NRSV: "the feet of the messenger who. . . ."

How *beautiful* upon the *mountains*
    are the *feet* of him who brings glad *tidings,*
Announcing *peace,* bearing *good news,*
    announcing *salvation,* and saying to *Zion,* ▪
    "Your God is *King!*" ▪ ▪

Do not shout "Hark."

NRSV: "sentinels" instead of "watchmen."

Hark! ▪ Your watchmen raise a *cry,*
    together they shout for *joy,*
For they see *directly,* before their *eyes,*
    the Lord *restoring* Zion. ▪
Break out together in *song,*
    O ruins of Jerusalem! ▪
For the Lord *comforts* his people,
    he *redeems* Jerusalem. ▪
The Lord has bared his holy *arm*
    in the sight of all the *nations;* ▪

Broad and expansive.

All the ends of the *earth* will behold
    the salvation of our *God.* ▪ ▪

READING II   Hebrews 1:1–6

A reading from the letter to the *Hebrews* ▪ ▪

NRSV: "our ancestors."

In times *past,* God spoke in *fragmentary* and *varied* ways to our fathers through the *prophets;* ▪ in this, the *final* age, he has spoken to us through his *Son,* whom he has made heir of all *things* and through whom he first created the *universe.* ▪ This *Son* is the reflection of the Father's *glory,* the exact representa- tion of the Father's *being,* and he sustains all *things* by his powerful *word.* ▪ ▪ When the Son had cleansed us from our *sins,* he took his seat at the right hand of the Majesty in *heaven,* as far superior to the *angels* as the *name* he has inherited is superior to theirs. ▪

Define carefully who this Son is.

This is one long rhetorical question. The mood is wonderment.

To which of the *angels* did God ever say, ▪
"You are my *son;* ▪ today I have *begotten* you"? ▪
Or again, ▪
"I will be his *father,* and he shall be my *son*"? ▪

READING I A great many passages from Isaiah have been set to music by composers and hymn writers — most mem- orably, perhaps, in Handel's *Messiah.* This brief text is chanted to a haunting and lovely melody in many monasteries on Christmas Eve. Once heard, it is never forgotten.

Try to read this stirring poem so that it will echo in the hearts of the assembly throughout the Christmas season. *You* are the messenger bringing the good news to the assembly today, and your "feet" (your approach, your presence) are welcome.

The truth of Christmas is that God has demonstrated sovereignty (kingship) over us and is restoring, redeeming and com- forting us. Those are very powerful verbs; they deserve a powerful rendering.

Many readers suffer from inhibitions when it comes to highly poetic texts such as this one. It's as though they feel foolish or silly when they are expected to commu- nicate the exalted emotion of the poet. Such feelings must be overcome to an extent before the full impact of the text can be felt by the listeners. Self-indulgence is not being recommended here, nor any- thing even approaching exhibitionism — just a bit of "soul," and the kind of courage that the Christmas message itself imparts.

READING II For the first time in this new liturgical year we have a reading from the richly-textured epistle to the Hebrews. The purpose of this entire letter is to demonstrate that all the partial revelations about God and the divine plan have come to fullness in Jesus, one who has a Son's relationship to a God who is Father.

Thus, the text you are reading today is meant to teach, albeit in an inspirational rather than a purely didactic tone. Some scholars feel that certain phrases and expressions are taken from an ancient hymn — so the passage seems to be a combination of information and exaltation. Your proclamation of it should take this into account.

The central truth here is that the Son, in whom we now see the glory of the Father revealed, ranks higher than the angels, and all the world is subject to him. The "babe of Bethlehem" is hardly the focal point in this Christmas reading! Rather, we see that the Incarnation (God becoming a human being in Jesus) is the beginning of the end—looking forward already to the death, resurrection and ascension of Christ.

This passage must be read with all the noble enthusiasm and solemnity you can muster. Relish the richness and the profundity of each phrase, so that the vast sweep of Christ's accomplishments and glory can be felt.

GOSPEL   These opening paragraphs of the gospel of John are from a hymn that the evangelist quotes and adapts. Beginning with the same words that open the book of Genesis, the text concerns itself with the Christ who existed before the world began and was active in its creation.

That same Christ entered the world (what we celebrate today), was rejected by many, but brought perfect love and redemption to all who accepted him. In other, and briefer, words: "The Word became flesh."

Pre-Vatican II Catholics will remember when this text was read at the end of every "Low Mass," and was called "The Last Gospel." A genuflection was prescribed at the words: "The Word became flesh and dwelt among us." Whatever reasons led to that practice, it is clear that these words have occupied a very special place in Christian liturgy and devotion. They seem to have a power of their own. They appear in the creed we recite at Mass—and today we are to genuflect when they are recited there.

This is not an easy reading—in part because it is so familiar, but perhaps more so because it is so rich. The option exists of using an abbreviated form. Unfortunately, the shorter form makes the thought even more difficult to follow.

And *again* when he leads his first-born *into the world*, he says, ▪
"Let all the angels of *God worship* him." ▪ ▪

GOSPEL   John 1:1–18

The beginning of the holy *gospel* according to *John* ▪ ▪

"In the beginning" reminds us of Genesis and the first words of the Bible. This is a summary of the mission of Jesus and his role in God's work of salvation. Read it with great care and deliberation.

In the beginning was the *Word;* ▪
the Word was in God's *presence,*
and the Word *was* God. ▪
He was *present* to God in the *beginning.*
Through *him* all things came into *being,*
and *apart* from *him nothing* came to be. ▪
Whatever came to be *in him,* found *life,*
life for the light of men. ▪

NRSV: "the light of all people."

The light shines on in *darkness,*
a darkness that did not *overcome it.* ▪ ▪
There was a man named *John* sent by *God,* who came as a *witness* to *testify* to the light, so that through him *all* men might believe— but only to *testify* to the light, for he *himself* was *not* the light. ▪ The *real* light which gives light to *every* man was coming into the world. ▪

NRSV: "all might believe through him."

NRSV: "everyone."

He was *in* the world,
and *through him* the world was *made,*
yet the world did not *know* who he *was.* ▪
To his *own* he came,
yet his own did not *accept* him. ▪
Any who *did* accept him
he empowered to become children of *God.* ▪
These are they who *believe* in his name— who were begotten *not* by blood, *not* by carnal desire, *nor* by man's *willing it,* but by *God.* ▪ ▪

NRSV: "or of the will of man," which still seems exclusive. Consider saying: "nor by human will."

The Word became *flesh*
and made his *dwelling* among us, ▪
and we have *seen* his glory:
the glory of an only *Son* coming
from the *Father,*
filled with *enduring* love. ▪ ▪
John *testified* to him by proclaiming, ▪ "This is he of whom I said, ▪ 'The one who comes *after* me ranks *ahead* of me, for he was *before* me.'" ▪
Of his *fullness*
we have all had a *share*—
love following upon *love.* ▪

The contrast between "law/ Moses" and "enduring love/Jesus Christ" should be stressed.

For while the *law* was a gift through *Moses,* this *enduring love* came through *Jesus Christ.* ▪ No one has ever seen *God.* It is God the only Son, ever at the Father's *side,* who has *revealed* him. ▪ ▪

[Shorter: John 1:5, 9–14]

THE HOLY FAMILY

LECTIONARY #17A

READING I   Sirach 3:2–6, 12–14

Sirach - SAI-rak

These poetic aphorisms demand an exalted proclamation. They are bold assertions that carry the guarantee of God's blessing. "Sons" can be "sons and daughters."

A reading from the book of *Sirach* ▪ ▪

The Lord sets a father in *honor* over his children; ▪
   a mother's *authority* he *confirms*
      over her sons. ▪
He who honors his *father* atones for *sins;* ▪
   he stores up *riches* who reveres his *mother.* ▪
He who honors his *father* is gladdened
      by *children,*
   and when he *prays* he is *heard.* ▪
He who *reveres* his father will live a long *life;* ▪
   he obeys the *Lord* who brings comfort
      to his *mother* ▪

The second paragraph is a poignant expansion on the first. Communicate the strength as well as the tenderness. Begin with "My child" to be inclusive.

My son, take *care* of your father
      when he is *old;* ▪
   grieve him *not* as long as he *lives.* ▪
Even if his *mind* fails, be *considerate*
      with him; ▪
   revile him *not* in the fullness
      of *your strength.* ▪
For kindness to a *father* will not be *forgotten,*
   it will serve as a *sin* offering— ▪
it will take lasting *root.* ▪ ▪

READING II   Colossians 3:12–21

The five virtues each must be given specific emphasis. "Bear with . . ." and "forgive whatever . . ." and "forgive . . ." must build to a peak. Pause before "over all these virtues put on love." Special emphasis here. It is the climax of the reading.

**A reading from the letter of *Paul*
to the *Colossians*** ▪ ▪

Because you are God's *chosen* ones, holy and beloved, ▪
clothe yourselves with heartfelt *mercy,* ▪ with
kindness, humility, meekness, and patience. ▪ *Bear*
with one another; ▪ forgive whatever *grievances* you
have against one another. *Forgive* as the Lord has forgiven *you.* ▪ Over all these virtues put on *love,* which
binds the rest *together* and makes them *perfect.* ▪
Christ's *peace* must *reign* in your hearts, since as
members of the one *body* you have been *called* to
that peace. ▪ Dedicate yourselves to *thankfulness.* ▪
Let the word of *Christ,* rich as it is, *dwell* in you. ▪

READING I The liturgy of the word today begins with a selection written by a school teacher. Sirach was a man of great learning and wide experience. His words of wisdom are the fruit of years of study and thought—and are modeled after the Book of Proverbs. This explains why the text of the first reading is cast in exalted verse-like aphorisms. Such style, even in modern literature, adds more than a hint of authority and weight. Who would dare deny a saying that begins, "He who honors his father . . ."?

To do justice to Sirach, you must realize that a conversational or informal manner of speaking is out of the question. The poetry/prose is exalted; the proclamation must be the same. As long as we remember that "exalted" does not mean "arrogant" or "cold" or "stuffy," we will find the proper tone for these treasured kernels of truth.

The way to prepare for proclamation of this reading is to study each sentence and meditate on the truth of it. Then analyze the grammatical structure—because the inverted word order can be tricky. But once the text is mastered, its timeless meaning and impact can startle even the most lethargic assembly into recognition.

READING II *Editor's note: In June 1992, the Bishops' Committee on the Liturgy issued a statement that permits a shorter version of this text to be proclaimed. The shorter version is highly recommended (Colossians 3:12–17).*

Paul's plea for oneness and harmony among Christians arises from the most basic thing we have in common: our bap-tism in Christ. It is difficult for us to remember that the unity we share in baptism is stronger than any other bond, bringing fellow Christians even closer together than blood relationships.

In baptism we become "God's chosen ones," so a certain kind of behavior fol-lows quite naturally. The strength of our union through baptism makes it clear how we are to treat one another. What makes it all possible, of course, is love, which binds all the other virtues together. Finally, the result of such loving unity is the peace that only Christ can give.

Clearly, Paul presents a difficult, though attractive, challenge to us. And the assembly who will hear this challenge will recognize at once that not all is as well as it could be—in the church or in families.

So as the reader, you will be encouraging your hearers to strive for greater success in the business of living together in love. Your voice will be completely sympathetic, because you know yourself how difficult it is sometimes to maintain peace. Above all, you will have mastered the ideas and advice in this text, so you can deliver it with confidence and peace.

GOSPEL The first two readings for this feast are the same for all three years of the lectionary cycle. The gospel is different so that three major events of Jesus' childhood may be recounted. Last year we read the account of the "Flight into Egypt." Next year we will read the story of the "Finding of the Child Jesus in the Temple." This year we hear the story of his "Presentation in the Temple."

The fact that a shorter form of this gospel narrative is provided indicates that the church wants today's feast to serve Christian families with a model of family life. The central point would then be that Mary and Joseph were obedient to the law in consecrating their first-born to the Lord. And, having fulfilled the law, they return to their home in Nazareth where we see Jesus growing to maturity in a simple and God-centered family setting.

If the longer form of this gospel narrative is read, the emphasis on familial domesticity is diminished somewhat, since Simeon and Anna take center stage and tell us a great deal about what this divine child means to human history. Certainly the most astonishing note sounded in Simeon's canticle is that this child (who *is* God's "saving deed") is a "revealing light to the Gentiles!" Luke is making the very clear and (to his contemporaries) amazing assertion that God's movement toward the world in love is universal. The good news is for all peoples of the earth, not only for the chosen people, Israel. Though it may be difficult for us to appreciate how radical such assertion is, we can see why Luke chooses the temple as the perfect setting for such a revelation. We can also understand why Simeon (a just and pious man who "awaited the consolation of Israel") is

In wisdom made *perfect*, instruct and *admonish* one another. ▪ Sing gratefully to God from your *hearts* ▪ in *psalms*, *hymns*, and inspired *songs*. ▪ *Whatever* you do, whether in *speech* or in *action*, ▪ do it in the name of the Lord *Jesus*. ▪ Give thanks to God the *Father* through *him*. ▪ ▪

See the commentary. This paragraph may be omitted.

You who are *wives*, ▪ be submissive to your husbands. ▪ This is your duty in the *Lord*. ▪ Husbands, ▪ *love* your wives. Avoid any bitterness toward them. You children, obey your *parents* in everything as the acceptable way in the Lord. And fathers, do not nag your children lest they lose heart. ▪ ▪

GOSPEL   Luke 2:22–40

A reading from the holy *gospel* according to *Luke* ▪ ▪

The first sentence is quite long. But it is easily broken up into thought patterns. In effect, it is a short story with commentary. Lots of vocal variety will enable you to distinguish the events from the significance of the events.

When the day came to *purify* them according to the law of *Moses*, Mary and Joseph brought Jesus up to *Jerusalem* so that he could be *presented* to the Lord, for it is written in the *law* of the Lord, ▪ "Every *first-born* male shall be consecrated to the *Lord*." ▪ They came to offer in sacrifice "a pair of *turtledoves* or two young *pigeons*," *in accord* with the dictate in the law of the *Lord*. ▪ ▪

A new section begins here—another short story. Prepare for it with a pause. Simeon = SIH-mee-uhn.

There lived in Jerusalem at the time a certain man named *Simeon*. ▪ He was *just* and *pious*, and awaited the consolation of *Israel*, and the Holy *Spirit* was upon him. ▪ It was *revealed* to him by the Holy Spirit that he would not experience *death* until he had seen the *Anointed* of the Lord. ▪ He came to the temple *now*, inspired by the Spirit; ▪ and when the parents brought in the child *Jesus* to perform for him the customary *ritual* of the *law*, he took him in his *arms* and blessed God in these words: ▪

This text is prayed at Compline, the church's official night prayer. Read it lovingly.

"*Now*, Master, you can *dismiss* your
    servant in *peace*; ▪
    you have fulfilled your *word*. ▪
For my eyes have witnessed your saving *deed*
    displayed for *all* the peoples to *see*: ▪
A revealing light to the *Gentiles*,
    the *glory* of *your* people *Israel*." ▪

The child's father and mother were *marveling* at what was being *said* about him. ▪ Simeon blessed them and said to Mary his mother: ▪ "This child is *destined* to be the *downfall* and the *rise* of *many* in Israel, a sign that will be *opposed* and you yourself shall be *pierced* with a *sword* so that the thoughts of many hearts may be laid *bare*." ▪ ▪

Another part of the story begins here. Prepare with a pause; begin with a fresh intonation. Phanuel = FAN-yoo-ehl, Asher = ASH-er.

There was also a certain *prophetess, Anna* by name, daughter of *Phanuel* of the tribe of *Asher.* ▪ She had seen many *days,* having lived *seven* years with her *husband* after her marriage and then as a *widow* until she was *eighty-four.* ▪ She was constantly in the *temple,* worshiping day and night in *fasting* and *prayer.* ▪ Coming on the scene at this moment, she gave thanks to God and *talked* about the *child* to all who looked forward to the deliverance of *Jerusalem.* ▪ ▪

The narrative begun in the first sentence is concluded. Communicate the calm and peaceful home scene described here.

When the pair had fulfilled all the *prescriptions* of the *law* of the *Lord,* they returned to *Galilee* and their *own* town of *Nazareth.* ▪ The child *grew* in *size* and *strength,* filled with *wisdom,* and the grace of *God* was upon him. ▪ ▪

[Shorter: Luke 2:22, 39–40]

the perfect spokesperson for God's great good news. Anna is another spokesperson for the people of Israel, long awaiting the coming of the Messiah, the anointed one who would deliver the chosen people from bondage.

The gospel text presented here is a story of fulfillment *par excellence*. Luke has assembled so many echoes from Israel's history that the temple scene is resonant with prophecies and promises. The prophet Malachi is most clearly evoked: "Suddenly there will come to the temple the Lord whom you seek." And for Luke's readers the two venerable witnesses who testify at this scene have strikingly convincing credentials.

READING I In recent years, the Solemnity of the Epiphany has been transferred from January 6 to the Sunday nearest that date. It is the fullness of Christmas, and it is good that we celebrate it now with a Sunday assembly.

There is a beautiful text from the church's Evening Prayer on this feast that summarizes what we celebrate: *"Three mysteries mark this holy day; today the star leads the Magi to the infant Christ; today water is changed into wine for the wedding feast; today Christ wills to be baptized by John in the river Jordan to bring us salvation."* The celebration of the Epiphany is concerned with theological meaning rather than historical events.

The gospel reading mentions only the first of these three mysteries: the lovely story of the three kings. (Happily, the Feast of the Baptism of the Lord is observed next Sunday, so we celebrate two of the great mysteries of the Epiphany in close proximity.) All three events have in common the manifestation of the divinity of Christ and the universality of his role as Messiah. The word "epiphany" means "to show forth."

The first reading (another gem from Isaiah) is preoccupied with the notion that God's glorious presence is now seen in the midst of Jerusalem (the holy city and God's holy people). In other words, though darkness may surround us, the glory of the Lord makes us shine like a bright dawn. That is the effect of the "restoration/redemption" which comes from God. That is the effect of Christmas, when the glory of God is manifested in Christ. And all the world (even the Gentiles) will see it and rejoice.

EPIPHANY

LECTIONARY #20

READING I   Isaiah 60:1–6

A reading from the book of the prophet *Isaiah* ▪▪

This poem deserves your brightest voice and most enthusiastic proclamation. Take it slowly and relish each image, so that the assembly will be caught up in the wonder and awe of the prophet's joy.

Make the parallel emphasis as indicated: "you . . . shines" and "you . . . glory."

Rise up in *splendor*, Jerusalem!
　　Your *light* has come,
　　the glory of the Lord *shines* upon you. ▪
See, *darkness* covers the earth,
　　and thick *clouds* cover the *peoples;* ▪
But upon *you* the Lord *shines,*
　　and over *you* appears his *glory.* ▪
Nations shall walk by your *light,*
　　and *kings* by your shining *radiance.* ▪
Raise your *eyes* and look *about;*
　　they all gather and *come* to you: ▪
Your sons come from *afar,*
　　and your daughters in the arms
　　　　of their *nurses.* ▪▪

Then you shall be *radiant* at what you see,
　　your heart shall *throb* and *overflow,* ▪
For the riches of the *sea* shall be *emptied out*
　　before you, ▪
　　the wealth of *nations* shall be *brought* to you. ▪
Caravans of *camels* shall fill you,
　　dromedaries from *Midian* and *Ephah;* ▪
All from *Sheba* shall come
　　bearing *gold* and *frankincense,*
　　and proclaiming the *praises* of the *Lord.* ▪▪

Midian = MIH-dih-uhn
Ephah = EE-phuh

READING II   Ephesians 3:2–3, 5–6

A reading from the letter of *Paul* to the *Ephesians* ▪▪

I am sure you have heard of the *ministry* which God in his goodness *gave* me in your regard. ▪ God's secret *plan*, as I have *briefly* described it, was *revealed* to me, unknown to men in *former* ages but now *revealed*

NRSV: "humankind."

by the *Spirit* to the holy *apostles* and *prophets*. ▪ It is no less than *this:* ▪ in Christ Jesus the *Gentiles* are now *co-heirs* with the *Jews*, ▪ members of the same *body* and *sharers* of the promise through the preaching of the *gospel*. ▪ ▪

"It is no less than this!" Such an expression demands that what follows be proclaimed mightily!

GOSPEL   Matthew 2:1–12

A reading from the holy *gospel* according to *Matthew* ▪ ▪

The story is familiar to the assembly. Your challenge is to make it live anew—in all its richness and tension. Resist the temptation to pass over even the smallest detail of this passage.

After Jesus' *birth* in Bethlehem of *Judea* during the reign of King *Herod*, astrologers from the *east* arrived one day in Jerusalem *inquiring*, ▪ "Where is the newborn king of the *Jews?* ▪ We observed his *star* at its rising and have come to pay him *homage.*" ▪ At this news King Herod became *greatly* disturbed, and with him all *Jerusalem*. ▪ Summoning all of the chief priests and scribes of the people, he inquired of them where the *Messiah* was to be born. ▪ "In Bethlehem of *Judea*," they informed him. "Here is what the *prophet* has written: ▪

'And *you*, Bethlehem, land of *Judah*,
are by no means *least* among the princes
   of Judah,
since from *you* shall come a *ruler*
who is to *shepherd* my people *Israel*.'" ▪

Here the conflict begins.

Herod called the astrologers *aside* and found out from them the exact *time* of the star's *appearance*. ▪ Then he sent them to *Bethlehem*, after having instructed them: ▪ "*Go* and get detailed *information* about the child. ▪ When you have *discovered* something, report your findings to *me* so that *I* may go and offer him homage *too.*" ▪

After their audience with the *king*, they set *out*. ▪ The star which they had observed at its *rising* went *ahead* of them until it came to a standstill over the place where the *child* was. ▪ They were *overjoyed* at seeing the star, and on entering the *house*, found the child with *Mary* his *mother*. ▪ They *prostrated* themselves and did him *homage*. ▪ Then they opened their coffers and presented him with *gifts* of *gold*, *frankincense*, and *myrrh*. ▪ ▪

Read the final sentence with a renewed sense of mystery. The implication is that more—and greater—conflict is to come.

They received a message in a dream *not* to return to *Herod*, so they went *back* to their own country by another *route*. ▪ ▪

READING II   Some scholars think that the letter to the Ephesians was not written by Paul, but by a later writer who takes pains to show how great Paul's mission was in getting the good news out to all the world—way beyond its Jewish origins. Certainly this is the point of today's feast: God's secret plan has not been kept secret! In Christ, all the world has "seen God," and all peoples have become coheirs of the ancient promises.

As you proclaim this passage, imagine yourself sharing an ambassador's delight over a successful mission, an effort at reconciliation that has exceeded even your highest hopes. Peoples with many differences have come together to embrace a common belief and goal. Your joy at this success is exceeded only by your gratitude to God for making it possible.

GOSPEL   Remember what Matthew's overall purpose is in this narrative: to demonstrate that all the prophecies about the promised Messiah have been fulfilled in the birth of Jesus. Then you will proclaim this dramatic story with a view toward convincing the assembly that their faith in Christ is indeed well placed.

Here is the evidence: The humble town of Bethlehem (the city of King David's ancestor, Ruth) would be the Messiah's birthplace; kings (non-Jews) from foreign lands would acknowledge his birth and be guided by a miraculous event (the star); and they would offer gifts. Although Matthew quotes the prophets for only one of these fulfilled promises, it is clear that he has many ancient texts in mind (including the last sentence of today's first reading).

The splendor of "Herod's city" (Jerusalem) is contrasted with the lowliness of Jesus' birthplace (Bethlehem), just as Herod's jealousy is contrasted with the humility of the foreign dignitaries. This gospel story is replete with conflict, drama and the inevitable struggle that God's manifestation in Christ implies for the world. Already, we see a hint of the inevitable sacrificial death of this "newborn king."

Finally, notice that although the story has a conclusion, it is far from a resolution. The astrologers have to slip past Herod by taking an alternate route. Danger still exists for them.

READING I Here we have the striking poetry of Isaiah. This reading is part of the first of four passages that are called the "Suffering Servant Songs." Bible scholars have much to debate about these songs, including the subject of them. Who is (was) this servant? For the gospel writers and for the liturgy today, however, it is clear that the servant is Jesus, and in today's feast we commemorate the beginning of his service.

Isaiah tells us about the election, the anointing and the objective of the servant's mission. He also describes the style or manner in which the servant will accomplish his goals. As you read these descriptions, it should be difficult for the assembly *not* to see the image of Jesus in his public ministry. As a matter of fact, next Sunday we begin to see in the gospel readings Jesus beginning his public ministry, so this "Servant Song" is a perfect bridge between the liturgy of Christmas and Ordinary Time.

Remember again that you are reading poetry—a form of literature that is particularly rich. Be sure to give each image its proper space and emphasis. Then your hearers will see a detailed portrait of the one on whom God's favor rests, the one whose mission they are called to share.

READING II For today's celebration the most important words in this second reading are these: "beginning in Galilee with the baptism John preached; of the way God anointed [Jesus] with the Holy Spirit and power." Here we have an example of the church's earliest teaching about Jesus and his mission. Peter's point is that it all began at the Jordan River when a divine anointing made manifest in Jesus the establishment of the reign of God on earth. In the power of the Spirit's anointing, Jesus begins his ministry—revealing himself, through good works, to be the Servant of God promised by Isaiah (the first reading). The point is this: God's presence in the world is demonstrated by Jesus, and God's plan to redeem the world through this anointed servant is set in motion at the moment of baptism.

You are proclaiming the words of a teacher. This brief passage is overflowing with important ideas and convictions. Let none of them escape your careful attention and your finest reading skills.

THE BAPTISM OF THE LORD

LECTIONARY #21

READING I   Isaiah 42:1–4, 6–7

A reading from the book of the prophet *Isaiah* ▪▪

"Here is my servant . . ." is a solemn pronouncement. Let it work its power!

Here is my *servant* whom I *uphold*,
   my *chosen* one with whom I am *pleased*, ▪▪
Upon whom I have put *my spirit*; ▪
   he shall bring forth *justice* to the *nations*,
Not crying out, *not* shouting,
   not making his *voice* heard in the *street*. ▪

Notice how the inverted word order makes the text stronger. "He shall not break a bruised reed" is not as memorable as "A bruised reed he shall not break."
Now the Lord speaks to the servant rather than about him. Let your voice signal the change.

A bruised *reed* he shall *not* break,
   and a smoldering *wick* he shall *not* quench,
Until he establishes *justice* on the *earth*; ▪
   the coastlands will *wait* for his *teaching*. ▪▪
I, the *Lord*, have called *you* for the victory
   of *justice*, ▪
   I have grasped *you* by the *hand*; ▪
I *formed* you, and set you
   as a *covenant of the people*,
   a *light* for the *nations*, ▪

"To open . . ." stands alone. But "to bring out . . ." and "from the dungeon . . ." are parts of a parallel construction. The second phrase echoes the first.

To *open* the eyes of the *blind*,
   to bring out *prisoners* from *confinement*, ▪
   and from the *dungeon*, those who live
     in *darkness*. ▪▪

The introductory sentence sets the scene and the identity of the speaker. Cornelius = kawr-NEE-lee-uhs

Now you are speaking in the person of Peter. Let his joy ring in your voice. To be inclusive: "Rather, anyone of any nation. . . ." and "people of Israel."

A reading from the *Acts* of the *Apostles* ▪ ▪

Peter addressed *Cornelius* and the people assembled at his *house* in these *words:* ▪ "I begin to *see* how *true* it is that God shows *no partiality.* ▪ Rather, the man of *any* nation who *fears* God and acts *uprightly* is *acceptable* to him. ▪ This is the message he has sent to the sons of *Israel,* ▪ 'the good news of *peace'* proclaimed through Jesus *Christ* who is *Lord of all.* ▪ I take it you *know* what has been reported all over Judea about Jesus of *Nazareth,* beginning in Galilee with the baptism *John* preached; ▪ of the way God *anointed* him with the Holy *Spirit* and *power.* ▪ He went about doing *good works* and *healing* all who were in the grip of the *devil,* ▪ and *God* was *with* him. ▪ ▪

"God was with him." A power-packed assertion! Let it ring out. God's special presence in Jesus was made clear at his baptism.

This is a brief chronicle of an historical event. The first half sets the scene; the second half gives it special meaning.

A reading from the holy *gospel* according to *Mark* ▪ ▪

The theme of John's *preaching* was: ▪ "One more *powerful* than *I* is to come *after* me. ▪ I am not fit to stoop and untie his *sandal* straps. ▪ *I* have baptized you in *water;* ▪ *he* will baptize you in the Holy *Spirit.*" ▪ ▪

Pause. Jesus appears on the scene. The focus sharpens.

During that time, Jesus came from *Nazareth* in Galilee and was *baptized* in the Jordan by *John.* ▪ *Immediately* on coming up out of the *water* he saw the sky *rent* in two and the Spirit *descending* on him like a *dove.* ▪ Then a voice came from the heavens: ▪ "*You* are my beloved *Son.* ▪ On *you* my *favor* rests." ▪ ▪

Mark's word (in Greek) for "rent in two" is almost brutal. Emphasize the phrase.

GOSPEL   With the feast of the baptism of Jesus we bring the sweep of Advent, Christmas and Epiphany to a close, and we witness the inauguration of Jesus' public ministry on earth.

Glance back at the first reading we heard on the First Sunday of Advent. There, in Isaiah, we heard the urgent cry, "Oh, that you would rend the heavens and come down." In today's brief gospel narrative from Mark we hear, "He saw the sky rent in two and the Spirit descending on him like a dove." As the lectionary interprets these two passages, the urgent cry has been heard. God has ripped the heavens open and drawn aside the veil that separated divinity from humanity. Jesus is designated as the chosen Son, the anointed Messiah, the beloved servant who will reunite heaven and earth with unbreakable bonds of love.

In this passage, Mark's contemporaries would have heard quite clearly a reference to Psalm 2, the great hymn that sings, "You are my son; this day have I begotten you." Finally, the Servant Songs of Isaiah (today's first reading) spring immediately to mind. These portions of the Hebrew Scriptures shed light on who the church understands Jesus to be and what the qualities of his mission are.

READING I Call and response: From the book of Genesis through the book of Revelation, this is the story of our relationship with God. Adam heard God's voice calling out to him in the Garden of Eden. Those who are marked for salvation hear God's angel call out to them at the end of time. In today's first reading we hear Samuel answer God's call with a perfect response: "Speak, Lord, for your servant is listening."

Notice, however, that the response comes only after discernment, even confusion. Because "Samuel was not familiar with the Lord," his response was not easily evoked. This is the drama of every vocation. The call is issued over and over, and our response each time becomes gradually more honest and sincere, more faithful, less confused.

The story of Samuel's call appears here in a formula often used in storytelling. The effect of the repeated dialogue ("Here I am, you called me." "I did not call you, my son.") is that the final response is more deeply impressed upon us. Ancient stories and fables use such repetition to fulfill the expectations of the hearers, and to make themselves memorable. Use your best storytelling technique to allow this reading to have its full effect.

The gospel narrative today also is concerned with call and response. Immediately after his own call to messiahship at his baptism, Jesus begins to gather disciples to share his mission. "Come and see," he says, and the disciples respond, "We have found the Messiah."

READING II Call and response: Those who have been called to share in the life of the Spirit must respond in a particular way. The dignity of "being called" makes certain lifestyles unthinkable. In this passage, Paul is telling the Corinthians to abandon pagan practices and to live in a way consistent with their new calling. The historical context of Paul's admonition makes it clear that he is faced with the challenge of persuading people to change their ways. Some Christians at Corinth felt they were above any strictures of the law. They believed their privileged spiritual status placed them beyond any moral code.

Paul recognizes the difficulty in altering people's beliefs, but insists on the consequences of being "joined to the Lord." He

SECOND SUNDAY IN ORDINARY TIME

LECTIONARY #66

READING I   1 Samuel 3:3–10, 19

The literary form here is a ritual short story. The call comes three times; only then is it understood. Let the classic structure of the tale work its effect. Eli = EE-lai

This sentence creates a pause in the narrative—to explain why Samuel has difficulty understanding that the Lord is calling him.

We might expect the Lord's message to come here. But no, the point of the story is the "calling." The story closes quietly, assuming that Samuel is now perfectly attentive to the Lord's voice.

A reading from the first book of *Samuel* ▪ ▪

Samuel was *sleeping* in the temple of the *Lord* where the ark of *God* was. ▪ The Lord called to Samuel, ▪ who answered, ▪ "*Here* I am." ▪ He ran to Eli and said, ▪ "*Here* I am. You *called* me." ▪ "*I* did not call you," Eli said. ▪ "Go back to sleep." ▪ So he went back to sleep. ▪ Again the Lord called Samuel, who rose and went to Eli. ▪ "*Here* I am," he said. ▪ "You *called* me." ▪ But he answered, ▪ "I did *not* call you, my son. ▪ Go back to sleep." ▪ At that time Samuel was not *familiar* with the Lord, because the Lord had not revealed *anything* to him as yet. ▪ The Lord called Samuel again, for the third time. ▪ Getting up and going to Eli, he said, ▪ "*Here* I am. ▪ You called me." ▪ Then Eli understood that the Lord was calling the youth. ▪ So he said to Samuel, ▪ "Go to sleep, and if you are called, reply, ▪ '*Speak*, Lord, for your *servant* is *listening.*'" ▪ When Samuel went to sleep in his place, the Lord came and *revealed* his *presence*, calling out as before, ▪ "Samuel, Samuel!" ▪ Samuel answered, ▪ "Speak, for your *servant* is *listening.*" ▪ ▪

Samuel grew up, and the Lord was *with* him, not permitting any word of *his* to be without effect. ▪ ▪

A reading from the first letter of *Paul* to the *Corinthians* ▪ ▪

The word "body" must be emphasized. It is the subject of the reading. The word "immorality" here is not as precise as the NRSV's "fornication," which is Paul's specific concern here.

The body is *not* for *immorality;* ▪ it is for the *Lord,* and the *Lord* is for the *body.* ▪ God, who raised up the *Lord,* will raise *us* also by his power. ▪ ▪

Do you not see that your *bodies* are members of *Christ?* ▪ Whoever is joined to the Lord becomes one *spirit* with him. ▪ ▪ Shun *lewd* conduct. ▪ Every other sin a man commits is *outside* his *body,* but the fornicator *sins* against his own *body.* ▪ You *must* know that your body is a temple of the Holy *Spirit,* who is within—the Spirit you have received from God. ▪ You are *not* your *own.* ▪ You have been purchased, and at *what* a price! ▪ So *glorify* God in your body. ▪ ▪

NRSV: "Every sin that a person commits is outside the body; but the fornicator sins against the body itself."

"You must know"—implying how unthinkable it is that we could defile the "temple of the Holy Spirit."

The final sentence should be emphasized thus: "So glorify God in your body," with the opposite implied: "don't insult God in your body."

GOSPEL   John 1:35–42

A reading from the holy *gospel* according to *John* ▪ ▪

This short passage is composed of three sections. This first identifies Jesus as God's Chosen One.

John was in Bethany across the Jordan with two of his disciples. ▪ As he watched *Jesus* walk by he said, ▪ *"Look!* ▪ There is the Lamb of *God!"* ▪ The two disciples heard what he said, and *followed* Jesus. ▪ When Jesus turned around and *noticed* them following him, he asked them, ▪ "What are you looking for?" ▪ They said to him, ▪ "Rabbi (which means Teacher), where do you *stay?"* ▪ "Come and *see,"* he answered. ▪ So they went to see where he was *lodged,* and *stayed* with him that day. ▪ (It was about four in the afternoon.) ▪ ▪

The second section begins here. The dialog is striking; it reveals the attraction to Jesus that the disciples felt. Let your voice convey their eagerness to be with him.

One of the two who had followed him after hearing John was Simon Peter's brother Andrew. ▪ The first thing *he* did was seek out his brother *Simon* and tell him, ▪ "We have found the *Messiah!"* (which means the Anointed). ▪ He brought him to Jesus, who looked at him and said, ▪ "You are *Simon,* son of John; ▪ your name shall be *Cephas* (which is rendered Peter)." ▪ ▪

The third section reveals Jesus' penetrating insight. His words to Peter are a thunderclap of revelation and a forecast of Peter's special place among the apostles. Cephas = SEE-fuhs.

insists on the unity of body and spirit, and points out that our very bodies are made holy by the indwelling of God's Spirit. Thus, everything we do must be an expression of our dignity and holiness. There is no separation between body and soul. Every part of us is infused with God's Spirit.

We belong body and soul to God, who bought us at the price of the Son, crucified for us, but now risen from the dead and glorified in the Spirit. Our very flesh and blood give glory to God.

GOSPEL   Call and response: John's calling was to point the way to the Messiah. In his response he becomes a perfect model for all who are called to official ministry: He makes sure that those who hear him preach are directed to Jesus and not to himself. Because there always have been religious leaders who seem to "get in the way" instead of "pointing the way," John's example is important in every age.

The gospel writer intends to show us a great deal in this passage. John the Baptist's role is made clear. He is to point toward the "Lamb of God," a title that reminds the reader of the "sacrificial lamb," the "suffering servant" of God, and even the "good shepherd" title so poignantly invoked by Jesus.

The dialogue between Jesus and the two disciples is a summary of the "call and response" challenge that every Christian must experience in some way. The question "What are you looking for?" is addressed to all of us. And all of us answer with another question: "Where do you stay?" (where is God found, where is lasting peace, where is the answer to life's most perplexing questions?). Then we are directed to "Come and see," which could just as easily read, "Follow me." When we heed that direction, we too are able to proclaim with Andrew, "We have found the Messiah!"

READING I   Jonah and Jesus have very similar missions in today's readings, and that is why the first reading and the gospel are set side by side in today's liturgy. Indeed, even the short second reading is about "being prepared" by separating ourselves from the attachments of earth. Thus, all three readings form a tightly woven meditation on the choice of a better way of life.

Jonah had difficulty believing that God really wanted him to preach to the people of Nineveh. After all, they were pagans! And because of their reputation for wickedness, Jonah found it hard to believe God's mercy could extend even to them, and approached his task with less than wholehearted enthusiasm. However, only one-third of the way into his mission, the people of Nineveh responded fully to his call to conversion. We see a parallel in the way the first disciples respond to Jesus. They "immediately" became his followers after hearing "Come after me." Jonah and Jesus both have something new and wonderful to announce: God's loving plan of salvation is universal, extended to every nation and every person on earth. Some people still have difficulty believing this, so your retelling of the Jonah story is urgently needed. Proclaim it with all the conviction it demands, and rejoice in the happy ending.

READING II   Is there anyone who does not realize that nothing is permanent in this life? Paul's words have great force today in the light of this universal realization. Whether or not Paul expected Jesus to return in just a few years, his advice to us is relevant. The virtue of detachment is perhaps more difficult in our culture than in others. We are bombarded with messages that security can be found in material things. Paul reminds us that such messages are false.

The rhetorical device employed in this reading is hyperbole—exaggeration for the sake of the point. Married people cannot *literally* live as though they had no spouse. The point is that we need to keep things in perspective and proportion. Nothing lasts forever, and the surest way to pave the way for disappointment is to live as if it did.

Ultimately, Paul's message is a totally positive one. The best guarantee of unshak-

THIRD SUNDAY IN ORDINARY TIME

LECTIONARY #69

READING I   Jonah 3:1–5, 10

This little story shows us Jonah's effectiveness as a preacher and the readiness of the people of Nineveh to take heed. Nineveh = NIHN-eh-veh.

"Now" signals important information; we need to know the immensity of the situation before we can appreciate the outcome.

A reading from the book of the prophet *Jonah* ▪▪

The word of the *Lord* came to Jonah *saying:* ▪ "Set out for the great city of Nineveh, and announce to it the message that I will tell you." ▪ So Jonah made ready and *went* to Nineveh, according to the Lord's *bidding.* ▪ Now Nineveh was an *enormously* large city; ▪ it took three *days* to go through it. ▪ Jonah began his journey through the city, and had gone but a *single* day's walk announcing, ▪ "Forty days *more* and Nineveh shall be *destroyed,*" ▪ when the people of Nineveh *believed* God; ▪ they proclaimed a *fast* and all of them, great and small, put on *sackcloth.* ▪▪

Here is the resolution. Your tone should communicate that God's response is typically generous.

When God saw by their actions how they *turned* from their evil way, he repented of the evil that he had threatened to do to them; ▪ he did not carry it *out.* ▪▪

READING II   1 Corinthians 7:29–31

NRSV: "brothers and sisters." The intended effect of this reading is to impress the hearer with the urgency of the situation. It is achieved by repetition: "let those . . . those . . . those . . . those." Let each "those" work its effect by slowly building the intensity. The final phrase is the whole point!

A reading from the first letter of *Paul* to the *Corinthians* ▪▪

I tell you, brothers, the time is *short.* ▪ From now on those with wives should *live* as though they *had* none; ▪ those who *weep* should live as though they were *not* weeping, ▪ and those who *rejoice* as though they were not *rejoicing;* ▪ buyers should conduct themselves as though they owned *nothing,* and those who make *use* of the world as though they were not *using* it, ▪ for the world as *we* know it is passing away. ▪▪

A reading from the holy *gospel* according to *Mark* ▪ ▪

After John's arrest, Jesus appeared in Galilee proclaiming God's good *news:* ▪ *"This* is the time of *fulfillment.* ▪ The reign of God is at *hand!* ▪ Reform your lives and believe in the good *news!"* ▪ ▪

As he made his way along the Sea of Galilee, he observed Simon and his brother Andrew casting their *nets* into the *sea;* ▪ they were fishermen. ▪ Jesus said to them, ▪ "Come after *me;* ▪ I will make you fishers of *men."* ▪ They *immediately* abandoned their nets and became his followers. ▪ Proceeding a little farther along, he caught sight of *James,* Zebedee's son, and his his *brother John.* ▪ They *too* were in their boat putting their nets in order. ▪ He *summoned* them on the *spot.* ▪ They abandoned their father *Zebedee,* who was in the boat with the hired men, and went off in his company. ▪ ▪

Section one: Jesus appears on the scene after John has left it—just as John had prophesied. Your emphasis must convey that Jesus (not his message) is the fulfillment, the kingdom and the gospel!

Section two: Jesus has an immediate and transforming effect on every life he touches. Convey the immediacy. NRSV: "I will make you fish for people."

Section three: Why wasn't Zebedee called too! Answering the call involves difficult choices: "they abandoned their father."

able peace is the realization that life is precious, fragile and transitory. We accept everything as a loving gift from God, we treat all creation with the boundless respect it deserves, and we let go readily, knowing that even greater (and permanent!) gifts are in store for us.

GOSPEL   In this short gospel passage Mark gives us Jesus' missionary objective in a nutshell. Jesus announces the "fulfillment" of all expectations and hopes. All that the prophets had to say about the coming of the Messiah and the restoration of God's sovereignty has come true in the person of Jesus. The "reign of God" is now established in him, and the conversion and faith urged upon us is centered in him.

Jesus is saying, in other words, "I am the fulfilled promises of God, I am the reign of God, I am the one to turn to in repentance, I am the good news to believe in." Because we tend to separate the person of Jesus from his message, we need to hear Mark clearly. Jesus *is* his message.

Notice how the call of the first disciples makes this clear. Jesus does not say, "Hear my words." He says, "Come after me." John the Baptist fulfilled his mission perfectly when he pointed out Jesus (not his message) as "the way." Only Jesus can say "*I* am the way, the truth, and the life." And that distinguishes him from all prophets—past, present and future. They *preach* the good news, but Jesus *is* the good news.

Common human experience demonstrates that genuine conversion (turning completely around and heading in a new direction) is most often the result of an encounter with a person who compels us with example, not words. Christian conversion is a matter of seeing that Jesus, his example, and his words are indistinguishable—and therefore irresistible.

READING I The writer of Deuteronomy is making the point here that the prophetic tradition in Israel will continue. After Moses there will be a succession of those chosen to speak for God and to guide the people. God promises to make the divine will clear to Israel through prophets whose words can be trusted, for they accurately relay God's wishes.

This first reading is obviously matched up with the gospel passage for today to make the point that Jesus is the ultimate prophet, the one who speaks for God with absolute and incontestable authority. The original intent of the text from Deuteronomy is thus reinterpreted through the eyes of Christian hindsight.

For our purposes, perhaps the most striking aspect of this text is the horrible fate of those who presume to speak for God, but do not represent the divine will honestly. They shall die. Every Christian is a prophet is the sense that we all speak for God in the way we live. The responsibility is an awesome one, and the result of not living up to that responsibility is terrifying!

READING II There is no need to shy away from this reading because it seems too challenging or because it seems to disparage marital union. Paul has a point to make: The ideal life for the Christian is to be entirely devoted to the Lord, in body and in mind. His personal conviction is that those who are unencumbered with the responsibilities of marriage can devote themselves to God more completely. The witness of monks and nuns throughout the ages (and in many non-Christian traditions) reflects the same conviction.

Paul clearly felt that celibacy is a higher way of life than marriage. But there is no indication whatever that he expected the majority of Christians to embrace his preference. The idea of enforced celibacy would have been completely abhorrent to Paul, as he himself says: "I have no desire to place restrictions upon you."

In this reading we glimpse the passion of a man whose faith has consumed him entirely. He wants to share that passion and to encourage us to place the highest priority on our devotion to the Lord. Nothing must displace that devotion, not even marriage—the kind of intimate union that most beautifully reflects God's relationship with us.

FOURTH SUNDAY IN ORDINARY TIME

LECTIONARY #72

READING I   Deuteronomy 18:15–20

Deuteronomy = dyoo-ter-AH-nuh-mee
The tone is one of assurance, despite the terrifying language. It is an awesome scene in which God promises to be present in the prophets. This first section is Moses speaking. The NRSV has "people" instead of "kinsmen."

From here on Moses is repeating God's words to him. The solemnity of "I will" continues throughout. NRSV: "people" instead of "kinsmen." And, "Anyone who does not heed the words that the prophet shall speak in my name, I myself will hold accountable."

A reading from the book of *Deuteronomy* ▪▪

Moses spoke to the people, saying: ▪ "A prophet like *me* will the Lord, your God, raise *up* for you from among your own *kinsmen;* ▪ to him you shall listen. ▪ This is exactly what you requested of the Lord, your God, at Horeb on the day of the assembly, when you said, ▪ 'Let us not again hear the voice of the *Lord,* our *God,* ▪ nor see this great *fire* any more, lest we *die.'* ▪ And the Lord said to me, ▪ 'This was well said. ▪ I will raise up for them a prophet like *you* from among their *kinsmen,* and will put *my* words into his mouth; ▪ he shall tell them all that *I* command him. ▪ If any man will not *listen* to my words which he speaks in my name, I myself will make him answer for it. ▪ But if a prophet *presumes* to speak in my name an oracle that I have not *commanded* him to speak, or speaks in the name of other *gods,* ▪ he shall *die.'"* ▪▪

READING II   1 Corinthians 7:32–35

Respect the tidy construction: "unmarried/married."

Paul gives his reason for this advice as a conclusion. Prepare for it with a pause, and finish with a sense of closure.

A reading from the first letter of *Paul* to the *Corinthians* ▪▪

I should like you to be free of all *worries.* ▪ The *unmarried* man is busy with the *Lord's* affairs, concerned with pleasing the *Lord;* ▪ but the married man is busy with *this* world's demands and is occupied with pleasing his *wife.* ▪ This means he is *divided.* ▪ The *virgin*—indeed, any *unmarried* woman—is concerned with things of the *Lord,* in pursuit of holiness in body *and* spirit. ▪ The married woman, on the other hand, has the cares of *this* world to absorb her and is concerned with pleasing her *husband.* ▪ I am going into this with you for your own good. ▪ I have no desire to place *restrictions* on you, but I do want to promote what is *good,* what will *help* you to devote yourselves *entirely* to the Lord. ▪▪

A reading from the holy *gospel* according to *Mark* ▪ ▪

Capernaum = kuh-PER-nay-uhm

"The people were spellbound." The drama begins here and climaxes when the unclean spirit leaves the afflicted man. Though you should not try to reenact the story, your vocal energy must be sustained at a very high level.

[In the city of Capernaum,] Jesus entered the synagogue on the sabbath and began to teach. ▪ The people were *spellbound* by his teaching because he taught with *authority* and not like the *scribes*. ▪ ▪

There appeared in their synagogue a man with an *unclean spirit* that shrieked: ▪ "What do you *want* of us, Jesus of Nazareth? ▪ Have you come to *destroy* us? ▪ I *know who* you are—the Holy One of God!" ▪ Jesus rebuked him sharply: ▪ "Be quiet! ▪ Come out of the man!" ▪ At that the unclean spirit convulsed the man violently and with a loud shriek came *out* of him. ▪ All who looked on were amazed. ▪ They began to ask one another: ▪ "What does this *mean?* ▪ A completely *new* teaching in a spirit of *authority!* ▪ He gives orders to unclean spirits and they obey him!" ▪ From *that* point *on* his reputation spread throughout the surrounding region of Galilee. ▪ ▪

"The people were amazed." The resolution of the drama begins here. The people have seen that Jesus acts on his own authority. Thus, the ultimate outcome is the spread of Jesus' fame. The final sentence is very strong!

GOSPEL   Jesus begins his public ministry with a very dramatic and miraculous healing. The people are spellbound because Jesus heals by his own power, unlike the scribes, whose teaching and ministry were appropriately second-hand—that is, they were attributed to the power of God. Even the unclean spirit recognizes Jesus' power: "You are the Holy One of God."

It is no wonder that the reputation of Jesus spread quickly and widely. Here was a man who claimed for himself the kind of authority and power that heretofore had been reserved to God alone. Mark's message is clear: Jesus is God.

Notice that the reading does not concentrate on the miracle; it concentrates on the authority of Jesus and his teaching, by word and example. Therein lies the true foundation of faith in Jesus: not in the *signs* of his power and authority, but in the authority itself. The miracles of Jesus have never converted anyone. It is the authority by which Jesus performed such signs that elicits our belief. He claims to be God, and his claim is incontestable, and therefore we believe.

It is worth noting, too, that the first demonstration of Jesus' power in Mark is a victory over unclean spirits. The point is that the powers of the dark side are subject to him and no longer have dominion over us. Hell has no force or influence in a world ruled by the authority of Jesus.

READING I   Here is a reading for those who believe that life should be all "sweetness and light." It reminds us of Henry David Thoreau's observation: "Most men lead lives of quiet desperation." In point of fact, there are probably more people who feel like Job than those who experience "sweetness and light." The suffering of many in modern times is as harsh and difficult to bear as it was for Job. And the question that plagued Job still plagues us: "Why is there evil in the world?" If God is all goodness, why do bad things happen to good people? These are questions we all wrestle with, if we are at all in tune with life. We place our contemporary achievements alongside the world's poverty and misery and we are shocked by the contrast. All the more reason for us to hear this text proclaimed with conviction.

Job's lament leads us to two realizations: (1) there is hope in the power and authority of God and, (2) that power and authority come to us out of sheer love and goodness. In no sense must our misery be overwhelming when we believe in love of God. And in no sense must we believe we can earn that love. There is no bargaining where God is concerned. How could there be? Everything is free!

Many spiritual writers have dwelt on the paradox that we can experience the power of God only when we have first experienced our own powerlessness. The justly famous Twelve Steps that guide Alcoholics Anonymous begin with just such an assertion: "I came to realize that I was powerless." True faith celebrates what has been done for us; it does not dwell on what we must do. Beware of cheap imitations that say otherwise.

READING II   Paul's passionate love for the good news lifts him to new heights of eloquence in this passage. We all admire men and women whose love for a noble cause seems to compel them to promote it unselfishly.

The historical situation here has to do with a mundane reality: Paul refused the stipend he could have rightfully accepted

FIFTH SUNDAY IN ORDINARY TIME

LECTIONARY #75

READING I   Job 7:1–4, 6–7

A reading from the book of *Job* ▪▪

The reading is one long lament, but respect the divisions. The first section progresses from the general (all human life) to the particular ("I have been assigned"). NRSV: "Do not human beings have a hard service on earth? Are not their days like the days of a laborer? Like a slave who longs for the shadow, and like laborers who look for their wages, so I. . . ."

The second section is a vivid instance of depression we've all experienced at one time or another.

The shortness of life is strikingly portrayed. This "heavy" reading records a very real aspect of life. Read it boldly.

Job spoke, saying: ▪
Is not man's *life* on earth a *drudgery?* ▪
   Are not his *days* those of a *hireling?* ▪
He is a slave who *longs* for the *shade,*
   a hireling who *waits* for his *wages.* ▪
So I have been assigned months of *misery,*
   and troubled *nights* have been told of
      for me. ▪

If in *bed* I say, ▪ "When shall I *arise?*" ▪
   then the night drags *on;* ▪
I am filled with restlessness until the *dawn.* ▪▪

My days are swifter than a weaver's shuttle; ▪
   they come to an *end* without *hope.* ▪
Remember that my *life* is like the *wind;* ▪
   I shall *not* see happiness *again.* ▪▪

READING II   1 Corinthians 9:16–19, 22–23

A reading from the first letter of *Paul* to the *Corinthians* ▪▪

Paul's point can be made clear in a careful proclamation. Let the language work its full effect.

A new section begins here. Pause, then launch into Paul's assertion about the need to adapt to one's audience and circumstances.

Preaching the gospel is not the subject of a *boast;* ▪ I am under *compulsion* and have no *choice.* ▪ I am ruined if I do *not* preach it! ▪ If I do it *willingly,* I have my *recompense;* ▪ if *unwillingly,* I am *nonetheless* entrusted with a charge. ▪ And this recompense of mine? ▪ It is simply this, ▪ that when preaching I offer the gospel *free of charge* and do not make full use of the *authority* the gospel gives me. ▪▪

Although I am not bound to *anyone,* I made myself the slave of *all* so as to win over as many as possible. ▪ To the weak I became a *weak* person with a view to

NRSV: "all things to all people."

winning the weak. ▪ I have made myself all *things* to *all* men in order to save at least *some* of them. ▪ In fact, I do *all* that I do for the sake of the *gospel* in the hope of having a share in its blessings. ▪▪

GOSPEL   Mark 1:29–39

A reading from the holy *gospel* according to *Mark* ▪▪

The narrative is divided into three nearly equal sections. The first is vivid with detail: "he grasped her hand and helped her up."

Upon leaving the synagogue, Jesus entered the house of Simon and Andrew with James and John. ▪ Simon's mother-in-law lay ill with a *fever*, and the first thing they *did* was to *tell* him about her. ▪ He went over to her and grasped her hand and helped her up, and the fever left her. ▪ She *immediately* began to *wait* on them. ▪▪

This section is more sweeping and general: "The whole town was gathered." Let the sweep of your voice communicate the breadth of the text.

After sunset, as evening drew on, they brought him all who were *ill* and those possessed by *demons*. ▪ Before *long* the whole *town* was gathered outside the door. ▪ Those whom he cured, who were variously afflicted, were *many*, and so were the *demons* he expelled. ▪ But he would not permit the demons to speak, because they *knew* him. ▪▪ Rising early the next morning, he went off to a lonely place in the *desert*; ▪ there he was *absorbed* in *prayer*. ▪ Simon and his companions managed to track him down; ▪ and when they found him, they told him, ▪ *"Everybody* is looking for you!" ▪ He said to them: ▪ "Let us move on to the neighboring villages so that I may proclaim the good news there *also*. ▪ That is what I have come to *do*." ▪ So he went into their synagogues preaching the good news and expelling demons throughout the *whole* of Galilee. ▪▪

The final section introduces a certain intimacy—or at least an attempt at it—but then depicts an even broader expanse. There is conviction in Jesus' statement of his universal goal. The final sentence is a summation of his healing mission. Let your proclamation match the vastness of the scene.

from the Corinthians in return for his ministry among them. And he refused because he wanted to make the parallel point that the good news is freely given by God. This wise decision placed Paul at an advantage over his opponents. It lent him, and his message, credibility.

This theme runs through the liturgy today: God's love and the salvation offered in Jesus is *gratis,* free (the same root word gives us the term "grace"). We do not deserve it and we cannot earn it. The more we realize this, the more enthusiastic will be the loving response we make in gratitude.

GOSPEL   Though we may be tempted to hear this gospel text as an account of Jesus' power as a miracle worker, the central concern of Mark is quite different. His purpose here is to indicate that Jesus is to be recognized as the one who brings the Kingdom of God to earth. His mission is to proclaim the arrival of salvation. The miracles he performs are nothing more than evidence that salvation (the word means "healing") accompanies him in that mission.

Notice that Jesus will not permit the evil spirits to acknowledge him as the Holy One of God, as we heard in last Sunday's gospel reading. The danger would be that Jesus would be recognized merely as a miracle worker; he is far more than that. Indeed, the ultimate healing he will work on the world will be at the most vulnerable and powerless moment of his life: his death on the cross. Mark's gospel is consistently intent upon keeping the true purpose of Jesus secret until such time as his disciples are capable of understanding it. They have to be disabused of their expectations of a conquering and warrior-like Messiah. And at this point in their education, the "scandal" of the cross would be too much to bear.

So Jesus must be able to escape any and all situations in which the people are too eager to acclaim his miracles. Such acclamation would compromise his much larger purpose. "Let us move on to the neighboring villages so that I may proclaim the good news there also. That is what I have come to do."

READING I Because we make such a clear and definite distinction between body and soul in our day, we do not usually associate physical maladies with spiritual illness. Such is not the case with the people we see in this first reading. They felt in many instances that bodily sickness involved spiritual sickness. Thus, the elaborate rituals for cleansing involved not only protection of the wider community from physical contagion, but the spiritual purification of the afflicted.

As a preparation for the gospel story we hear today, this first reading is perfect in the contrast it offers. Here we see the implication of moral guilt associated with illness, painful quarantine and exclusion from community life, and the inevitable shame that must have accompanied such a condition. We also see a detailed cleansing ritual that could only have created further suffering for the person stricken. In the gospel passage, all these horrors are stripped away.

READING II In this very brief passage, Paul is responding to those who were worried about eating meat that had been sacrificed to idols. Paul makes the very important distinction between what we consume and what we do: Our behavior toward others is more important than what we eat or drink. When one remembers how obsessed organized religion can get with dietary matters, Paul's distinction is refreshing.

The larger concern here is stated clearly: "Give no offense to Jew or Greek or to the church of God." Unfortunately, it is not uncommon to hear members of one faith try to build themselves up by ridiculing members of a different faith. Nothing could be further from the mind of Paul and the heart of Jesus.

SIXTH SUNDAY IN ORDINARY TIME

LECTIONARY #78

READING I   Leviticus 13:1–2, 44–46

Leviticus = leh-VIH-tih-koos. The very repulsiveness of the subject of this text is part of its power. Do not shy away from it.

The switch to the plural form here makes for easier listening. The NRSV uses the plural form throughout the text, making it inclusive.

A reading from the book of *Leviticus* ▪▪

The Lord said to Moses and Aaron, ▪ "If someone has on his skin a scab or pustule or blotch which appears to be the sore of *leprosy*, he shall be brought to Aaron, the priest, or to one of the priests among his *descendants*. ▪ If the man is leprous and unclean, the priest shall *declare* him unclean by reason of the sore on his head. ▪▪

"The one who bears the sore of leprosy shall keep his *garments rent* and his *head bare*, and shall muffle his beard; he shall cry out, 'Unclean, unclean!' ▪ As long as the sore is on him he shall *declare* himself *unclean*, ▪ since he is in *fact* unclean. He shall dwell *apart*, making his abode *outside* the camp." ▪▪

There is power in brevity here. Proclaim this lesson in tolerance and respect with the kind of "largesse" it deserves. The final sentence should be set off with a preceding pause and a strong sense of closure.

A reading from the first letter of *Paul* to the *Corinthians* ▪▪

Whether you eat or drink—*whatever* you do—you should do *all* for the glory of *God*. ▪ Give no offense to Jew or Greek or to the church of God, ▪ just as *I* try to please *all* in any way I *can* ▪ by seeking not my own advantage, but that of the *many* ▪ that they may be saved. ▪ Imitate *me* as *I* imitate Christ. ▪▪

GOSPEL   Mark 1:40—45

The tenderness here is heartrending! The humility of the leper is striking: "If you will. . . ." Let your proclamation carry the man's firm but quiet trust and the profound compassion in Jesus' response.

The tone changes here. The stern warning is for the man's own good.

There should be no hint of condemnation of the man for not heeding Jesus' warning. The point is that he couldn't restrain himself for pure joy.

A reading from the holy *gospel* according to *Mark* ▪▪

A *leper* approached Jesus with a *request*, kneeling down as he addressed him: ▪ "If you *will* to do so, you can *cure* me." ▪ Moved with pity, Jesus stretched out his hand, touched him, and said: "I *do* will it. ▪ Be cured." The leprosy left him then and there, and he was cured. ▪▪ Jesus gave him a stern *warning* and sent him on his way. ▪ "Not a word to *anyone* now," he said, ▪ "Go off and present yourself to the *priest* and offer for your cure what Moses *prescribed*. That should be a *proof* for them." ▪▪ The man went off and began to *proclaim* the whole matter *freely*, making the story *public*. ▪ As a result of this, it was no longer *possible* for Jesus to enter a town *openly*. ▪ He stayed in *desert* places; yet people *kept* coming to him from all *sides*. ▪▪

GOSPEL   We have seen Jesus at work as a healer for the past three Sundays. Today's story is especially touching and, perhaps, elusive for some hearers.

Notice the dramatic contrast with the first reading from Leviticus. There the afflicted were banished from the community; here the leper approaches Jesus. There anyone who touched the afflicted became unclean; here Jesus eagerly reaches out to touch the leper. There the cleansing process was complex and lengthy; here the healing comes in an instant.

The second half of the passage deals with Mark's concern about the "secret" of Jesus' real mission. The warning to the healed leper is Mark's way of showing us that Jesus is far more than a miracle worker, and that healing at this point is a mere foreshadowing of the ultimate healing he will accomplish on the cross. Likewise, the leper's inability to keep the secret is Mark's way of showing us how great the secret is. It's too wonderful and powerful to be contained! One can hardly blame the leper for finding it impossible to heed the stern warning. But the consequence of his joy has negative results for Jesus. He is no longer able to enter a town openly. Even here, Mark's purpose is to show us that the greatness of Jesus cannot be contained. Notice that even when he hides in desert places, the people find him.

From the long-range point of view, we see already that Jesus is becoming such a well-known figure (and often for the wrong reason) that only the ultimate horror of the cross and the wonder of the resurrection will serve to establish his true identity for his followers.

This gospel passage is an excellent illustration of one thing we must always keep in mind when reading the scriptures: *How* the writer tells the story is more revealing of the purpose than *what* is told. True dramatist that he is, Mark relates the *significance* of Jesus' life, not a chronological or merely factual account of it.

READING I We say we dread Lent, with its abstinence and severity, but we know it is significant and we come to church for the ashes. The assembly is in a receptive mood, expecting a message that will help them to live up to their lenten resolutions. You, the lector, have a wonderful opportunity to fulfill their expectations.

Notice, first of all, that this reading is poetry. The prophet Joel is calling the people to conversion, and he does so in language that is exalted and beautiful. When you proclaim these words with exaltation and communicate their beauty, you will create in the assembly the same effect Joel hoped for.

The first words ("Even now . . .") could be translated "Even with things as bad as they are. . . ." Joel is describing a bad situation, in which it is clear that the people's only recourse is to God. That is always our situation, of course, but Lent reminds us that we need to concentrate on the fundamentals once in a while. We need to get back to basics. We need to take another look at our priorities, and perhaps rearrange them.

"Blow the trumpet in Zion!" This is another way of saying: "Rally the troops for action!" The intention is to get us excited about reforming our lives. It's not an easy thing to do, but we all feel better when we've done it. And in fact, it *is* easier to do when we all do it together. That's what "church community" is all about.

READING II The point of this reading is that there is a time when we must all choose to be representatives of God's goodness, and that time is now. Lent is the season that calls us back to an honest appraisal of ourselves as followers of Jesus. And although every day is a day of salvation, we need to look forward (as Lent does) to that ultimate day, that final day, and prepare for it.

Readings that use the first person ("I" and "we") have a special force—and an advantage for you, the reader. There is an identity with your hearers that enables them to listen more closely. Make that identity real—in your heart and in your voice. Then when you proclaim "We implore . . ." and "We beg . . . ," you will effectively encourage them.

ASH WEDNESDAY

LECTIONARY #220

READING I   Joel 2:12–18

A reading from the book of the prophet *Joel* ▪▪

Begin with high energy, in a voice full of encouragement and hope. The whole point is that we can "return to the Lord" with confidence, "for gracious and merciful is he."

Even now, says the Lord, ▪
  return to me with your whole *heart*,
    with *fasting*, and *weeping*, and *mourning*; ▪
Rend your *hearts*, not your *garments*,
  and return to the Lord, your *God*. ▪
For *gracious* and *merciful* is he,
  slow to *anger*, rich in *kindness*,
    and relenting in *punishment*. ▪
Perhaps he will *again relent*
  and leave behind him a *blessing*,
Offerings and libations
  for the Lord, your *God*. ▪▪

Pause before this section and let your voice ring out anew. Take your time; otherwise, the short phrases will be lost. Let each sink in before you speak the next one.

Blow the trumpet in *Zion!*
  proclaim a *fast*,
    call an *assembly*; ▪
Gather the *people*,
  notify the congregation; ▪
Assemble the *elders*,
  gather the children
    and the infants at the *breast*; ▪
Let the bridegroom *quit* his room,
  and the bride her *chamber*. ▪
Between the *porch* and the *altar*
  let the *priests*, the ministers of the Lord,
    weep,
And say, ▪ "*Spare*, O Lord, your *people*,
  and make not your *heritage* a reproach,
    with the nations *ruling* over them! ▪
Why should they say among the peoples, ▪
  'Where is their *God?*'" ▪▪

Pause again. Total assurance here. The Lord is taking pity on us even as you proclaim these words.

Then the Lord was stirred to *concern* for his land and took *pity* on his people. ▪▪

**A reading from the second letter of *Paul*
to the *Corinthians* ▪ ▪**

Announce this first sentence with energetic pride!

We are *ambassadors for Christ,* ▪ God as it were *appealing* through *us.* ▪ We *implore* you, in Christ's name: ▪ be *reconciled* to God! ▪ ▪ For our sakes God made him who did not *know sin* to *be sin,* so that in *him* we might become the very holiness of *God.* ▪ ▪

At this point you have built up to an exalted tone of voice. Pause before continuing with the second paragraph.

As your fellow *workers* we beg you *not to receive* the grace of God in *vain.* ▪ For he says, ▪ "In an acceptable time I have *heard* you; ▪ on a day of *salvation* I have *helped* you." ▪ ▪ *Now* is the acceptable time! ▪ *Now* is the day of salvation! ▪ ▪

"Now!" "Now!" The emphasis on this powerful word should convey enthusiasm and opportunity, not a threat.

GOSPEL   Matthew 6:1–6, 16–18

**A reading from the holy *gospel* according
to *Matthew* ▪ ▪**

The first two sentences contain the whole point of the reading. Three examples follow.

Jesus said to his disciples: ▪ "Be on guard against performing religious acts *for people to see.* ▪ Otherwise expect no *recompense* from your heavenly *Father.* ▪ When you *give alms,* for example, do not blow a *horn* before you in synagogues and streets like *hypocrites* looking for *applause.* ▪ You can be sure of *this* much, they are *already* repaid. ▪ In giving *alms you* are not to let your left hand know what your right hand is *doing.* ▪ Keep your deeds of mercy *secret,* and your Father who *sees in secret* will *repay* you. ▪ ▪

Pause before "When you give alms . . ." and before "In giving alms. . . ."

Pause before "When you are praying . . ." and before "Whenever you pray. . . ." "No man" could be "no one."

"When *you are praying,* do not behave like the *hypocrites* who love to stand and pray in synagogues or on street corners in order to be *noticed.* ▪ I give you my word, they are *already* repaid. ▪ Whenever *you pray,* go to your *room,* close your *door,* and pray to your Father in *private.* ▪ Then your Father, who sees what no man sees, will *repay* you. ▪ ▪

Pause before "When you fast . . ." both times.

"When *you fast,* you are not to look glum as the *hypocrites* do. ▪ They change the appearance of their faces so that others may *see* they are fasting. ▪ I assure you, they are *already* repaid. ▪ When *you fast,* see to it that you *groom* your hair and *wash* your face. ▪ In that way no one can *see* you are fasting but your *Father* who is *hidden;* ▪ and your Father who *sees* what is hidden will *repay* you." ▪ ▪

GOSPEL   This reading is not about hypocrites. It is about us. Jesus intends to teach us that fasting and other forms of penance are directed toward God, as signs of humility, not toward our neighbor, as signs of piety. On the other hand, our sacrifices ("giving things up for Lent") are directly related to almsgiving ("charity"). We give things *up* so that we are able to give things *to* those who are in greater need. And this we do quietly, without fanfare.

So this reading is not a condemnation of the hypocrites. It is a lesson in Christian attitudes toward lenten sacrifice and conversion of heart. And, as always, the ideal is presented to us for our encouragement and our imitation.

With the above in mind, then, you will be able to proclaim this reading in a bright tone of voice. Your purpose is to strengthen the assembly in their lenten resolutions by reminding them of the most noble way of carrying them out.

The reading is divided into three parallel sections, each composed of three parts: (1) "When you give alms (pray) (fast) . . . (2) don't behave like the hypocrites . . . (3) but do it secretly." The pattern should be discernible, almost predictable, like a formula. The effect is in the way the reading builds upon itself, so the lesson becomes clearer and clearer.

Begin each section with a strong, bright intonation, and let each section come to a close on a note of calm resolution. Readings like this one are very familiar, and part of their strength lies in that familiarity. Allow the familiarity to assist you; enable the assembly to welcome this encouraging reminder like the old friend it is.

READING I Lent means many things to many different people. From a liturgical point of view, however, one meaning is dominant: It is a preparation for baptism for catechumens, and for the renewal of baptismal vows (and life!) for the faithful in the celebration of Easter. Because Noah and the flood always have been seen as a prefigurement of baptism, we begin Lent with that story.

The event related in this passage takes place immediately after the flood waters have receded. God is resolved to make a covenant with Noah and his descendants, and the burden of that covenant is that the whole earth and all its inhabitants will be placed under the saving hand of God—a God of life and salvation, not a God of death and destruction.

The covenant of baptism carries the same burden. Through the waters of the baptismal font, God lifts us from the depths of sin, preserves us from destruction, and makes us heirs of the promise of salvation. The beauty of a rainbow can remind us of the tender compassion of God and the universality of divine love, both of which are ours through the dignity of our baptism.

READING II The scripture scholars tell us that Peter is adapting an early Christian hymn in this summary of the paschal mystery. Placed here at the beginning of Lent, it gives us a thumbnail sketch of what we will celebrate during the Triduum (Holy Thursday, Good Friday, Easter Vigil and Easter Sunday) and the Easter season.

The overall point of this passage is that our experience as Christians parallels Jesus' experience. Our old selves are put to death when we "go down" into the waters of baptism and rise to new life—resurrected life. And it is our destiny, too, to be in the presence of God for all eternity. As the risen Christ is victorious over sin and death, so too are we, having been raised from the waters of baptism as completely new beings, fortified against every evil.

Peter's specific reference to Noah and the waters of the flood clearly indicates that the Genesis story we heard in the first reading has long been seen as a fore-shadowing of Christian baptism. As he says, "You are now saved by a baptismal bath which corresponds to this exactly."

Those who are catechumens this Lent will pay particular attention to Peter's

FIRST SUNDAY OF LENT

LECTIONARY #23

READING I   Genesis 9:8–15

A reading from the book of *Genesis* ▪ ▪

A big, solemn, energetic tone is a must for this reading. God is renewing the covenant after the devastating flood. The listing of creatures makes the covenant specific and complete. Your proclamation should get Lent off to a good start!

God said to Noah and to his sons with him: ▪ "See, I am now establishing my *covenant* with you and your descendants *after* you and with every living creature that was *with* you: ▪ all the birds, and the various tame and wild animals that were with you and came out of the *ark*. ▪ I will establish my covenant with you, that never *again* shall all bodily creatures be destroyed by the waters of a *flood;* ▪ there shall not be *another flood* to devastate the earth." ▪ God added: ▪

This new section reveals the sign (proof) of the covenant. Pause before it, then renew the energy level. "Bow" is pronounced as in "rainbow," which is what it refers to. Sustain the feeling of "solemn promise" through to the end.

"*This* is the sign that I am giving for all ages to *come*, of the covenant between me and you and every living creature with you: ▪ I set my *bow* in the clouds to serve as a *sign* of the covenant between me and the earth. ▪ When I bring clouds over the earth, and the *bow* appears in the *clouds*, I will recall the covenant I have made between me and you and all living beings, so that the waters shall *never again* become a *flood* to destroy all mortal beings." ▪ ▪

A reading from the first letter of *Peter* ▪ ▪

This is why Christ *died* for sins once for *all*, a just man for the sake of the unjust: ▪ so that he could lead you to *God*. ▪ He was put to death insofar as *fleshly* existence goes, but was given life in the realm of the *spirit*. ▪ It was in the spirit also that he went to preach to the spirits in *prison*. ▪ They had disobeyed as long ago as *Noah's* day, while God patiently waited until the *ark* was built. ▪ At that time, a few persons, eight in all, escaped in the ark through the water. ▪ *You* are now saved by a *baptismal bath* which *corresponds* to this exactly. ▪ *This* baptism is no removal of *physical* stain, but the pledge to *God* of an irreproachable *conscience* through the resurrection of Jesus *Christ*. ▪ *He* went to *heaven* and is at God's right *hand*, with angelic rulers and powers subjected to him. ▪ ▪

GOSPEL   Mark 1:12—15

A reading from the holy *gospel* according to *Mark* ▪ ▪

The Spirit sent Jesus out toward the *desert*. ▪ He stayed in the wasteland forty *days*, put to the test there by *Satan*. ▪ He was with the wild *beasts*, and angels waited on him. ▪ ▪

After John's arrest, Jesus appeared in *Galilee* proclaiming God's good *news:* ▪ "*This* is the time of fulfillment. ▪ The reign of God is at *hand*! ▪ Reform your *lives* and believe in the good *news!*" ▪ ▪

definition of baptism as far more than the removal of physical stain. No, it is a pledge to God. And that pledge comes from a conscience made clear by the saving resurrection of Jesus. Again the point is made that the resurrection of Jesus makes it all possible—and baptism is not something we undertake so much as an offering of love and life that we accept gratefully.

GOSPEL   The First Sunday of Lent always presents us with the story of Jesus' temptation in the desert. Mark's account is extremely brief, omitting even the specifics of Satan's three tempting offers. Nevertheless, for Mark and his contemporaries, this short passage would evoke parallels with many figures and events in the Hebrew Scriptures: The Chosen People wandered in the desert 40 years; Jesus is the new People of Israel. As they ate manna, which was heavensent, so is Jesus fed by angels. The prophet Elijah endured a 40-day fast and was fed by ravens. Those who rely on God are protected from wild beasts and are provided for by the angels. Thus, a great wealth of traditional Hebrew history is hinted at in Mark's well-chosen words and images.

This event takes place immediately after Jesus' baptism—and it is his preparation for the public ministry that we see him beginning immediately after the temptation experience. All three readings today allude to baptism and its consequences, offering us a springboard into Lent.

READING I The sacrifice of Isaac is a story so compelling that it has been a favorite with painters, composers, and dramatists throughout the centuries. Interpreted as a prefigurement of the sacrifice of Jesus, it appears everywhere in Christian literature, and is perhaps even in Paul's mind in that portion of the Letter to the Romans which serves as today's second reading.

In Genesis the story clearly is meant to be a striking test of Abraham's faith—a test he passes and for which he is rewarded far beyond any expectations he could have had. He becomes "our father in faith," a phrase we used to hear at every celebration of the eucharist—and still hear when Eucharistic Prayer I is proclaimed.

But the story existed before the author of Genesis wrote it down, and probably dealt with Israel's movement away from human sacrifice. Later scholars chose to highlight the role of Isaac in the story, seeing him as a willing victim and therefore a symbol of the lamb sacrificed at passover.

For us today, the story cannot but remind us of how God has acted in our behalf. The God who rewarded Abraham for not withholding even his only son is the same God who said of Jesus at his baptism, "You are my beloved Son."

READING II This reading is almost certainly a text that existed before Paul addressed it to the Romans. It has all the signs of an ancient Christian formulation of fundamental beliefs.

The charm of the passage (and the challenge, to the reader) lies in its appeal as a list of rhetorical questions. The answer to each question is so obviously "Of course not!" that the text becomes a special kind of encouragement. We see this rhetorical device often in the scriptures, as in, "Can a mother forget her child?" Paul is encouraging the Romans to stand firm in the face of temptation and difficulty—perhaps even

SECOND SUNDAY OF LENT

LECTIONARY #26

READING I   Genesis 22:1–2, 9, 10–13, 15–18

You're reading a classic of biblical literature. Use your best storytelling technique. The first three very brief sentences will not seem "blunt" if you give each one strong emphasis and "space."

In this paragraph the drama progresses through climax to resolution. Use sufficient vocal range to communicate the range of feeling.

The final section shows the result of Abraham's obedience. It is the first solemn proclamation of the covenant between God and Israel. It deserves your most dignified and solid delivery!

A reading from the book of *Genesis* · ·

God put Abraham to the test. · He called to him, · "Abraham!" · "Ready!" he replied. · Then God said: · "Take your son Isaac, your only *one*, whom you *love*, and go to the land of *Moriah*. · *There* you shall offer him *up* as a *holocaust* on a height that I will point out to you." · ·

When they came to the place of which God had told him, Abraham built an *altar* there and arranged the *wood* on it. · Then he reached out and took the knife to slaughter his *son*. · But the Lord's messenger called to him from heaven, · "Abraham, Abraham!" · "Yes, Lord," he answered. · "Do not lay your hand on the boy," said the messenger. · "Do not do the least *thing* to him. · I know *now* how *devoted* you are to God, since you did not withhold from me your own beloved *son*." · · As Abraham looked about, he spied a ram caught by its horns in the thicket. · So he went and took the ram and offered it up as a holocaust in place of his *son*. · ·

Again the Lord's messenger called to Abraham from heaven and said: · "I swear by myself, declares the Lord, that because you acted as you *did* in not withholding from me your beloved *son*, · I will bless you abundantly and make your descendants as countless as the stars of the sky and the sands of the seashore; · *your* descendants shall take possession of the gates of their *enemies*, and in *your* descendants all the nations of the *earth* shall find blessing— · all *this* because you obeyed my *command*." · ·

A reading from the letter of *Paul* to the *Romans* ▪ ▪

A series of rhetorical questions. This is Paul's way of emphasizing the point. Make sure your reading includes the question marks.

If *God* is for us, who can be *against* us? ▪ Is it possible that he who did not spare his own *Son* but handed him over for the sake of us all will not grant us all things *besides?* ▪ Who shall bring a charge against God's *chosen* ones? ▪ God, who *justifies?* ▪ Who shall condemn *them?* ▪ Christ Jesus, who died or rather was raised *up,* who is at the right hand of *God* and who *intercedes* for us? ▪ ▪

GOSPEL   Mark 9:2–10

A reading from the holy *gospel* according to *Mark* ▪ ▪

This story is complete with plot, characters, conflict and resolution. The first section sets the scene quite dramatically. Be sure to separate the sections with pauses and new vocal inflection.

Peter's response begins the second section. The comment on his confusion must stand out from the story itself.

The mystery is explained in section three with the appearance of God, whose voice is more comforting than awesome.

Jesus took Peter, James and John off by themselves with him and led them up a high mountain. ▪ He was *transfigured* before their *eyes* and his clothes became dazzlingly *white*— whiter than the work of any bleacher could *make* them. ▪ *Elijah* appeared to them along with *Moses;* ▪ the two were in conversation with *Jesus.* ▪ Then Peter spoke to Jesus: ▪ "Rabbi, how *good* it is for us to *be* here. ▪ Let us erect three booths on this site, one for you, one for Moses, and one for Elijah." ▪ He hardly knew *what* to say, for they were *all* overcome with *awe.* ▪ A cloud came, overshadowing them, and out of the cloud a voice: ▪ "This is my *Son,* my beloved. ▪ *Listen* to him." ▪ Suddenly looking around they no longer saw anyone with them— ▪ only Jesus. ▪ ▪

A hint of all that follows in Jesus' life and death. Let your voice convey a feeling of suspense ("to be continued") at the end.

As they were coming down the mountain, he strictly *enjoined* them not to tell *anyone* what they had seen before the Son of Man had risen from the dead. ▪ They kept this word of his to themselves, though they continued to discuss what ▪ "to rise from the dead" meant. ▪ ▪

---

the threat of brutal persecution for their beliefs. Such a frightening situation calls for strong encouragement, and Paul seems to have found just the right words in this revered text.

As the reader, your challenge is to proclaim the questions boldly and confidently, so that your hearers will be strengthened for the inevitable conflict that will pervade their lives as committed Christians.

GOSPEL   On the Second Sunday of Lent, we always hear the story of the Transfiguration. This year we have Mark's account, which differs in some ways from Matthew (Year A) and Luke's (Year C). As we have noted in earlier commentaries for this year, Mark is very much concerned about the true identity and mission of Jesus. More particularly, he is concerned about mistaken notions about Jesus. In Mark, Jesus silences the demons he casts out, so they will not draw attention to his divine power. Mark notes that Jesus warned the leper he healed not to tell anyone about it. In today's reading, he tells of Jesus silencing the apostles so they will not overemphasize the glory of his relationship with God.

The secret yet to be revealed is that this Jesus is not going to fulfill messianic expectations that center on glory and majesty and triumph. No, the secret is that this Messiah is going to accomplish his mission by undergoing the agony of death on a cross. And that secret must be guarded until such time as the evidence of the resurrection will make it believable.

It is not difficult to understand that a suffering and dying savior would be hard to accept if we were expecting a conquering hero. But Mark also makes the point that the secret of Jesus' ultimate triumph (indeed, the secret of who he is) is too astounding to keep hidden. The demons he cast out managed at least once to shriek: "You are the Holy One of God." The healed leper could not contain the news of his good fortune. And in today's reading the disciples who heard "This is my Son, my beloved," cannot help continuing to discuss what "to rise from the dead" means.

The thing to remember when reading Mark is that he reveals the story of Jesus like a playwright. The resolution of the conflict on the stage comes only at the end, but it is hinted at in every scene.

READING I When you read the Ten Commandments you are proclaiming a summary of duties toward God and neighbor that have been (along with the Golden Rule) the foundation of all Judeo-Christian instruction since the calling of Israel as the Chosen People. It is one of the most sacred and revered and widely known of all printed texts. Notice, too, that the writer of Exodus places these words in the mouth of God. No passage deserves more careful and loving proclamation.

Notice that half the commandments are "you shall" and half are "you shall not." We are enjoined to do good and avoid evil; we are instructed in our dealings with God and in our dealings with our neighbor. Those who object to the tone of harshness in "you shall not" should realize that each "shall not" has positive implications as well. The injunction not to kill, for example, is a commandment to respect life; to avoid adultery is to respect the commitments made in human relationships; to refrain from stealing is to respect private ownership and the needs of others.

Though a shorter form of this reading is provided, take the longer form if at all possible. It contains elaborations that make the reading much more clear, and, indeed, easier to understand.

READING II Paul took great delight in speaking of the "folly" and "scandal" of the cross as opposed to the "wisdom" of the world. It was a paradox he relished, and so can we. It reminds us of a basic tenet of Christianity as well as other religions, namely, that faith is a gift of God and cannot be forced upon anyone. Nor can faith in Jesus be arrived at by pure reason. We might be able to prove logically the existence of a Supreme Being, but there is no logical proof for a God of boundless compassion and mercy who would become flesh and dwell among us.

In accepting the gift of faith, "those who are called" find themselves capable of seeing beyond what reason reveals, and imbued with the ability to see the weakness of the cross as the power of love.

Perhaps the best tone to adopt in proclaiming this lovely passage is utter confidence, tinged with awed humility.

MARCH 6, 1994

THIRD SUNDAY OF LENT

LECTIONARY #29

READING I   Exodus 20:1–17

A reading from the book of *Exodus* ··

A well-known and revered text. Give it your most careful proclamation.

God delivered all these commandments: · "I, the Lord, am your *God*, who brought you out of the land of Egypt, that place of slavery. · You shall not have other gods besides me. · You shall not carve idols for yourselves in the shape of anything in the sky *above* or on the earth *below* or in the waters beneath the earth; · you shall not bow down before them or worship them. · For I, the Lord, your God, am a *jealous* God, inflicting *punishment* for their fathers' wickedness on the children of those who hate me, down to the *third* and *fourth generations*; · but bestowing *mercy* down to the *thousandth generation*, on the children of those who *love* me and keep my *commandments*. ··

God reveals something of the divine nature. NRSV: "parents." Emphasize the contrast between "third and fourth generations" and "thousandth generation."

"You shall not take the name of the Lord, your *God*, in *vain*. · For the Lord will not leave unpunished him who takes his name in vain. ··

A tone of instruction, not reprimand, is most appropriate. Substitute "anyone" for "him."

"Remember to keep holy the *sabbath* day. · *Six* days you may *labor* and do all your *work*, · but the seventh day is the sabbath of the *Lord*, your *God*. No work may be done *then* either by you, or your son or daughter, or your male or female slave, or your beast, or by the alien who lives with you. · In six days the Lord made the heavens and the earth, the sea and all that is *in* them; · but on the *seventh* day he *rested*. · That is why the Lord has blessed the sabbath day · and made it *holy*. ··

Explain the reason for the sabbath tradition.

"Honor your *father* and your *mother*, that you may have a long *life* in the land which the Lord, your God, is giving you. ·

The rest of the commandments are in brief form. Do not rush through them. Each one should be heard distinctly.

"You shall not kill. ·

"You shall not commit adultery. ·

"You shall not steal. ·

"You shall not bear false witness against your neighbor. ·

NRSV: "You shall not covet your neighbor's house; you shall not covet your neighbor's wife, or male or female slave, or ox, or donkey, or anything that belongs to your neighbor."

"You shall not covet your neighbor's *house*. · You shall not covet your neighbor's *wife*, nor his male or female *slave*, nor his *ox* or *ass*, nor anything *else* that belongs to him." ··

[Shorter: Exodus 20:1–3, 7–8, 12–17]

A reading from the first letter of *Paul* to the *Corinthians* ▪▪

Paul loves the paradox of the cross. Your tone should be exultant.

Jews demand *"signs"* and Greeks look for *"wisdom,"* ▪ but we preach *Christ crucified,* ▪ a stumbling block to *Jews,* and an absurdity to *Gentiles;* ▪ but to those who are *called,* Jews and Greeks alike, Christ is the power of *God* and the *wisdom* of God. ▪ For God's *folly* is *wiser* than men, ▪ and his *weakness* more *powerful* than men. ▪▪

NRSV: "For God's foolishness is wiser than human wisdom, and God's weakness is stronger than human strength."

GOSPEL   John 2:13–25

A reading from the holy *gospel* according to *John* ▪▪

A dramatic scene. John's purpose is to show the scriptures fulfilled. The real drama is in the fulfillment.

As the Jewish *Passover* was near, Jesus went up to *Jerusalem.* ▪ In the temple *precincts* he came upon people engaged in selling oxen, sheep and doves, and *others* seated changing *coins.* ▪ He made a [kind of] whip of cords and drove them all out of the temple area, sheep and oxen alike, and knocked over the moneychangers' tables, spilling their coins. ▪ He told those who were selling doves: ▪ "Get them *out* of here!" ▪ Stop turning my Father's house into a marketplace!" ▪ His disciples recalled the words of Scripture: ▪ "Zeal for your house *consumes* me."▪▪▪

Do not imitate Jesus' anger. Tell the story; don't reenact it.

The challenge in the question should be clear, so that Jesus' response sounds all the more bold.

At this the Jews responded, ▪ "What *sign* can you show us authorizing you to *do* these things?" ▪ "Destroy this *temple,*" was Jesus' answer, ▪ "and in three days I will raise it *up.*" ▪ They retorted, ▪ "This *temple* took forty-six *years* to build, and you are going to 'raise it up in three *days*'!" ▪ Actually *he* was talking about the temple of his *body.* ▪ Only after Jesus had been raised from the *dead* did his disciples recall that he had *said* this, and come to believe the *Scripture* and the word he had spoken. ▪▪

Here, again, the purpose is "fulfillment."

While he was in Jerusalem during the Passover festival, *many* believed in his name, for they could see the *signs* he was performing. ▪ For his part, Jesus would not trust himself to them because he knew them all. ▪ He needed no one to give him testimony about human nature. ▪ He was well *aware* of what was in man's *heart.* ▪▪

The final comment strongly asserts Jesus' divine origin. Make it strong. NRSV: "for he himself knew what was in everyone."

GOSPEL   We have been reading from the gospel of Mark for the Sundays in Lent, but now we turn to the evangelist John. On Passion (Palm) Sunday we will return to Mark for his account of Jesus' passion and death.

John's account of the cleansing of the temple is placed at the beginning of Jesus' public ministry, whereas in the other gospel, this event comes later. The reason for the switch is probably that John wants to reveal the ultimate mission of Jesus rather early on. The prediction of his own resurrection is indirect and was misunderstood by those who heard it. But the commentary supplied by John ("Actually he was talking about the temple of his body") rids the passage of any vagueness for the reader. And he asserts that the disciples understood the reference as well, but only after the resurrection.

John is at pains throughout his gospel to show that, with the coming of Jesus into the world, an entirely new kind of worship has been established. In another part of his gospel (the passage assigned to this Sunday in Year A), he has Jesus make the point explicitly: "An hour is coming, and is already here, when authentic worshipers will worship the Father in Spirit and truth." The temple is no longer relevant in John's theology; it has been replaced by the temple that is the body of the risen Christ, a spiritual body.

When we notice that the cleansing of the temple is placed in the context of the Jewish Passover, and that Jesus refers to the temple as "my Father's house," and, finally, that the three days Jesus refers to parallel the three days of his suffering, death, and resurrection, it becomes evident that John's intent is to reveal Jesus as the divine Son of God—and to do so at the beginning of his ministry.

The final paragraph of the reading contains more of John's commentary, which further reveals the all-knowing divinity of Jesus, and his complete sovereignty over the human heart.

READING I It may be difficult for us to appreciate the water imagery that saturates today's readings. First we hear of "water in the wilderness"—a sign of God's presence in adversity. Then Paul uses the expression "poured out" to describe how the Spirit fills our hearts with love. Finally, we have the gospel story, so well-known that it has acquired a popular name: the woman at the well. If we could live in arid Palestine for a while, we might be able to appreciate better this precious element of water. We certainly would have a clearer understanding of why it is so central in our scriptures and liturgy.

In this first reading we witness a serious confrontation between Moses and the unruly people he is leading through the desert. They are panicky with thirst; Moses is frightened for his life. The real problem, of course, is that the people doubt that the Lord will be with them in their trial. Thus they ask a question that echoes in the heart of every believer who has undergone severe temptation or suffering: "Is the Lord in our midst or not?"

The words Massah and Meribah are practically synonymous with "quarrel" and "test," and you can indicate this by reading them with parallel emphasis. Don't shy away from the chilling question with which this reading ends. It's a fact of life that we doubt and question—especially during the difficult times. This reading acknowledges our weakness, and then demonstrates that the Lord does appear in our midst. Having doubts is not sinful; it is part of the struggle inherent in a life of faith—the kind of struggle we hear a lot about during the Lent/Easter seasons.

READING II In a way, Christianity is in the passive voice—meaning that it is more about *what has been done for us* than about *what we are to do.* The good news, as Paul summarizes it here, is that we *have been* justified, we *have gained* access and the Holy Spirit *has been* poured out in our hearts. Our Christian life is a response to something that has already been accomplished on our behalf by a loving God.

How different such an attitude is from one of grinding duty and restrictions by which we mistakenly think we earn God's love. That difference in attitude should

MARCH 6, 1994

THIRD SUNDAY OF LENT, YEAR A

LECTIONARY #28

READING I   Exodus 17:3–7

Do not try to imitate the angry whine of the people. Liturgical proclamation is different from "dramatic interpretation."

Horeb = HAWR-ehb

Pause between the story and the added commentary.

Massah = MAH-suh
Meribah = MEHR-ih-bah

The final sentence (question) is a rare example of an ending that is abrupt—and effective.

A reading from the book of *Exodus* ▪▪

In their thirst for *water,* the people *grumbled against Moses,* saying, ▪ "Why did you ever make us leave *Egypt?* ▪ Was it just to have us *die* here of *thirst* with our *children* and our *livestock?*" ▪ So Moses *cried out to the Lord,* ▪ "What shall I *do* with this people? ▪ A little *more* and they will *stone* me!" ▪ The Lord answered Moses, ▪ "Go over there in front of the people, along with some of the elders of Israel, holding in your hand, as you go, the *staff* with which you *struck the river.* ▪ I will be standing there in *front* of you on the rock in *Horeb.* ▪ *Strike* the rock, and the water will *flow* from it for the people to *drink.*" ▪ This Moses *did,* in the presence of the elders of Israel. ▪ The place was called *Massah* and *Meribah,* because the Israelites *quarreled* there and *tested* the Lord, saying, ▪ *"Is* the Lord in our midst or *not?"* ▪▪

READING II   Romans 5:1–2, 5–8

This is a strong opener—full of confidence. "Now that we have been justified. . . ." Then Paul explains how and why this is the case.

NRSV: "For while we were still weak, at the right time Christ died for the ungodly. Indeed, rarely will anyone die for a righteous person—though perhaps for a good person someone might actually dare to die."

A reading from the letter of *Paul* to the *Romans* ▪▪

Now that we have been *justified by faith,* we *are at peace* with God through our Lord Jesus *Christ.* ▪ Through *him* we have gained *access* by faith to the *grace* in which we now *stand,* and we *boast of our hope* for the glory of God. ▪ And this hope will not leave us *disappointed,* because the love of God has been *poured out* in our hearts through the Holy *Spirit* who has been *given* to us. ▪ At the appointed *time,* when we were *still powerless,* Christ *died* for us godless men. ▪ It is rare that anyone should lay down his life for a *just* man, though it is barely *possible* that for a *good* man someone may have the courage to die. ▪ It is *precisely in this* that God proves his *love* for us: ▪ that *while we were still sinners,* Christ died for us. ▪▪

A reading from the holy *gospel* according to *John* ▪ ▪

Begin quietly. Set the scene and the mood of fatigue.
Samaria = suh-MEHR-ih-uh
Shechem = SHEE-kehm

Jesus had to pass through *Samaria*, and his journey brought him to a Samaritan *town* named *Shechem* near the plot of land which *Jacob* had given to his son *Joseph*. ▪ This was the site of Jacob's *well*. ▪ *Jesus*, tired from his *journey*, sat down at the well. ▪

Though "Give me a drink" seems abrupt, it should not sound harsh; Jesus is tired and makes an earnest request. Likewise, the woman's question is asked in surprise, not outrage.

The hour was about *noon*. ▪ When a Samaritan *woman* came to draw *water*, Jesus said to her, ▪ "Give me a *drink*." ▪ (His disciples had gone off to the town to buy provisions.) ▪ The Samaritan woman said to him, ▪ "You are a *Jew*. ▪ How can you ask me, a *Samaritan* and a *woman*, for a *drink?* ▪ (Recall that Jews have nothing to do with Samaritans.) ▪ Jesus replied: ▪

"If only you recognized God's *gift*,
and *who it is* that is asking you for a drink,
you would have asked *him instead*,
and he would have given you *living* water." ▪

The point is that Jesus is greater than Jacob. Great leaders were often noted for the good wells they dug to provide for their followers. Jesus has a source of water that surpasses all others.

"Sir," she challenged him, ▪ "you don't have a *bucket* and this well is *deep*. ▪ Where do you expect to get this *flowing water?* ▪ Surely you don't pretend to be *greater than our ancestor Jacob*, who *gave* us this well and *drank* from it with his sons and his *flocks?*" ▪ Jesus replied: ▪

NRSV employs the plural: "Everyone who drinks of this water will be thirsty again, but those who drink of the water that I will give them will never be thirsty. The water that I will give will become in them a spring of water gushing up to eternal life."

"Everyone who drinks *this* water
will be *thirsty again*. ▪
But whoever drinks the water *I* give him
will *never* be thirsty; ▪
no, the water *I* give
shall become a *fountain* within him,
leaping up to provide eternal *life*." ▪
The woman said to him, ▪ "*Give* me this water, sir, so that I won't grow *thirsty* and have to keep coming here to draw *water*." ▪

A set-up so that Jesus can reveal his true nature to the woman. "You are right . . ." is the moment of truth. The point is not to scold, but to reveal himself as one who knows all.

He told her, ▪ "Go, call your *husband*, and then come *back* here." ▪ "I *have* no husband," replied the woman. ▪ "You are *right* in saying you *have* no husband!" Jesus exclaimed. ▪ "The fact is, you have had *five*, and the man you are living with *now* is *not* your husband. ▪ What you said is true *enough*." ▪

NRSV: "men" = "people."

"Sir," answered the woman, ▪ "I can see you are a *prophet*. ▪ Our ancestors *worshiped* on this mountain, but you people claim that *Jerusalem* is the place where men ought to worship God." ▪ Jesus told her: ▪

characterize your joyful (even slightly incredulous) reading of this text. The underlying feeling is: "Can you believe this? It's almost too good to be true."

To demonstrate his point, Paul illustrates the difference between the human and the divine. Yes, on rare occasions we hear of one human being giving up life itself for another (deserving) human being. Well, it's very different with God. Christ died for us even though we were undeserving. What better proof of love? Notice, also, the delightful presumption that we are no longer undeserving; we have been made deserving (the passive voice again)!

GOSPEL   Don't even think about abbreviating this long reading, even though a shorter version is provided. The story is too important and too rich to excise certain parts. If you are worried about Mass "taking too long," use other legitimate ways to shorten the liturgy on this day. If you are worried about the assembly's boredom, use your best lector—or have the reading proclaimed by three readers (as has been done for centuries in the reading of the Passion narratives during Holy Week). The three would read the parts of the narrator (who would also read the disciples' and the Samaritans' words), the woman and Jesus. (I hope it is not necessary to insist that a woman read the woman's dialogue!)

Though this story has much to say about water and all its associations for us (baptism, Red Sea, Jordan, new life and grace), it would probably be more insightful to describe the encounter between Jesus and the woman as a lesson in seeing at deeper levels. There is water and then there is living water; bread and the food that is God's will; Jacob and Jesus; the promised Messiah and Jesus; notions about worship and genuine worship; and the list goes on. The reading is, in its effect, a series of epiphanies (manifestations of God in Jesus). The homilist has much to do in applying this gospel story to our lives.

The readers also have much to do, but a sensitive and careful proclamation will accomplish the task. Respect the natural divisions of the story: the introduction, which sets the scene and mood; the dialogue with the Samaritan woman, which has many colors of challenge and response; the final revelation of Jesus as Messiah; the lesson for the disciples in evangelization; and the Samaritans' belief in Jesus as Savior of the world.

There is no need for this challenge to sound condemnatory. It is a statement of fact, and the woman is clearly not incensed by it.

This is a thunderclap. It is a repetition of God's voice in the book of Exodus, "I am!" to all who heard it, who read it and to John who wrote it. Pause before starting the next section.

NRSV: "The reaper is already collecting wages . . ." and "One sows and another reaps."

"*Believe* me, woman,
an hour is coming
when you will worship the Father
neither on this mountain
nor in Jerusalem. ▪ ▪
You people worship what you do *not understand*,
while we *understand* what *we* worship; ▪
after all, salvation is from the *Jews*. ▪
Yet an hour is *coming*, and is already *here*,
when *authentic* worshipers
will worship the Father *in Spirit and truth*. ▪
Indeed, it is just such worshipers
the Father *seeks*. ▪ ▪
God is *Spirit*,
and those who *worship* him ▪
must worship *in Spirit and truth*." ▪ ▪
The woman said to him: ▪ "I know there is a *Messiah* coming. ▪ (This term means *Anointed*.) ▪ *When he comes*, he will tell us *everything*." ▪ Jesus replied, ▪ "*I* who *speak* to you *am he*." ▪ ▪

His *disciples*, returning at this point, were *surprised* that Jesus was speaking with a *woman*. ▪ No one put a *question*, however, such as ▪ "What do you *want* of him?" or "Why are you *talking* with her?" ▪ The woman then *left her water jar* and went off into the *town*. ▪ She said to the people: ▪ "Come and see someone who told me everything I ever *did*! ▪ Could this not be the *Messiah*?" ▪ With that they set out from the town to *meet* him. ▪ ▪

Meanwhile the disciples were urging him, ▪ "Rabbi, *eat* something." ▪ But he told them: ▪
"I have food to eat
of which you do not *know*." ▪

At this the disciples said to one another, ▪ "You do not suppose anyone has *brought* him something to eat?" ▪ Jesus explained to them: ▪
"Doing the will of *him who sent me*
and *bringing his work* to completion
is *my* food. ▪
Do you not have a saying: ▪
'Four months more
and it will be *harvest*'? ▪
Listen to what *I* say: ▪
Open your eyes and *see*! ▪
The fields are *shining* for harvest! ▪
The reaper *already* collects his wages
and gathers a yield for eternal *life*,
that sower and reaper may rejoice *together*. ▪
Here we have the saying verified: ▪
'One man *sows*; another *reaps*.' ▪

I sent you to *reap*
what you had not *worked* for. ▪
Others have done the *labor,*
and *you* have come into their *gain.*" ▪▪
Many Samaritans from that town *believed* in him on
the strength of the *woman's* word of *testimony:* ▪
"He told me everything I ever *did.*" ▪ The result was
that, when these Samaritans *came* to him, they
begged him to *stay* with them awhile. ▪ So he stayed
there two days, and through *his own spoken word*
many *more* came to faith. ▪ As they told the *woman:*
▪ "No longer does our faith depend on *your story.* ▪
We have heard *for ourselves,* and we know that this
really is the Savior *of the world.*" ▪▪

[Shorter: John 4:4–15, 19–26, 39, 40–42]

Here is the ultimate payoff. The woman spreads the good news, the Samaritans come to hear Jesus, and then move from secondhand belief to personal faith. And John has made the striking point that Jesus' mission is universal; he is the savior of the whole world.

A chronicler is one who records historical events (Greek *chronos* = time). Clearly, however, the writer of this passage is more than a recorder; there is an obvious attempt to interpret events and explain their significance: "All this was to fulfill the word of the Lord spoken by Jeremiah." In this summary sentence, the writer attributes Judah's sufferings and exile to the infidelity of its people. God's punishment is seen as a justly severe sentence in response to the worst crimes of all: unfaithfulness and idolatry. Seventy years of enforced exile must be endured because Judah abandoned the sabbath (seventh day) rest. The irony is bitter.

Further irony is apparent in the final paragraph. A pagan king becomes Judah's savior—a profound embarrassment for this monotheistic nation, and yet at the same time a tribute to the power of God to bring good out of any situation.

MARCH 13, 1994

FOURTH SUNDAY OF LENT

LECTIONARY #32

READING I   2 Chronicles 36:14–17, 19–23

A reading from the second book of *Chronicles* ▪ ▪

A grim announcement, but proclaim it boldly.

All the princes of Judah, the priests and the people added infidelity to infidelity, practicing all the abominations of the *nations* and polluting the Lord's *temple* which he had consecrated in Jerusalem. ▪ ▪

A hint of sadness here; God's love and compassion toward Israel are rebuffed. NRSV: "the God of their ancestors."

Early and often did the Lord, the God of their fathers, send his *messengers* to them, for he had compassion on his people and his dwelling place. ▪ But they *mocked* the messengers of God, despised his *warnings,* and scoffed at his *prophets,* until the anger of the Lord against his people was so inflamed that there was no remedy. ▪ Then he brought up against

The punishment is swift and horrifying. Chaldeans = kal-DEE-uhnz.

them the king of the *Chaldeans,* who slew their young men in their own sanctuary building, sparing neither *young* man nor *maiden,* neither the *aged* nor the *decrepit;* ▪ he delivered all of them over into his grip. ▪ Finally, their enemies burnt the house of *God,* tore down the walls of *Jerusalem,* set all its *palaces* afire, and destroyed all its precious *objects.* ▪ Those who escaped the *sword* he carried captive to *Babylon,* where they became his and his sons' servants until the kingdom of the *Persians* came to power. ▪ All this was to fulfill the word of the Lord spoken by *Jeremiah:* ▪ "Until the land has retrieved its lost

Speak Jeremiah's prophecy with absolute conviction.

sabbaths, during all the time it lies waste it shall have rest while *seventy years* are fulfilled." ▪ ▪

A new section begins with a pause. Cyrus = SAI-ruhs.

In the first year of *Cyrus,* king of Persia, in order to fulfill the word of the Lord spoken by *Jeremiah,* the Lord inspired King Cyrus of Persia to issue *this* proclamation throughout his kingdom, both by word of *mouth* and in *writing:* ▪ "Thus says Cyrus, king of Persia: ▪ '*All* the kingdoms of the *earth* the Lord, the

A grim situation is now filled with hope. Finish with a tone of exaltation. Use the plural form for the final sentence: "Therefore, let those among you who belong to any part of his people go up, and may their God be with them."

God of heaven, has given to *me,* ▪ and he has also charged me to build him a *house* in *Jerusalem,* which is in Judah. ▪ Whoever, therefore, among you belongs to any part of his *people,* let him go *up,* and may his God be *with* him!'" ▪ ▪

A reading from the letter of *Paul* to the *Ephesians* ▪ ▪

This is a hymn of praise, recalling God's goodness. Let your voice be bright and strong throughout.

God is rich in *mercy:* ▪ because of his great *love* for us he brought us to life with *Christ* when we were dead in *sin.* ▪ By this *favor* you were saved. ▪ Both with and in Christ Jesus he raised us up and gave us a place in the heavens that in the ages to come he might display the great wealth of his *favor,* manifested by his *kindness* to us in Christ Jesus. ▪ I repeat, it is owing to *his* favor that salvation is yours through *faith.* ▪ This is not your own doing, it is God's *gift;* ▪ neither is it a *reward* for anything you have *accomplished,* so let no one *pride* himself on it. ▪ We are truly his handiwork, created in Christ Jesus to lead the life of *good* deeds which God prepared for us in advance. ▪ ▪

"I repeat" must receive special emphasis, followed by a slight pause.

NRSV: "This is not the result of works, so that no one may boast." Or: "let none pride themselves on it."

READING II One of the great controversies in Christianity has to do with "faith *vs.* good works." Are we saved by the gift of faith, an entirely gratuitous action on God's part, or do our good works win God's favor? The answer is more "both/and" rather than "either/or." However, in this reading the emphasis is on "salvation through God's favor," and the recipients of the letter are being cautioned to avoid any notion that the grace of God is a reward for their goodness.

It is an emphasis we need to hear frequently, because of our tendency to forget that Christianity is the story of what an all-loving God has done for us, and not the story of what we must do to be saved. In no way does the writer of Ephesians encourage passivity or presumption. The point is that once we realize fully how much we have been loved by God, our response in loving deeds will be whole-hearted and spontaneous.

It is difficult to understand why so many preachers concentrate on our sinfulness and our duty. To do so reveals inadequate theology and bad psychology. The whole point of Jesus' life, death and resurrection is heard in these words: "This is not your own doing, it is God's gift." A gift is, by definition, free—with no strings attached. This is where the emphasis must lie in all our ministry. Likewise, we need to be attentive to human psychology, which clearly shows that we respond well to being loved, not to being told how sinful we are.

GOSPEL We should be ever grateful for the curiosity of Nicodemus, a leader in the community who came to Jesus at night, so as to avoid risk to his reputation. Despite his caution, Nicodemus had the courage to seek the truth—and in so doing drew from Jesus, through the evangelist John, perhaps the most memorable words in the Bible: "God so loved the world . . ." (John 3:16).

This verse from John is about as simple a formulation of Christianity as one can imagine, and yet it contains all the essential elements. Most important, during our observance of Lent, it puts things in perspective. If we are tempted to concentrate a bit too much on our lenten penance or good works (in other words, *our duty*), we need to read John 3:16 again. It makes clear to us that our salvation is accomplished for us by the goodness of an all-loving God, whose movement toward the world through the Son is entirely motivated by love, not condemnation. The only duty we have is to *believe* in such overwhelming love; then penance and good works will arise spontaneously from our grateful hearts.

In this reading, verse 16 is bordered by two rich images. First, the image of the crucified Jesus is seen as prefigured in the bronze serpent upon which Israel gazed and then found healing. Second, light is a symbol of Jesus, penetrating the dark world with illuminating truth.

A reading from the holy *gospel* according to *John* ▪▪

Jesus said to Nicodemus: ▪

You are quoting Jesus for the entire reading. The tone is one of patient and loving explanation.

"Just as *Moses* lifted up the serpent
   in the desert, ▪
so must the Son of *Man* be lifted up, ▪
that all who believe
may have eternal *life* in *him*. ▪
Yes, God so *loved* the world

"Yes" prepares for a much-loved verse: John 3:16. Read it with special care.

that he gave his only *Son*,
that whoever *believes* in him may not *die*
but may have eternal *life*. ▪▪
God did not send the Son into the world
   to *condemn* the world,
but that the world might be *saved*
   through him. ▪

An easy riddle: Non-believers condemn themselves to a terrible loss, namely, the loss of joy in believing.

Whoever believes in *him* avoids
   condemnation,
but whoever does *not* believe is *already*
   condemned
for *not* believing in the name of God's
   only *Son*. ▪▪
The judgment in question is *this:* ▪
the light came into the *world*,
but men loved darkness rather than *light*

NRSV: "men" = "people."

because their deeds were wicked. ▪
Everyone who practices evil
hates the light; ▪

Employ the plural to be inclusive: "All who practice evil hate the light; they do not come near it for fear their deeds will be exposed. But those who act in truth come into the light, to make clear that their deeds are done in God."

he does not come near it
for fear his deeds will be *exposed*. ▪
But he who acts in *truth*
comes *into* the light,
to make clear
that his deeds are done in *God*." ▪▪

FOURTH SUNDAY OF LENT, YEAR A

LECTIONARY #31

READING I   1 Samuel 16:1, 6–7, 10–13

A reading from the first book of *Samuel* ▪ ▪

The Lord said to *Samuel:* ▪ "I am sending you to *Jesse of Bethlehem*, for I have chosen *my king* from among *his sons.*" ▪

As Jesse and his sons came to the *sacrifice*, Samuel looked at *Eliab* and thought, ▪ "Surely the Lord's anointed is here *before* him." ▪ But the Lord said to Samuel: ▪ "Do not judge from his *appearance* or from his lofty *stature*, because I have *rejected* him. ▪ Not as *man sees* does *God see*, because man sees the *appearance* but the Lord looks into the *heart*." ▪

In the same *way* Jesse presented *seven sons* before Samuel, but Samuel said to Jesse, ▪ "The Lord has not chosen *any one of these*." ▪ Then Samuel asked Jesse, ▪ "Are these *all* the sons you *have?*" Jesse replied, ▪ "There is still the *youngest*, who is tending the *sheep*." ▪ Samuel said to Jesse, "Send for *him*; ▪ we will not begin the sacrificial banquet until *he arrives* here." ▪ Jesse sent and had the young man *brought* to them. ▪ He was *ruddy*, a youth handsome to *behold* and making a *splendid* appearance. ▪ The Lord said, ▪ "*There*—anoint *him*, for this is *he!*" ▪ Then Samuel, with the horn of *oil* in hand, *anointed* him in the midst of his *brothers*; ▪ and from that day *on*, the spirit of the Lord *rushed upon David.* ▪ ▪

Eliab = ee-LAI-ab

NRSV: "The Lord does not see as mortals see; they look on the outward appearance, but the Lord looks on the heart."

Because this sentence is the proof of the validity of God's choice, it deserves special emphasis.

READING I   This is one of those scripture passages that demonstrate clearly why a literal reading of the story is insufficient. The account of David's anointing here is contradicted elsewhere in the Bible. And although the Lord advises Samuel that he must not make the choice of king on the basis of appearance, the one who is chosen (David) is described at some length as "handsome to behold and making a splendid appearance." The NRSV translation is even more specific, telling us that David had beautiful eyes. Clearly, then, the author of this passage has something more than a drawn out election process in mind.

The point is, of course, that God's ways are different from our own, and choices made by the divine are not to be questioned—the presumption being that God sees the ultimate outcome of such things far more clearly than we do. It is not difficult to communicate this larger message, because the framework for it has a definite feeling of literary formula. Seven of Jesse's sons are paraded by Samuel; all are rejected. David, the youngest, has to be sent for because Jesse obviously felt he couldn't be the right choice. And, of course, he is the one who is chosen. The story is formulaic and predictable (more clearly so when verses 8 and 9 are not excised, as they are here). But the underlying message is crucial. And the formula couches the message in memorable terms.

The proof of the validity of David's anointing is recorded in the final sentence: "The spirit of the Lord rushed upon David." All the messianic promises associated with David's house (culminating in Christ) are now given credibility and force.

READING II This passage from Ephesians is an inspiring meditation on darkness and light, comparing these elements to our situation before and after receiving Christ in baptism. When we remember that Lent is the time for preparing catechumens for baptism, the reading becomes particularly appropriate. So closely is "light" associated with baptism that the early church referred to the newly baptized as "those who have been illumined."

The theme of light continues, and is brought to fullness, in the gospel narrative. Jesus proclaims publicly, "I am the light of the world." All the more reason, then, to proclaim this brief reading with special care, giving attention to the rather jumbled — but ultimately very beautiful — images of light and darkness.

The final lines are a portion of an ancient baptismal hymn. We awake and arise from the dead when we emerge from the waters of baptism and are filled with the light of Christ.

GOSPEL If this seems to you like a long reading, think of it instead as a short story — for that is what it is. And it is a wonderful story. It is about not seeing the light, being afraid to see the light, seeing the light, and refusing to see the light.

The man born blind could not see the light until Jesus, "the light of the world," covered his eyes with mud, sent him to the pool to wash, and restored his sight. A veritable treasure chest of lenten/baptismal/messianic images tumble out before us in this story. The very mudpack Jesus uses as a salve reminds us of the dust we came from and to which we shall return. The pool of Siloam (which means "one who has been sent") reminds us of the waters of baptism as well as the Christ who has been sent from God — and who sends us forth through our baptismal commission to bring light into the world.

But there are other characters in the story who are blind — and remain that way. The Pharisees are downright annoying in their reluctance to believe the simple story of this simple man. He tells the story of his cure over and over to no avail: "I was blind. I did what this Jesus told me to do. Now I see." The Pharisees refuse to see. The bystanders refuse to believe that the man was blind in the first place.

READING II   Ephesians 5:8–14

Paul's expression here is strongly put. He uses the strength of metaphor, not simile. We were darkness (not simply in the dark); we are light (not simply enlightened).

The things too shameful to mention are no doubt pagan sexual practices; even they will be corrected when brought into the light of day.

You are reading a hymn. Proclaim it broadly, poetically and beautifully. Above all, it must be heard as a strong and confident summons!

A reading from the letter of *Paul* to the *Ephesians* ▪▪

There was a *time* when *you were darkness*, but *now* you are *light* in the *Lord*. ▪ Well, then, *live* as children of *light*. ▪ Light produces every kind of *goodness* and *justice* and *truth*. ▪ Be *correct* in your judgment of what *pleases the Lord*. ▪ Take no part in vain deeds done in *darkness*; ▪ rather, *condemn* them. ▪ It is shameful *even to mention* the things these people do in secret; ▪ but when such deeds are *condemned*, they are seen in the light of *day*, and all that then appears *is* light. ▪ That is why we *read:* ▪

"*Awake*, O sleeper,
    arise from the *dead*,
        and *Christ* will give you *light*." ▪▪

GOSPEL   John 9:1–41

"Blind from birth" is a symbolic refrain in this reading. Be sure we hear its deeper implication each time.

Siloam = sih-LO-uhm

Three remarks by the man born blind have been translated so colloquially that, when read aloud and in context, they make him sound flippant. Do your best to avoid the trivializing effect of these renderings — or choose the

A reading from the holy *gospel* according to *John* ▪▪

As Jesus walked along, he saw a man who had been *blind from birth*. ▪ His disciples asked him, ▪ "Rabbi, was it *his* sin or his *parents'* that caused him to be *born blind?*" ▪ "*Neither*," answered Jesus: ▪
    "It was *no* sin, either of this *man*
        or of his parents. ▪
    Rather, it was to let *God's works*
        show *forth* in him. ▪
    We must do the deeds of *him who*
        sent me while it is *day*. ▪
    The *night* comes on
        when *no one* can work. ▪
    While *I* am *in the world*
        I am the *light of the world*." ▪
With that Jesus spat on the *ground*, made mud with his *saliva*, and smeared the man's *eyes* with the mud. ▪ Then he told him, ▪ "*Go*, wash in the pool of *Siloam*." ▪ (This name means "One who has been *sent*.") ▪ So the man went *off* and *washed*, and came back *able* to see. ▪▪

His *neighbors* and the people who had been accustomed to see him *begging* began to ask, ▪ "Isn't this the fellow who used to sit and *beg?*" ▪ Some were

NRSV, which maintains some dignity: For "I'm the one, all right," the NRSV has: "I am the man." For "I have no idea," the NRSV has: "I do not know." For "Well, this is news," the NRSV has: "Here is an astonishing thing!"

Mark each new section with a pause and a fresh intonation. The Pharisees are blinded by legalism. The wonder of this healing escapes them because they are obsessed with the notion that Jesus broke the sabbath rest. It was not permitted to heal on the sabbath.

"The Jews" could be "the religious leaders." (Everyone in the story is a Jew.)

Instead of "the Jews," say "the authorities."

Transition into a new section.

claiming it was he; ▪ others maintained it was *not* but someone who *looked* like him. ▪ The man himself said, ▪ "I'm the one, all right." ▪ They said to him then, ▪ "How were your *eyes opened?*" ▪ He answered: ▪ "That man they call *Jesus* made mud and smeared it on my eyes, telling me to go to *Siloam* and *wash.* ▪ When I *did* go and wash, I was able to *see.*" ▪ "Where *is* he?" they asked. ▪ He replied, ▪ "I have no idea." ▪ ▪

Next, they took the man who had been born blind to *the Pharisees.* ▪ (Note that it was *on a sabbath* that Jesus had made the mud paste and opened his eyes.) ▪ The Pharisees, in turn, began to inquire *how* he had recovered his sight. ▪ He told them, ▪ "He put *mud* on my eyes. ▪ I washed it *off,* and now I can *see.*" ▪ This prompted some of the Pharisees to assert, ▪ "This man *cannot be from God* because he does *not keep the sabbath.*" ▪ Others objected, ▪ "If a man is a *sinner,* how can he perform *signs like these?*" ▪ They were sharply *divided* over him. ▪ Then they addressed the *blind* man again: ▪ "Since it was *your* eyes he opened, what do you have to *say about him?*" ▪ "He is a *prophet,*" he replied. ▪ ▪

The Jews *refused to believe* that he had really been *born* blind and had begun to *see,* until they summoned the *parents* of this man who now could see. ▪ "Is this your *son?*" they asked, ▪ "and if *so,* do you attest that he was *blind at birth?* ▪ How do you account for the fact that he *now can see?*" ▪ His parents answered, ▪ "We know this is our *son,* and we know he was blind at *birth.* ▪ But how he can see *now,* or who *opened his eyes,* we have no *idea.* ▪ Ask *him.* ▪ He is old enough to speak for *himself.*" ▪ (His parents answered in this fashion because they were afraid of the Jews, who had *already agreed among themselves* that anyone who acknowledged Jesus as the *Messiah* would be put out of the *synagogue.* ▪ That was why his parents said, ▪ *"He* is of age—ask *him.")* ▪ ▪

A *second* time they summoned the man who had been born blind and *said* to him, ▪ "Give glory to *God!* ▪ First of all, we know this man is a *sinner.*" ▪ "I would not know whether he is a sinner or *not,*" he answered. ▪ "I know *this* much: ▪ I was *blind* before; ▪ now I can *see.*" ▪ They persisted: ▪ "Just what *did he do* to you? ▪ *How* did he open your eyes?" ▪ "I have told you *once,* but you would not *listen* to me," he answered them. ▪ "Why do you want to hear it all *over* again? ▪ Do not tell me *you* want to become his

The parents of the blind man are afraid to see clearly what Jesus did (and afraid to get involved), knowing that the Pharisees can cause them trouble. We inevitably are struck with the degree of resistance to something wonderful. How many people find the good news too good to be true?

Perhaps the most exciting development in the story is that the beggar, blind from birth, became an ambassador for Jesus, insisting that he must be from God or he could not perform such wonderful works. For this brave act of apostleship he is excommunicated. But Jesus seeks him out and takes his belief one step further— into faith in the Son of God, the ultimate kind of seeing.

The story ends on a sad note. The old expression, "There are none so blind as those who will not see," is wrong. There are some even more blind than that. They are the ones who are blind but are convinced they see.

Note: Some margin notes here deal with John's use of "the Jews," which has fostered anti-Semitism by implying that the Jewish people as a whole were responsible for Christ's death. This issue requires thoughtful preaching as well as proclamation. For more background, consult the 1988 statement of the Bishops' Committee on the Liturgy, "God's Mercy Endures Forever: Guidelines on the Presentation of Jews and Judaism in Catholic Preaching." Another helpful resource is "Criteria for the Evaluation of Dramatizations of the Passion," issued by the Bishops' Committee for Ecumenical and Interreligious Affairs. Both documents are available from the National Conference of Catholic Bishops, Office of Publishing and Promotion Services, 3211 Fourth Street NE, Washington DC 20017.

disciples *too?*" ▪ They retorted scornfully, *"You* are the one who is *that man's* disciple. ▪ *We* are disciples of *Moses.* ▪ We *know* that God spoke to *Moses,* but we have no idea where *this man* comes from." ▪ He came *back* at them: ▪ "Well, this *is* news! ▪ You do not know where he *comes* from, yet he opened my *eyes.* ▪ We know that God does not hear *sinners,* but that if someone is *devout* and obeys his *will* he listens to him. ▪ It is unheard of that *anyone* ever gave sight to a person *blind from birth.* ▪ If this man were not from *God,* he could never have *done* such a thing." ▪ *"What!"* they exclaimed, ▪ "You are *steeped* in sin from your *birth,* and you are giving *us* lectures?" ▪ With that they threw him out *bodily.* ▪▪

When Jesus *heard* of his expulsion, he sought him *out* and asked him, ▪ "Do you believe in the Son of *Man?"* ▪ He answered, ▪ *"Who is he,* sir, that I may *believe in him?"* ▪ "You have *seen* him," Jesus replied. ▪ "He is speaking to you *now."* ▪ ["I *do* believe, Lord," he said, ▪ and bowed down to *worship* him. ▪ Then Jesus said:] ▪

"I *came into this world* to *divide* it,
to make the sightless *see*
and the seeing *blind."* ▪

Some of the *Pharisees* around him picked this *up,* saying, ▪ "You are not counting *us* in with the *blind,* are you?" ▪ To which Jesus replied: ▪

"If you *were* blind
there would be no sin in *that.* ▪
'*But we see,'* you say,
and your sin *remains."* ▪▪

[Shorter: John 9:1, 6–9, 13–17, 34–38]

The final section is a kind of resolution of the conflict. The poor man has been expelled from the synagogue, but he has found faith. The final words of Jesus are awful to hear, but must be read with firm conviction—even awe.

FIFTH SUNDAY OF LENT

LECTIONARY #35

READING I   Jeremiah 31:31–34

A reading from the book of the prophet *Jeremiah* ▪ ▪

"The days are coming" is a very strong opener. Make it big!

NRSV: "fathers" = "ancestors."

"But this" signals a strong contrast. The law is no longer written in stone, but on human hearts.

"I will be their God...." There is no more moving way of describing how close God is to us. Make much of this sentence. "Kinsmen" could be "kin."

The days are coming, says the Lord, when I will make a *new covenant* with the house of *Israel* and the house of *Judah.* ▪ It will not be like the covenant I made with their *fathers* the day I took them by the hand to lead them forth from the land of *Egypt:* ▪ for *they* broke my covenant, and I had to show myself their *master,* says the Lord. ▪ But *this* is the covenant which I will make with the house of Israel *after* those days, says the Lord. ▪ I will place my law *within* them, and write it upon their *hearts:* ▪ I will *be* their God, and they shall *be* my people. ▪ No longer will they have need to *teach* their friends and kinsmen how to know the Lord. ▪ *All,* from least to greatest, shall know me, says the Lord, for I will forgive their *evildoing* and remember their sin no *more.* ▪ ▪

READING II   Hebrews 5:7–9

A reading from the letter to the *Hebrews* ▪ ▪

A brief reading, but two lengthy sentences. Proceed slowly and deliberately, letting each thought sink in. A great deal of vocal variety, careful pauses, and attention to sense units will enable the assembly to hear the fullness of the good news in this brief passage.

In the days when Christ was in the *flesh*, he offered prayers and supplications with loud cries and tears to God, who was able to save him from *death,* ▪ and he was *heard* because of his *reverence.* ▪ Son though he *was,* he learned obedience from what he *suffered;* ▪ and when perfected, he became the source of eternal salvation for all who *obey* him. ▪ ▪

READING I   It is becoming a custom today to refer to the two parts of the Bible as the First Testament and the Second Testament, rather than the "Old" and the "New." The reason for this is obvious: "Old" can have a perjorative connotation, as though the Hebrew Scriptures were no longer relevant, or less important to Christians than the "New" Testament. Nothing could be further from the truth. It would be impossible to make sense of the Second Testament without the First!

The "new covenant" (covenant = testament) Jeremiah speaks of is a development from the "old covenant," and could not exist without its predecessor. The growth from an exterior law (on tablets of stone) to an interior law (engraved on our hearts) is a common enough phenomenon in many aspects of human life. Rules become habits, good deeds become virtues, etiquette becomes loving respect.

From a more immediate point of view, this prophecy of Jeremiah (spoken to Israel in exile) can serve as a model for the Lent/Easter experience. We strive to move from mere external observance of our religion toward a more interior experience of our faith. As Jeremiah puts it, we move from "learning about" the Lord toward "knowing" the Lord.

READING II   The controlling image of Jesus in the letter to the Hebrews is that of "high priest." Keep that image in mind as you read this short passage, because the actions attributed to Christ here are those of priestly intercession.

Notice, too, the distinction between "the days when Christ was in the flesh" and his priestly intercession for us now in heaven. The writer is showing us why Christ's priesthood in our behalf is efficacious. It was because of his *reverence*— which enabled him to learn *obedience* in suffering on earth—that his priestly work was "perfected" (consummated). By this process, the writer says, "he became the source of eternal salvation for all who [in imitation of his obedience] obey him."

GOSPEL   In both the second reading and the gospel today, we hear hints of Gethsemane, the garden where Jesus suffered such spiritual torment that his sweat became like drops of blood. The letter to the Hebrews spoke of his "loud cries and tears." John quotes Jesus saying, "My soul is troubled now." Clearly, we stand at the threshold of Passiontide. "The hour has come." Next Sunday (Passion [Palm] Sunday) we will hear Mark's account of the suffering, death, and burial of Jesus.

The gospel reading begins with a request on the part of some Greeks to see Jesus. Apparently, their request is not granted—perhaps because John the evangelist feels that it is impossible to *really* see Jesus in his true nature until after the resurrection. Certainly it is true that the spread of Christianity beyond Palestine was severely limited until after the risen Christ had empowered his disciples to "go forth into all the world."

In any event, it is interesting that Jesus' response to the request of the Greeks becomes a prediction of his death and the results of it: the grain of wheat must die before it can produce fruit. Is he saying that it is impossible for the good news to spread (impossible, that is, for the Greeks and the whole world to see him) until after he has died and risen? The question is implied again later in the assertion that before he can draw "all men [humankind]" to himself, he must be lifted up from earth (on the cross and from the grave).

The voice that is heard indistinctly by the bystanders is heard very clearly by Jesus. It was divine confirmation that God would be glorified in the death of Jesus and in the consequent salvation of the world.

The solemnity of the final parenthetical comment should be heard just as clearly by the assembly with whom you are sharing this rich and mysterious text. It is the perfect preparation for Passiontide and the rapidly approaching drama of the Paschal Triduum.

A reading from the holy *gospel* according to *John* ▪▪

The first paragraph is an interesting preface to Jesus' long discourse. It sets the scene. Bethsaida = behth-SAY-ih-duh.

Among those who had come up to worship at the feast of Passover were some *Greeks.* ▪ They approached Philip, who was from Bethsaida in Galilee, and put this request to him: ▪ "Sir, we should like to see *Jesus.*" ▪ Philip went to tell Andrew; ▪ Philip and Andrew in turn came to inform Jesus. ▪ Jesus answered them: ▪

Prepare for this passage with a pause. Then use a bright, vigorous tone.

"The hour has come
for the Son of Man to be *glorified.* ▪
I solemnly assure you,
unless the grain of wheat falls to the earth
    and *dies,*
it remains just a grain of *wheat.* ▪
But if it *dies,*
it produces much *fruit.* ▪
The man who loves his life
loses it, ▪

NRSV: "Those who love their life, lose it, and those who hate their life in this world will keep it for eternal life. Whoever serves me must follow me."

while the man who hates his life in this world
preserves it to life eternal. ▪
If anyone would serve *me,*
let him *follow* me; ▪
where I am,
there will my servant be. ▪
Anyone who serves *me,*
the Father will honor. ▪

Pause. The tone changes here.

My soul is troubled now,
yet what should I say— ▪
Father, *save* me from this hour? ▪
But it was *for* this that I *came* to this hour. ▪
Father, *glorify* your name!" ▪
Then a voice came from the sky: ▪

Slightly louder, perhaps, but no sense of imitating God's voice!

"I *have* glorified it,
and will glorify it *again.*" ▪
When the crowd of bystanders heard the voice, they said it was thunder. ▪ Others maintained, "An angel was speaking to him." ▪ Jesus answered, ▪ "That voice did not come for *my* sake, but for *yours.*" ▪

Jesus speaks again, in an even more solemn tone. The reading peaks at "draw all men to myself." NRSV: "will draw all people to myself."

"Now has *judgment* come upon this *world,*
now will this world's *prince* be driven *out,*
and I—once I am lifted up from earth—
will draw all men to myself." ▪

Pause. The parenthetical commentary is added only after the previous sentence has had a chance to sink in.

(This statement of his indicated the sort of death he was going to die.) ▪▪

FIFTH SUNDAY OF LENT, YEAR A

LECTIONARY #34

READING I   Ezekiel 37:12–14

A reading from the book of the prophet *Ezekiel* ▪▪

"Thus says the Lord God" is a trumpet fanfare to catch our attention and enable us to listen with special care.

"O my people . . . ," "O my people . . ." are solemn incantations to reassure us.

Consider eliminating the final "says the Lord." This will make the formula "The word of the Lord," and the assembly's response much stronger.

Thus says the Lord *God:* ▪ O my *people,* ▪ I will *open your graves* and have you *rise* from them, and *bring you back* to the land of *Israel.* Then you shall know that *I am the Lord,* when I open your *graves* and have you *rise* from them, O my people! ▪ I will *put my spirit* in you that you may *live,* and I will *settle you upon your land;* ▪ thus you shall *know* that I am the Lord. ▪ I have *promised,* and *I will do it,* says the Lord. ▪▪

READING II   Romans 8:8–11

A reading from the letter of *Paul* to the *Romans* ▪▪

Begin slowly, to give yourself and the assembly time to relish the contrast between "in the flesh" and "in the spirit."

NRSV: "Anyone who does not have the Spirit of Christ does not belong to him."

The last sentence is long and begins with an "if" statement. Take a deep breath and proceed with care— so you can tie it all together.

Those who are *in the flesh* cannot please *God.* ▪ But you are *not in the flesh;* ▪ you are *in the spirit,* since the Spirit of God *dwells in you.* ▪ If anyone does *not* have the Spirit of Christ, he does not *belong* to Christ. ▪ If Christ is *in* you, the body is indeed *dead* because of *sin,* while the spirit *lives* because of *justice.* ▪ If the Spirit of him who raised Jesus from the dead *dwells in you,* then he who raised Christ from the dead will *bring your mortal bodies to life* also through his Spirit *dwelling* in you. ▪▪

GOSPEL   John 11:1–45

A reading from the holy *gospel* according to *John* ▪▪

Lazarus = LAZ-er-uhs
Bethany = BEHTH-uh-nee

There was a certain man named *Lazarus* who was *sick.* ▪ He was from *Bethany,* the village of *Mary* and her sister *Martha.* ▪ (This Mary whose brother Lazarus was sick was the one who *anointed* the Lord

READING I A reading as brief (and packed with good news) as this one must be read slowly and deliberately. Every line contains a promise that we rejoice to hear. The words are strangely beautiful, too. "Bring you back" is loaded with meaning and nuance. "Open your graves" is slightly horrifying, but we know it is a promise of life beyond death. When God says, "I will put my spirit in you," we know something tremendous—beyond our understanding—is being promised.

All of these wonderful occurrences will convince us once and for all that God is truly the Lord of life and death. And to comfort us further, God promises to *keep* these awesome promises. The same theme of death and resurrection appears in all of today's readings. And there is a progression in the quality of our belief in God's promises.

The words you are reading come from a situation very different from our own. Ezekiel is in the famous "valley of dry bones," foreseeing a day when Israel's exile will be ended and their suffering vindicated. To be restored to the land that is their birthright would be very much like being raised from the dead. Anything approaching our modern belief about resurrection of the body was to come much later. Nevertheless, the loving care God exhibits for the Chosen People is seen as extending beyond destruction and death. In the end (whatever that end may be), the love of God (and the startling reality that God's spirit lives in us) will enable us to triumph.

READING II Two weeks from today is Easter Sunday. Already we are inundated with words about death and life, flesh and spirit, grave and resurrection. Paul is at pains to explain that the Spirit of God dwelling in us is our guarantee that life does not end; it changes.

And the evidence for the truth of our belief is the resurrection of Jesus. Most challenging for the reader here is a deft handling of the paradox that Paul presents. Our bodies are dead (to sin) because our spirits are alive (in God). And our mortal bodies, which carry in them many signs of death (illness, pain, sin), are nonetheless enlivened by the spirit we received at baptism.

The evidence that we have God's Spirit in us is found in the way we lead our lives even now—not according to the flesh, a symbol of weakness and sin. No, we lead lives of holiness because we are "in the spirit" and the spirit is in us. Enjoy the wordplay.

GOSPEL Note: Some margin notes here deal with John's use of "the Jews," which has fostered anti-Semitism by implying that the Jewish people as a whole were responsible for Christ's death. This issue requires thoughtful preaching as well as proclamation. For more background, consult the 1988 statement of the Bishops' Committee on the Liturgy, "God's Mercy Endures Forever: Guidelines on the Presentation of Jews and Judaism in Catholic Preaching." Another helpful resource is "Criteria for the Evaluation of Dramatizations of the Passion," issued by the Bishops' Committee for Ecumenical and Interreligious Affairs. Both documents are available from the National Conference of Catholic Bishops, Office of Publishing and Promotion Services, 3211 Fourth Street NE, Washington DC 20017.

John's strange and wonderful story about the raising of Lazarus is filled with strong emotions, dramatic scenes and profound teaching about the person of Jesus. The combination of narrative with discussion is explained by the fact that John has taken a preexisting account of Lazarus being brought back to life and has overlaid it with his own special brand of teaching.

The Lazarus story appears in John's gospel shortly before Jesus is captured, tried and crucified. It is the event that most directly results in his condemnation by those who were seeking to kill him. In the other gospels it is another event that turns the officials against Jesus: the cleansing of the temple. The effect of John's arrangement is striking, since immediately before his death and resurrection Jesus proclaims those words that form the very heart of today's story: "I am the resurrection and the life." All the elements of the story point toward these words and put them in bold relief.

We learn first that Lazarus is a special friend, so we might think that Jesus would hasten to his side in his sickness. But his delay gives the author of the story the opportunity to point out that time is irrelevant.

"The one you love is sick" is a striking way of naming a dear friend; not even the name is necessary.

"Yet . . . he stayed . . . for two days more." Jesus is confident of his mastery over death. Instead of "the Jews," say "the people there."

An elusive passage, but surely indicating that the disciples would understand why Jesus has to go back to Judea if they could see more clearly what his ultimate mission is to be. The light of faith enables us to see that the apparent obstacles to Jesus' safety are really the stepping stones toward his final triumph over sin and death.

The "sleep vs. death" discussion is John's way of emphasizing that Lazarus is really dead—and that Jesus will do far more than wake him from slumber.

"In the tomb four days" is another way of impressing us that Lazarus is really dead—and that Jesus is the master of the situation.

Here is the heart of John's account. It falls precisely in the center of the narrative. These words must be proclaimed with special conviction.

with *perfume* and dried his *feet* with her *hair.)* ••
The sisters sent word to Jesus to inform him, • "Lord, the one you *love* is *sick.*" • Upon *hearing* this, Jesus said: •
   "This sickness is *not to end in death;* •
   rather it is for God's *glory,*
   that through it the *Son of God* may
      be *glorified.*" ••
Jesus *loved* Martha and her sister and Lazarus very *much.* • Yet, after hearing that Lazarus was *sick,* he stayed on where he was for *two days more.* • Finally he said to his disciples, • "Let us go back to *Judea.*" • "Rabbi," protested the disciples, • "with the Jews only recently trying to *stone* you, you are going back up there *again!*" • Jesus answered: •
   "Are there not *twelve hours* of daylight? •
   If a man goes walking *by day* he does
      not *stumble,*
   because he sees the world bathed in *light.* •
   But if he goes walking at *night*
      he will *stumble,*
   since there is no *light* in him." •
After uttering these words, he added, • "Our beloved Lazarus has *fallen asleep,* but I am going there to *wake* him." • At this the disciples *objected,* • "Lord, if he is asleep his life will be *saved.*" • Jesus had been speaking about his *death,* but they thought he meant sleep in the sense of *slumber.* • Finally Jesus said plainly, "Lazarus is *dead.* • For *your sakes* I am glad I was not there, that you may *come to believe.* • In any event, let us *go* to him." • Then *Thomas* (the name means "Twin") said to his fellow disciples, • "Let us go along, to *die with him.*" ••

When Jesus arrived at *Bethany,* he found that Lazarus had already been in the tomb *four days.* • The village was not far from *Jerusalem*—just under two *miles*—and many *Jewish people* had come out to *console* Martha and Mary over their *brother.* • When Martha heard that *Jesus* was coming she went to *meet* him, while Mary sat at *home.* • Martha said to Jesus, • "Lord, if *you had been here,* my brother would never have *died.* • Even *now,* I am sure that God will give you whatever you *ask* of him." • "Your brother will *rise* again," Jesus assured her. • "I *know* he will rise again," Martha replied, • "in the *resurrection on the last day.*" • Jesus told her: •
   "I am the resurrection and the life: •
   whoever believes in *me,*
   though he should *die,* will come to *life;* •

and whoever is *alive* and *believes in me*
will *never* die. ▪
Do you *believe* this?" ▪ "Yes, Lord," she replied. ▪ "I
have come to believe that you *are* the Messiah, the
Son of *God:* ▪ he who is to come *into the world.*" ▪ ▪

When she had said this she went back and called her
sister *Mary.* ▪ "The *Teacher* is here, *asking* for you,"
she whispered. ▪ As soon as Mary heard this, she got
up and started out in his *direction.* ▪ (Actually Jesus
had not yet come into the village but was still at the
spot where *Martha* had *met* him.) ▪ The Jews who
were in the house with Mary *consoling* her saw her
get up quickly and go out, so they *followed* her,
thinking she was going to the *tomb* to *weep* there. ▪
When Mary came to the place where *Jesus* was,
seeing him, she fell at his feet and *said* to him, ▪
"Lord, *if you had been here* my brother would never
have *died.*" ▪ ▪ When Jesus saw her *weeping,* and the
Jewish folk who had accompanied her *also* weeping,
he was troubled in *spirit,* moved by the deepest
emotions. ▪ ▪ "Where have you *laid* him?" he asked. ▪
"Lord, come and *see,*" they said. ▪ Jesus began to
weep, which caused the Jews to remark, ▪ "See how
much he *loved* him!" ▪ But some said, ▪ "He opened
the eyes of that *blind* man. ▪ Why could he not have
done something to stop this man from *dying?*" ▪ ▪
Once *again* troubled in spirit, Jesus approached the
tomb. ▪

It was a *cave* with a *stone* laid across it. ▪ "Take away
the *stone,*" Jesus directed. ▪ *Martha,* the dead man's
sister, said to him, ▪ "Lord, it has been four *days* now; ▪
surely there will be a *stench!*" ▪ Jesus replied, ▪ "Did I
not *assure* you that *if you believed* you would *see the
glory of God?*" ▪ They then took away the stone and
Jesus looked upward and said: ▪

"Father, I *thank* you for *having heard me.* ▪
I know that you *always* hear me
but I have said this for the sake of the *crowd,*
that *they may believe* that you *sent* me." ▪

Having said this, he called *loudly,* ▪ "Lazarus, come
out!" ▪ ▪ The dead man came *out,* bound hand and
foot with linen *strips,* his face wrapped in a *cloth.* ▪
"*Untie* him," Jesus told them, ▪ "and let him go *free.*" ▪ ▪

This caused *many* of the Jews who had come to visit
Mary, and had *seen* what Jesus *did,* to put their *faith
in him.* ▪ ▪

[Shorter: John 11:3–7, 17, 20–27, 33–45]

Emotions run high in this section. Even Jesus is "troubled in spirit." And the shortest verse in the Bible (11:35) reveals the Lord of Life in tears. In the Latin Vulgate and the King James version, two words are used: "Jesus flevit (Jesus wept)." The brevity of the verse makes it much stronger than our modern translation.

The drama reaches its climax. Nothing could make death more vivid than the "stench." The King James version is even more blunt: "Lord, by this time he stinketh." In a masterful literary and theological stroke, John juxtaposes the horror of bodily corruption with the glory of victory over it. The final command, "Come out," is preceded by a prayer by which Jesus reminds us of his relationship with the Author of Life.

The purpose of the entire event is fulfilled. Those who witnessed it put their faith in Jesus.

The degree of Lazarus' illness is also irrelevant. Jesus is the master of life and death.

When the disciples protest Jesus' decision to go back to Judea (where he is in trouble with the authorities), the author has the opportunity to show that this too is irrelevant. What does the master of life and death have, ultimately, to fear from such dangers?

The strange poetic response of Jesus to the apostles' protest is difficult to understand. It certainly means that Jesus is seeing the outcome of the situation more clearly than his followers do. And there is also something of the feeling of: "Open your eyes and see what I have been trying to teach you: you have been enlightened by belief in me; you have nothing to fear from anyone. If you still feel unequal to the risk and challenge of being my follower, believe more strongly—and the light within you will increase."

Thomas, the Twin, responds either with real courage or impulsive enthusiasm—or perhaps "Oh, what the heck!" resignation. Whatever the motive behind this energetic response, it is obviously a decision to take the consequences of being a disciple.

The discussion about the difference between sleep and death is John's way of impressing us even further that Jesus is actually going to raise the dead—not merely revive the seriously ill. And the fact that Lazarus has been dead for four days impresses the witnesses of the miracle even more. Custom and law required burial within 24 hours, because modern means of preserving a corpse were not available. The central point is further stressed: *Nothing* can hinder the master of life and death.

It is also John's intent in this story to prefigure the imminent suffering of Jesus himself. The personal grief and emotional stress that Jesus expresses at the loss of his friend is a prediction of his own passion and death. But that suffering and death too will be overcome, when God raises Jesus from the dead.

Finally, John points out to us in the last sentence of this reading that all the signs had their intended effect: "This caused many of the Jews . . . to put their faith in him." In your reading of John's account of this wonderful occurrence, realize that it is packed with instruction for the hearers.

PROCESSION GOSPEL We hear from Mark twice today. This brief gospel passage that recounts the triumphant entry of Jesus into Jerusalem prepares us for the proclamation of his suffering and death later in the liturgical celebration. The contrast between the acclamations of the crowd now and their curses later should not escape us. The liturgy places both acclamation and curse on our lips today, and thus dramatically reveals to us how fickle the human heart is.

In the book of the prophet Zechariah we find the text that Mark alludes to in this scene: "Rejoice greatly, O daughter Zion! Shout aloud, O daughter Jerusalem! Lo, your king comes to you; triumphant and victorious is he, humble and riding on a donkey, on a colt, the foal of a donkey."

The humility of the messiah-king is apparent in Jesus as he is borne into the city astride the lowly colt. But it is more than apparent later when he bears his cross out of the city to the place of his crucifixion. The prophecy is fulfilled, but the sudden shift in its emphasis is wrenching!

READING I Who is speaking in this first-person passage? As Christians celebrating Palm Sunday, we see Jesus in the role described. But the voice also belongs to the God of heaven and earth, now revealed to be a God of compassion, intimately involved with creation. It is also the voice of those who spoke on God's behalf throughout history: Jeremiah (a prophet appointed to live out in his person the suffering of his people), the whole people of Israel, and, indeed, men and women of every age who have borne the pain of the suffering poor and carried the burden of straying sinners.

You speak for all these as you proclaim this text. The ideal response of the assembly will be that they hear themselves speaking these words — and experience a renewal of their oneness with (and responsibility for) a pain-ridden world.

READING II You are privileged to proclaim one of ancient Christianity's most moving and beautiful summaries of Christ's person and mission. Your purpose is to move your hearers to live lives in imitation of their noble model.

Most striking of all is the clear indication that the model is God. God is just as

MARCH 27, 1994

PASSION (PALM) SUNDAY

LECTIONARY #37B

PROCESSION GOSPEL   Mark 11:1–10

A reading from the holy *gospel* according to *Mark* ▪ ▪

Bethphage = BEHTH-fuh-dzhee
Bethany = BEHTH-uh-nee

A drama is about to unfold. Set the scene calmly. Jesus' instructions should be read with a profound feeling of sureness.

Pause after Jesus' words. The following dialogue is an almost word-for-word fulfillment of Jesus' prediction.

Pause. Another stage in the drama has arrived.

Do not imitate the shouts of the crowd. Slightly more volume and intensity is sufficient.

As the crowd drew near *Bethphage* and *Bethany* on the Mount of *Olives*, close to *Jerusalem*, Jesus sent off two of his disciples with the instructions: ▪ "Go to the village straight *ahead* of you, and as soon as you *enter* it you will find tethered there a *colt* on which no one has *ridden*. ▪ *Untie* it and bring it *back*. ▪ If anyone says to you, ▪ 'Why are you *doing* that?' ▪ say, ▪ 'The *Master* needs it but he will send it *back* here at *once*.'" ▪ So they went *off*, and finding a colt tethered out on the street near a *gate*, they *untied* it. ▪ Some of the bystanders *said* to them, ▪ "What do you *mean* by untying that *colt?*" ▪ They answered as Jesus had *told* them to, and the men let them *take* it. ▪ They brought the colt to *Jesus* and threw their *cloaks* across its *back*, and he *sat* on it. ▪ *Many people* spread their cloaks on the *road*, while others spread *reeds* which they had cut in the *fields*. ▪ Those *preceding* him as well as those who *followed* cried out: ▪

"*Hosannah!* ▪
Blessed be he who comes
    in the name of the *Lord!* ▪
Blessed be the reign of our father *David*
    to *come!* ▪
God *save* him from on *high!*" ▪

READING I   Isaiah 50:4–7

A reading from the book of the prophet
Isaiah ••

The lector's creed! Your tongue has been most effectively trained by your own faith experience of joy and pain.

The Lord God has given me
   a well-trained *tongue*,
That I might know how to *speak to the weary*
   a word that will *rouse* them. •

Every day, every moment, is an opportunity to "hear" more clearly.

Morning after *morning*
   he opens my *ear* that I may *hear;* •
And I have not *rebelled,*
   have not turned *back.* •

The poetry demands an exalted delivery. The meaning is bigger than the actual words.

I gave my *back* to those who *beat* me,
   my *cheeks* to those who plucked my *beard;* •
My *face* I did not *shield*
   from *buffets* and *spitting.* ••
The *Lord God* is my help,
   therefore I am not *disgraced;* •
I have set my face like *flint,*
   knowing that I shall *not be put to shame.* ••

READING II   Philippians 2:6–11

A reading from the letter of *Paul*
to the *Philippians* ••

The text is neatly divided into two sections: (1) empty, slave, human, humbled, obedient, death; and (2) exalted, name above every other, knees bend, tongues proclaim, glory, Lord.

Your attitude must be *Christ's:* •
   though he was in the *form of God*
   he did not deem *equality with God*
   something to be *grasped* at. •

NRSV: "Being born in human likeness."

Rather, he *emptied* himself
   and took the form of a *slave,*
   being born in the likeness of men. •
He was known to be of *human* estate,
   and it was thus that he *humbled himself,*
   obediently accepting even *death,*
   death on a *cross!* ••
Because of this,
   God highly *exalted* him
   and bestowed on him *the name*
   above every other name, •

Despite the capital letters, the reading does not end in a shout. A whisper would be a more sensitive human response—and yet this too is inappropriate in the liturgical context. Strive for confidence, but be awed by your realization of the consequences of the message.

So that at Jesus' *name*
   every knee must *bend*
   in the *heavens,* on the *earth,*
   and *under* the earth,
   and every tongue *proclaim*
   to the glory of God the *Father:* •
JESUS CHRIST IS LORD! ••

---

much God in suffering as in glory. Suffering is not merely something endured for a time because it leads to glory. No, suffering and glory are the natural mixture that define God—and Jesus—and us.

When we proclaim "to the glory of God the Father" that "Jesus Christ is Lord," we are accepting the apparent contradiction of a Christian life. Since Jesus is the perfect model of perfect acceptance of the paradox, "every knee must bend" to acknowledge—and to imitate—that perfection.

Here is the Easter "mystery" in a nutshell. And, indeed, it is a mystery. How well can any of us live up to Paul's challenge to make Christ's attitude our own? Why do our hearts rise to the challenge and sink in the face of it at the same moment? Have we come face to face with the reason why this observation has been made: "It's too early to tell whether or not Christianity will work; it hasn't yet been tried"?

As you read this amazing text, try to enable the assembly to ask themselves such questions.

PASSION   It is not inconceivable that the entire Passion Gospel can be effectively read by one person. Liturgical practice through the ages, however, has preferred a group—not only because it adds variety, but because it adds dynamism and power. If you are approaching the "senior citizen" time of life, you no doubt remember the Passion accounts being sung in Latin by three cantors (one as Narrator, one as Crowd and one as Jesus). This is still done in some places (though usually in the language of the hearers). Able-bodied members of the assembly also stood throughout the proclamation.

Today the forms of proclamation vary widely. The assembly may be seated, and usually is. Whatever practice is decided upon in your community, please try to meet the challenge of a long proclamation (potentially tedious for the assembly) and avoid the excesses of a presentation so elaborate and literal that the assembly is preoccupied with the medium at the expense of the message.

The story of Christ's passion and death is told by all four evangelists. Over the three-year cycle of the lectionary we read Matthew, Mark and Luke on Passion Sunday. John's version is read every year on

Good Friday. It is very important to realize that each of the four writers had more in mind than a literal telling of the events. Each had a particular point of view and a particular purpose. Thus, the accounts differ. Thus the importance of choosing a mode of proclamation that serves the faith-building insight offered rather than the events related. To this end, we should not be timid in our experimentation, but we do need to be quite sensitive. Above all, we need to remember that liturgical proclamation is very different from dramatic (theatrical) reenactment (granting the obvious similarities). To ignore this difference is to reduce the word of God to a history lesson, and the assembled worshipers to an emotionally manipulated audience.

Perhaps the most striking characteristic of Mark's account of the passion is its severity and bleakness. It feels like a bare-bones narrative, yet it clearly intends to show Jesus to us as the "suffering servant" so poignantly portrayed and cruelly mistreated in the prophecy of Isaiah. The suffering Jesus in Mark is always and dramatically "alone," with no one to comfort him. And his struggle is seen as one involving the entire universe—a battle between the forces of good and evil, between darkness and light.

By contrast, Luke's account seems intent on letting God's mercy show through and emphasizing the cross as the means by which divine love enters the world. Matthew, on the other hand, and by no means only in the passion narrative, is guided by his intent to see a fulfillment of scripture in every detail of Jesus' suffering and death.

Any proclamation of the passion narrative will benefit from readers who are alert to the specific aims of the individual gospel writers. Pay close attention to the margin notes beside the text. These point out features of the story that are peculiar to Mark, or to which he attaches a special significance. Noted passages can then be given a special emphasis in proclamation.

(1) To place Jesus' obedient suffering and death in the context of the Passover is to connect it forever with the Passover themes of exile and liberation. The implication that Jesus is unjustly condemned (like the "suffering servant" in Isaiah) is clear: The leaders must resort to trickery to arrest him, and his popularity with the

The *Passion* of our *Lord Jesus Christ* according to *Mark* ··

The reading begins quietly with a sinister darkness. The malice is palpable, as those who plot to kill Jesus also recognize his popularity with the people. Be sure to pause appropriately between the clearly-marked sections of the narrative.

(1) The feasts of *Passover* and Unleavened *Bread* were to be observed in two days' *time,* and therefore the chief *priests* and *scribes* began to look for a way to *arrest* Jesus by some *trick* and *kill* him. · Yet they pointed out, · "Not during the *festival,* or the *people* may *riot.*" ··

Light relieves the darkness here. This is a "story within a story." The woman's lovely gesture is scorned by smaller minds. Keep the woman's gentle goodness in your tone here. Jesus' rebuke to those who criticize her will be most effective if spoken calmly and tenderly.

(2) When Jesus was in *Bethany* reclining at table in the house of Simon the *leper,* · a *woman* entered carrying an alabaster jar of *perfume* made from expensive aromatic *nard.* · *Breaking* the jar, she began to pour the perfume on his *head.* · Some were saying to themselves indignantly: · "What is the *point* of this extravagant waste of *perfume?* · It could have been sold for over three hundred *silver* pieces and the *money* given to the *poor.*" · They were *infuriated* at her. · But *Jesus* said: · "Let her *alone.* · Why do you *criticize* her? · She has done me a *kindness.* · The *poor* you will *always* have with you and you can be generous to them whenever you *wish,* but you will not always have *me.* · She has done what she *could.* · By perfuming my *body* she is anticipating its preparation for *burial.* · I *assure* you, wherever the good news is proclaimed throughout the *world,* what she has *done* will be told in her *memory.*" ··

The entrance of Judas darkens the picture again. The tone is conspiratorial.

(3) Then Judas *Iscariot,* one of the *Twelve,* went off to the chief *priests* to hand Jesus *over* to them. · Hearing what he had to *say,* they were *jubilant* and promised to give him *money.* · He for *his* part kept looking for an opportune way to *hand him over.* ··

Another "story within a story," the lengthy account of the Last Supper. It begins very brightly, with no hint of the horror to come.

(4) On the first day of Unleavened *Bread,* when it was customary to sacrifice the paschal *lamb,* his disciples said to him, · "Where do you wish us to go to prepare the *Passover supper* for you?" · He sent two of his disciples with these instructions: · "Go into the *city* and you will come upon a man carrying a *water* jar. · *Follow* him. · Whatever house he *enters,* say to the *owner,* · 'The *Teacher* asks, · Where is my *guestroom* where I may eat the Passover with my *disciples?*' · Then he will show you an upstairs *room,* spacious, furnished, and all in *order.* · *That* is the place you are to get *ready* for us." · The disciples went off. · When they reached the city they found it just as he had *told* them, and they prepared the Passover supper. ··

(5) As it grew *dark* he arrived with the *Twelve*. ▪ They reclined at *table*, and in the course of the meal Jesus said, ▪ "I give you my *word*, one of you is about to *betray* me, yes, one who is *eating* with me." ▪ They began to say to him *sorrowfully*, one by one, ▪ "Surely not *I!*" ▪ He said, "It is one of the *Twelve*—a man who dips into the *dish* with me. ▪ The Son of Man is going the way the Scripture *tells* of him. ▪ Still, *accursed* be that man *by whom* the Son of Man is *betrayed*. ▪ It were better for him had he never been *born*." ▪ ▪

(6) During the *meal* he took *bread*, blessed and broke it, and *gave* it to them. ▪ "*Take* this," he said, "*this* is my *body*." ▪ He likewise took a *cup*, gave thanks and *passed* it to them, ▪ and they all *drank* from it. ▪ He said to them: ▪ "*This* is my *blood*, the blood of the *covenant*, to be poured out on behalf of *many*. ▪ I solemnly *assure* you, I will never again drink of the fruit of the *vine* until the day when I drink it in the reign of *God*." ▪ ▪

(7) After singing songs of *praise*, they walked out to the Mount of *Olives*. ▪

Jesus then said to them: ▪ "Your faith in me shall be *shaken*, for Scripture has it, ▪

'I will strike the *shepherd*
and the *sheep* will be dispersed.' ▪

But after I am raised *up*, I will go to Galilee *ahead* of you." ▪ Peter said to him, "Even though *all* are shaken in faith, it will not be that way with *me*." ▪ Jesus answered, ▪ "I give you my *assurance*, ▪ this very night before the cock crows *twice*, you will deny me three *times*." ▪ But Peter kept reasserting vehemently, ▪ "Even if I have to *die* with you, I will not *disown* you." ▪ They all said the *same*. ▪ ▪

(8) They went then to a place named *Gethsemani*. ▪ "Sit down here while I *pray*," he said to his disciples; ▪ at the same time he took along with him Peter, James, and John. ▪ Then he began to be filled with *fear* and *distress*. ▪ He said to them, ▪ "My heart is filled with *sorrow* to the point of *death*. ▪ *Remain* here and stay *awake*." ▪ He advanced a little and fell to the *ground*, praying that if it were possible this hour might pass him *by*. ▪ He kept saying, ▪ "*Abba* (O Father), you have the power to do *all things*. ▪ Take this cup *away* from me. ▪ But let it be as *you* would have it, not as *I*." ▪ When he returned he found them *asleep*. ▪ He said to Peter, ▪ "Asleep, Simon? ▪ You could not stay awake for even an *hour?* ▪ Be on *guard* and pray that *you* may not be put to the test. ▪ The *spirit* is willing but *nature* is *weak*." ▪ Going

people forces them to time their treachery carefully.

(2) Here Jesus is the victor for a moment. The woman's generosity contrasts with the pettiness of her accusers. The intention here is not to explain away poverty, or to say that the poor can be taken for granted, but that the presence of Jesus is an opportunity not to be missed through shortsightedness.

(3) Jesus is the victim of the godless. The scandal of Judas's betrayal is made all the more horrible because he is "one of the Twelve," those who were on most intimate terms with Jesus. The horror is further impressed upon us at the Last Supper. It is bad enough to be betrayed by one's enemies, but Jesus was betrayed by a friend.

(4) In Jesus' predictions regarding the preparation of the Passover supper, Mark makes it clear that Jesus is in control of all that is happening to him—whether the point is Jesus' supernatural foreknowledge or his careful arrangement of details. In other words, it is important to Mark that Jesus is a "willing victim," for that is the main characteristic of the suffering servant, choosing obedience freely—even unto death.

(5) At the Passover meal, ordinarily a joyous celebration, the darkness of betrayal enters. Jesus is a victim. The worst kind of betrayal is depicted, reminding hearers of Psalm 41: "All my foes whisper together against me. . . . Even my friend who had my trust and partook of my bread, has raised his heel against me." And the betrayer must bear responsibility for his treachery—even though all is taking place according to the scriptures (God's will). The irony is difficult to understand, yet Mark makes a point of it.

(6) In very few words, the account of the meal draws on a wealth of Jewish theology and scripture. Mark associates the sacrifice of Jesus with ancient sacrificial traditions ("the blood of the covenant") as well as the future messianic banquet at the end of time ("the reign of God"). The meaning of the words "in behalf of many" is not exclusive. The phrase literally means "for all."

(7) The "songs of praise" were part of the Passover ritual and brought it to a close. What follows is a literary device (foreshadowing) in which Mark prepares

us for the triple denial of Jesus by Peter. The strength of Peter's promise to be faithful makes his later denial all the more poignant and painful. Notice, too, that Jesus is master of the situation here, foretelling the events that surround his apparent defeat—another instance of the victor/victim tension.

(8) Inexorably, Jesus is becoming more and more isolated as he approaches the ultimate sacrifice. He must watch and pray by himself. There is no one to comfort him. He will endure his trial as a suffering servant: abandoned and alone. It is important to Mark to portray Jesus as completely alone in both roles—victimized by all, victorious over all. Jesus finds his followers asleep three times—a parallel to the three predictions of his passion made earlier in Mark's gospel. Reduced to its simplest terms, the message is clear: All is going according to plan.

(9) The arrest is a frenzied moment, in contrast to the quiet of Jesus' solitary and agonized prayer. Disorder seems to reign. The horror of Judas's betrayal is intensified by the gesture of affection he employs. In other accounts of the passion, Jesus responds both to Judas's kiss and to the violence inflicted on the high priest's slave. In Mark he responds to neither—and the effect is to elevate Jesus above the frenzy, above even the betrayal. He does, however, make it clear that his arrest is based on a false charge, pointing out that he has never acted in secret and was open about his mission. He explains the irony in his statement: "But now, so that the Scriptures may be fulfilled. . . ." It explains everything.

Whoever the young man is who flees the scene naked, he serves the purpose here of emphasizing the abandonment Jesus must endure. All will flee from him, and he himself will be stripped naked.

(10) Mark paints a picture of desperate legal minds trying to build a case where no evidence is available. They are frustrated on two counts: the lack of evidence, and the inability to find agreement on the little evidence offered. The point, of course, is that the case is false and the prosecutors' motives are dishonest. The more subtle point: All that is happening is in accord with a divine plan, not a human one.

(11) The silence of Jesus at his trial enables Mark to make several points. First,

The entire drama turns on this paragraph. We are shocked each time we hear of the "Judas kiss." The mild protest Jesus raises is for the benefit of his captors, to point out their treachery. "But now, so that the Scriptures may be fulfilled. . . ." is an incomplete sentence—as though nothing further be said. The meaning is clear: no resistance is appropriate, so "now let it all come to pass as it has been predicted."

This section concentrates on the futility and dishonesty of the case against Jesus. There is a feeling of it all being "beside the point." Jesus is going to die. Try to communicate the emptiness of the case against Jesus.

This section rises from orderly interrogation to frenzied hatred. Build slowly to a climax at "guilty." Then slowly return to a narrative tone.

back *again* he began to pray in the same *words.* ▪ Once *again* he found them *asleep* on his *return.* ▪ They could not keep their *eyes* open, nor did they know what to *say* to him. ▪ He returned a *third* time and said to them, ▪ "Still sleeping? ▪ Still taking your ease? ▪ It will have to do. ▪ The hour is *on* us. ▪ You will see that the Son of Man is to be handed over into the clutches of *evil men.* ▪ *Rouse* yourselves and come along. ▪ *See!* My betrayer is *near.*" ▪▪

(9) Even while he was still speaking, *Judas,* one of the *Twelve,* made his appearance accompanied by a *crowd* with *swords* and *clubs;* ▪ these people had been sent by the chief *priests,* the *scribes,* and the *elders.* ▪ The *betrayer* had arranged a *signal* for them, saying, ▪ "The man I shall *embrace* is the one; ▪ arrest *him* and lead him *away,* taking every precaution." ▪ He then went directly over to him and said, ▪ *"Rabbi!"* and embraced him. ▪ At this, they laid *hands* on him and *arrested* him. ▪ One of the *bystanders* drew his *sword* and struck the high priest's *slave,* cutting off his *ear.* ▪ Addressing himself to them, *Jesus* said, ▪ "You have come out to arrest me armed with *swords* and *clubs* as if against a *brigand.* ▪ I was within your reach *daily,* teaching in the temple *precincts,* yet you *never* arrested me. ▪ But *now,* so that the *Scriptures* may be fulfilled. . . ." ▪ With that, all *deserted* him and *fled.* ▪ There was a young man following him who was covered by nothing but a linen *cloth.* ▪ As they *seized* him he left the cloth *behind* and ran off *naked.* ▪▪

(10) Then they led Jesus off to the *high* priest, and *all* the chief priests, the *elders* and the *scribes* came *together.* ▪ Peter followed him at a distance right into the high priest's *courtyard,* where he found a seat with the temple *guard* and began to *warm* himself at the *fire.* ▪ The chief *priests* with the whole *Sanhedrin* were busy *soliciting testimony* against Jesus that would lead to his *death,* but they could not *find* any. ▪ *Many* spoke against him *falsely* under *oath* but their testimony did not *agree.* Some, for instance, on taking the stand, testified falsely by alleging, ▪ "We heard him declare, 'I will destroy this *temple* made by *human* hands,' and 'In three days I will construct another *not* made by human hands.'" ▪ Even *so,* their testimony did not *agree.* ▪▪

(11) The *high* priest rose to his *feet* before the court and began to *interrogate* Jesus: ▪ "Have you no *answer* to what these men *testify* against you?" ▪ But Jesus remained *silent:* ▪ he made no *reply.* ▪ Once again the *high* priest interrogated him: ▪ "Are you the *Messiah,* the Son of the *Blessed One?*" ▪ Then Jesus

answered: ▪ "I *am*; ▪ and you will *see* the Son of Man seated at the *right hand* of the Power and coming with the clouds of *heaven.*" ▪ ▪ At that the *high* priest tore his *robes* and said: ▪ "What further need do we have of *witnesses?* ▪ You have heard the *blasphemy.* ▪ What is your *verdict?*" ▪ They all concurred in the verdict "*guilty,*" ▪ with its sentence of *death.* ▪ Some of them then began to *spit* on him. ▪ They *blindfolded* him and *hit* him, saying, ▪ "Play the *prophet!*" ▪ while the officers *manhandled* him. ▪ ▪

(12) While *Peter* was down in the *courtyard,* one of the servant girls of the *high* priest came along. ▪ When she noticed Peter *warming* himself, she looked more *closely* at him and said, ▪ "You *too* were with Jesus of Nazareth." ▪ But he *denied* it: ▪ "I don't know what you are *talking* about! ▪ ▪ What are you *getting* at?" ▪ Then he went out into the *gateway.* ▪ At that moment a *rooster* crowed. ▪ The servant girl, keeping an *eye* on him, started again to tell the bystanders, ▪ "*This* man is *one* of them." ▪ Once *again* he denied it. ▪ A little *later* the bystanders said to Peter once *more,* ▪ "You are *certainly one* of them! ▪ You're a *Galilean,* are you not?" ▪ He began to *curse,* and to swear, "I don't even *know* the man you are talking about!" ▪ Just then a *second* cockcrow was heard and Peter recalled the prediction *Jesus* had made to him, ▪ "Before the cock crows *twice* you will *disown* me three *times.*" ▪ He *broke down* and began to *cry.* ▪ ▪

(13) As soon as it was *daybreak* the chief priests, with the elders and scribes (that is, the whole *Sanhedrin*), reached a *decision.* ▪ They *bound* Jesus, led him away, and handed him over to *Pilate.* ▪ Pilate interrogated him: ▪ "Are you the *king* of the *Jews?*" ▪ "*You* are the one who is *saying* it," Jesus replied. ▪ The chief priests, meanwhile, brought many *accusations* against him. ▪ Pilate interrogated him again: ▪ "Surely you have some *answer?* ▪ See how many *accusations* they are leveling against you." ▪ But greatly to Pilate's *surprise,* Jesus made no further response. ▪ ▪

(14) Now on the occasion of a *festival* he would release for them one *prisoner*—any man they *asked for.* ▪ There was a prisoner named *Barabbas* jailed along with the rebels who had committed murder in the *uprising.* ▪ When the crowd came up to press their *demand* that he honor the *custom,* Pilate rejoined, ▪ "Do you want me to release the *king* of the *Jews* for you?" ▪ He was aware, of course, that it was out of *jealousy* that the chief priests had handed him *over.* ▪ Meanwhile, the chief priests incited the crowd to

NRSV: "The guards also took him over and beat him." Another subplot begins here— Peter's denial. The tone is one of agitation and fear, until the final sentence, which is heartrending. A lengthy pause is a must before the next section.

The trial continues. It is marked by Jesus' silence— either in answering indirectly or not answering at all. There is an air of mystery.

The in-fighting and tension between Pilate and the religious leaders account for the cat-and-mouse game being played here, all at Jesus' expense. Pilate is taunting his enemies arrogantly. The horror is that it all ends with the sentence of crucifixion. Barabbas = bar-RAB-uhs.

that Jesus is the "suffering servant" of Isaiah who is led "dumb to the slaughter, not opening his mouth." Second, the protestations of Peter (in the following section) seem all the more cowardly when contrasted with Jesus' silence. Third, everything is going according to God's plan; there is nothing that can be said to alter the outcome. Jesus does assert his special relationship to God (invoking the great "I AM" of Exodus), and is inevitably accused of blasphemy. It is a spurious charge, but sufficient for those who are desperate to find one.

(12) Peter's three-fold denial builds in intensity. His first response is confusion. The second response is a simple denial. The third becomes frantic, accompanied by cursing and phrased in terms of an oath. The effect is vivid. As our horror mounts with the intensity of the three denials, so does our pity become overwhelming when Peter remembers Jesus' prediction and collapses in grief.

(13) It seems important to Mark that the entire Sanhedrin be responsible for the judgment against Jesus. Pilate is merely the political and legal entity they must influence to carry out their conviction. In Pilate's presence, Jesus is completely silent. His lack of response contrasts with the "many accusations against him." The pattern seems to be that the more serious the charges, the more silent Jesus becomes. The effect, again, is to show the futility of the plot against him. It is by the will of God that Jesus will give his life, not by the will of human judges.

(14) Pilate "wished to satisfy the crowd." His motive in handing Jesus over to be crucified is a political one. And when a convicted criminal (Barabbas) is allowed to go free, the injustice done to Jesus is further highlighted.

(15) In the torture inflicted by the soldiers, more is implied than Jesus' physical suffering. The irony is not lost on succeeding generations of believers who claim Jesus as their king. Though the soldiers intend only to mock, they are precisely correct when they robe Jesus in purple, place a crown upon his head, salute him as king, and kneel before him in homage. Mark recounts an event here, but he is

more concerned with its significance than its historical details.

(16) Mark does not dwell on the details of the crucifixion scene. And he mentions Jesus' physical agony hardly at all. The wine drugged with myrrh was intended to lessen the pain of the crucified. The fact that Jesus refuses it may indicate uncompromising dedication to his role as "suffering servant." Once the inevitable has been set in motion, the actual death take place swiftly. There is a clear allusion to Psalm 22 in the rolling dice: "They divided my garments among them, and for my clothing they cast lots."

There are three sets of taunters here: the people going by, the chief priests and scribes, and the two insurgents crucified with him. Again, the irony is palpable. Indeed, Jesus *will* rebuild the temple (of his body) in three days. From Mark's point of view Jesus *is* the King of the Jews. And the two insurgents are guilty of mocking the innocent.

(17) Whatever explains the darkness that covered the countryside at noon, the gospel writer's point is that "darkness" characterizes that awful moment when the Son of God is put to death. The cry of Jesus is a quotation from Psalm 22, the prayer assigned to the suffering servant, and already alluded to in the casting of lots for Jesus' clothing. It further establishes Jesus as the suffering servant. The mention of Elijah (by those who confuse "Eloi" with the prophet's name) brings into the play that prophet's role as harbinger of the promised kingdom.

The curtain in the sanctuary (the Temple) divided the holy of holies from the outer sanctuary. Torn from top to bottom, it is a symbol, for Mark, of the end of the old covenant with Israel and the beginning of the new. It may also signify the end of God's distance from us and a new and more intimate mode of the divine presence in the world, seen principally, of course, in Jesus. The centurion (a Gentile) utters an act of faith, also signaling the universality of the new covenant. The mention of the women followers of Jesus comes as something of a surprise here, since there fidelity at this point (and their discovery of the empty tomb later) certainly adds a note of comfort.

The feeling here is one of profound irony and sadness. The mocking soldiers have no idea who it is they are making sport of. And that is why the passage is so affecting.

Cyrene = sai-REE-ne

Golgotha = GAHL-guh-thuh

The juxtaposition of "crucified" with "rolling dice" is shocking.

Further taunting makes the scene all the more bitter. Feel free to omit the "Ha, ha!" It is almost impossible to say it without sounding ridiculous and childish. The NRSV has "Aha," which is somewhat more usable, but probably still inadequate for the solemnity of the moment.

Pause before this section. The cosmic drama is bad enough, but Jesus' cry is filled with pathos and grief. Pause significantly after "why have you forsaken me!" Eloi, Eloi, lama sabachthani = AY-lo-ee, AY-lo-ee, lah-MAH sah-BAHK-thah-nee.

have him release Barabbas *instead.* ▪ Pilate again asked them, ▪ "What am I to do with the man you call the *king* of the *Jews?*" ▪ They shouted back, ▪ "Crucify him!" ▪ Pilate protested, ▪ *"Why?* What *crime* has he committed?" ▪ They only shouted the louder, ▪ "Crucify him!" ▪ So Pilate, who wished to satisfy the *crowd,* released *Barabbas* to them, and after he had had Jesus *scourged,* he handed him over to be *crucified.* ▪▪

(15) The soldiers now led Jesus away into the hall known as the *praetorium;* ▪ at the same time they assembled the whole cohort. ▪ They dressed him in royal *purple,* then wove a *crown of thorns* and put it on him, and began to *salute* him, ▪ "All *hail!* King of the *Jews!*" ▪ Continually striking Jesus on the head with a reed and *spitting* at him, they genuflected before him and pretended to pay him *homage.* ▪ When they had finished *mocking him,* they stripped him of the purple, dressed him in his own clothes, and led him out to *crucify* him. ▪▪

(16) A man named *Simon of Cyrene,* the father of Alexander and Rufus, was coming in from the fields and they pressed him into service to carry the *cross.* ▪ When they brought Jesus to the site of *Golgotha* (which means "*Skull* Place"), they tried to give him *wine* drugged with *myrrh,* but he would not *take* it. ▪ Then they *crucified* him and divided up his garments by rolling *dice* for them to see what each should *take.* ▪ It was about nine in the *morning* when they crucified him. ▪ The *inscription* proclaiming his offense read, ▪ "The *King of the Jews.*" ▪▪

With him they crucified two *insurgents,* one at his *right* and one at his *left.* ▪ People going by kept *insulting* him, tossing their *heads* and saying, ▪ "Ha, ha! ▪ So you were going to destroy the *temple* and rebuild it in three *days!* ▪ Save *yourself* now by coming down from that *cross!*" ▪ The chief priests and the scribes *also* joined in and jeered: ▪ "He saved *others* but he cannot save *himself!* ▪ Let the '*Messiah,*' the '*king of Israel,*' come down from that *cross* here and *now* so that we can *see* it and *believe* in him!" ▪ The men who had been crucified with him *likewise* kept taunting him. ▪▪

(17) When *noon* came, *darkness* fell on the whole countryside and lasted until midafternoon. ▪ At that time Jesus cried in a loud voice, ▪ "Eloi, Eloi, lama sabachthani?" ▪ which means, ▪ "My God, my God, why have you forsaken me?" ▪▪ A few of the bystanders who heard it remarked, ▪ "Listen! He is calling on Elijah!" ▪▪ Someone ran off, and soaking a

sponge in sour *wine*, stuck it on a *reed* to try to make him *drink*. ▪ The man said, ▪ "Now let's see whether *Elijah* comes to take him *down*." ▪ ▪

The anticlimax. A feeling of exhaustion seems appropriate here. The onlookers are stunned into silence. The centurion's recognition seems nearly whispered. The faithful women lend a strong but silent poignancy to the scene.

Joses = DZHO-seez
Salome = suh-LO-mee

Arimathea = ehr-uh-muh-THEE-uh
Sanhedrin = san-HEE-drihn
The burial preparations take on a certain briskness—the necessary work must be done before the sabbath falls, and may even bring a brief respite from the pain. There probably should be a tone of "matter-of-factness" in your voice—until the final sentence, which clearly carries a hint of "to be continued."

Then *Jesus*, uttering a loud *cry*, breathed his *last*. ▪ ▪ At that moment the curtain in the *sanctuary* was *torn in two* from top to *bottom*. ▪ The *centurion* who stood *guard* over him, on seeing the *manner* of his death, declared, ▪ "Clearly this man *was* the Son of *God!*" ▪ There were also *women* present looking on from a *distance*. ▪ *Among* them were Mary Magdalene, Mary the mother of James the younger and Joses, and Salome. ▪ These women had *followed* Jesus when he was in *Galilee* and attended to his *needs*. ▪ There were *also* many *others* who had come up with him to Jerusalem. ▪ ▪

(18) As it grew *dark* (it was *Preparation* Day, that is, the eve of the *sabbath*), Joseph from *Arimathea* arrived—a distinguished member of the *Sanhedrin*. ▪ He was *another* who looked forward to the reign of God. ▪ He was bold enough to seek an audience with *Pilate*, and urgently requested the *body* of Jesus. ▪ Pilate was *surprised* that Jesus should have died so *soon*. ▪ He summoned the *centurion* and inquired whether Jesus was already *dead*. ▪ Learning from him that he *was* dead, Pilate *released* the corpse to *Joseph*. ▪ Then, having bought a linen *shroud*, Joseph took him *down*, wrapped him in the *linen*, and laid him in a *tomb* which had been cut out of *rock*. ▪ Finally he rolled a *stone* across the *entrance* of the tomb. ▪ Meanwhile, Mary Magdalene and Mary the mother of Joses *observed* where he had been *laid*. ▪ ▪

[Shorter: Mark 15:1–39]

(18) It was necessary to proceed with the burial in haste, in order to accomplish it before the Sabbath rest. The exchange between Joseph of Arimathea and Pilate is Mark's way of confirming, beyond any doubt, that Jesus was really dead. No doubt this is to anticipate any possible claim after the resurrection that he had not really died. The final sentence of the passion narrative has a clear feeling of "to be continued." The fact that the women observe where Jesus was buried prepares us for their visit to the tomb later and their discovery that it was empty.

READING I All three readings today are suffused with the dynamic symbolism of a meal taken in common. With this kind of emphasis we begin the three greatest days of the church calendar.

The first reading is a detailed description of the ritual Passover seder meal commemorating the Israelites' escape from their bondage in Egypt. But notice that it was a communal (family) meal. Sometimes it even brought together smaller families. The notion of sacrifice in an earlier age has developed into a notion of participation by eating the sacrificial lamb in a communal setting. From this setting it is not too great a leap to the eucharistic meal that lies at the heart of our worship.

The intricate details of the reading are not as important as the significance of the overall event. It is obviously a form of the meal that Jesus shared with his disciples on the night before he died, and should enable us to experience a gratifying link with our ancient past.

Strive to create an atmosphere of solemn significance as you proclaim this record of our ancestors' most sacred feast. Ceremonies made holy by time and devout practice deserve our attention—as we carry out the Lord's command to observe them.

HOLY THURSDAY: EVENING MASS OF THE LORD'S SUPPER

LECTIONARY #40

READING I   Exodus 12:1–8, 11–14

Your first words make it clear that the Paschal Triduum, the solemnity of solemnities, has begun. We begin at the ancient beginnings of our heritage. We will witness the progression of thousands of years in the next three days. Make a good beginning!

A reading from the book of *Exodus* ▪▪

The Lord said to Moses and Aaron in the land of Egypt, ▪ *"This month* shall stand at the *head of your calendar;* ▪ you shall reckon it the *first month of the year.* ▪ Tell the whole community of *Israel:* ▪ On the *tenth* of this month every one of your families must procure for itself a *lamb,* one apiece for each household. ▪ If a family is too *small* for a whole lamb, it shall join the nearest household in procuring one and shall *share* in the lamb in proportion to the number of persons who *partake* of it. ▪ The lamb must be a year-old male and without blemish. ▪ You may take it from either the *sheep* or the *goats.* ▪ You shall keep it until the *fourteenth* day of this month, and *then,* with the whole assembly of Israel *present,* it shall be slaughtered during the evening *twilight.* ▪ They shall take some of its *blood* and apply it to the two *doorposts* and the *lintel* of every house in which they *partake* of the lamb. ▪ *That same night* they shall eat its roasted *flesh* with unleavened *bread* and bitter *herbs.* ▪▪

The urgency of the situation is clear. Stand ready (loins girt) because God is about to do a marvelous thing!

"This is how you are to *eat* it: ▪ with your loins *girt, sandals* on your feet and your staff in *hand,* you shall eat like those who are in *flight.* ▪ It is the Passover of the *Lord.* ▪ For on this *same night* I will go through Egypt, striking down every *first-born* of the land, both *man* and *beast,* and executing *judgment* on all the gods of *Egypt*—I, the Lord! ▪ But the *blood* will mark the houses where *you* are. ▪ *Seeing* the blood, I will *pass over you;* ▪ thus, when I strike the land of Egypt, no destructive blow will come upon *you.* ▪▪

NRSV: "Both human beings and animals. . . ."

Recall that you are looking back over all the generations since Moses as you read these words. And forward to all the generations yet to come.

"This day shall be a memorial *feast* for you, which all your generations shall *celebrate* with *pilgrimage* to the *Lord,* as a perpetual institution." ▪▪

A reading from the first letter of *Paul* to the *Corinthians* ▪▪

The reading is made up of very short phrases, each one important. They cannot be rushed.

I received from the *Lord* what *I handed on to you,* ▪ namely, that the Lord *Jesus* on the night in which he was *betrayed* ▪ took *bread,* and after he had given *thanks,* broke it and said, ▪ "This is my *body,* which is for *you.* ▪ Do this in *remembrance of me.*" ▪ In the same way, after the supper, he took the *cup,* saying, ▪ "This cup is the *new covenant* in my *blood.* ▪ Do this, whenever you drink it, in *remembrance of me.*" ▪ Every *time,* then, you eat this *bread* and drink this *cup,* ▪ you proclaim the *death of the Lord* until he *comes!* ▪▪

A solemn reminder of what we do when we celebrate eucharist. Read it so that the assembly will "hear it again for the first time."

GOSPEL   John 13:1–15

A reading from the holy *gospel* according to *John* ▪▪

Let it be clear that you hear the echo of "Passover" in Jesus' realization that the hour had come for him to "pass from this world."

Before the feast of *Passover,* Jesus realized that the hour had come for him to *pass from this world* to the *Father.* ▪ He had *loved* his own in this world, and would *show* his love for them to the *end.* ▪ The devil had already induced Judas, son of Simon Iscariot, to *hand Jesus over;* ▪ and so, during the *supper,* Jesus— fully *aware* that he had *come* from God and was *going* to God, the Father who had *handed everything over to him*—rose from the meal and took off his cloak. ▪ He picked up a towel and tied it around himself. ▪ Then he poured water into a basin and began to *wash* his disciples' *feet* and *dry* them with the *towel* he had around him. ▪ Thus he came to Simon *Peter,* who said to him, ▪ "Lord, are *you* going to wash *my* feet?" ▪ Jesus answered, ▪ "You may not realize *now* what I am doing, but later you will *understand.*" ▪ Peter replied, ▪ "You shall *never* wash my feet!" ▪ "If I do not *wash* you," Jesus answered, ▪ "you will have no share in my *heritage.*" ▪ "Lord," Simon Peter said to him, ▪ "then not only my *feet,* but my *hands* and *head* as *well.*" ▪▪ Jesus told him, ▪ "The man who has bathed has no need to wash [except for his feet]; ▪ he is entirely cleansed, just as *you* are; ▪ though not *all.*" ▪ (The reason he said, "Not *all* are washed clean," was that *he knew his betrayer.)* ▪▪

The variation on the expression "to hand over" needs to be brought out clearly: Judas hands Jesus over; God the Father had handed everything over to Jesus.

READING II   Here we have the eucharistic tradition in Paul's words. How rich is this word tradition, from the Latin "*tradere.*" It means "to hand on," or to "hand over," and is used in both senses here. Paul has "handed on" to us the tradition that relates what Jesus did at the Last Supper. And Jesus was using the context of the ancient ceremony that was "handed on" through his Jewish culture. And Jesus did all this on the night that he was "handed over" in betrayal by Judas. The point of all this is that a good lector ought to be very sensitive to an intricately woven text!

Paul's main emphasis here is not on what Jesus did, but on what the assembled community does when it gathers to do it in his memory. We know this because of the difficulties among the Corinthians that had led to rival factions, and the exclusion of the poor from the agape meal. Paul is reminding the church at Corinth that this holy meal is for the purpose of proclaiming the Lord's death until the end of time—a duty that must certainly not be exclusive, and must certainly not be confused with less significant gatherings.

GOSPEL   Have you ever wondered why, when we celebrate the Last Supper, the liturgy does not select a gospel reading that records Jesus' command to "Take and eat" and "Take and drink"? Matthew, Mark and Luke all record these words. John does not, although the events we read from his gospel this evening are clearly within the context of a meal.

John does, however, record the dramatic and moving gesture of Jesus washing the feet of his disciples. And this gives us profound insight into the *meaning* and *consequence* of celebrating the eucharist. We can put it quite plainly: Eucharist means we wash each other's feet. Because we hear the "Take and eat" in the first reading, we are prepared to hear the consequences of that command in the gospel.

The washing of feet is made all the more striking in the presence of Judas, the betrayer. He is not excluded from the washing, even though Jesus refers to him as "unclean." And because the washing of feet is a symbol of the ultimate act of love (Christ's sacrificial death), an even deeper level of the meaning of eucharist is revealed to us.

And there is more: Peter's refusal to allow Jesus to wash his feet (on the grounds of unworthiness, we must presume) indicates that he does not yet fully comprehend the implications of eucharist and ministry. Full understanding will come, as Jesus tells him, only later, when the sacrificial death of Jesus is validated in his resurrection.

The final words of Jesus amount to a definition of authentic ministry.

After he had washed their feet, he put his cloak back on
and reclined at table once more. ▪ He said to them: ▪
"Do you *understand* what I just *did* for you? ▪
You address me as *'Teacher'* and *'Lord,'*
and fittingly *enough,*
for that is what *I am.* ▪
But if *I* washed *your* feet—
I who am *Teacher* and *Lord*—
then *you* must wash each *other's* feet. ▪
What I just did was to give you an *example:* ▪
as *I* have done, so *you* must do." ▪ ▪

GOOD FRIDAY

LECTIONARY #41

READING I   Isaiah 52:13 — 53:12

A reading from the book of the prophet
Isaiah ▪ ▪

"See" is a very difficult word to begin with. Try substituting "Behold." This first section is bright and upbeat.

See, my servant shall *prosper*,
   he shall be raised *high* and greatly *exalted*. ▪
Even as many were *amazed* at him—
   so marred was his look beyond that of man,
   and his appearance beyond that of mortals— ▪
So shall he *startle* many nations,
   because of him kings shall stand *speechless*; ▪
For those who have not been *told* shall see, ▪
   those who have not *heard* shall ponder it. ▪

Disbelief is the rhetorical tool here. Your tone of voice should sustain a feeling of "How can this be?"

Who would *believe* what we have heard? ▪
   To whom has the arm of the Lord
     been *revealed?* ▪
He grew up like a sapling before him,
   like a shoot from the parched earth; ▪
There was in him no *stately* bearing to make us
    look at him,
   nor appearance that would *attract* us to him. ▪

NRSV: "men" = "others."

He was spurned and avoided by men,
   a man of *suffering*, accustomed to *infirmity*,
One of those from whom men hide their faces,
   spurned, and we held him in no esteem. ▪ ▪

"Yet . . ." is your signal that deeper insight is coming. The suffering servant has a mission and it is for our benefit; and it is our sin that he carries.

Yet it was *our infirmities* that he bore,
   our sufferings that he endured,
While we thought of him as *stricken*,
   as one *smitten* by God and *afflicted*. ▪
But he was pierced for *our offenses*,
   crushed for *our sins*; ▪
Upon him was the chastisement that
    makes us whole,
   by his *stripes* we were *healed*. ▪
We had all gone astray like sheep,
   each following his own way; ▪

NRSV: "his" = "our."

But the Lord laid upon him
   the guilt of us all. ▪

The central idea in this section is patient and quiet endurance of suffering—suffering accepted in obedience.

Though he was harshly treated, he *submitted*
   and opened not his *mouth*; ▪
Like a *lamb* led to the *slaughter*
   or a *sheep* before the *shearers*,

READING I   There are four "songs" in Isaiah devoted to the subject of a "Suffering Servant." The first reading for the Good Friday liturgy is the fourth and the most significant of these. Obviously, the liturgy applies the text and the term "suffering servant" to Jesus and his redemptive mission. But this in no way cancels the original application of the term to the whole people of Israel. The "servant" is really "God's servants" and the language of poetry has personified the term and collected the people of God into one. Even the most superficial awareness of the history (both ancient and modern) of the Jewish people enables us to hear a poignant rendition of the Suffering Servant Songs.

It is uncertain whether Jesus actually applied this text to himself. It is crystal clear, however, that the text has been applied to him since the earliest Christian writers began to record and interpret his life, mission, passion and death. He is seen as the culmination of the suffering servant, fulfilling the Isaiah prophecy in every detail. No other scriptural text is more suited to Good Friday.

One implicit idea must be communicated: Obedience is the key to the suffering servant's ultimate victory, for himself and for those whose sin he bore. It is obedience to God that ennobles the servant's agony and wins the allegiance and contrition of all who witness his pain. In the second reading of today's liturgy, we will hear these words in reference to Christ: "Son though he was, he learned obedience from what he suffered."

READING II It helps to realize that the author of this letter is writing to comfort Jewish Christians who have been alienated from the Jewish practices they had combined with their faith in Jesus. The point of this part of the letter, then, is to point out that Jesus is the perfect high priest whose perfect sacrifice has rendered all others superfluous.

The effect of hearing this passage read on Good Friday is that we understand more clearly the *way* that Jesus functions as the source of eternal salvation. The priest is a human being who is a mediator between other human beings and God. Jesus, as both God and human being, is the perfect priest-mediator. He identifies completely with us and completely with God—to whom he is totally obedient.

Jesus knows our temptations—he underwent them; he knows our suffering—he learned obedience from his own. This is why we can approach the throne of grace with utter confidence: We know we will be heard and understood by the one who has experienced all that we experience.

he was *silent* ▪ and opened not his *mouth.* ▪
Oppressed and condemned, he was
    taken away, ▪
  and who would have thought any more
    of his *destiny?* ▪
When he was cut off from the land of the living,
  and smitten *for the sin of his people,*
A grave was assigned him among the *wicked*
  and a burial place with *evildoers,* ▪
Though he had done *no* wrong
  nor spoken *any* falsehood. ▪
[But the Lord was pleased
  to crush him in *infirmity.*] ▪▪

There is a reward for his sacrifice!

If he gives his life as an offering for *sin,*
  he shall see his descendants in a long life,
  and the will of the *Lord* shall be *accomplished*
    through him. ▪▪

Here is the good news for us. We are justified by his suffering.

Because of his *affliction*
  he shall see the *light* in fullness of *days;* ▪
Through his *suffering,* my servant shall
    justify many,
  and their *guilt* he shall *bear.* ▪▪
Therefore I will give him his portion
    among the *great,*
  and he shall divide the spoils with the *mighty,*
Because he *surrendered* himself to death
  and was *counted* among the *wicked;* ▪
And he shall take away the sins of *many,*
  and win *pardon* for their *offenses.* ▪▪

READING II   Hebrews 4:14–16; 5:7–9

A reading from the letter to the *Hebrews* ▪▪

There is an implied "therefore" between "Son of God" and "let us hold fast."

We have a great *high priest* who has passed through the heavens, *Jesus,* the Son of God; ▪ let us hold fast to our profession of faith. ▪ For we do not have a high priest who is *unable to sympathize* with our weakness, but one who was *tempted in every way that we are,* yet never sinned. ▪ So let us *confidently* approach the throne of grace to receive *mercy* and *favor* and to find help in time of need. ▪▪

These two sentences are packed with good news about our identification with Christ. Read them broadly.

In the days when he was in the *flesh,* Christ offered *prayers* and *supplications* with loud *cries* and *tears* to God, who was able to *save* him from death, and he was heard *because of his reverence.* ▪ Son though he was, he *learned* obedience *from what he suffered;* ▪ and when perfected, he became the source of eternal salvation for all who *obey him.* ▪▪

Kidron = KIHD-ruhn

It will be helpful, whatever the mode of proclamation, to analyze the structure of John's account of the passion very carefully. It is easy to see how the action moves from place to place, and inexorably toward Golgotha. In each location there is an important revelation, the dynamic interplay of characters, and a kind of resolution—before the action moves on. Many writers have commented on the "dramatic action" of the text. The various stages of this action must be set off by clear transitions.

The *Passion* of our *Lord Jesus Christ* according to *John* ▪ ▪

(1) Jesus went out with his disciples across the Kidron valley. ▪ There was a *garden* there, and he and his disciples entered it. ▪ The place was familiar to *Judas* as well (the one who was to hand him over) because Jesus had often *met* there with his disciples. ▪ Judas took the cohort as well as police supplied by the chief priests and the Pharisees, and *came there* with lanterns, torches and weapons. ▪ Jesus, *aware of all that would happen to him*, stepped forward and said to them, ▪ "Who is it you want?" ▪ "Jesus the Nazorean," they replied. ▪ *"I am he,"* he answered. ▪ (Now Judas, the one who was to *hand him over*, was right there with them.) ▪ As Jesus said to them, "I am he," they *retreated* slightly and fell to the ground. ▪ Jesus put the question to them *again*, ▪ "Who is it you *want*?" ▪ "Jesus the Nazorean," they repeated. ▪ "I have told you, I am he," Jesus said. ▪ "If *I* am the one you want, let *these men* go." (This was to fulfill what he had said, ▪ "I have not lost one of those you gave me.") ▪

(2) Then Simon Peter, who had a sword, drew it and *struck* the slave of the *high priest*, severing his right *ear.* ▪ (The slave's name was Malchus.) ▪ At that Jesus said to Peter, ▪ "Put your sword back in its sheath. ▪ Am I not to drink the cup the *Father has given me?*" ▪ ▪

The action moves to the residence of Annas. Then to the high priest Caiaphas.

Then the soldiers of the cohort, their tribune, and the Jewish police *arrested* Jesus and *bound* him. ▪ They led him first to Annas, the father-in-law of Caiaphas who was high priest that year. ▪ (It was Caiaphas who had proposed to the Jews the advantage of having one man die for the people.) ▪ ▪

Instead of "the Jews," say "the Jewish leaders."

(3) Simon Peter, in company with another disciple, kept following Jesus closely. ▪ This disciple, who was known to the high priest, *stayed* with Jesus as far as the high priest's courtyard, while Peter was left standing at the gate. ▪ The disciple known to the high priest came out and spoke to the woman at the gate, and then brought *Peter* in. ▪ This servant girl who kept the gate said to Peter, ▪ "Aren't you one of this man's *followers?*" ▪ "Not *I*," he replied. ▪ ▪

Now the night was cold, and the servants and the guards who were standing around had made a charcoal fire to warm themselves by. ▪ Peter *joined* them and stood there warming himself. ▪

through the ages, however, has preferred a group—not only because it adds variety, but because it adds dynamism and power. If you are approaching the "senior citizen" time of life, you no doubt remember the Passion accounts being sung in Latin by three cantors (one as Narrator, one as Crowd and one as Jesus). This is still done in some places (though usually in the language of the hearers). Able-bodied members of the assembly also stood throughout the proclamation.

Today the forms of proclamation vary widely. The assembly may be seated and usually is. Whatever practice is decided upon in your community, please try to meet the challenge of a long proclamation (potentially tedious for the assembly) and avoid the excesses of a presentation so elaborate and literal that the assembly is preoccupied with the mode at the expense of the message.

The story of Christ's passion and death is told by all four evangelists. Over the three-year cycle of the lectionary we read Matthew, Mark and Luke on Passion Sunday. John's version is read every year on Good Friday. It is very important to realize that each of the four writers had more in mind than a literal telling of the events. Each had a particular point of view and a particular purpose. Thus the accounts differ. Thus the importance of choosing a mode of proclamation that serves the faith-building insight offered rather than the events related. To this end, we should not be timid in our experimentation, but we do need to be quite sensitive. Above all, we need to remember that liturgical proclamation is very different from dramatic (theatrical) reenactment (granting the obvious similarities). To ignore this difference is to reduce the word of God to a history lesson, and the assembled worshipers to an emotionally manipulated audience.

In the version of the Passion offered by John, there is clear evidence that the evangelist downplays the physical suffering of Jesus to emphasize his true identity, his origins and his function. The entire gospel of John is preoccupied with these issues, and his revelation of Jesus as king and priest has set him apart from the other three gospel writers.

You will notice as you read the narrative that Jesus is much more in control of the situation—even, and perhaps especially, when he would seem by human terms to be most vulnerable.

Note: Some margin notes here deal with John's use of "the Jews," which has fostered anti-Semitism by implying that the Jewish people as a whole were responsible for Christ's death. This issue requires thoughtful preaching as well as proclamation. For more background, consult the 1988 statement of the Bishops' Committee on the Liturgy, "God's Mercy Endures Forever: Guidelines on the Presentation of Jews and Judaism in Catholic Preaching." Another helpful resource is "Criteria for the Evaluation of Dramatizations of the Passion," issued by the Bishops' Committee for Ecumenical and Interreligious Affairs. Both documents are available from the National Conference of Catholic Bishops, Office of Publishing and Promotion Services, 3211 Fourth Street NE, Washington DC 20017.

(1) The encounter with the cohort and police in the garden is an opportunity for the divinity of Jesus to be revealed. Jesus takes the initiative, steps forward and demands, "Who is it you want?" In response to the name they supply, Jesus answers, "I am he"—a clear echo of the great "I am" spoken by God to Moses. The cohort falls to the ground at this flash of divinity. Even in surrendering himself, Jesus is in charge when he demands that his disciples be let free.

(2) Peter's impulsive move to protect Jesus is fraught with symbolic meaning. By mutilating the ear of the high priest's servant, he has symbolically rendered the high priest himself unfit for office—according to ancient Jewish law. The evangelist is saying, in effect, the old order is passing away; a new order is being established. And Jesus' rebuke to Peter highlights the obedience of the Son to the Father's will for him.

(3) The most striking thing about Peter's denial in John's account is that it is interwoven with Jesus' bold statement of fidelity to the truth. This mingling of truth and falseness serves to make Peter's denial all the more shameful. It also puts Jesus' courage in bold relief.

(4) In his dialogue with the high priest, Jesus speaks quite freely in defending his

The action moves to the praetorium—and, symbolically, into the world of the Gentiles.

Instead of "the Jews answered," say "they replied."

(4) The high priest *questioned* Jesus, first about his *disciples*, then about his *teaching*. ▪ Jesus answered by saying: ▪

"I have spoken *publicly* to any who
would listen. ▪
I always taught in a *synagogue*
or in the *temple* area
where all the Jews come *together*. ▪
There was nothing *secret* about
anything I said. ▪

"Why do you *question me?* ▪ Question those who *heard* me when I *spoke*. ▪ It should be obvious they will know what I said." ▪ At this reply, one of the guards who was standing nearby gave Jesus a sharp blow on the face. ▪ "Is that any way to answer the *high priest?*" he said. ▪ Jesus replied, ▪ "If I said anything *wrong* produce the *evidence*, but if I spoke the *truth* why *hit* me?" ▪ Annas next sent him, bound, to the high priest Caiaphas. ▪ ▪

All through this, Simon Peter had been standing there warming himself. ▪ They said to him, "Are you not a *disciple* of his?" ▪ He denied: "I am *not!*" ▪ "But did I not see you with him in the *garden?*" insisted one of the high priest's slaves— as it happened, a relative of the man whose ear Peter had severed. ▪ Peter denied it *again*. ▪ At that moment a *cock* began to crow. ▪

At daybreak they brought Jesus from Caiaphas to the praetorium. ▪ They did not enter the praetorium *themselves*, for they had to avoid ritual impurity if they were to eat the *Passover* supper. ▪ Pilate came out to them. ▪ "What *accusation* do you bring against this man?" he demanded. ▪ "If he were not a *criminal*," they retorted, "we would certainly not have *handed him over* to you." ▪ At this Pilate said, ▪ "Why do *you* not take him and pass *judgment* on him according to your *law?*" ▪ "We may not put anyone to *death*," the Jews answered. ▪ (This was to fulfill what Jesus had said, indicating the sort of death he would die.) ▪ ▪

(5) Pilate went back into the praetorium and summoned Jesus. ▪ "Are you the *King* of the *Jews?*" he asked him. ▪ Jesus answered, ▪ "Are you saying this on your *own*, or have others been *telling* you about me?" ▪ "I am no *Jew!*" Pilate retorted. ▪ "It is *your own people* and the chief priests who have *handed you over* to me. ▪ What have you *done?*" ▪ Jesus answered:

"*My* kingdom does not belong to *this* world. ▪
If my kingdom were of *this* world,
my subjects would be fighting
to save me *from being handed over* to the Jews. ▪
As it is, *my* kingdom is not *here*." ▪▪

Instead of "the Jews," say "the Jewish authorities."

At this Pilate said to him, ▪ "So, then, you *are a king?*" ▪ Jesus replied:
"It is *you* who say I am a king. ▪
The reason I was *born*,
the reason why I *came* into the world,
is to testify to the *truth*. ▪
Anyone committed to the *truth* hears
  my voice." ▪▪
"*Truth!*" said Pilate, ▪ "What does that *mean?*" ▪

(6) After this remark, Pilate went out again to the Jews and told them: ▪ "Speaking for myself, I find *no case against this man*. ▪ Recall your custom whereby I *release* to you someone at Passover time. ▪ Do you want me to release to you the *king of the Jews?*" ▪ They shouted back, ▪ "We want *Barabbas*, not *this* one!" ▪ (Barabbas was an insurrectionist.) ▪▪

Instead of "the Jews," say "the Jewish leaders."

(7) Pilate's next move was to take Jesus and have him *scourged*. ▪ The soldiers then wove a crown of *thorns* and fixed it on his *head*, throwing around his shoulders a cloak of royal *purple*. ▪ Repeatedly they came up to him and said, ▪ "All hail, *King* of the *Jews!*" ▪ slapping his face as they did so. ▪▪

Pilate went out a second time and said to the crowd: ▪ "Observe what I *do*. ▪ I am going to bring him out to you to make you realize that I find *no case against him*." ▪ When Jesus came out wearing the crown of thorns and the purple cloak, Pilate said to them, ▪ "*Look* at the man!" ▪ As soon as the chief priests and the temple police saw him they shouted, "*Crucify* him! *Crucify* him!" ▪ Pilate said, ▪ "Take him and crucify him *yourselves*; ▪ I find *no case against him*." ▪ "We have our *law*," the Jews responded, ▪ "and *according* to that law he must *die* because he made himself God's *Son*." ▪ When Pilate heard *this* kind of talk, he was more afraid than *ever*. ▪▪

Instead of "the Jews," say "the Jewish leaders."

Going back into the praetorium, he said to Jesus, "Where do you *come* from?" ▪ Jesus would not give him any answer. ▪ "Do you refuse to *speak* to me?" Pilate asked him. "Do you not know that I have the power to *release* you and the power to *crucify* you?" ▪ Jesus answered:
"You would have no power over me *whatever*
  unless it were *given you from above*. ▪

public record and even calls on witnesses to his preaching as proof of the openness of his teaching. For this he is slapped, but vindicates himself again in the name of truth.

(5) But it is in Jesus' exchange with Pilate that John most clearly reveals the kingship that is his interest. Jesus speaks at some length of his kingdom not of this world. And in the same speech he boldly asserts his purpose and mission. Later, Pilate is frightened when Jesus reminds him of the source of all power.

(6) The name "Barabbas" means, literally, "son of the father" (bar = son; abbas = father). Jesus is, of course, also "Son of the Father," and the point is made that the people choose the wrong "son of the father" for release.

(7) The mockery by the soldiers stems from their perception of Jesus as just another pathetic protester of Roman power—a puny claimant of power that only the emperor can have. How very different from the Jewish interpretation of "King of the Jews," which to them is tantamount to the claim of being the Messiah. Thus two worlds, the Roman and the Jewish, reject this "king"—but for entirely different reasons. The irony of this passage is all the more complex because we, the hearers, recognize the "kingship" of Jesus in yet another way.

(8) ". . . carrying the cross by himself." In John's account of the crucifixion, no one helps Jesus carry the cross. Here is yet another detail of difference that emphasizes the sovereignty of Jesus throughout John's narrative. Other details are the seamless garment (which the soldiers cast lots for) and Jesus' thirst, both of which provide opportunities for specific scriptural passages to be fulfilled. Notice too that there are no mocking crowds at the foot of the cross. Instead, we see a group of devoted women (including Mary his mother) and the beloved disciple "near the cross." Jesus is not abandoned by all, as he is in the other gospel accounts.

Instead of "the Jews," say "the Jewish leaders."

Instead of "the Jews," say "the Jewish leaders."

Jesus carries his own cross as the action moves toward Golgotha (pronounced GAHL-guh-thuh), Calvary.

That is why he who *handed me over* to you is guilty of the greater sin." ▪

After this, Pilate was *eager* to release him, but the Jews shouted, ▪ "If you *free* this man you are no 'Friend of *Caesar.*' ▪ Anyone who makes himself a king *becomes Caesar's rival.*" ▪ Pilate heard what they were saying, then brought Jesus outside and took a seat on a judge's bench at the place called the Stone Pavement— Gabbatha in Hebrew. ▪ (It was the Preparation Day for Passover, and the hour was about noon.) ▪ He said to the Jews, ▪ "Look at *your king!*" At this they shouted, ▪ *"Away* with him! ▪ *Away* with him! ▪ *Crucify* him!" ▪ *"What!"* Pilate exclaimed. ▪ "Shall I crucify *your king?*" ▪ The chief priests replied, ▪ "We *have* no king but *Caesar.*" ▪ In the end, Pilate handed Jesus over to be crucified. ▪ ▪

(8) Jesus was led away, and carrying the cross *by himself*, went out to what is called the Place of the *Skull* (in Hebrew, Golgotha). ▪ There they crucified him, and two *others* with him: one on either side, Jesus in the middle. ▪ Pilate had an inscription placed on the cross which read, ▪
   JESUS THE NAZOREAN,
   THE KING OF THE JEWS.

This inscription, in Hebrew, Latin and Greek, was read by many of the Jews, since the place where Jesus was crucified was near the city. ▪ The chief priests of the Jews tried to tell Pilate, ▪ "You should not have written, 'The *King* of the *Jews.*' ▪ Write instead, ▪ 'This man *claimed* to be king of the Jews.'" ▪ Pilate answered, ▪ "What I have *written*, I have *written.*" ▪ ▪

After the soldiers had crucified Jesus they took his *garments* and divided them four ways, one for each soldier. ▪ There was also his *tunic*, but this tunic was woven in one piece from top to bottom and *had no seam.* ▪ They said to each other, ▪ "We shouldn't *tear* it. ▪ Let's throw dice to see who *gets* it." ▪ (The purpose of this was to have the Scripture fulfilled: ▪
   "They *divided my garments* among them; ▪
   for my clothing they cast *lots.*") ▪
And this was what the soldiers did. ▪ ▪

Near the cross of Jesus there stood his mother, his mother's sister, Mary the wife of Clopas, and Mary Magdalene. ▪ Seeing his *mother* there with the *disciple* whom he *loved*, Jesus said to his mother, ▪

"Woman, there is your *son*." ▪ In turn he said to the disciple, ▪ "There is your *mother*." ▪ From that hour onward, the disciple took her into his care. ▪▪ After that, Jesus, realizing that everything was now finished, *to bring the Scripture to fulfillment* said, "I am thirsty." ▪ There was a jar there, full of common wine. ▪ They stuck a sponge soaked in this wine on some hyssop and raised it to his lips. ▪ When Jesus took the wine, he said, ▪ "Now it is *finished*." ▪ Then he bowed his head, ▪ and *delivered over his spirit*. ▪▪

Instead of "the Jews," say "the Jewish leaders."

Since it was the Preparation Day the Jews did not want to have the bodies left on the cross during the *sabbath*, for *that* sabbath was a *solemn feast day*. ▪ They asked Pilate that the *legs* be broken and the bodies be taken *away*. ▪ Accordingly, the soldiers came and broke the legs of the men crucified with Jesus, first of one, then of the other. ▪ When they came to Jesus and saw that he was already dead, *they did not break his legs*. ▪ One of the soldiers ran a lance into his side, and immediately *blood* and *water* flowed out. ▪ (This testimony has been given by an *eyewitness*, and his testimony is *true*. ▪ He tells what he *knows* is true, so that you may believe.) ▪ These events took place for the fulfillment of *Scripture*: ▪

"Break none of his bones." ▪
There is still *another* Scripture passage which says: ▪
"They shall look on him
whom they have pierced." ▪▪

Instead of "the Jews," say "the Jewish authorities."

Afterward, Joseph of Arimathea, a disciple of Jesus (although a *secret* one for fear of the *Jews*), asked Pilate's permission to remove Jesus' body. ▪ Pilate granted it, so they came and took the body away. ▪ Nicodemus (the man who had first come to Jesus at night) *likewise* came, bringing a mixture of myrrh and aloes which weighed about a hundred pounds. ▪ They took Jesus' *body*, and in *accordance with Jewish burial custom* bound it up in wrappings of cloth with perfumed oils. ▪ In the place where he had been crucified there was a *garden*, and in the garden a new *tomb* in which no one had ever been *laid*. ▪ Because of the Jewish Preparation Day they laid Jesus there, for the tomb was close at hand. ▪▪

At the tomb, the dead Christ is anointed and given an elaborate burial according to Jewish custom.

In summary, it is a much more voluble and assertive Jesus than we saw in Mark on Passion Sunday. And he is treated differently. The inscription on the cross ("King of the Jews") appears in three languages, an indication that this king's reign is universal. Even the Jews' protest about the inscription cannot get it changed.

Jesus in John's Passion narrative *reigns* from his cross, sending out the decree that his mother and John are to care for one another, realizing when the moment had come to fulfill the scriptures and declare his thirst, announcing his own death with the words "It is finished" and, most significantly, delivering over his spirit. Nothing was taken from Jesus; he surrendered everything in obedience to the divine plan.

The proclamation of the Passion must attempt to emphasize these elements that are peculiar to John, so that we get another view and a fuller picture of Jesus: king, priest, obedient ruler.

READING I We read from this "book of beginnings" on the First Sunday of Lent. Now, as the celebration of the paschal mystery begins to peak, we read from it again—to sum up all of creation in the great work Jesus is about to accomplish.

There is one controlling idea throughout this wonderful passage: God the Almighty is the source of all life, the cause and the goal of every living thing, and the one who sustains everything in existence. But what a colorless way to assert this belief! The author of Genesis knows by instinct that great truths must be told in memorable ways. And what is more memorable than the first chapter of Genesis?

You are reading something huge here. Resist any notions that you need to make it less formal—or more intimate. It is a ringing proclamation of (literally) cosmic events, and deserves to be delivered with all the nobility and grandeur it contains.

The text is filled with refrains—phrases repeated over and over again. The overall effect is hypnotic. It marches through the seven days with gratifying predictability, relying precisely on the familiarity that makes for enjoyable listening. Each time you proclaim the words "And so it happened," you assert the sovereignty of God's creative will. The power of this refrain lies in the assembly's awareness that it comes with soothing regularity.

Let your presentation be guided by your awareness that one truth underlies this account of creation: It all comes from God, and all of it is good!

EASTER VIGIL

LECTIONARY #42

READING I Genesis 1:1—2:2

A reading from the book of *Genesis* ··

Begin very strongly as though a trumpet blast is required to capture the attention of the assembly. But "strongly" does not mean "harshly." It means "with unshakable conviction."

"Then God said": A lower voice (in pitch and volume) will give you the space to modulate up a notch at every new section.

In the beginning, · when God created the heavens and the earth, the earth was a formless wasteland, and darkness covered the abyss, · while a mighty wind swept over the waters. ··

Then God said, · "Let there be *light,*" ·· and there was *light.* · God saw how *good* the light was. · God then separated the light from the darkness. · God called the light "day," and the darkness he called "night." · Thus evening came, and morning followed—the *first* day. ··

A fresh attack, in a slightly higher key. "Let there be . . ." is a command that knows it will be obeyed. It is uttered with conviction, not hardness.

Then God said, · "Let there be a *dome* in the middle of the waters, to separate one body of water from the other." ·· *And so it happened:* · God made the dome, and it separated the water above the dome from the water below it. · God called the dome "the sky." ·· Evening came, and morning followed—the *second* day. ··

There are two sections in this paragraph. Separate them by modulating up another notch.

Then God said, · "Let the water under the sky be gathered into a single basin, so that the *dry land* may appear." ·· *And so it happened:* · the water under the sky was gathered into its basin, and the dry land appeared. · God called the dry land *"the earth,"* · and the basin of the water he called *"the sea."* · God saw how *good* it was. ·· Then God said, · "Let the earth bring forth *vegetation:* every kind of plant that bears seed and every kind of fruit tree on earth that bears fruit with its seed in it." ·· *And so it happened:* · the earth brought forth every kind of plant that bears seed and every kind of fruit tree on earth that bears fruit with its seed in it. · God saw how *good* it was. ·· Evening came, and morning followed—the *third* day. ··

Renew your energy level. Don't be afraid to pause between sections.

Then God said: · "Let there be *lights* in the dome of the sky, to separate day from night. · Let them mark the fixed times, the days and the years, and serve as luminaries in the dome of the sky, to shed light upon the earth." ·· *And so it happened:* · God made the two great lights, the greater one to govern the *day*, and the lesser one to govern the *night*; and he made the *stars*. God set them in the dome of the sky, to shed light upon the earth, to govern the day and the night, and to separate the light from the darkness. ▪ God saw how *good* it was. ▪▪ Evening came, and morning followed—the fourth day. ▪▪

Communicate the prodigality of nature here. "Let the water teem . . ."—a wonderful word! Remember that the energy is still building, ever so slightly, but perceptibly.

Then God said, ▪ "Let the water *teem* with an abundance of *living creatures*, and on the earth let *birds* fly beneath the dome of the sky." ▪▪ *And so it happened:* ▪ God created the great sea monsters and all kinds of swimming creatures with which the water teems, and all kinds of winged birds. ▪ God saw how *good* it was, ▪ and God blessed them, saying, ▪ "Be fertile, multiply, and fill the water of the seas; ▪ and let the birds multiply on the earth." ▪▪ Evening came, and morning followed—the *fifth* day. ▪▪

Then God said, ▪ "Let the *earth* bring forth all kinds of living creatures: cattle, creeping things, and wild animals of all kinds." ▪▪ *And so it happened:* ▪ God made all kinds of wild animals, all kinds of cattle, and all kinds of creeping things of the earth. ▪ God saw how *good* it was. ▪▪ Then God said: ▪ "Let us make *man* in our image, *after our likeness.* ▪ Let them have dominion over the fish of the sea, the birds of the air, and the cattle, and over all the wild animals and all creatures that crawl on the ground." ▪

This is the climax, the creation of humankind. The NRSV is inclusive: "Then God said, 'Let us make humankind in our image.'" "So God created humankind in his image, in the image of God he created them; male and female he created them."

God created man *in his image*; ▪
  in the *divine* image he created him; ▪
  male and female he created them. ▪

God blessed them, saying: ▪ "Be fertile and multiply; ▪ fill the earth and *subdue* it. ▪ Have *dominion* over the fish of the sea, the birds of the air, and all the living things that move on the earth." ▪ God also said: ▪ "See, I give you every seed-bearing plant all over the earth and every tree that has seed-bearing fruit on it to be your food; ▪ and to all the animals of the land, all the birds of the air, and all the living creatures that crawl on the ground, I give all the green plants for food." ▪▪ *And so it happened.* ▪▪ God looked at everything he had made, ▪ and he found it *very good.* ▪▪ Evening came, and morning followed—the *sixth* day. ▪▪

A significant pause should precede this final section. Then deliver it with slow resolution.

Thus the heavens and the earth and all their array were *completed.* ▪▪ Since on the *seventh* day God was finished with the work he had been doing, he *rested* on the seventh day from all the work he had undertaken. ▪▪

[Shorter: Genesis 1:1, 26–31]

READING II   Though our immediate reaction to this reading may be revulsion, we need to remind ourselves of the *purpose* of the story and what the writer wants us to take from it. This is always the case with scripture. It is always more than history.

By the time the Abraham and Isaac story was written, human sacrifice was no longer practiced among the Israelites. That's part of the point of the story. The firstborn of every creature belonged to God—a way of proclaiming God's sovereignty. But that firstborn was "redeemed" by the alternative animal sacrifice.

The emphasis throughout is on Abraham's willingness to relinquish all things to attest to God's sovereignty. It is the ultimate test for all believers—to arrive at the kind of faith that relinquishes control and affirms God as in charge of life, and as a provident guardian. Indeed, this is the meaning of the name that Abraham bestows on the site of the sacrifice. The translation here ("On the mountain the Lord will see") does not do the meaning justice. Better would be "the Lord will see to it." The NRSV translation is best: "So Abraham called that place 'The Lord will provide'; as it is said to this day, 'On the mount of the Lord it shall be provided.'"

The reward for Abraham's obedience and service is the beautiful blessing that concludes the passage. It should be read with breadth and conviction. Your hearers will instinctively draw the parallel between Abraham (and his son Isaac) and God (and his son Jesus). For this account is one of the most favored prefigurations of Jesus' sacrifice in obedience to his Father's will. The blessing now takes on new meaning for us—the descendants of Jesus, beloved Son of God.

"Ready!" is almost impossible to read without sounding trivial. You may wish to use the NRSV translation: "Here I am." Moriah = maw-RAI-uh.

Notice that there is no record of hesitation or anxiety in Abraham's response to this horrific command. The point is not that he is heartless, but that he is faithful.

"God himself will provide . . .": This prefigures the final resolution of the story.

Thus the firstborn that belongs to God is redeemed by the substitution of the ram. We cannot help thinking at this point of the Lamb of God, Jesus, who was sacrificed to redeem us.

The great blessing—the reward for obedience and fidelity.

A reading from the book of *Genesis* ▪▪

God put Abraham to the test. ▪ He called to him, ▪ "Abraham!" ▪ "Ready!" he replied. ▪ Then God said: ▪ "Take your son *Isaac*, your only one, *whom you love*, and go to the land of Moriah. ▪ There you shall offer him up as a *holocaust* on a height that I will point out to you." ▪ Early the next morning Abraham saddled his donkey, took with him his son Isaac, and two of his servants as well, and with the wood that he had cut for the holocaust, set out for the place of which God had told him. ▪▪

On the third day Abraham got *sight* of the place from afar. ▪ Then he said to his servants: ▪ "Both of you stay here with the donkey, while the boy and I go on over yonder. ▪ We will *worship* and then come *back* to you." ▪ Thereupon Abraham took the wood for the holocaust and laid it on his son Isaac's shoulders, while he *himself* carried the fire and the *knife*. ▪ As the two walked on together, Isaac spoke to his father Abraham. ▪ "Father!" he said. ▪ "Yes, son," he replied. ▪ Isaac continued, ▪ "Here are the *fire* and the *wood*, but where is the *sheep* for the holocaust?" ▪ "Son," Abraham answered, ▪ "God *himself* will provide the sheep for the holocaust." ▪ Then the two *continued going forward.* ▪

When they came to the place of which God had *told* him, Abraham built an *altar* there and arranged the wood on it. ▪ Next he tied up his son *Isaac*, and put *him* on top of the wood on the altar. ▪ Then he reached out and took the knife to *slaughter* his son. ▪ But the Lord's messenger called to him from heaven, ▪ "Abraham, Abraham!" ▪▪ "Yes, Lord," he answered. ▪ "Do *not* lay your *hand* on the boy," said the messenger. ▪ "Do not do the *least thing* to him. ▪ I know now how devoted you are to God, since you did not withhold from me *your own beloved son*." ▪ As Abraham looked about, he spied a *ram* caught by its horns in the thicket. ▪ So he went and took the *ram* and offered it up as a holocaust *in place of his son.* ▪▪ Abraham named the site Yahweh-yireh; ▪ hence people now say, ▪ "On the mountain the Lord will *see*." ▪▪

Again the Lord's messenger called to Abraham from heaven and said: ▪ "I *swear* by myself, declares the Lord, that because you acted as you *did* in not withholding from me *your beloved son*, I will *bless* you *abundantly* and make *your descendants* as countless as the stars of the *sky* and the sands of the *seashore*; ▪

your *descendants* shall take possession of the gates of their enemies, and in *your descendants* all the nations of the *earth* shall find blessing—all this because you obeyed my *command.*" ▪ ▪

[*Shorter: Genesis 22:1–2, 9, 10–13, 15–18*]

READING III   Exodus 14:15 — 15:1

We see a people cowering in fright, afraid to move forward until their leadership instructs them in no uncertain terms to put their trust in God and "go forward!" The feeling of resolve is palpable from the very beginning of this adventure.

A reading from the book of *Exodus* ▪ ▪

The Lord said to Moses, ▪ "Why are you crying out to me? ▪ Tell the Israelites to go *forward.* ▪ And *you*, lift up your *staff* and, with hand outstretched over the sea, split the sea in two, that the Israelites may pass through it on *dry land.* ▪ But I will make the Egyptians so *obstinate* that they will go in after them. ▪ Then I will receive *glory* through Pharaoh and all his army, his chariots and charioteers. ▪ The Egyptians shall know that *I am the Lord,* when I receive *glory* through Pharaoh and his chariots and charioteers." ▪ ▪

An unusual way for God to receive glory—through the defeat of Pharaoh and his troops. The point is that the hand of God is at work on both sides of the struggle.

The *angel of God,* who had been leading Israel's camp, now moved and went around *behind* them. ▪ The *column of cloud* also, leaving the front, took up its place *behind* them, so that it came between the camp of the Egyptians and that of Israel. ▪ But the cloud now became *dark,* and thus the night passed without the rival camps coming any closer together all night long. ▪ ▪ Then Moses stretched out his hand over the sea, and the Lord swept the sea with a strong east wind throughout the night and so turned it into *dry land.* ▪ When the water was thus *divided,* the Israelites marched into the midst of the sea on *dry land,* with the water like a wall to their right and to their left. ▪

The Lord becomes Israel's rear guard and vanguard. Your proclamation should be solid, strong, deliberate.

The Egyptians followed in pursuit; all Pharaoh's horses and chariots and charioteers went after them right into the midst of the sea. ▪ In the night watch just before dawn the Lord through the *column of the fiery cloud* cast upon the Egyptian force a glance that threw it into a *panic*; and he so clogged their chariot wheels that they could hardly drive. ▪ With that the Egyptians sounded the *retreat* before Israel, because the *Lord* was fighting for them *against* the Egyptians. ▪

The odd word order makes reading it aloud very difficult. Try this instead: "In the night watch just before dawn, the Lord—through the column of the fiery cloud—cast a glance upon the Egyptian force that threw it into a panic."

Then the Lord told Moses, ▪ "Stretch out your hand over the sea, that the water may flow back upon the

---

READING III   Here is the story of one of the most memorable and vivid events in the life of God's Chosen People. The deliverance from captivity in Egypt has come to signify various kinds of deliverance for peoples and cultures throughout the world. The crossing of the Red Sea has become a symbol of transition from any kind of slavery to the freedom that is the birthright of every human being.

The central assertion in every detail of this familiar passage is that God's intervention in the life of the Chosen People is the reason for their deliverance. God's hand is the motivating force behind every power at work here. And everyone involved (including the Egyptians) is to know that God is the Lord. The angel of the Lord, the column of cloud, the fiery cloud, the staff of Moses, the strong east wind—*all* are manifestations of God's unshakable resolve to deliver Israel from bondage.

The mood of this story is clearly one of excitement, panic and noisy confusion. There is even a thrilling "chase" in which the enemy is routed. It will take an energetic reader to do this reading justice. Which is not to say that a literal imitation of the frenzied activity is recommended. Rather, the voice must be capable of suggesting many different moods, while communicating as clearly as possible that the central theme of this adventure is the irresistible power and will of the Lord.

Presuming that the response given in the lectionary to follow this reading will be sung (find this out from the music director or musicians far in advance of the Vigil), the last three lines of the reading (which are part of the response) should be omitted by the reader—as well as "This is the word of the Lord." The effective order of things, then, would be:
Reader:"Then Moses and the Israelites sang this song to the Lord."
Cantor: *[Immediately, without pause]* "Let us sing to the Lord; he has covered himself in glory."
People:*[Repeat]*
Cantor:"I will sing to the Lord . . . ," and so forth.

READING IV It would be difficult to find a more tender proclamation of love than this one. And it is a poem of intimacy between God and Jerusalem—the holy city, the people who belong there, the Chosen People, Israel. What a contrast to the warrior-hero-lover in the previous reading!

In this love song, we see evidence of a stormy relationship. This does not surprise us. Any relationship that strives for genuine union between two independent hearts will have its stormy times. But in this reading, as in our experience, the difficulties encountered in genuine love serve only to make the love stronger.

The theme of Israel's exile is clear in the "abandoned wife" imagery. And the promise of deliverance and prosperity is just as clear in the "peace of your children." The marital bond is very often employed in scripture as the only one intimate enough to describe God's love for Israel.

The same bond is used to describe the love between Christ and his church. He is the bridegroom who has rescued his beloved from every danger and has given his life for her happiness. Marital bliss is an appropriate image as we celebrate this holiest of nights.

Keep the momentum up, even though the second half of this paragraph may seem tame by comparison. The writer wants us to be very clear that "the Lord saved Israel," and to show us how they responded.

Egyptians, upon their chariots and their charioteers." ▪ So Moses stretched out his hand over the sea, and at dawn the sea flowed back to its normal depth. ▪ The Egyptians were *fleeing* head on toward the *sea*, when the Lord hurled them into its *midst*. ▪ As the water flowed *back*, it covered the chariots and the charioteers of Pharaoh's *whole army* which had followed the Israelites into the sea. ▪ Not a single *one* of them escaped. ▪ But the Israelites had marched on *dry land* through the midst of the sea, with the water like a wall to their right and to their left. ▪ Thus the Lord *saved* Israel on that day from the power of the Egyptians. ▪ When Israel saw the Egyptians lying dead on the seashore and beheld the great power that the Lord had shown against the Egyptians, they *feared* the Lord and *believed* in him and in his servant *Moses*. ▪ ▪

Then Moses and the Israelites sang this *song* to the Lord: ▪

I will sing to the Lord,
    for he is gloriously triumphant; ▪
    horse and chariot he has cast into the sea. ▪ ▪

READING IV   Isaiah 54:5–14

A reading from the book of the prophet *Isaiah* ▪ ▪

How striking these words are! The revelation they contain is humbling, moving and exhilarating, all at the same time.

He who has become your *husband*
    is your *Maker*; ▪
    his name is the Lord of *hosts*; ▪
Your redeemer is the *Holy One of Israel*,
    called God of all the *earth*. ▪
The Lord calls you back,
    like a wife forsaken and grieved in spirit,
A wife married in *youth* and then cast *off*,
    says your God. ▪

God speaks in the frailty of human language. Despite all the difficulties and infidelities, the desire for intimacy remains.

For a brief moment I *abandoned* you,
    but with great tenderness *I will*
        take you back. ▪
In an outburst of wrath, for a *moment*
    I hid my *face* from you; ▪
But with enduring love *I take pity on you,*
    says the Lord, your redeemer. ▪
This is for me like the days of *Noah*,
    when I swore that the waters of Noah
    should *never again* deluge the earth; ▪

So I have sworn *not* to be *angry* with you,
or to *rebuke* you. ▪

Though the mountains leave their *place*
and the hills be *shaken,*

My *love* shall never leave *you*
nor my covenant of *peace* be shaken, ▪

says the Lord, *who has mercy on you.* ▪▪

O afflicted one, storm-battered and unconsoled,
I lay your pavements in *carnelians,*
and your foundations in *sapphires;* ▪

I will make your battlements of *rubies,*
your gates of *carbuncles,*
and all your walls of precious *stones.* ▪

All your sons shall be taught by the *Lord,*
and great shall be the peace of your *children.* ▪

In *justice* shall you be *established,*
far from the fear of *oppression,*
where destruction cannot come *near* you. ▪▪

The feeling here is that something akin to a marriage vow is being sworn. The realization should be that our goodness comes not from ourselves but from God's faithful love for us.

NRSV: "All your children shall be taught by the Lord, and great shall be the prosperity of your children." This is inclusive, but the repetition of the word "children" is weak. Consider using "all your offspring" or "all your sons and daughters."

READING V   Isaiah 55:1–11

A reading from the book of the prophet *Isaiah* ▪▪

Thus says the Lord: ▪
All you who are *thirsty,*
come to the *water!* ▪

You who have no *money,*
come, receive grain and *eat;* ▪

Come, without *paying* and without *cost,*
drink *wine* and *milk!* ▪

Why spend your money for *what is not bread;*
your wages for *what fails to satisfy?* ▪

Heed me, and you shall eat *well,*
you shall delight in *rich* fare. ▪

Come to me heedfully,
listen, that you may have *life.* ▪

I will renew with you the *everlasting covenant,*
the benefits assured to *David.* ▪

As I made him a *witness* to the peoples,
a leader and commander of *nations,*

So shall you summon a nation *you knew not,*
and nations that *knew you not* shall run
to you,

Because of the Lord, your God,
the Holy One of Israel, who has
glorified you. ▪▪

Seek the Lord *while he may be found,*
call him *while he is near.* ▪

"Thus says the Lord" always begins a solemn pronouncement. Do not dismiss the formula lightly. You are reading a poem, which calls for a more exalted and deliberate delivery. The lines are carefully constructed and packed with importance. Read them lovingly.

The "bread" is a symbolic term here, representing the nourishment of wisdom. Why spend your money on what will not last . . . and fails to satisfy! The implication is that the only lasting and satisfying "food" is doing the will of God. Recall Jesus' words: "My food is to do the will of God who sent me."

"So shall you summon . . .": Be wary of this line. It's a tongue-twister.

READING V   The scholars tell us that the author of these verses of poetry lived in the midst of a very poor community. One would expect the images of a banquet, and the consoling message that no money is needed to partake in it. One writes in a way one's audience can understand.

The broader view of these poetic lines reveals the kind of sustenance that comes from trust in the God who provides. And it is clear that a future time of peace and prosperity is implied. Again we are confronted with a vision of the "end times"— and encouraged to see the signs that indicate their imminent arrival: the mercy and redemptive love of God.

The kind of faith that sees the reign of God at work on a very imperfect earth is the faith that comes with conversion, with change. Turning to the Lord for mercy is our best guarantee of deeper insight. Then we will see how very different our ways are from God's ways.

Finally, we are reminded that God's word is irrevocable and will accomplish the purpose for which it has been proclaimed. The evidence for this in our immediate situation is the paschal mystery we are celebrating. We are keeping vigil for the resurrection—the most dramatic demonstration that God's will on our behalf will be accomplished.

The poetry of Baruch (pronounced BEHR-ook, not bar-OOK) is a call to awareness. The cosmic and astronomical imagery create a sense of the immensity and universality of God's domain. Above all, it is a call to find *wisdom,* that most beautiful of virtues, which enables us to see things aright.

Wisdom comes from the self-revealing God. And God is revealed in every aspect of creation—from the four-footed beasts to the stars at their posts. The myopic will never find wisdom; only the far-sighted will be able to see her as a manifestation of God.

Specifically, the prophet calls out to Israel, dispersed as she is throughout the pagan world. If they are concerned that they cannot serve God well in the midst of foreigners, they must be reminded that their exile is the result of not serving God well in their homeland. This may seem a harsh indictment, but the prophet is more eager to point out that wisdom is available wherever we are. And that is because God has revealed the law and the word by which we can guide our behavior and our devotion. It is discernible in nature, yes, but even more in the hearts of the just who have loved the law.

In a dramatic way, Baruch is discouraging us from needing tidy answers to specific questions. And he is reminding us of a much more faith-motivated approach: to seek Divine Wisdom is already to serve God!

"Let the scoundrel": You can make this inclusive by using the plural: "Let scoundrels forsake their ways, and the wicked their evil thoughts. Let them turn to the Lord. . . ."

NRSV: "Giving seed to the sower and bread to the eater. . . ."

In the paschal mystery (the life and death and resurrection of Jesus) we see the word of God achieving the end for which it was sent.

Let the scoundrel *forsake* his way,
and the *wicked* man his *thoughts;* ▪
Let him turn to the Lord for *mercy;* ▪
to our God, who is *generous* in forgiving. ▪
For *my* thoughts are not *your* thoughts,
nor are *your* ways *my* ways, says the Lord. ▪
As high as the heavens are *above the earth,*
so high are my ways *above your ways*
and my thoughts *above your thoughts.* ▪ ▪
For just as from the heavens
the rain and snow come down
And do not *return* there
till they have *watered* the earth,
making it fertile and fruitful,
Giving *seed* to him who *sows*
and *bread* to him who *eats,* ▪
So shall my *word* be
that goes forth from my mouth; ▪
It shall not return to me *void,*
but shall do my *will,*
achieving the end for which I *sent* it. ▪ ▪

READING VI   Baruch 3:9–15, 32 — 4:4

A reading from the book of the prophet
Baruch ▪ ▪

"Hear, O Israel" is a formula that signals something of importance, and must always remind us of the most fundamental of Jewish beliefs (the Shema): "Hear, O Israel, the Lord our God is One!"

It is possible to "dwell in enduring peace" no matter how miserable our situation— if we walk in the way of God.

The rhetorical questions and the answers center on God as Creator and sustainer of all things.

Hear, O Israel, the commandments of *life:* ▪
listen, and know *prudence!* ▪
How is it, Israel,
that you are in the land of your *foes,*
grown old in a *foreign* land,
Defiled with the *dead,* ▪
accounted with those destined for the
nether world? ▪
You have forsaken the *fountain of wisdom!* ▪
Had you walked in the *way of God,*
you would have dwelt in enduring *peace.* ▪
Learn where *prudence* is,
where *strength,* where *understanding;* ▪
That you may know also
where are the length of *days,* and *life,*
where light of the *eyes,* and *peace.* ▪ ▪

Who has found the place of *wisdom,*
who has entered into her *treasuries?* ▪
He who knows *all* things knows *her;* ▪
he has *probed* her by his *knowledge—*
He who established the earth for all *time,*
and filled it with four-footed *beasts;* ▪
He who dismisses the *light,* and it *departs,*

calls it, and it *obeys* him *trembling;* ▪
Before whom the stars at their posts
  shine and *rejoice;* ▪
When he *calls* them, they *answer,* ▪
  "Here we are!"
  shining with *joy* for their *Maker.* ▪
Such is *our* God; ▪
  no *other* is to be compared to *him:* ▪
He has traced out all the way of *understanding,*
  and has given her to *Jacob,* his servant, ▪
  to *Israel,* his beloved son. ▪

Since then she has *appeared on earth,*
  and *moved among men.* ▪
She is the book of the precepts of God,
  the law that endures *forever;* ▪
All *who cling to her* will live,
  but those will die *who forsake her.* ▪
Turn, O Jacob, and *receive her:* ▪
  walk by her light toward *splendor.* ▪
Give not your glory to *another,*
  your privileges to an *alien* race. ▪
Blessed are we, O Israel; ▪
  for what pleases *God* is *known* to us! ▪ ▪

Wisdom has appeared on earth in the revealed will and providence of God.

READING VII Ezekiel 36:16–28

A reading from the book of the prophet *Ezekiel* ▪ ▪

"Thus the word of the Lord came to me": The prophet, by definition, speaks for God. Listen carefully.

Because our culture does not look upon menstruation as in any way a defilement, some lectionaries omit this line. It is strongly recommended that you omit it, even though it is printed here. Delete the words in brackets.

Thus the word of the Lord came to me: ▪ Son of man, when the house of Israel lived *in their land,* they *defiled* it by their conduct and *deeds.* ▪ [In my sight their conduct was like the defilement of a menstruous woman.] ▪ Therefore I poured out my *fury* upon them [because of the blood which they poured out on the ground, and because they defiled it with idols]. ▪ I *scattered* them among the *nations,* dispersing them over foreign *lands;* ▪ according to their conduct and *deeds* I judged them. ▪ But when they came *among the nations* [wherever they came], they served to profane my holy name, because it was said of them: ▪ "These are the people of the *Lord,* yet they had to *leave their land."* ▪ So I have relented because of my holy name which the house of Israel *profaned* among the nations where they came. ▪ Therefore say to the house of Israel: ▪ Thus says the Lord *God:* ▪ Not for *your* sakes do I act, house of Israel, but for the sake of *my holy name,* which you profaned among

READING VII   Readings that dwell on the exile of Israel and their return to the land of their ancestors are common in the First Testament, just as the experience was central to Israel's faith experience. The prophet Ezekiel places a very harsh tone in God's mouth here. But the facts of the case are harsh.

Israel's infidelity is no worse than human infidelity at any age, but that's bad enough! What is most distressing is that a Chosen People have profaned the name of the God who chose them. It is no different with us. Chosen as we are by a merciful and loving God, our infidelity is all the more horrible.

But again God relents, as we have come to expect, since mercy seems always to triumph over justice where God is concerned. Although the homecoming is said to be for the sake of "the holiness of my great name" among the foreign nations—and not because God pities us—nevertheless we are to be reestablished as the People of the Covenant.

The point is that neither our good deeds, nor our bad deeds nor our repentance *earn* the love of God. It is gratuitous, always a gift and always spontaneously given. God *makes* us holy. On this night, of all nights, we need to be reminded that the sacrificial love demonstrated in Christ's death and resurrection is a totally free act of love. We can accept redemptive love; we can reject redemptive love; but there is no way we can *earn* redemptive love. We can, however, respond to it with the new natural hearts God has given us.

EPISTLE The rhetorical question demands the answer: "Of course we are aware of that!" Thus begins a masterful comparison between baptism and death, and between Jesus' bodily resurrection and our spiritual resurrection. But it's a little more complex than that. Paul's argument is not very tidy, nor was it meant to be. He immerses his thought in images of life, death, baptism, resurrection and sin in order to emerge with the clear conviction that baptism has changed us into completely different beings, just as Jesus emerges from the grave a totally new being.

We know by experience that in many ways we appear to be the same as we were before baptism. Likewise with Jesus after the resurrection. But the spiritual insight we must capture here is that, appearances notwithstanding, we are totally changed by baptism. And the reason is this:

Baptism is union with Christ in his death and resurrection. It is a death to our old selves; a new life in our new selves. Sin no longer has any power over us because "His death was death to sin, once for all."

Look at persons who are physically dead. They certainly are outside the power of sin. They cannot sin. It is just as true of us, because our union with Christ's death has killed that part of us that was subject to sin.

The central truth (and the great good news) is that we also will be united with Christ in his resurrection. The age-old promise of victory over death and sin has come to fruition in the paschal mystery we have gathered to celebrate this very night.

The purification is a necessity before reentering the holy land of promise. We cannot help but be reminded of our celebration of water and the renewal of our baptismal vows at tonight's vigil.

The concluding words are unsurpassed in "blessed assurance." Read them with special care. NRSV: "ancestors" instead of "fathers."

the nations to which you came. ▪ I will prove the *holiness of my great name*, profaned among the nations, in whose midst you have profaned it. ▪ Thus the nations shall know that *I am the Lord*, says the Lord God, when in their sight *I prove my holiness through you*. ▪ For I will take you *away* from among the nations, gather you from *all* the foreign lands, and bring you back to your *own* land. ▪ I will sprinkle clean *water* upon you to *cleanse* you from all your impurities, and from all your idols I will *cleanse* you. ▪ I will give you a *new* heart and place a *new* spirit within you, taking from your bodies your *stony* hearts and giving you *natural* hearts. ▪ I will put *my spirit* within you and make you live by *my statutes*, careful to observe *my decrees*. ▪ You shall live in the land I gave your fathers; ▪ you shall be *my people*, and I will be *your God*. ▪ ▪

EPISTLE   Romans 6:3–11

This is a difficult reading. You must be very careful to bring sensitive emphasis to images that are being compared and contrasted throughout Paul's discourse. It will require a great deal of vocal variety. Above all, read slowly, so that you have sufficient space to place the emphases effectively.

NRSV: "Whoever has died is freed from sin."

A reading from the letter of *Paul* to the *Romans* ▪ ▪

Are you not aware that we who were *baptized into Christ Jesus were baptized into his death?* ▪ ▪ Through baptism into his death we were *buried* with him, so that, just as *Christ* was raised from the dead by the glory of the Father, we too might *live a new life*. ▪ If we have been united with him through likeness to his *death*, so shall we be through a like *resurrection*. ▪ This we *know*: ▪ our *old* self was *crucified* with him so that the sinful body might be destroyed and we might be slaves to sin no longer. ▪ A man who is dead has been freed from sin. ▪ If we have *died with Christ*, we believe that we are also to *live with him*. ▪ We know that Christ, once raised from the dead, will never die again; ▪ death has no more *power* over him. ▪ *His* death was death to *sin*, once for *all*; ▪ his *life* is life for *God*. ▪ ▪ In the same way, you must consider *yourselves* dead to sin but alive for God in Christ *Jesus*. ▪ ▪

A reading from the holy *gospel* according to *Mark* ▪ ▪

As you begin, remember that this story ends with bewilderment and trembling. The mood is mysterious, not triumphant.

When the *sabbath* was over, Mary Magdalene, Mary the mother of James, and Salome bought perfumed *oils* with which they intended to go and *anoint* Jesus. ▪ Very *early*, just after sunrise, on the first day of the week they came to the *tomb*. ▪ They were saying to one another, ▪ "Who will roll back the *stone* for us from the entrance to the *tomb?* ▪ When they looked, ▪ they found that the stone *had* been rolled back. ▪ (It was a huge one.) ▪ On *entering* the tomb they saw a young man sitting at the *right*, dressed in a white *robe*. ▪ This frightened them *thoroughly*, but he reassured them: ▪ "You need not be *amazed!* ▪ You are looking for *Jesus* of *Nazareth*, the one who was *crucified*. ▪ He has been *raised up;* ▪ he is not *here*. ▪ See the *place* where they *laid* him. ▪ Go now and tell his *disciples* and *Peter*, ▪ 'He is going *ahead* of you to *Galilee*, where you will see him just as he *told* you.' " ▪ ▪ They made their way out and fled from the tomb *bewildered* and *trembling;* ▪ and because of their great *fear*, ▪ they said nothing to *anyone*. ▪ ▪

"It was a huge one" could sound too colloquial. The NRSV has more dignity: "They saw that the stone, which was very large, had already been rolled back."

The words "just as he told you" deserve special emphasis.

The story ends abruptly. Fear is dominant; the revelation of what all this means must come later.

GOSPEL   Perhaps the most revealing words in Mark's account of the empty tomb are these: "just as he told you." Remember that throughout his gospel, Mark sustains the tension between "secret" and "surprise." That is, the reader is constantly being held in suspense between questions and answers. Who is Jesus? What meaning underlies his strange words? The miracles he works are surely more than the isolated marvels of a wonder-worker. The tension is Mark's ingenious way of slowly revealing the deeper meaning of Jesus' life and death—and resurrection. Only when we hear the words "He is not here; he has been raised," can we understand all those cryptic passages that raised so many questions during Jesus' short ministry.

The women who hear the messenger's words do not experience a sudden flash of understanding, however. They are bewildered and frightened and silent—traditional scriptural responses to a divine revelation. The fact that they tell no one of their experience, despite the messenger's directions, seems strange. But remember, Mark presumes the reader's awareness of post-resurrection appearances by Jesus.

The process of understanding (or better, believing) has just begun. The Risen Lord will be seen again in Galilee (where, in Mark's tradition, the proclamation of the resurrection must begin), even as he prophesied he would. When the disciples see him there, they will be confirmed in their mission to tell the story of faith throughout the world. When Jesus appeared to the disciples, they understood for the first time the deeper significance of all that he had done and taught. The secret is no more; the word is out!

But not entirely, of course. Even today we speak of the "mystery" of salvation. The Reign of God is here and our salvation is accomplished. But the fullness of that Reign is not yet part of our experience. We are still a pilgrim people, walking by faith and not by sight. Mark's way of telling the story of Jesus still best describes the tension of our faith experience: "already, but not yet." The Reign of God is already among us, but it is not yet fully revealed.

READING I The paschal mystery has been celebrated in its fullness. The culmination was reached in last night's vigil. Today we begin the great 50 days that prolong the joy of the resurrection.

And we begin the scripture readings with Peter's summary of the life, work, death and resurrection of Jesus. It is a reminder of what the Easter season makes present in the assembly.

The recurrent theme here is that Peter and the others who received their commission from the Risen Lord were eyewitnesses. And of particular note is that their commission included the teaching that Jesus is judge of the living and the dead. The concern about the "last days" and the end of time reminds us that the Risen Christ is now in the glory of the Father—his work having been accomplished. The words of the creed are brought to mind: "He will come again in glory to judge the living and the dead."

The final sentence points out Peter's conviction that all the prophets who spoke of the coming Messiah were testifying about Jesus, and their expectations have been fulfilled.

READING II (Colossians) These words of Paul make it clear that we are living an entirely new life as the result of our baptism—and the renewal of our baptismal vows at last night's vigil or today's Mass. "Our life is hidden now with Christ . . . ": That is, there is more to come and the work of salvation is not complete until the "end time." Scholars speak of "partially realized eschatology," a formidable phrase which means that the kingdom of God is established on earth but has not reached perfection. Less scholarly types call this the "already, but not yet" principle!

We will no longer be hidden when Christ comes in glory. When *he* appears, our lives, too, will appear in the glory with which they have been mysteriously imbued since baptism.

There is a choice of second readings today. Check with the lector chairperson or a parish staff member to see which one you should read.

EASTER SUNDAY

LECTIONARY #43

READING I   Acts 10:34, 37–43

A reading from the *Acts* of the *Apostles* ▪ ▪

This is a very concise summary of Jesus' life and work. In effect it is a list. Be sure that you avoid making it sound like a list! The tone is more conversational than declamatory. And the personal "we" adds a note of intimacy.

Peter addressed the people in these words: ▪ "I take it you *know* what has been reported all over Judea about Jesus of *Nazareth*, beginning in Galilee with the baptism *John* preached; ▪ of the way God *anointed* him with the Holy Spirit and *power*. ▪ He went about *doing good works* and healing all who were in the grip of the devil, ▪ and *God was with him.* ▪ We are witnesses to all that he did in the land of the Jews and in Jerusalem. ▪ They *killed* him finally, 'hanging him on a *tree*,' only to have *God raise him up* on the third day and grant that he be *seen*, not by all, but only by such witnesses as had been chosen beforehand by God— ▪ by *us* who ate and *drank* with him after he rose from the *dead*. ▪ He commissioned us to *preach* to the people and to *bear witness* that he is the one set apart by God as judge of the living and the dead. ▪ To him all the *prophets* testify, saying that everyone who believes in *him* has forgiveness of sins through his *name*." ▪ ▪

READING II   Colossians 3:1–4

A reading from the letter of *Paul* to the *Colossians* ▪ ▪

Let the words that point "up" work their charm: raised up, higher realms, above.

Be sure the relationship between the last two sentences is made clear by your inflection and emphasis. (See the commentary.)

Since you have been raised up *in company with Christ*, set your heart on what pertains to *higher realms* where Christ is seated at God's right hand. ▪ Be intent on *things above* rather than on *things of earth*. ▪ After all, you have *died!* ▪ Your life is *hidden* now with Christ in *God*. ▪ When Christ our *life* appears, then *you* shall appear with him in *glory*. ▪ ▪

Many images are at work. Study the commentary for an explanation of Paul's choices here, and proclaim this very brief reading slowly—with understanding.

A reading from the first letter of *Paul* to the *Corinthians* ▪ ▪

Do you not know that a little *yeast* has its effect all through the *dough?* ▪ Get rid of the *old yeast* to make of yourselves *fresh dough,* ▪ *unleavened* loaves, as it were; ▪ Christ our Passover has been *sacrificed.* ▪ Let us celebrate the feast not with the old *yeast,* that of corruption and wickedness, but with the *unleavened* bread of *sincerity* and *truth.* ▪ ▪

GOSPEL   John 20:1–9

The time is early on a Sunday morning—not the seventh day of rest, but the first day of the week. The Christian observance of Sunday rather than the Sabbath begins here.

Notice Mary's presumption that the body of Jesus had been stolen. How very different from John's response to the empty tomb.

Read these details carefully. All are significant; all contain a message larger than themselves.

A reading from the holy *gospel* according to *John* ▪ ▪

Early in the morning on the first day of the week, while it was still dark, Mary Magdalene came to the tomb. ▪ She saw that the *stone* had been moved *away,* ▪ so she ran off to Simon *Peter* and the *other* disciple (the one Jesus loved) and told them, ▪ "The Lord has been taken from the *tomb!* We don't know where they have *put* him!" ▪ At that, Peter and the other disciple started out on their way toward the tomb. ▪ They were running *side by side,* but then the other disciple *outran Peter* and reached the tomb first. ▪ He did not enter but bent down to peer in, and saw the wrappings lying on the ground. ▪ Presently, Simon *Peter* came along *behind* him and *entered* the tomb. ▪ He observed the wrappings on the ground and saw the piece of cloth which had covered the head *not* lying with the *wrappings,* but rolled up in a place by *itself.* ▪ Then the disciple who had arrived *first* at the tomb went in. ▪ ▪ He saw ▪ and *believed.* ▪ ▪ *(Remember,* as yet they did not understand the Scripture that Jesus had to rise from the *dead.)* ▪ ▪

READING II (Corinthians) The situation in Corinth that prompted Paul to write these words had to do with a person of evil influence in the community. Paul is reminding the Corinthians that one bad apple can spoil the whole barrel. However, he uses the image of yeast instead— a little yeast leavens all the dough— an image not infrequently employed to describe a corruptive influence.

In the context of the Easter celebration, the passage is meant to remind us of the need to restore our baptismal innocence. The images begin to pile up as Paul refers to Christ as "our Passover," and the immediate association of "unleavened bread" (no yeast) comes to mind. Unleavened bread was eaten at the Passover meal in memory of the command to be ready (loins girt) for a speedy escape from Egypt. There was no time for the dough to rise.

The overall effect of the reading is to make a good case for the need to purify ourselves of wickedness and live renewed lives of sincerity and truth.

GOSPEL John's account of the resurrection contains some unique features. The account of the race between Peter and John has John arriving first. More than an indication that he is the younger of the two, it is a sign of his special position as the "disciple whom Jesus loved." The same point is made when John enters the empty tomb after Peter. This put him in the position of making the act of faith: "He saw and believed."

The detail concerning the burial cloths (the head cloth folded up neatly by itself) is a way of offering evidence that the body had not been stolen; there is order here, not the chaos one would expect to be left by grave robbers.

Their full understanding of the scripture that Jesus had to rise from the dead will come when Jesus completes his work on earth and ascends to the Father's right hand, his rightful place.

The overall purpose in the way John describes the resurrection scene is to demonstrate the faith arrived at by the disciple when he saw the empty tomb. No further proof was necessary for him. And indeed, the same is true of us. No amount of physical evidence can force us into believing. Faith is always a free choice.

READING I For the seven Sundays of the Easter Season, the first reading is a selection from the Acts of the Apostles, giving us an extended view of the risen Christ moving among the early believers.

Today's passage offers an ideal picture of social justice being put into practice. But we should be aware that this social justice is the inevitable result of Christian love. Everything was held in common *because* the community of believers was of one mind and one heart. The contemporary slogan, "If you want peace, work for justice," may well be flawed. When true love and peace are present, justice can be presumed. Is the reverse really true, human nature being what it is? Our notions about justice are probably far more diverse than our understanding of unselfish love.

Despite the complexity of many large parish situations, the description of Christian community in this reading should remain our ideal. In other words, we cannot dismiss fundamental notions of Christian community as naive and unrealistic for our time. Nor can we leave pursuit of that ideal up to charitable organizations and programs. Personal and mutual responsibility for each other in the Christian community is as basic as baptism!

In these faith-filled days of Easter, this reading can serve as an impetus toward genuine renewal, and it deserves the most sensitive and powerful rendition we can muster. It should not surprise you that your careful reading of this passage could bring someone in the congregation to a new realization of what "Christian community" means—and move your hearers toward greater zeal in living the Christian ideal in their homes and work places.

READING II You may want to consult later commentaries on this letter to get a broader sense of John's purpose in writing it. Today's brief selection is packed with essential truths about Jesus and his followers. Notice where the reading is headed, even before you get there. John is eager to make the point that it is the death of Jesus that proves his origin and guarantees the validity of his mission. Though we may tend to place the words and works of Jesus at the center of our Christian endeavors, they

SECOND SUNDAY OF EASTER

LECTIONARY #45

READING I   Acts 4:32–35

A reading from the *Acts* of the *Apostles* ▪ ▪

The community of believers were of *one heart* and *one mind.* ▪ None of them ever claimed anything as his *own;* ▪ rather everything was held in *common.* ▪ With power the apostles bore *witness* to the *resurrection* of the Lord Jesus, and great respect was paid to them all; ▪ nor was there anyone *needy* among them, for all who owned property or houses *sold* them and donated the proceeds. ▪ They used to lay them at the feet of the *apostles* to be distributed to everyone according to his *need.* ▪ ▪

NRSV: "No one claimed private ownership of any possessions, but everything they owned was held in common."

NRSV: "They laid it at the apostles' feet, and it was distributed to each as any had need."

READING II   1 John 5:1–6

A reading from the first letter of *John* ▪ ▪

Everyone who believes that *Jesus* is the *Christ*
    has been begotten by *God.* ▪ ▪
Now, everyone who loves the *father*
    loves the *child* he has *begotten.* ▪ ▪
We can be sure that we love God's *children*
    when we love *God*
    and do what he has commanded. ▪ ▪
The love of God consists in *this:* ▪
    that we keep his *commandments*— ▪
    and *his* commandments are *not* burdensome. ▪
Everyone begotten of *God* conquers the world,
    and the *power* that has conquered the world
    is this *faith* of ours. ▪ ▪
Who, then, is *conqueror* of the world? ▪
    The one who believes that *Jesus* is the
        Son of *God.* ▪
Jesus Christ it *is* who came through water
    and blood— ▪
    not in water *only,*
    but in water and in *blood.* ▪ ▪
It is the *Spirit* who testifies to this, ▪
    and the Spirit is *truth.* ▪ ▪

Read slowly and deliberately. This is a free-flowing meditation on basic Christian living.

A new section begins here. Pause before it.

"Jesus Christ it is . . ." The inverted word order gives this sentence emphasis and a poetic strength.

With absolute confidence, for who would not believe the Spirit of God!

A reading from the holy *gospel* according to *John* ▪▪

This is an amazing story. Tell it with joy and wonder.

On the evening of that first day of the week, even though the disciples had locked the *doors* of the place where they were for fear of the Jews, ▪ Jesus *came* and stood *before* them. ▪▪ *"Peace* be with you," he said. ▪ When he had said this, he showed them his *hands* and his *side.* ▪ At the sight of the Lord the disciples *rejoiced.* ▪▪ *"Peace* be with you," he said again. ▪

Emphasize the word "peace" (not "with") each time Jesus says "Peace be with you."

"As the *Father* has sent *me,*
so *I* send *you."* ▪▪
Then he breathed on them and said: ▪
"Receive the Holy *Spirit.* ▪
If you *forgive* men's sins,
they are *forgiven* them; ▪
if you hold them *bound,*
they are held *bound."* ▪▪

NRSV: "If you forgive the sins of any, they are forgiven them; if you retain the sins of any, they are retained."

It happened that *one* of the Twelve, *Thomas* (the name means "Twin"), was *absent* when Jesus came. ▪ The *other* disciples kept *telling* him: ▪ "We have seen the *Lord!"* ▪ His answer was, ▪ "I'll never *believe* it without probing the *nail-prints* in his *hands,* without putting my *finger* in the nail-marks and my *hand* into his *side."* ▪▪

Pause before the new section begins. Into this scene of wonder and joy is introduced the struggle involved in believing.

A week *later,* the disciples were once *more* in the room, and this time Thomas was *with* them. ▪ Despite the locked *doors,* Jesus came and stood *before* them. ▪ *"Peace* be with you," he said; ▪ then, to Thomas: ▪ *"Take* your finger and *examine* my hands. ▪ *Put* your hand into my *side.* ▪ Do not persist in your *unbelief,* but *believe!"* ▪ Thomas said in response, ▪ "My *Lord* and my *God!"* ▪ Jesus then said to *him:* ▪ *"You* became a believer because you *saw* me. ▪ Blest are they who *have not* seen and
have *believed."* ▪▪

And now the climax! Thomas's act of faith ("My Lord and my God!") is the victory cry of anyone who has doubted.

There is no hint of rebuke here.

Jesus performed many *other* signs as well— ▪ signs not *recorded* here—in the presence of his disciples. ▪ But *these* have been recorded to help you *believe* that *Jesus* is the Messiah, the Son of *God,* so that through this faith you may have *life* in *his name.* ▪▪

Consider altering the word order: "Jesus performed many other signs as well in the presence of his disciples— signs not recorded here." The final sentence is John's offering, in love, to all future generations.

mean nothing without the burden of proof that his death provides.

John's way of explaining his convictions here may seem odd to us, but the meaning is clear: Jesus was sent to us from God through water (his baptism) and through blood (his crucifixion and death). To become a Christian is simply to *believe* in Jesus' origins and his accomplishments on our behalf. Simply believe! How different from the impression we get sometimes that being Christian is based on *doing.* Not so. We are Christians not because of what we have done; we are Christians because of what Jesus has done. Our only duty is to believe deeply and personally in Jesus; good deeds will then spring from us spontaneously.

GOSPEL   Here is a conflict-filled situation that is resolved by the end of the passage. In fact, we have a story within a story here: the appearance of Jesus to encourage the fearful disciples, and the resolution of Thomas's doubts. He believes only when he hears the Lord's call to belief. It is not so much his eyes as his ears that call him to faith. For all but a few of the earliest Christians, faith comes through hearing.

Paint the scene for your hearers so they get a clear, fresh picture of the situation. We are about to witness the first public appearance of Jesus since the resurrection—and the bestowing of the Holy Spirit on the apostles.

Make sure that a significant pause follows the words "they are held bound," because we now launch into the story-within-the-story. Thomas is often made to sound like a bullish and stubborn unbeliever by hitting the word "never" too hard: "I'll *never* believe. . . ." But Thomas's problem is doubt—as the phrase "doubting Thomas" makes clear. Read this passage with more emphasis on "believe"—implying "I want to, but I *can't* believe without some physical evidence." "I'll never *believe* it without. . . ."

When Jesus appears again a week later, Thomas gets the evidence he needs. There is no sense of rebuke in Jesus' reply to Thomas's affirmation of faith. Rather, the reply is for all succeeding generations of Christians who are challenged to believe without having seen.

READING I The entire reading is in quotation marks, and the author of Acts (St. Luke) represents the thoughts here as part of a sermon preached by Peter. Whether or not they are Peter's actual words (probably not) is beside the point. The truth being proclaimed here is that God's will for us will be carried out, despite any and all attempts to thwart it. Thus, the writer's purpose here is not to condemn those who were responsible for Jesus' death, but to show them that all things come to pass in accord with God's will, and that Jesus is the fulfillment of the ancient promises.

Jesus is referred to here as the Holy and Just One. In more contemporary usage, we might use the words "innocent" and "obedient," for that is the point being made. As God's worthy servant, obedient unto death, Jesus is again seen as the embodiment of those qualities of the Messiah that were foretold in Israel's history. The reference to Jesus as "the Author of Life" reminds us that his death and resurrection ushered in a new era of right relationship with God. No longer need we be estranged from God, for now we have a new leader (like Moses) to show us the way to the promised land.

READING II This is the second of six consecutive Sundays on which we read from the First Letter of John. You may want to consult previous and later commentaries. The *fact* is that, despite the perfect sacrifice of Jesus, there is still sin in the world. The *point* is that, despite the presence of sin, there is ongoing forgiveness available to all who seek it. We need to remember, as we read this letter of John, that he had to deal with a theological movement that denied that people who had been baptized could sin. They were called "gnostics" (related to the word "knowledge") and they saw themselves as being above the reality of sin—and, indeed, even above the responsibility to strive for greater goodness.

John makes it very clear that such notions are incompatible with true Christian faith. Yes, he says, it would be great if none of you ever sinned again, but, thank God, we have Jesus to intercede for us and continue to forgive us when we do sin—and repent. Further, he says, there's

THIRD SUNDAY OF EASTER

LECTIONARY #48

READING I   Acts 3:13–15, 17–19

A solemn proclamation that requires great vocal energy. Be sure it rings out to the assembly. NRSV: "the God of our ancestors."

A reading from the *Acts* of the *Apostles* ▪▪

Peter said to the people: ▪ "The 'God of *Abraham*, of *Isaac*, and of *Jacob*, ▪ the God of our fathers,' has *glorified* his Servant Jesus, whom *you* handed *over* and *disowned* in Pilate's presence when Pilate was ready to release him. ▪ You *disowned* the Holy and Just One and preferred *instead* to be granted the release of a *murderer*. ▪ *You* put to *death* the Author of *life*. ▪ But *God raised* him from the dead, and *we* are his *witnesses*. ▪▪

No need to shy away from this awful charge; our sins identify us with those who "put to death the Author of life."

"Yet I *know*, my brothers, that you acted out of *ignorance*, just as your *leaders* did. ▪ God has brought to *fulfillment* by this means what he announced *long ago* through all the *prophets:* ▪ that his Messiah *would* suffer. ▪ Therefore, reform your *lives!* ▪ Turn to *God*, that your sins may be *wiped away!*" ▪▪

NRSV: "And now, friends, I know that you acted in ignorance." A dramatic change of tone must be heard here: empathy and explanation.

Pause before "therefore," and allow the sense of closure to work its effect.

READING II   1 John 2:1–5

A reading from the first letter of *John* ▪▪

My little ones,
    I am *writing* this to keep you from *sin*. ▪
But *if* anyone should sin,
    we have, in the presence of the Father,
Jesus *Christ*, an intercessor who is *just*. ▪
    He is an *offering* for our sins,
    and not for our sins *only*,
    but for those of the whole *world*. ▪▪
The way we can be sure of our *knowledge* of him
    is to keep his *commandments*. ▪
The man who claims, ▪ "*I* have known him,"
    without keeping his commandments,
    is a *liar;* ▪ in such a one there is no *truth*. ▪
But whoever keeps his *word*
    truly *has* the love of God made *perfect* in him. ▪▪

The tenderness and reassurance here are quite poignant. Emphasize the word "if" rather than "should"— which can sound like "ought to." The NRSV solves the problem: "But if anyone does sin."

A new section, explaining carefully and with patience.

NRSV: "Whoever says . . ." and "But whoever obeys his word, truly in this person the love of God has reached perfection."

A reading from the holy *gospel* according to *Luke* ▪ ▪

Emmaus = eh-MAY-uhs. This is a wonderful story, full of Easter joy. Read it lovingly.

The disciples recounted what had happened on the road to Emmaus and how they had come to *know* Jesus in the breaking of *bread.* ▪ ▪

"Peace to you" is too abrupt. Say "Peace be with you," and emphasize the word "Peace," not "with."

Jesus' words must have a calming effect; no sense of rebuke here.

While they were still *speaking* about all this, he himself stood in their *midst* [and said to them, *"Peace to you."*] ▪ In their panic and fright they *thought* they were seeing a ghost. ▪ He said to them, ▪ "Why are you disturbed? ▪ Why do such ideas cross your mind? ▪ Look at my *hands* and my *feet;* ▪ it is really *I.* ▪ Touch me, and see that a ghost does not have flesh and bones as I do." ▪ [As he said this he *showed* them his hands and feet.] ▪ They were still incredulous for sheer *joy* and *wonder,* so he said to them, ▪ "Have you anything here to *eat?*" ▪ ▪ They gave him a piece of cooked fish, which he took and ate *in their presence.* ▪ Then he said to them, ▪ "Recall those words I spoke to you when I was still *with* you: ▪ everything written about *me* in the law of Moses and the prophets and psalms had to be *fulfilled."* ▪ Then he opened their minds to the *understanding* of the Scriptures. ▪ ▪

The "panic and fright" have now turned to "joy and wonder."
The point of the gospel writer that Jesus ate in their presence is very significant. Emphasize it.

Jesus is teaching, and then commissioning his hearers. You are doing the same thing.

He said to them: ▪ "Thus it is likewise written that the Messiah *must* suffer and rise from the *dead* on the third day. ▪ In his name, penance for the remission of *sins* is to be preached to *all* the nations, *beginning* at Jerusalem. ▪ *You* are *witnesses* of this." ▪ ▪

more to being a Christian than an intellectual assent to Jesus. Our behavior must make it evident that we put our faith into action. Here is the cure for the horror of hypocrisy.

GOSPEL   If we are familiar with the plan of the lectionary, we will be surprised to see today's gospel taken from Luke. Ordinarily we would expect John to appear during Lent and Easter, and it is Mark's narrative that provides the gospel reading at other times during Year B. The reason for this change is that Luke's account of Jesus' appearance in the "upper room" in Jerusalem parallels the account we read from John last Sunday. Also, this is Luke's last recorded instance of Jesus appearing to the disciples after his resurrection from the dead. It is appropriate that it be read early in the Easter Season.

The story here is filled with human emotions and responses to the extraordinary. We read that the disciples were frightened, as though they were seeing a ghost. To prove that he was no ghost, Jesus takes food in their presence. The implication is that eating is certain proof that Jesus in his risen body is more than spirit. In other words, he is truly risen from the dead—which implies far more than that he has crossed over from earthly to spiritual existence. There is almost certainly a hint of the eucharist here too, for the partaking of a meal is never without profound significance in Luke. Taken together, then, the two aspects of "real flesh and blood" and proof of his reality through "eating" make a profound impression on the disciples—and on us as well.

Once that impression has been made, the Risen Lord resumes his role as teacher, instructing the disciples regarding the implications of his resurrection. First of all, it is the ultimate fulfillment of the scriptures—"the law of Moses and the prophets and psalms"—echoing Peter's teaching in today's first reading. Second, it makes clear that we can have every confidence as "witnesses"—that is, as people who know the power of the resurrection in our own lives and can joyfully proclaim it to the world in all we say and do.

READING I *Non nobis, Domine, non nobis, sed nomini tuo da gloriam!* Luke surely had this first verse of Psalm 115 in mind in recording Peter's eagerness to attribute the cripple's healing to Jesus and not to himself. It translates: "Not to us, Lord, not to us, but to your name give the glory." The Latin text has inspired musicians and poets through the centuries, for there are many musical settings of it. Every Christian does well to remember that God's glory is the object of worship and the very reason for our existence.

Luke quotes directly from another Psalm (118) to make the point that Jesus is the "stone rejected by the builders" which has become the "cornerstone" of the church. And we sing this psalm again today as the response to the reading. So the writer is still intent on persuading his readers that, in Jesus, all prophecies regarding the messiah have been fulfilled.

Peter's urgent tone in this sermon makes two things clear: Despite all human attempts to discredit or discourage the saving mission of Jesus, God, who raised *him* from the dead, will prevail and will raise the *world* from sickness and death. And the healed cripple signifies a saved world—made whole and new by the only one capable of such an achievement: Jesus the Christ.

READING II This is the third of six consecutive Sundays on which we read from the First Letter of John. You may want to consult previous and later commentaries. In this brief passage, John addresses a problem that every Christian has encountered—the world's failure to recognize the nature of Jesus and his disciples. It should not surprise us that we are often misunderstood and criticized. After all, what we truly are "has not yet come to light," as John says.

How often have you heard people say they don't go to church because the church is full of hypocrites? And how do you respond to such a comment? John can help us here. The reason the world sees hypocrites instead of saints is that it sees Jesus as a great figure of history instead of a vibrant spiritual presence now, and because our redeemed natures are not fully visible yet. The world sees a community of people who can't live up to what they profess to believe. We see ourselves

FOURTH SUNDAY OF EASTER

LECTIONARY #51

READING I   Acts 4:8–12

Except for the first sentence, the entire reading is a quotation from Peter's sermon. The second sentence is quite long—an "if . . . then" construction. Convey this with your voice. The word "cripple" may seem harsh to some; the NRSV has "someone who was sick."

"Name" is the important word here.

The final sentence is the strongest yet. Proclaim it with vigor. Better than "given to men," is the NRSV translation: "given among mortals."

A reading from the *Acts* of the *Apostles* ▪ ▪

Peter, *filled* with the Holy *Spirit*, spoke up: ▪ "Leaders of the people! ▪ Elders! ▪ If we must *answer* today for a *good deed* done to a *cripple* and explain how he was restored to *health*, ▪ then *you* and *all* the people of Israel must realize that it was done in the name of Jesus *Christ* the Nazorean whom *you crucified* and whom *God raised* from the dead. ▪ In the power of that *name* this man stands before you perfectly *sound*. ▪ This *Jesus* is 'the stone *rejected* by you the builders which has *become* the *cornerstone*.' ▪ There is *no* salvation in anyone *else*, for there is no *other* name in the whole *world* given to men by which we are to be *saved*." ▪ ▪

READING II   1 John 3:1–2

"See" has the sense of "behold" here. It is an exclamation.

Pause before "dearly beloved," and then proceed slowly. The theology presented here is in poetic form.

Utter confidence and peace should be heard as you bring this lovely text to a broad and expansive close.

A reading from the first letter of *John* ▪ ▪

See what *love* the Father has *bestowed* on us
    in letting us be called children of *God!* ▪ ▪
Yet that *is* what we *are.* ▪
    The reason the world does not *recognize* us
    is that it never recognized the *Son.* ▪ ▪
Dearly beloved,
    we are God's *children now;* ▪
    what we shall *later* be has not yet
        come to *light.* ▪
We know that *when* it comes to light
    we shall be *like* him,
    for we shall *see* him as he *is.* ▪ ▪

A reading from the holy *gospel* according to *John* ▪▪

The reading has four sections. Pause between them. Emphasize the word "good" here rather than "shepherd," so that it is clear from the beginning that a contrast is being drawn: "good shepherd" vs. "bad shepherd."

Jesus said: ▪

"I am the *good* shepherd; ▪

the *good* shepherd lays down his *life*

    for the sheep. ▪

The *hired hand*, who *is* no shepherd

nor *owner* of the sheep,

catches sight of the *wolf* coming

and runs *away*, leaving the *sheep*

to be snatched and scattered by the *wolf*. ▪

That is because he works for *pay*; ▪

he has no *concern* for the *sheep*. ▪▪

Pause. The second section. Mutual knowledge is the test of the true "sheep/shepherd" relationship.

"I am the *good* shepherd. ▪

I know *my* sheep

and my sheep know *me*

in the same way that the *Father* knows me

and *I* know the *Father*; ▪

for these sheep I will give my *life*. ▪

I have *other* sheep

that do not belong to *this* fold. ▪

I must lead them, *too*,

and they shall hear my *voice*. ▪

There shall be *one* flock *then, one* shepherd. ▪▪

Pause. The third section. The sheepfold is not yet complete.

The Father loves me for *this*: ▪

that I lay down my *life*

to take it *up* again. ▪

No one *takes* it from me; ▪

I lay it down *freely*. ▪

I have *power* to lay it down,

and I have power to take it *up* again. ▪

This command I *received* from my *Father*." ▪▪

Pause. The fourth section. Jesus tells us that his obedience to the Father explains the infinite love between them. Pay particular attention to the emphasis marks in this final section.

as *saints* who haven't yet lived up to the title! We are heirs to the kingdom of heaven, but right now we are living on a relatively modest allowance. The full inheritance is ours, but we haven't come into it yet.

Jesus saved us in love. But that salvation and that love are yet to be seen in their fullness. If we don't understand this, then our present imperfection will blind us to the fullness of perfection that lies ahead. We truly are a pilgrim people, and pilgrims are covered with the dust and grime of the journey. The present dust and grime, however, don't make us any less pilgrims, nor do they mean that our destination will be any less glorious.

GOSPEL   Of all the images of Jesus throughout the ages, what has inspired more tenderness and compassion than the Good Shepherd? Though we have become accustomed to the image, perhaps we can renew our understanding of it by looking closely at the reason Jesus gives for the shepherd's goodness.

Unlike the hired hand, who works for pay, the good shepherd devotes his life to the sheep out of pure love. The sheep are far more than a responsibility to the good shepherd—who is also their owner. They are the object of his love and concern. Thus, his devotion to them is completely unselfish, and he is willing to put his own life in jeopardy rather than abandon them. To the hired hand, the sheep are merely a commodity, to be watched over only so they can provide him with wool and meat.

What a lesson for those in positions of spiritual leadership! What a judgment on religious leaders who have been caught "fleecing" their flock! Unfortunately, there are wolves always ready to prey on the sheep; some of them are difficult to detect, because they wear sheep's clothing and do their dirty work from inside the fold. As a model of religious leadership, Jesus shows us that love can be the only motivation for ministry. He also shows us that there must be no exclusiveness on the part of the religious leader. There are sheep outside the fold who also must hear the good shepherd's voice. And they must be brought in, so that there will be one flock under one shepherd. And again, the motivation for inclusion must be love, not impressive statistics.

READING I

To understand this narrative passage from Acts, we have to remember that Saul (later renamed Paul) was a fierce persecutor of the young Christian church. It is not difficult to understand why the disciples would find it difficult to trust him. It takes one of their trusted own—Barnabas—to convince them that Saul has, indeed, seen the true light of faith. Once they are convinced, they accept Saul completely, and even band together to protect him against enemies of the good news.

This first reading is a glimpse into the early adventures of the young church at a time when it was growing quite rapidly and coping with all the vicissitudes of becoming established. There are threats everywhere, but there are exciting and encouraging developments as well. The final paragraph draws a picture of an expanding body of believers at peace with one another, despite the conflict and struggle that surrounded them. In fact, the peace that reigned within their ranks may have been the result of their need to band closely together against their persecutors—as well as the less dramatic but challenging struggle of becoming the community of believers Jesus promised they would be.

Again, the early Christian community depicted in Acts provides us with a model for our contemporary communities. The difficulties we encounter as we grow in faith should bring us closer together in genuine peace, not divide us into rival camps. Such peace *is* the consolation of the Holy Spirit.

READING II

This is the fourth of six consecutive Sundays on which we read from the First Letter of John. You may want to consult previous and later commentaries.

One of the most delightful feelings one gets in reading the letters of John is that he presumes we are good and worthy of loving encouragement. There is a gentle rambling tone to this reading that makes him sound like a kindly parent, eager to recognize his children's goodness, and resolved to urge the budding progeny on to greater virtue.

John is a realist, though, for all his tender talk. Notice the presumption that we may be burdened with a conscience which accuses us of sin. Such a burden could keep us from growing; indeed, such

FIFTH SUNDAY OF EASTER

LECTIONARY #54

READING I   Acts 9:26–31

A reading from the *Acts* of the *Apostles* · ·

You are telling a story of conflict, struggle and ultimate resolution.

"Then" signals a new section. Renew the vocal energy.

When Saul arrived back in *Jerusalem* he tried to join the *disciples* there; · but it turned out that they were all *afraid* of him. · They even refused to believe that he was a *disciple.* · Then Barnabas took him in charge and introduced him to the apostles. · He explained to them how on his journey Saul had seen the *Lord,* who had *conversed* with him, and how Saul had been speaking out fearlessly in the *name* of *Jesus* at Damascus. · Saul stayed on with them, moving freely about Jerusalem and *expressing* himself quite *openly* in the name of the *Lord.* · He even addressed the *Greek*-speaking Jews and *debated* with them. · They for their part *responded* by trying to *kill* him. · When the brothers learned of *this,* some of them took him down to *Caesarea* and sent him off to Tarsus. · ·

Barnabas's testimony in Saul's behalf was convincing. Your voice carries a tone of "consequently" in this section.

A subplot in this story. Let your voice signal surprise at Saul's boldness—and no surprise that the Greeks reject Saul's message.

The resolution. The narrative ends with solid peace and hope. The future is bright.

Meanwhile throughout all Judea, Galilee and Samaria the *church* was at *peace.* · It was being built *up* and was making steady *progress* in the fear of the *Lord;* · at the same *time* it enjoyed the increased *consolation* of the Holy *Spirit.* · ·

READING II   1 John 3:18–24

A reading from the first letter of *John* · ·

John's tenderness is touching. The voice should rise, not fall, on "Little children." The contrast between "deed/truth" and "talk about it" is quite strong. There is no stronger message of consolation than this: "God is greater than our hearts."

Little children,
let us love in *deed* and in *truth*
and not merely *talk* about it. ·
This is our way of *knowing* we are committed
to the truth
and are at *peace* before him
no matter *what* our consciences may
charge us with; ·
for God is *greater* than our *hearts*
and all is known to *him.* · ·

Pause. A new section. Let your voice rise on "Beloved." The rhetorical "Why?" is gentle.

Beloved,
if our consciences have nothing
to *charge* us with,

we can be *sure* that God is *with* us
and that we will receive at his hands
  whatever we *ask.* ▪

Why? ▪ Because we are keeping
  his *commandments*
and doing what is *pleasing* in his sight. ▪

His commandment is *this:* ▪
we are to believe in the name of his *Son,*
  Jesus *Christ,* ▪
and are to love one another as he
  commanded us. ▪

Those who keep his commandments *remain*
  in him
and he in *them.* ▪

And this is how we *know* that he remains in us: ▪
from the *Spirit* that he gave us. ▪ ▪

Pause. The final section. Explain carefully and slowly.

GOSPEL John 15:1–8

A reading from the holy *gospel* according to *John* ▪ ▪

The entire reading is a vivid metaphor. Read it carefully and sensitively. The first section deals with the necessity of suffering (pruning).

Jesus said to his disciples: ▪
"I am the true *vine*
and my Father is the vine*grower.* ▪
He prunes away
every *barren* branch,
but the *fruitful* ones
he trims clean
  to increase their *yield.* ▪ ▪

An aside to the disciples, indicating the cleansing (pruning) effect of Jesus' words to them. Then we are led to the heart of the metaphor (Jesus = vine, we = branches). Announce it with great strength.

You are clean *already,*
thanks to the *word* I have spoken to you. ▪
Live *on* in me, as *I* do in *you.* ▪
No more than a branch can bear fruit of *itself*
apart from the vine,
can *you* bear fruit
apart from *me.* ▪

I am the *vine, you* are the *branches.* ▪

To be inclusive: Instead of "he who lives," etc., say "Those who live in me and I in them will produce abundantly." Instead of "a man who does not," say, "whoever does not," etc.

He who *lives* in me and I in *him,*
will produce abundantly,
for *apart* from me you can do *nothing.* ▪

A man who does not live in *me*
is like a withered, rejected *branch,*
picked up to be thrown in the *fire*
  and *burnt.* ▪ ▪

If you live in *me,*
and my *words* stay *part* of you,
you may ask what you *will*— ▪
it will be *done* for you. ▪

Pause. Here is a strong guarantee and a word of encouragement.

My Father has been glorified
in your bearing much *fruit*
and becoming my *disciples.*" ▪ ▪

is often the case with those whose education in the faith concentrated on sin rather than love. So John knows we need to be reminded that God is greater than our hearts—a lovely way of saying that God can conquer even craven doubts and painful remorse, bitter resentments and paralyzing scruples.

John seems to be saying here that it is in our very nature (transfigured in baptism) to do the right thing. Perhaps this is a far healthier attitude than the presumption that we tend toward sin and weakness. Any experienced teacher knows that students tend to perform according to the teacher's expectations of them. If they know the teacher expects them to do well, they tend to do well. If they know the teacher expects them to do poorly, they tend to do poorly.

John's theology can soar like the eagle. But he is also good at distilling our faith down to the simplest and most memorable terms: "His commandment is this: We are to believe . . . and love." Then we know we are "in" Jesus and Jesus is "in" us.

GOSPEL John is quite fond of the notion of "mutual indwelling," and the imagery of the vine and branches is a vivid instance of that fondness. There hardly can be a more complete oneness than that between a vine and its branches. Think of a tree and its trunk. Although it is rather clear where one stops and the other begins, it is also clear that the transition is merely one of appearance, not substance. The trunk and the branches of the tree are identical in their make-up. Both are bark and sap and woody center. Yet the difference between them is obvious, too. The same can be said for the grapevine and its branches.

The point, like the image, is clear: We are so much a part of Christ, and he so much a part of us, that separation can only mean death. The intimacy is so total that apart from him there can be no life. "Mutual indwelling" is an absolute necessity.

And the consequences of oneness are obvious too. Firmly joined to the vine, we can bear much fruit. Pruned of our debris and encumbering dead wood, we can bear even more fruit.

READING I Two things about this reading are striking. First, a Gentile is converted to the Christian way of life. Second, Luke wants us to see how important it is that the message of Jesus has now gone beyond the Jewish culture and is on its way to becoming worldwide—as Jesus himself promised it would. If Peter's new understanding of the universality of Christianity seems curious to us, we must remember that our faith began with the Jews and the idea of the "chosen people" was still very much restricted. The earliest Christians were all Jews, "the circumcised believers" mentioned in this passage. It was difficult for them to embrace the notion that Jesus' mission was to all the world. Peter himself had earlier denied membership in the "new faith" to non-Jews.

The second striking event recorded here is the descent of the Holy Spirit upon the unbaptized. Surely we are to learn from this that nothing can inhibit God's will to bestow grace and redemption upon every race and nation. Our theologians may speak in dogmatic tones about a "sacramental system," but the Spirit of God cannot be enclosed by it. Sometimes in our efforts to codify our faith, we can forget that God's love and mercy are beyond any code or system. If the accustomed order of things needs to be rearranged to shake us from our prejudice or narrow view of God's plan, rest assured that the Holy Spirit will intervene. And that's what happens here.

READING II This is the last of six consecutive Sundays on which we read from the First Letter of John. You may want to consult previous commentaries. One word characterizes this final selection, and sums up the entire letter: love. But something different from our immediate understanding of "love" is offered here. Yes, we know that the greatest commandment is to love. But what we perhaps tend to forget is how much we have *been loved*. That's what John wants to point out to us in the words, "Love, then, consists in this."

Christianity seems to tend toward an emphasis on "duty." Though we constantly use words like "grace" (which means "free"), we still are inclined to concentrate on what we must do to earn God's love (impossible, of course). John wants to straighten out our thinking here. The whole point of Jesus' life, death and resurrection

MAY 8, 1994

SIXTH SUNDAY OF EASTER

LECTIONARY #57

READING I   Acts 10:25–26, 34–35, 44–48

A reading from the *Acts* of the *Apostles* ▪ ▪

Cornelius = kawr-NEE-lee-uhs. This is a narrative—a little short story. Tell it as such, moving from one event to the next with renewed vocal energy.

Peter entered the house of *Cornelius* who *met* him, dropped to his *knees* before Peter and bowed *low*. ▪ Peter said as he helped him to his feet, ▪ "Get *up!* ▪ I am only a man *myself*." ▪ ▪

Peter proceeded to address [the *relatives* and *friends* of Cornelius] in these words: ▪ "I begin to see how *true* it *is* that *God* shows no *partiality*. ▪ Rather, the man of *any nation* who fears *God* and acts *uprightly* ▪ is *acceptable* to him." ▪ ▪

NRSV: "in every nation anyone who fears him and does what is right is acceptable to him."

The "circumcised" are the Jews. They begin to learn that God's loving plan of salvation is for the whole world.

Peter had not finished these words when the Holy *Spirit* descended upon all who were *listening* to Peter's *message*. ▪ The *circumcised* believers who had accompanied Peter were surprised that the gift of the Holy Spirit should have been poured out on the *Gentiles also*, whom they could hear speaking in *tongues* and glorifying *God*. ▪ Peter put the question at that point: ▪ "What can stop these people who have received the Holy *Spirit*, even as *we* have, from being baptized with *water?*" ▪ So he gave orders that they *be* baptized in the name of Jesus *Christ*. ▪ After *this* was *done*, they asked him to *stay* with them for a few days. ▪ ▪

Peter's question could be momentarily misunderstood and taken literally. It is a rhetorical question, as the NRSV translation makes clear: "Can anyone withhold the water for baptizing from these people?"

READING II   1 John 4:7–10

A reading from the first letter of *John* ▪ ▪

Be-lov-ed. Three syllables. As an "opener," it demands this pronunciation.

Beloved,
    let us *love* one another
    because love is of *God;* ▪
    everyone who loves is *begotten* of God
    and has *knowledge* of God. ▪

The message is tender and cosmic at the same time.

The man without *love* has known nothing of *God*, for God *is* love. ▪ ▪

NRSV: "Whoever does not love, does not know God."

God's love was *revealed* in our midst in *this* way: ▪

he sent his only *Son* to the world
that we might have *life* through him. ▪
Love, then, consists in *this*: ▪
not that *we* have loved *God*,
but that *he* has loved *us* ▪
and has sent his *Son* as an offering
for our *sins*. ▪ ▪

Here is an all-important lesson we have not yet learned fully. Proclaim it with all the vigor you can muster. God took the initiative in our regard!

GOSPEL   John 15:9–17

A reading from the holy *gospel* according to *John* ▪ ▪

The spirit of this reading is quiet and profound. Each phrase requires your total attention.

Jesus said to his disciples: ▪
"As the *Father* has loved *me*,
so *I* have loved *you*. ▪
Live *on* in my love. ▪
You *will* live in my love
if you keep my *commandments*,
even as *I* have kept my Father's *commandments*,
and live in *his* love. ▪

Stay fresh! Familiar expressions suffer most from predictable or off-hand treatment.

All this I tell you
that *my* joy may be *yours*
and *your* joy may be *complete*. ▪ ▪

Let this be a convincing explanation: "because I want you to be full of joy."

This is *my* commandment: ▪
love one another
as I have loved *you*. ▪

Here it is! In a sense, the only commandment.

There is no *greater* love than *this*: ▪
to lay down one's *life* for one's *friends*. ▪
You *are* my friends
if you *do* what I *command* you. ▪
I no longer speak of you as *slaves*,
for a slave does not know what his
    master is *about*. ▪

"His" could be "the."

Instead, I call you *friends*
since I have made *known* to you *all*
    that I heard from my *Father*. ▪

Another explanation: "because we share the Father's good news."

It was not *you* who chose *me*,
it was *I* who chose *you*
to go forth and bear *fruit*. ▪
Your fruit must *endure*,
so that *all* you ask the Father in *my* name
he will *give* you. ▪ ▪
The *command* I give you is *this*: ▪
that you *love* one another." ▪ ▪

In a nutshell. Now we know how to be Christians.

is *not* that we love God in return, but that God has loved us freely and given us the Son as redemption for our sins. The only real duty we have is to accept such overwhelming love. What could be easier?

In truth, nothing could be harder. Human nature has great difficulty in believing that complete love—no strings attached—is possible. There seems to be a trace of cynicism in all of us. "What's the catch?" we ask, revealing our stubborn conviction that "something for nothing" is impossible. Perhaps this inability to *believe fully* that we are *loved totally* accounts for our sinfulness. It keeps us from responding with a similar kind of unselfish love. Thus, we need to hear John's "theme song" over and over, until we get it: God has loved us! That's the point.

GOSPEL The theme of love is taken up again in this gospel passage. It seems important, however, to realize that the writer here has Jesus speaking of an event, an action on God's part, rather than a state of being or ongoing relationship. Yes, the enduring relationship between God and Jesus is included here, but the emphasis is on the great act of love that we call "the redemption," an event that took place at a point in human history—an event that has consequences.

The consequences are that we have been loved into a new existence. We are no longer slaves, but friends of God. There is no longer any question of what we must do in return: We must love one another. There is a kind of poetic logic at work here. We might put it this way: "Because the Father loved me, I loved you. And because I loved you (and proved it beyond any doubt by laying down my life for you), you must love one another. By loving one another, you keep my commandment."

The emphasis, as always in John, is on what has been done for us: God has loved us. The emphasis is not, as we so often seem to think, on what we must do. Duty-bound Christianity always seems to deteriorate into bargain-counter religion or score-keeping or concentration on sin. As there is only one commandment—to love one another—so there is only one sin—refusal to love one another.

READING I The speaker here is Luke. His first account is, of course, his gospel. And Theophilus (which translates "one who loves God") may not be a specific person, but any and all readers of good will. Announce this reading with "The beginning of the Acts of the Apostles," rather than in the usual way.

The point of this first section of the book of Acts is to show that God's plan to save us continues in one great sweep from the time of Jesus' ministry on earth, through his suffering and resurrection and ascension, and beyond. "Yes," Jesus says, "you will be my witnesses even to the ends of the earth." The good news of Jesus' victory on our behalf will radiate out from Jerusalem to Samaria and around the world.

And when will the rule of Israel be restored? The gentle answer is that only God knows. The question is asked in sincerity, but Jesus must point out that it is irrelevant. The business at hand is to get the word out that Jesus is truly the Messiah and the Reign of God upon earth has begun. When it will come to completion no one knows.

In effect, Luke teaches us here what a life of faith is. It is not a life of certainty, of knowing. It is a life of believing, and acting on what we believe. Thus, Jesus disappears from bodily view. Only in his physical separation from the historical scene can his spiritual union with all the world for all time be complete.

The angels' question brings the point home. "Why stand here looking up at the skies? Go now and tell the world all that Jesus did and taught."

READING II We have in this reading a celebration of the role of Christ in God's plan to save. It should be proclaimed with the highest energy and joy. The first paragraph is a greeting and a blessing and a prayer.

In the second paragraph we hear the writer celebrate the completion of Christ's earthly ministry and his return to the glory of God's right hand.

In the final paragraph we see Christ as ruler of the world, head of the church (his body). We also see the fullness of the believers who fill every corner of the universe. It is a victory hymn as we approach

THE ASCENSION OF THE LORD

LECTIONARY #59

READING I   Acts 1:1–11

Notice: "The beginning of the Acts of the Apostles."

Theophilus = thee-AH-fih-luhs

The narrative begins with a sweeping summary. Let your delivery be broad and expansive.

The story of the ascension begins here. Prepare for it with a pause, then resume with a new tone of voice.

Pause slightly after the apostles' question—to give weight to Jesus' response.

Ask the angels' question simply. Avoid any tone of reprimand.

The beginning of the *Acts* of the *Apostles* ▪ ▪

In my *first* account, Theophilus, I dealt with all that Jesus *did* and *taught* until the day he was taken up to *heaven*, having first instructed the *apostles* he had chosen through the Holy *Spirit*. ▪ In the time after his *suffering* he showed them in *many* convincing ways that he was *alive*, appearing to them over the course of *forty days* and *speaking* to them about the reign of *God*. ▪ On *one* occasion when he met with them, he *told* them *not* to leave Jerusalem: ▪ "Wait, rather, for the fulfillment of my Father's *promise*, of which you have heard me *speak*. ▪ John baptized with *water*, but within a few days *you* will be baptized with the Holy *Spirit*." ▪

While they were *with* him they asked, ▪ "Lord, are you going to restore the *rule* to *Israel* now?" ▪ His answer was: ▪ "The exact *time* it is not yours to *know*. ▪ The Father has reserved that to *himself*. ▪ You will receive *power* when the Holy *Spirit* comes down on you; ▪ *then* you are to be my *witnesses* in Jerusalem, throughout Judea and Samaria, *yes*, even to the ends of the *earth*." ▪ No sooner had he *said* this ▪ than he was lifted *up* before their *eyes* in a *cloud* which took him from their *sight*. ▪

They were still gazing up into the *heavens* when two *men* dressed in *white* stood *beside* them. ▪ "Men of Galilee," they said, ▪ "why do you stand here looking up at the *skies*? ▪ This *Jesus* who has been *taken* from you will *return*, just as you saw him *go up* into the heavens." ▪ ▪

A reading from the letter of *Paul* to the *Ephesians* ▪ ▪

The first paragraph is two sentences in the subjunctive mood ("May the God . . . ," "May he enlighten . . .") and the second is very long. Read slowly, deliberately, and divide the text into sense units. Let your tone be bright and warm.

May the God of our Lord Jesus Christ, the Father of *glory*, grant you a spirit of wisdom and insight to *know* him *clearly*. ▪ May he enlighten your innermost *vision* that you may *know* the great *hope* to which he has called you, the *wealth* of his glorious *heritage* to be distributed among the members of the church, ▪ and the immeasurable *scope* of his *power* in us who believe. ▪ It is like the *strength* he showed in raising Christ from the *dead* and seating him at his right hand in *heaven*, high *above* every principality, power, virtue, and domination, and every name that can be *given* in *this* age or the age to come. ▪

Another long sentence. Pause between sense units.

He has put *all* things under Christ's *feet* and has *made* him thus *exalted, head* of the *church,* which is his *body:* ▪ the fullness of him who fills the universe in all its *parts.* ▪ ▪

After the colon (:), read the concluding words broadly and with a note of triumph.

GOSPEL   Mark 16:15–20

The *conclusion* of the holy *gospel* according to *Mark* ▪ ▪

Notice: "The conclusion of the holy gospel according to Mark."

[Jesus appeared to the Eleven and] said to them: ▪ "Go into the whole *world* and *proclaim* the good news to all *creation*. ▪ The man who *believes* in it and accepts *baptism* will be *saved;* ▪ the man who *refuses* to believe in it will be *condemned*. ▪ Signs like *these* will accompany those who have professed their faith: ▪ they will use my name to expel *demons*, they will speak *entirely* new *languages*, they will be able to handle *serpents*, they will be able to drink deadly *poison* without *harm*, ▪ and the sick upon whom they lay their *hands* will *recover*." ▪ ▪ Then, after *speaking* to them, the Lord Jesus was taken up into *heaven* and took his seat at God's right *hand*. ▪ The *Eleven* went forth and preached *everywhere*. ▪ The Lord continued to *work* with them *throughout* and *confirm* the message through the signs which *accompanied* them. ▪ ▪

NRSV: "The one who believes and is baptized will be saved; but the one who does not believe will be condemned." Not only more inclusive, but more straightforward.

Do not run the list of "signs" together. Let each one be heard.

Significant pause before "Then."

Very high energy level here— and through to the end.

the end of the Easter Season: "The strife is o'er, the battle done."

Anything less than a powerful declamation of this beautiful text will not do it justice.

GOSPEL   Notice that the announcement of the reading is different today: "The *conclusion* of the holy gospel according to Mark. Today's gospel is taken from what is called, in the *New Revised Standard Version* of the Bible, "The Longer Ending of Mark." The original form of Mark's gospel almost certainly ended at the empty tomb. The fact that a longer ending was added early in Christian history simply bears witness to the ancient teaching that Jesus ascended to God's right hand after his resurrection. It is useless, and beside the point, to argue about when the ascension occurred or whether it took place in a dramatic and literal way. The Eastern mentality confuses us Westerners again, because of our need or inclination to impose literal meanings on everything. Even the "forty days" between the resurrection and the ascension (mentioned in Acts) is a symbolic number of perfection or fullness.

The ascension means that Christians have always believed that Jesus, having completed his earthly mission, returned to God, from whom he was sent, and now takes up his continuing role as priest, prophet and king. That is the meaning of the words: "took his seat at God's right hand." There is no implication that Jesus is no longer present in the world or is inactive. We believe quite the opposite. Jesus has not gone to a specific place; rather, he has taken on the role of intermediary in a new way.

The emphasis on the mission of the Eleven at the conclusion of the reading further demonstrates the continuing activity of the Risen Christ. There is great comfort and confirmation in the evidence that the Lord manifests himself through the work of the apostles.

Clearly, we are approaching the end of the Easter season and are reaching the fullness of Pentecost (Pentecost means "fifty days"). Ten days hence we will celebrate the coming of the Holy Spirit—the ultimate and enduring manifestation of the Risen Lord's presence in the world.

READING I During these weeks after Easter we have been reading from various sections of the Acts of the Apostles. Now we return to the beginning section, in which the author, Luke, is intent on bringing the apostolic band back to its original complement of twelve. Judas Iscariot abandoned his calling. His position had to be assigned to another—and it had to be someone who had witnessed the resurrection, for bearing the good news will be the primary duty of the apostles henceforth.

Why must the Eleven be restored to the Twelve? One reason given by the author is that the words of scripture must be fulfilled, and he quotes a relevant passage from the Psalms to demonstrate this objective. Another reason may not be so obvious to the casual reader: the new faith in Christ is the fulfillment of the older faith of Israel. And the full complement of Israel is composed of the twelve tribes. Symbolically, then, the original twelve chosen by Jesus represent the "new" Israel and the completion of God's plan for the Chosen People. They were primarily a symbol of Israel, brought back in fullness and in accord with God's promise of restoration.

Later, of course, the Twelve were seen as the earliest missionaries, charged with the duty to spread the news of Jesus throughout the world. In this work they were joined by many others—for example, the "further seventy-two" we hear commissioned elsewhere in scripture. The "apostolic band" must be understood in two ways, then: as the original Twelve chosen by Jesus as a sign of the restored twelve tribes of Israel, and as a host of early missionaries.

READING II A theme very common in John is that of "mutual indwelling." It describes a relationship by which God lives in us and we live within God. It is a relationship that is seen between God and Jesus, first of all, but one in which we can participate by accepting the love of God and then showing that acceptance in our love for one another.

Particularly fascinating in this text is the way John anticipates our need for proof or evidence. Yes, he acknowledges that God is invisible to the human eye, but there is still evidence of the divine presence. That evidence is our love for one another. It is the guarantee that we are

SEVENTH SUNDAY OF EASTER

LECTIONARY #61

READING I   Acts 1:15–17, 20–26

A reading from the *Acts* of the *Apostles* ▪ ▪

Except for the first and last sentences, the reading is in Peter's words. He is explaining, so let your tone be explanatory. The NRSV uses "believers" instead of "brothers." And Peter's greeting is "friends" rather than "brothers."

In those days Peter stood up in the midst of the brothers—there must have been a hundred and twenty gathered together. ▪ "Brothers," he said, ▪ "the saying in Scripture uttered long ago by the Holy *Spirit* through the mouth of *David* ▪ was destined to be *fulfilled* in *Judas*, the one that *guided* those who arrested *Jesus*. ▪ He was one of *our* number and he had been given a *share* in this *ministry* of ours. ▪ ▪

"It is written in the Book of Psalms, ▪
'May *another* take his *office*.' ▪

Explain the situation carefully.

"It is entirely *fitting*, therefore, that one of those who was of our company while the Lord *Jesus* moved *among* us, from the baptism of *John* until the day he was taken *up* from us, should be named as *witness* with us to his *resurrection*." ▪ At that they nominated *two*, Joseph (called Barsabbas, also known as Justus) and Matthias. ▪ Then they prayed: ▪ "O Lord, you read the hearts of men. ▪ Make *known* to us which of these two you choose for this apostolic *ministry*, replacing *Judas*, who *deserted* the cause and went the way he was *destined* to go." ▪ They then drew *lots* between the two men. ▪ The choice fell to *Matthias*, who was added to the eleven apostles. ▪ ▪

*Barsabbas = BAHR-suh-buhs
Justus = DZHUHS-tuhs
Matthias = muh-THAI-uhs
NRSV: "Lord, you know everyone's heart."*

The resolution of the situation. Let the sound of closure be clear.

A reading from the first letter of *John* ▪ ▪

"Beloved" (be-lov-ed) should be three syllables here (not be-loved).

Beloved, ▪
  if God has loved *us* so,
  we must have the *same* love for one *another*. ▪
No one has ever *seen God.* ▪
Yet if we *love* one another
  God *dwells* in us,
  and his love is brought to *perfection* in us. ▪

This text is best rendered by letting each sentence stand as an aphorism, a kernel of truth.

The way we *know* we remain in him
  and he in *us*
  is that he has given us of his *Spirit.* ▪
We have seen for ourselves, and can testify,
  that the Father has *sent* the Son as *savior*
    of the world. ▪

NRSV: "God abides in those who confess that Jesus is the Son of God, and they abide in God."

When anyone *acknowledges* that Jesus is
    the Son of God,
  God *dwells* in him
  and he in *God.* ▪
We have come to *know* and to *believe*
  in the love God *has* for us. ▪

Proclaim this lovingly. It is a much loved text. NRSV: "God is love, and those who abide in love abide in God, and God abides in them."

God *is* love,
  and he who abides in *love*
  abides in God,
  and God in *him.* ▪ ▪

dwelling in God and God is dwelling in us. Simple logic makes it clear, too, that if we do not love one another, we forego the life of God within ourselves.

John is eager to assure us here. He offers himself as an eyewitness to the great act of love by which God sent Jesus to save the world. "Believe me," he says, "I can testify to this greatest of all events, and those who acknowledge it have already begun to share in the life of God."

Finally, we get the message in the simplest of terms: "God is love." But we must not be too philosophical in our understanding of this most popular Christian truth. "Love" can be a pretty slippery term, and it would be a mistake (often made) to equate love with God in some simplistic, romantic way. John makes it clear earlier in this passage that God is love in a particular way: God is that *great act of love* that gave Jesus as redeemer of the world.

GOSPEL   In all the readings today there is a "gathering of forces" in preparation for launching the great missionary endeavor of the Christian church. In the first reading, the full complement of apostles is restored. In the second reading, we are reminded of the intimate relationship we have with God and the Spirit, the relationship which is the proof and the source of our missionary effort. In this gospel passage, Jesus prays the great prayer that is clearly a commission as well.

All three readings explain something of the adventure involved in being a Christian, something of the power of love at our disposal. And they explain quite a lot about the guarantee of our success.

The language here (as is often the case in John) is not particularly easy. It is exalted and poetic, the language of formal but urgent prayer. The earliest cue for this tone is "Father most holy," an unusually formal mode of address, and very different from "Abba," which is quite intimate and warm. The solemnity of the occasion accounts for the solemnity of Jesus' tone.

"Protect them with your name. . . ." We must remember that the "name" and the "person named" are practically inseparable in scripture. Jesus is asking for the most intimate and powerful kind of protection for his disciples. He also prays for the kind of unity among them that he shares with God his Father. The implication is that the oneness between Jesus and God is the *source* of the unity among the disciples.

"That they may share my joy. . . ." The joy comes from reliance on God's promises, that beyond suffering and death lies the sure hope of resurrection. Beyond the difficulties and dangers of missionary involvement lies the inevitability of God's kingdom becoming established throughout the world. God's will and his call are irrevocable. To know this is to possess invincible joy.

"Not one of them was lost. . . ." We are reminded of the possibility—perhaps even the inevitability—of danger involved in discipleship. Under the watchful love of Jesus, no danger befell the disciples. The recognition that the world will not always be eager for the Christian message is important for us to hear. A message of love is not always welcomed, for the challenge underlying it can be quite threatening. It always means conversion, and conversion is difficult.

"I consecrate myself. . . ." Jesus' total consecration of himself through death is the fundamental consecration of all who are united with him. It is also their guarantee of ultimate joy in sharing his resurrection.

A reading from the holy *gospel* according to *John* ▪▪

Simplicity and strength are the most effective qualities to communicate in this prayer of Jesus.

The "name" is identical to the power and the person of God.

Pause. The tone becomes more urgent perhaps.

Pause. This sentence stands out from the rest.

The final sentence is perfectly balanced; the two pairs of assertions should be accented carefully so the balance is felt.

Jesus looked up to heaven and prayed: ▪
   "O Father most holy, ▪
   protect them with your *name* which you
      have *given* me, ▪
   [that they may be *one*, even as *we* are one.] ▪
   As long as I was *with* them,
   I *guarded* them with your name which you
      gave me. ▪
   I kept careful *watch*,
   and not *one* of them was lost,
   none but him who was *destined* to be lost—
   in fulfillment of *Scripture*. ▪
   Now, however, I *come* to you; ▪
   I say all this while I am still in the *world*
   that they may *share* my joy *completely*. ▪
   I gave them your *word*,
   and the world has *hated* them for it; ▪
   they do not belong to the *world*,
   [any more than *I* belong to the world.] ▪▪
   I do not ask you to take them *out* of the world,
   but to *guard* them from the *evil* one. ▪
   They are not *of* the world,
   any more than *I* am of the world. ▪
   Consecrate them by means of *truth*— ▪
   'Your *word* is truth.' ▪
   As you have sent *me* into the world,
   so I have sent *them* into the world; ▪
   I consecrate myself for *their* sakes now,
   that *they* may be consecrated in *truth*." ▪▪

PENTECOST VIGIL

LECTIONARY #63

READING I   Genesis 11:1–9

This short story makes the point that God is responsible for all that happens. Tell the story simply.

NRSV: "And as they migrated from the east."

Shinar = SHAI-nahr

A reading from the book of *Genesis* ▪▪

At that time the whole world spoke the same *language*, using the same *words*. ▪ While men were migrating in the east, they came upon a *valley* in the land of Shinar and *settled* there. ▪ They said to one another, ▪ *"Come,* let us mold *bricks* and harden them with *fire."* ▪ They used bricks for *stone,* and bitumen for *mortar.* ▪ Then they said, ▪ *"Come,* let us build ourselves a *city* and a *tower* with its top in the *sky,* and so make a *name* for ourselves; ▪ otherwise we shall be scattered all over the *earth."* ▪▪

NRSV: "The Lord came down to see the city and the tower, which mortals had built."

The *Lord* came down to see the city and the tower that the men had built. ▪ Then the Lord said: ▪ "If now, while they are one people, all speaking the same *language,* they have started to do *this,* nothing will later stop them from doing whatever they *presume* to do. ▪ Let us then go *down* and there *confuse* their language, so that one will not understand what another *says."* ▪ Thus the Lord *scattered* them from there all over the *earth,* and they stopped *building* the city. ▪

Babel = BAY-b'l (or BAB-b'l)

That is why it was called *Babel,* because there the Lord confused the *speech* of all the *world.* ▪ It was from *that* place that he *scattered* them all over the *earth.* ▪▪

READING I   Exodus 19:3–8, 16–20

This is the first part of the story of the giving of the Ten Commandments. It is quite a spectacle. Give the text your best storytelling effort, but avoid anything like mimicry of the thunder and trumpet b!ast. Proclaim the text; do not reenact it.

A reading from the book of *Exodus* ▪▪

Moses went up the mountain to God. ▪ Then the Lord called to him and said, ▪ "Thus shall you say to the house of *Jacob;* tell the Israelites: ▪ You have seen for yourselves how I treated the *Egyptians* and how I bore you up on *eagle* wings and brought you here to *myself.* ▪ Therefore, if you hearken to my *voice* and keep my *covenant,* ▪ you shall be my special

READING I (Genesis) The story of the Tower of Babel is one of the options for the vigil celebration because it is alluded to in the first reading (Acts 2:1–11) of tomorrow's feast. Whereas the sin of pride in those who built the tower is punished by an angry God who "confuses their language," the linguistic divisions among peoples are bridged by the unifying power of the Spirit in the fire of Pentecost.

In this story from Genesis we see a traditional explanation for the many different tongues spoken by the peoples of the earth. In the story from Acts we see a traditional explanation for the universal spread of the gospel. It helps us understand the "jealousy" of God in the Genesis reading when we realize that the people defied God's command to scatter and settle each in their respective homelands. It is their disobedience that brings on their punishment. It is their willful pride that creates division among them.

Read this story with all the gusto of a good storyteller. It is the classic fable: constructed for our benefit to teach us a moral lesson.

> There is a choice of first readings today. Check with the lector chairperson or a parish staff member to see which one you should read.

READING I (Exodus) The second option for today's first reading contains the same kind of theophany (marvelous demonstration of God's power) that we find in the Pentecost story in Acts: smoke, cloud, fire, the roar like thunder. It is another instance of the revelation of God's power on behalf of the people (though terrifying in its force).

In this reading we encounter the awesome occasion on which the law is given to the people through Moses. The chapter following the one from which this reading is taken lists the Ten Commandments. The parallels between the giving of the Law and the coming of the Spirit are not difficult to see, nor are the differences between the two events.

In both instances the people are brought together into a covenant relationship with God. And both events are characterized by the "marvels" of divine power. In the first, the fundamental laws by which the Israelites will live are entrusted to them. In the second, the power to preach the gospel to every nation is entrusted to an assembly made up of peoples from many parts of the world.

Thus the point is made: The news of the new covenant will not be limited to one chosen people but will spread to every corner of the earth.

READING I (Ezekiel) The third option for today's first reading is the justly famous story of the Valley of the Dry Bones. It is filled with dramatic tension and marvelous imagery. Ezekiel foresees the day (the final day) when the spirit of the Lord will revive the people and will breathe into them the new life for which they now long so poignantly.

That day comes, in a new and unforeseen way, on the feast of Pentecost. The Lord's promise to place a new spirit within the people takes on a whole new meaning in the marvelous event described in the first reading for tomorrow's feast (Acts 2:1–11). Ezekiel foresaw the fulfillment of God's promises at the end of time. The Pentecost event in Acts sees the fulfillment of that promise and the inauguration of that end-time even now!

The very familiarity of this wonderful story is part of its charm. Master every element of suspense, awe, climax and resolution so that the assembly will hear it anew.

The final sentence is anticlimactic. Consider omitting it here.

possession, dearer to me than all *other* people, though all the *earth* is *mine.* • *You* shall be to me a kingdom of *priests,* a *holy* nation. • That is what you must tell the *Israelites."* • So Moses went and summoned the *elders* of the people. • When he set before them all that the Lord had *ordered* him to tell them, the people all answered *together,* "Everything the Lord has *said,* we will *do."* • •

On the morning of the third day there were peals of *thunder* and *lightning,* and a heavy *cloud* over the mountain, • and a very loud *trumpet blast,* so that all the people in the camp *trembled.* • But Moses led the people *out* of the camp to meet *God,* and they stationed themselves at the *foot* of the mountain. • Mount *Sinai* was all wrapped in *smoke,* for the Lord came down upon it in *fire.* • The smoke rose from it as though from a *furnace,* and the whole *mountain* trembled *violently.* • The *trumpet blast* grew louder and *louder,* while Moses was speaking and God *answering* him with thunder. • •

When the *Lord* came down to the top of Mount *Sinai,* he summoned *Moses* to the top of the mountain. • •

READING I Ezekiel 37:1–14

A reading from the book of the prophet *Ezekiel* • •

The story of the "Valley of the Dry Bones" has always captured imaginations. Do the story justice by reading it with all the vocal variation necessary. It is written in the first person ("I"); this should help you.

The *hand* of the *Lord* came upon me, • and he led me *out* in the *spirit* of the *Lord* and set me in the center of the *plain* which was now filled with *bones.* • He made me walk among them in every *direction* so that I saw how *many* they were on the surface of the *plain.* • How *dry* they were! • He asked me: • Son of man, • can these bones come to *life?* • "Lord God," I answered, • "you *alone* know *that."* • Then he said to me: • *Prophesy* over these bones, and say to them: • Dry bones, • hear the word of the *Lord!* • Thus says the Lord *God* to these bones: • *See!* • I will bring *spirit* into you, that you may come to *life.* • I will put *sinews* upon you, make *flesh* grow over you, cover you with *skin,* and put *spirit* in you so that you may come to *life* and know that *I* am the *Lord.* • • I prophesied as I had been *told,* • and even as I was prophesying I heard a *noise;* • it was a rattling as the bones came *together*, bone joining *bone*. ▪ I saw the *sinews* and the *flesh* come upon them, and the *skin* cover them, but there was no *spirit* in them. ▪ Then he said to me: ▪ Prophesy to the *spirit*, *prophesy*, son of man, and say to the spirit: ▪ Thus says the Lord *God:* ▪ From the four winds *come*, O spirit, and breathe into these slain that they may come to *life*. ▪ I prophesied as he told me, ▪ and the spirit came *into* them; ▪ they came *alive* and stood upright, a vast *army*. ▪ Then he said to me: ▪ Son of man, ▪ these bones are the whole house of *Israel*. ▪ They have been saying, ▪ "Our bones are dried *up*, our hope is *lost*, and we are cut *off*." ▪ Therefore, prophesy and say to them: ▪ Thus says the Lord God: ▪ O my people, ▪ I will open your *graves* and have you *rise* from them, ▪ and bring you back to the land of *Israel*. ▪ Then you shall know that *I* am the Lord, ▪ when I open your *graves* and have you *rise* from them, O my people! ▪ I will put my *spirit* in you that you may *live*; ▪ and I will settle you upon your *land*; ▪ thus you shall know that *I* am the *Lord*. ▪ I have *promised*, ▪ and I will *do* it, says the Lord. ▪ ▪

The last few lines are the Lord's words. Do not be afraid to give the repeated "O my people" the grandeur it deserves.

READING I   Joel 2:28–32

A reading from the book of the prophet *Joel* ▪ ▪

A solemn proclamation in the mouth of the Lord God. Let it ring with solemnity and power. NRSV: "all flesh."

To render these two venerable lines more inclusively, take the simplest approach: "Your old shall dream dreams, your young shall see visions."

Thus says the Lord: ▪
I will pour out
   my *spirit* upon all mankind. ▪
Your sons and daughters shall *prophesy*, ▪
   your old men shall dream *dreams*,
   your young men shall see *visions*; ▪
Even upon the *servants* and the *handmaids*,
   in those days, I will pour out my *spirit*. ▪
And I will work *wonders* in the heavens and
     on the earth, ▪
   blood, ▪ *fire*, ▪ and columns of *smoke*; ▪
The sun will be turned to *darkness*,
   and the moon to *blood*,
At the coming of the *Day of the Lord*,
   the great and *terrible* day. ▪ ▪
Then everyone shall be *rescued*
   who calls on the name of the *Lord*; ▪
For on Mount *Zion* there shall be a *remnant*,
   as the *Lord* has said,
And in *Jerusalem* survivors
   whom the *Lord* shall call. ▪ ▪

READING I (Joel) Here, in this fourth option for the first reading, we see the same kind of theophany (marvelous demonstration of God's power) presented in the story of Pentecost related in the first reading of tomorrow's feast (Acts 2:1–11). There is fire and smoke and the outpouring of God's spirit.

It is a description of the end of Israel's suffering and degradation, a time when all the people (not just the great prophets and chosen leaders) will be filled with a portion of the Lord's spirit.

The same kind of event takes place at Pentecost, but the circle widens even more: All the world, people of every race and tongue, will receive that spirit and speak of the marvels God has accomplished.

READING II This selection from Paul's letter to the Romans is striking in its vivid portrayal of our present spiritual condition. Anyone who has felt efforts at prayer to be a bumbling, awkward experience should take great comfort in these words: "The Spirit too helps us in our weakness, for we do not know how to pray as we ought."

The most striking thing about this passage, however, is the enormous dignity that Paul accords hopeful believers. The Spirit, which has come to dwell in us, gives our efforts, our suffering, our weakness the same nobility that we see in the sufferings of Christ.

We should not regret the fact that we must live in hope, subject to all the miseries of the flesh. How can it be otherwise? Is it possible to hope for something we already have? No. We hope for what we cannot see and we do so in patient endurance—the same patient endurance we see in Jesus. It is the Spirit dwelling within us that ennobles our hope.

GOSPEL The festival referred to here is the great Feast of Tabernacles, which included a ceremonial drawing of water and scripture readings that foretold the great day of restoration—when "You will draw water joyfully from the springs of salvation" (Isaiah 12:3). We sang this very text at the Easter Vigil. Jesus may have been inspired to cry out his dramatic invitation in response to these words. He surely is the spring of salvation.

The parenthetical comment by John equates the "living water" with the outpouring of the Holy Spirit at Pentecost which, of course, occurred after Jesus' resurrection and ascension. Remember, too, that John records that water and blood poured from Jesus' side when the Roman soldier pierced him with a lance at the crucifixion.

John sees the connection between Jesus' cry and all the coming events through hindsight as he records the life of Jesus, and he makes the central point that it is the sacrificial death of Jesus that makes the Spirit's coming possible.

READING II   Romans 8:22–27

A lovely and comforting text. Notice that it begins with "we," giving you, the reader, immediate identification with your hearers. Make the most of Paul's rhetorical devices here: "Not only that," "But hope is not hope," "how is it possible . . . !"

Read the second paragraph very slowly. The thought is complex.

A reading from the letter of *Paul* to the *Romans* ▪▪

We know that *all creation* groans and is in *agony* even until *now*. ▪ Not only *that*, but we ourselves, although we have the Spirit as first fruits, groan *inwardly* while we await the redemption of our *bodies*. ▪ In *hope* we were *saved*. ▪ But hope is *not* hope if its object is *seen;* ▪ how is it *possible* for one to *hope* for what he *sees?* ▪ And hoping for what we *cannot* see means awaiting it with patient *endurance*. ▪

The Spirit *too* helps us in our *weakness*, ▪ for we do not *know* how to pray as we ought; ▪ but the Spirit *himself* makes intercession for us with groanings which cannot be expressed in *speech*. ▪ He who searches *hearts* knows what the Spirit *means*, ▪ for the Spirit *intercedes* for the saints ▪ as God *himself* wills. ▪▪

GOSPEL   John 7:37–39

A brief gospel reading that makes up in power what it lacks in length. There should be a very clear contrast between Jesus' words and John's parenthetical comment.

NRSV: "Let anyone who is thirsty come to me, and let the one who believes in me drink. As the scripture has said, 'Out of the believer's heart shall flow rivers of living water.'"

A reading from the holy *gospel* according to *John* ▪▪

On the last and greatest day of the *festival*, Jesus stood up and cried *out:* ▪
"If anyone *thirsts*, let him come to *me;* ▪
Let him *drink* who believes in *me*. ▪
Scripture has it: ▪
'From *within* him rivers of living *water* shall flow.'" ▪

(Here he was referring to the *Spirit*, whom those that came to *believe* in him were to *receive*. ▪ There was, of course, ▪ no Spirit as *yet*, ▪ since Jesus had not yet been *glorified*.) ▪▪

PENTECOST

LECTIONARY #64

READING I   Acts 2:1–11

A reading from the *Acts* of the *Apostles* ▪ ▪

A very dramatic narrative. It will require your best efforts to convey the awe and delight of those who witnessed this event.

All these signs of God's power appear in the Hebrew scriptures. They are familiar, yet never fail to startle us.

When the day of *Pentecost* came it found the brethren gathered in one *place.* ▪ Suddenly from up in the *sky* there came a noise like a *strong, driving wind* which was heard all through the *house* where they were *seated.* ▪ Tongues as of *fire* appeared which parted and came to *rest* on *each* of them. ▪ All were filled with the Holy *Spirit.* ▪ They began to express themselves in foreign *tongues* and make bold proclamation as the Spirit *prompted* them. ▪ ▪

This paragraph makes the point that the Spirit's aim is to reach "every nation under heaven."

"His" can be "his or her."

Galileans = gal-ih-LEE-uhnz
Parthians = PAHR-thee-uhnz
Medes = meeds
Elamites = EE-luh-maits
Mesopotamia = mehs-o-po-TAY-mih-uh
Judea = dzhoo-DEE-uh
Cappadocia = kap-ih-DO-shee-uh
Pontus = PAHN-tuhs
Phrygia = FRIH-dzhih-uh
Pamphylia = pam-FIHL-ih-uh
Libya = LIH-bih-uh
Cyrene = sai-REE-nee
Cretans = KREE-tihnz
Arabs = EHR-uhbz (not AY-rabz!)

Staying in Jerusalem at the time were devout *Jews* of every nation under *heaven.* ▪ *These* heard the sound, and assembled in a large *crowd.* ▪ They were *much* confused because each one heard these men speaking his own *language.* ▪ The whole occurrence *astonished* them. ▪ They asked in utter *amazement,* ▪ "Are not all of these men who are speaking *Galileans?* ▪ How is it that each of us hears them in his native *tongue?* ▪ We are Parthians, Medes, and Elamites. ▪ We live in Mesopotamia, Judea, and Cappadocia, ▪ Pontus, the province of Asia, Phrygia and Pamphylia, ▪ Egypt, and the regions of Libya around Cyrene. ▪ There are even visitors from Rome—*all Jews,* or those who have come *over* to Judaism; ▪ Cretans and Arabs too. ▪ Yet each of us hears them speaking in his *own* tongue about the marvels *God* has accomplished." ▪ ▪

READING I   Remember the story of the Tower of Babel in the book of Genesis? Today's reading from Acts reverses the situation. Whereas the people who built the Tower (in prideful disobedience) had their one language split into many, the people who experience the coming of the Spirit hear their many languages made intelligible to all. The point is clear: The coming of the Holy Spirit is a unifying force that binds all peoples together.

When did this marvelous event take place? In this reading it is on the Jewish feast of Pentecost (when Jewish tradition had come to commemorate the giving of the Law on Mount Sinai—also accompanied by wind and fire). In today's gospel reading, John places the event when the resurrected Jesus first appears to his sequestered disciples. The writers of scripture have their reasons for situating the occurrence at different times. In any case, the coming of the Spirit cannot be limited to any particular moment in history. It is a constant and dynamic reality.

And most important are the consequences of that reality. The God who gave the Law now gives the Divine Spirit, the very "self" of God. And that Spirit is given not only to a chosen few—it fills the entire world.

READING II   To understand this reading, we must realize that Paul is addressing a community that struggled mightily with disagreeing factions and divided loyalties. Paul's intent here is to encourage them to unify themselves under the one true Lord, Jesus the Christ.

Any squabbling over who has the greatest gift from the Spirit makes no sense at all for Christians. All true gifts come from the one God, and the test of their authenticity is the degree to which they build up the common good and bring different peoples together in unity of belief.

The matter of speaking in tongues led the Corinthians to rank themselves inappropriately. Speaking in tongues is a gift; those who do not receive it have no doubt received a different gift, perhaps less spectacular, but certainly no less important for the community. The one Spirit has filled all of us.

GOSPEL In this brief passage the Holy Spirit has been given to the disciples, and the progression of the Easter celebration comes full circle. With the bestowal of the Holy Spirit, the work of Jesus is complete. The disciples are now empowered to continue the work of redemption in full awareness of the presence of Christ.

Perhaps the most immediately fascinating part of this reading is John's painstaking eagerness to let us know that the Jesus who appears to his disciples is no mere mortal. The doors of the place were locked, yet Jesus comes before them. He is not a spirit, for he shows the disciples his hands and his side. But his body clearly has a composition different from our own—John's way of noting Jesus' new mode of existence.

Then comes quite an understatement! "At the sight of the Lord the disciples rejoiced." As reader, you will have to make more of this than what the simple words carry on their own. Let your voice and demeanor be joyful.

Finally, the giving of the Holy Spirit. The power to forgive sins or to hold them bound is most clearly a commission to spread the news of Jesus and to bring all people to belief through baptism. Baptism is the great sign of the forgiveness of sin and the incorporation into the fold of Christ. Jesus' mission is accomplished, but his work of redemption continues through those he sends forth in the power of the Spirit.

READING II 1 Corinthians 12:3–7, 12–13

A reading from the first letter of *Paul* to the *Corinthians* ▪ ▪

Be sure the assembly is settled and ready before you begin. The first sentence is crucial. The very effective structure should be stressed: "There are . . . but . . . ; there are . . . but . . . ; there are . . . ; but. . . ."

No one can say: "Jesus is *Lord*," ▪ except in the Holy *Spirit*. ▪

There are different *gifts*, but the same *Spirit*; ▪ there are *different* ministries but the *same* Lord; ▪ there are different *works* but the same *God* who accomplishes all of them in *every one*. ▪ To each person the manifestation of the Spirit is given for the common *good*. ▪ ▪

Take special care—and plenty of time—to read this paragraph. It is complex and rich with meaning.

The body is *one* and has many *members*, ▪ but all the members, *many* though they *are*, are one *body*; ▪ and so it is with *Christ*. ▪ It was in one *Spirit* that all of *us*, whether Jew or Greek, slave or free, were baptized into one *body*. ▪ *All* of us have been given to drink of the one *Spirit*. ▪ ▪

GOSPEL John 20:19–23

A reading from the holy *gospel* according to *John* ▪ ▪

A brief gospel; therefore proclaimed with extra care and breadth.

Emphasize "Peace" each time—not "with."

On the evening of that first day of the week, even though the disciples had locked the *doors* of the place where they were for fear of the *Jews*, ▪ Jesus came and stood *before* them. ▪ ▪ "*Peace* be with you," he said. ▪

When he had said this, he showed them his *hands* and his *side*. ▪ At the sight of the *Lord* the disciples *rejoiced*. ▪ "*Peace* be with you," he said *again*. ▪

A divine commission. Let it ring in the assembly's ears, not with volume but with intensity.

"As the Father has sent *me*,
so I send *you*." ▪
Then he *breathed* on them and said: ▪
"Receive the Holy *Spirit*.

NRSV: "If you forgive sins, they are forgiven."

If you *forgive* men's sins, ▪
they are *forgiven* them; ▪
if you hold them *bound*, ▪
they are held *bound*." ▪ ▪

TRINITY SUNDAY

LECTIONARY #166

READING I   Deuteronomy 4:32–34, 39–40

A reading from the book of *Deuteronomy* ▪▪

This is a wonderful text, full of exaltation and confidence. More than half of it is made up of rhetorical questions. Ask them vigorously! NRSV: "human beings" instead of "man."

This very long question does not sound like a question at the end. The question mark should be "heard" after the word "terrors." Then the remainder is more like a statement.

Pause. The questions have been leading up to this point— which must be made strongly and clearly.

Moses said to the people: ▪ *"Ask* now of the days of *old*, before your time, ever since God *created* man upon the earth: ▪ *ask* from *one* end of the sky to the *other:* ▪ Did anything so great ever *happen* before? ▪ Was it ever *heard* of? ▪ Did a people ever hear the voice of *God* speaking from the midst of *fire,* as *you* did, ▪ and *live?* ▪ Or did any *god* venture to go and take a *nation* for himself from the midst of *another* nation, by testings, by signs and wonders, by war, with his strong hand and outstretched arm, and by great *terrors, all* of which the *Lord, your* God, did for *you* in *Egypt* before your very *eyes?* ▪ *This* is why you must *now* know, and *fix* in your heart, ▪ that the *Lord* is God in the heavens *above* and on earth *below*, and that there is no *other.* ▪ You must keep his *statutes* and *commandments* which I enjoin on you today that you and your children *after* you may *prosper*, and that you may have *long life* on the *land* which the Lord, your God, is *giving* you *forever."* ▪▪

READING II   Romans 8:14–17

A reading from the letter of *Paul* to the *Romans* ▪▪

This is one of Paul's poetic proclamations. Make it big. Instead of "sons," say "children."

"Abba" is a very tender and intimate title.

A series of short phrases— adding up to a profound truth.

All who are led by the *Spirit* of God are *sons* of God. ▪ You did not receive a spirit of *slavery* leading you back into *fear,* but a spirit of *adoption* through which we cry out, ▪ *"Abba!"* (that is, "Father"). ▪ The Spirit himself gives *witness* with *our* spirit that we *are* children of God. ▪ But if we are *children,* we are *heirs* as *well:* ▪ heirs of *God,* heirs with *Christ,* if only we *suffer* with him so as to be *glorified* with him. ▪▪

READING I   The doctrine of the Holy Trinity (one God in three persons: Creator, Redeemer, Holy Spirit) is not expounded in any direct way in scripture. It is an implication drawn from the ways people have seen God revealed. And in this first reading from Deuteronomy, we can see in Moses' words the different manifestations of God at work among the Chosen People. Thus it was chosen for today's feast.

The literary device at work here is the rhetorical question. It is an effective way to emphasize the obvious—by asking questions to which no answer is expected because the answer is so obvious. "Did anything so great ever happen before?" The implied answer is, "Of course not!" Moses is encouraging the people under his leadership to be mindful of the many ways in which God has appeared in their midst: as the sustaining Creator who keeps them in existence, as the worker of signs and wonders, and as the loving parent who chooses a special people for particular favors.

And the reason for Moses' encouragement is to elicit a response of obedience, respect and love from Israel at times when they are tempted to doubt that God is really in their midst in all these different ways. Further motivation is provided in the promise God has made to Israel: that they will inherit the promised land and live long, prosperous lives.

It is the promise that gives birth to hope—and hope enables us to live grateful and reverent lives, obedient to the commandments given us by the God who is Creator, the God who is Redeemer, the God who is Comforter.

READING II   The traditional designations for God as a Trinity are employed in this brief selection from Paul's letter to the Romans: Father, Son (Christ) and Spirit. Thus, this reading is particularly appropriate for today's celebration.

The kernel of this passage is not so much that we are children of God because we were created by divine power; rather, it is that we have been adopted (chosen in love) by a divine being so loving that we can respond with the intimate term "Abba" (that is, Father). The analogy is clear. There are unwanted children in the world, born to parents who did not make a direct choice to have them. But the adopted child is always sought out by parents who clearly make a direct choice motivated by love and concern. Thus, our status as adopted children of God tells us a great deal about the loving concern of our "Abba."

And, as adopted children, we are heirs. That is, we have a right to inherit the promised kingdom—just as Christ did through his obedient suffering. The Spirit of God dwelling in us is the best proof of our status as heirs with Christ.

The God who is Three in One is revealed quite vividly in this brief reading. The Father has sent the Son to make us coheirs of the kingdom with him. And even now the Spirit gives witness to our status as children of God, enabling us to bear the suffering that leads to glory.

GOSPEL Matthew concludes his gospel with a dramatic scene, indeed. It is filled with significance far beyond the specific events and words we read. First of all, the meeting takes place on a mountain. In Matthew, who sees Jesus as the second Moses, several important events take place on a mountaintop: the sermon on the mount, the transfiguration and the crucifixion. The scene itself tells us something of the significance of this event.

The resurrected Jesus reveals himself in a new way; this explains why "those who had entertained doubts fell down in homage." He is now the Christ, Ruler of the Universe, with all authority. And it is in that authority that he utters the great missionary challenge to the eleven who remained faithful. The word "therefore" is extremely important: "Full authority has been given me . . . go, *therefore,* and make disciples."

The fundamental sign of our incorporation into the life of the risen Christ (and therefore the Holy Trinity) is baptism. When the church baptizes, it precedes and follows the sacrament with instruction in the commandments. Thus, the final charge which makes the apostles (and all of us) teachers. We cannot escape this charge. If the universal obligation to evangelize fills us with dread or feelings of insecurity, we need to take to heart the final promise of this reading: "I am with you always."

A reading from the holy *gospel* according to *Matthew* ▪▪

A dramatic scene, indeed. The tone is one of awe.

This sentence is translated by the NRSV thus: "When they saw him, they worshipped him; but some doubted."

The eleven disciples made their way to *Galilee,* to the mountain to which Jesus had *summoned* them. ▪ At the *sight* of him, those who had entertained doubts fell *down* in homage. ▪▪ Jesus came forward and addressed them in *these* words: ▪

It is the Risen Christ who speaks in this reading. Proclaim his words triumphantly.

> "*Full* authority has been given to *me*
>   both in *heaven* and on *earth;* ▪
> go, therefore, and make disciples
>   of *all* the *nations.* ▪
> *Baptize* them in the name
>   'of the Father
>   and of the Son,
>   and of the Holy Spirit.' ▪
> *Teach* them to carry out *everything*
>   I have *commanded* you. ▪

What a promise! Be sure it rings in the assembly's ears.

> And *know* that I am with you *always,*
>   until the *end* of the *world!*" ▪▪

THE BODY AND BLOOD OF CHRIST

LECTIONARY #169

READING I Exodus 24:3–8

Such a solemn and ritual scene requires a bold, broad delivery.

A reading from the book of *Exodus* ▪ ▪

When Moses came to the *people* and related all the words and ordinances of the *Lord*, they all answered with one *voice*, ▪ "We will do *everything* that the Lord has *told* us." ▪ Moses then wrote *down* all the words of the Lord and, rising early the next *day*, he erected at the foot of the *mountain* an *altar* and twelve *pillars* for the twelve *tribes* of *Israel*. ▪ Then, having sent certain young men of the Israelites to offer *holocausts* and sacrifice young *bulls* as *peace* offerings to the Lord, ▪ Moses took *half* of the blood and put it in the large *bowls*; ▪ the *other* half he splashed on the *altar*. ▪ Taking the book of the *covenant*, he read it *aloud* to the people, who answered, ▪ "All that the Lord has *said*, we will *heed* and *do*." ▪ Then he took the blood and sprinkled it on the people, saying, ▪ "This is the blood of the *covenant* which the Lord has made with *you* in accordance with *all* these *words* of his." ▪ ▪

This is a gory ordeal by our standards, but your tone will make it clear that we are recalling an ancient ritual with modern parallels.

A solemn proclamation. Read slowly and deliberately.

Let the concluding sentence ring out!

READING II Hebrews 9:11–15

This is dense theology. Proclaim it slowly.

A reading from the letter to the *Hebrews* ▪ ▪

When Christ came as *high* priest of the good things which came to *be*, he entered *once* for *all* into the *sanctuary*, passing through the *greater* and more *perfect* tabernacle not made by *hands*, that is, not belonging to this *creation*. ▪ He entered not with the blood of *goats* and *calves* but with his *own* blood, and achieved *eternal redemption*. ▪ For if the blood of *goats* and *bulls* and the sprinkling of a heifer's *ashes* can sanctify those who are defiled so that their *flesh* is cleansed, how much *more* will the blood of *Christ*, who through the eternal spirit offered *himself* up

The contrast is the point here. Jesus entered with his own blood. The redemption he achieved is eternal.

Again, hear the contrast: blood of bulls vs. blood of Christ. It's a long sentence; take it slowly and broadly.

READING I Do not presume that readings such as this one have less power in our civilized age. The idea of animal sacrifice (not to mention human sacrifice) is repugnant to us only because it is no longer customary. Though repelled by such sacrifices we are capable, nevertheless, of understanding them, along with the culture in which the shedding of blood seemed to be the most powerful context in which oaths and vows were made. There are even contemporary references to the power of blood. We can speak quite comfortably, albeit figuratively, of "signing in blood" when we sense that a weighty obligation is about to be placed on us—or when we want our assent to seem especially solemn.

The word "covenant" carries the central idea of this reading, as indeed it sums up today's celebration. The old covenant was solemnized and effected by the shedding of blood, for there is finality in it. The Body and Blood of Christ is also a covenant—the *new* covenant. And because Christ's sacrifice and bloodshed effected the eternal covenant, no further bloody sacrifice is necessary. Hearing of the old covenant increases our understanding of the new.

READING II This reading could serve as a commentary on the first reading, explaining as it does the difference between the old and new covenants. The writer of Hebrews has a specific ritual in mind here. Every year on the Day of Atonement, the high priest entered the Holy of Holies in order to atone for the sins of the people. But now the writer assigns to Christ the role of ultimate high priest, entering the Holy of Holies (that is, entering the presence of God through death, resurrection and ascension), and atoning for the sins of the people *once and for all*. In other words, what used to be a yearly ritual, required again and again for forgiveness, has been rendered unnecessary by the perfect atonement achieved by Jesus.

The striking difference between the high priest of old and Christ, the eternal high priest, is that the blood of unblemished animals was shed to achieve forgiveness of sins. In shedding his own blood, Jesus—the unblemished, sinless one—achieved *eternal* forgiveness of sins. The Sunday eucharist is a reenactment of Jesus' sacrifice, a meal in which the sacrificial Lamb of God's flesh is eaten and blood is drunk. And the words, "This is the blood of the new and everlasting covenant," remind us each time of the sacrifices that preceded Jesus' own.

GOSPEL The first half of the reading, describing preparations for the passover meal, reveals Jesus to be like the prophets of old, who had foreknowledge of coming events. The purpose of revealing Jesus in this light was to enhance his credibility as the culmination of all the prophets who had gone before him, and to show that he was in complete control of his destiny as a suffering redeemer.

The actual description of the course of the meal provides us with one of the earliest forms of the eucharist—as it was celebrated at the time Mark wrote his gospel narrative. It varies from other accounts by John and by Paul in his first letter to the Corinthians. But the essentials are the same, with Mark identifying the cup with the blood covenant of old. In drinking from the cup, the disciples (through all ages) share in the vast sweep of salvation history right down to the present moment.

The final remark of Jesus points to the time when the reign of God will be fully established and all are united in the banquet of heaven. All the meals that Jesus shared during his life on earth (with sinners, with friends, with disciples) point toward that final and unending unity of love and shared fellowship.

The songs of praise that concluded the meal were traditional. The final words of this reading, however, have an ominous ring: "they walked out to the Mount of Olives." Here Jesus will be handed over like a criminal and the great ordeal of his suffering will begin. Thus, as we celebrate the last of a series of feasts at the end of the Lent, Easter and Pentecost seasons, we sense the cycle beginning all over again. Jesus died and rose once for all. But our liturgical remembrance of this great drama must be enacted over and over again, each time bringing us closer to that final day when we too will drink of the fruit of the vine—and drink it new—in the reign of God.

unblemished to God, cleanse our *consciences* from dead *works* to worship the living *God!* ▪▪

This is why he is mediator of a *new* covenant: ▪ since his *death* has taken place *for deliverance* from transgressions committed under the *first* covenant, those who are *called* may receive the promised *eternal inheritance.* ▪▪

More dense theology. Wider vocal variety (carefully placed emphasis) will enable you to make the meaning clearer.

GOSPEL Mark 14:12–16, 22–26

A reading from the holy *gospel* according to *Mark* ▪▪

This is Mark's account of the Last Supper. Proclaim it lovingly.

On the first day of Unleavened *Bread*, when it was customary to sacrifice the paschal *lamb*, the disciples said to *Jesus*, ▪ "Where do you wish us to go to prepare the *Passover* supper for you?" ▪ He sent two of his disciples with these instructions: ▪ "Go into the *city* and you will come upon a man carrying a *water* jar. ▪ *Follow* him. ▪ Whatever house he *enters*, say to the owner, ▪ 'The *Teacher* asks, ▪ Where is my *guestroom* where I may eat the *Passover* with my *disciples?*' ▪ Then he will show you an upstairs *room*, spacious, furnished, and all in order. ▪ *That* is the place you are to get ready for us. ▪ The disciples went *off.* ▪ When they reached the city they found it *just* as he had *told* them, and they prepared the Passover *supper.* ▪▪

Jesus' foreknowledge is striking; pronounce his prediction with utter calm and certainty.

Pause. The familiarity of this text demands a fresh and careful treatment. Avoid predictable patterns.

During the *meal* he took *bread*, blessed and broke it, and *gave* it to them. ▪ "*Take* this," he said, ▪ "*this* is my *body.*" ▪ He likewise took a cup, gave thanks and passed it to them, ▪ and they all *drank* from it. ▪ He said to them: ▪ "*This* is my *blood* the blood of the *covenant*, to be poured out on behalf of *many.* ▪ I solemnly *assure* you, I will never again drink of the fruit of the *vine* until the day when I drink it *new* in the reign of *God.*" ▪▪

A feeling of foreboding is appropriate here.

After singing songs of *praise* they walked out to the Mount of *Olives.* ▪▪

ELEVENTH SUNDAY IN ORDINARY TIME

LECTIONARY #93

READING I   Ezekiel 17:22–24

A reading from the book of the prophet *Ezekiel* ··

This reading is an extended metaphor. It is poetry, so read phrases—beyond traditional considerations of punctuation or capitalization.

Thus says the Lord God: ·
I, too, will take from the crest of the cedar,
  from its *topmost branches* tear off
    a tender *shoot,*

Notice the parallelism: the second line echoes the first.

And plant it on a high and lofty *mountain;* ·
  on the mountain heights of *Israel* I will plant it. ·
It shall put forth branches and bear fruit,
  and become a majestic *cedar.* ·

A classic example of parallelism: "birds" = "every winged thing."

Birds of every *kind* shall dwell beneath it,
  every winged *thing* in the shade of its boughs. ·
And all the trees of the *field* shall know
  that I, the *Lord,*

Articulate the poetic contrast vigorously.

Bring low the *high* tree,
  lift *high* the *lowly* tree,
Wither up the *green* tree,
  and make the *withered* tree *bloom.* ·

A final stamp of assurance. Let the conclusion be strong.

As I, the Lord, have *spoken,* so will I *do.* ··

READING II   2 Corinthians 5:6–10

A reading from the second letter of *Paul* to the *Corinthians* ··

Begin strongly. Emphasizing "continue" more than "confident" may result in a more effective opening.

We *continue* to be confident. · We *know* that while we dwell in the *body* we are away from the *Lord.* · We walk by *faith,* not by *sight.* · I repeat, · we are full of *confidence,* and would much rather be *away* from the body and at *home* with the *Lord.* · This being *so,*

Pause. What follows is the result of what has gone before.

we make it our aim to *please* him whether we are *with* him or *away* from him. · The lives of all of us are to be *revealed* before the tribunal of *Christ* so that

NRSV: "so that each may receive recompense for what has been done in the body, whether good or evil."

each one may receive his *recompense,* good or bad, according to his life in the *body.* ··

READING I   With the resumption of Ordinary Time, we hear a lovely poetic promise of restoration and exaltation. The prophet Ezekiel foretells a day when poor, exiled Judah (a geographical region) will once again be the envy of all, the Lord's chosen, and the benevolent protector of weaker peoples. The selection we read today is part of a much longer allegory in which specific historical references to people and places are made in a poetic way.

The cedar is the house of David, and the tender shoot torn from the topmost branch is a new king. From this remnant of the former house, a new house will grow and become even greater than its source. The birds that will rest in its branches are the lesser nations or kings who will know the benevolence of the greater.

All the trees (all the kingdoms and nations of the earth) must know that God can bring down the mighty, lift up the lowly, wither the prosperous and prosper the withered! The point, obviously, is that the Lord is in charge, and the Lord is to be credited for the prosperity of whoever is chosen for blessing. The point is not, however, that God is fickle or arbitrary. No, Ezekiel's allegory is a description of the careful and inscrutable plan of God. All the more reason for Judah to rejoice! "As the Lord has spoken, so the Lord will do!" In today's gospel reading, we hear the same message: God's plan *will* be brought to fulfillment.

READING II   In this reading, the tension between heaven and earth is palpable. Paul is no doubt addressing a discussion among the Corinthians. Is it better to be dead and beyond the sufferings of this present life, or is it better to be alive, even though this means we must live by faith instead of by sight? It's an ancient question, asked over and over again by devout Christians as well as scoundrels. The famous "To be or not to be" speech in *Hamlet* manifests the same concerns.

Paul admits that being "in the body" has its drawbacks. It means we cannot be completely united with the Lord Jesus. Yet Jesus wouldn't want us to denigrate or demean our bodies, seeing them merely as burdens that hamper us on our way to God. By no means. It is precisely according to the lives we live in our bodies that we will be judged before the "tribunal of

Christ." Thus, it is best to accept both life and death—striving to please the Lord in both.

The frustration remains, then, but the prescription for our discomfort lies in the acceptance of Paul's assertion that "we walk by faith, not by sight." That is, our faith leads us, because we can't possibly see into the future in any literal way. Having faith that a loving God has a wonderful destiny planned for us makes it possible to live in spiritual peace—regardless of how much we are subjected to bodily warfare. We are confident; more, we are *full* of confidence.

GOSPEL The unrelenting and inexorable will of God we heard Ezekiel speak of in the first reading is echoed here in Mark's description of the "reign of God" inaugurated by Jesus. Throughout his gospel, Mark is also preoccupied with the "secret" of the kingdom and the messiahship of Jesus. Unseen by most, this kingdom is like the seed sown by the farmer. It lies hidden at first. As it grows, the growth is almost imperceptible. Nevertheless, it matures eventually and becomes ready for harvest—a hint of the "end times."

The second comparison is with a mustard seed—smallest of all seeds. Again, in its beginning stages, the seed goes unnoticed. Who could imagine that such a small seed could become the largest of shrubs, with branches large enough to harbor the birds of the air?

It may seem strange to us that Jesus would speak only in parables to the crowds, but explain things when speaking privately to his disciples. Is he intentionally hiding his mission from the people? No, but we have to remember Mark's purpose here: to demonstrate the slow but inevitable revelation of God's saving plan, to teach us that the kingdom is in our midst but that we have to look carefully with eyes of faith or it will escape us. And Jesus cannot reveal himself as Messiah until we have been prepared to accept the *kind* of messiah he will be—very different from our expectations, and impossible to discern except through the special vision only faith can provide.

A reading from the holy *gospel* according to *Mark* ▪▪

Two parables—extended metaphors—constitute this reading. The images are vivid and rich. Your proclamation should unfold slowly and broadly—just like the seed does.

Jesus said to the crowd: ▪ *"This* is how it is with the reign of *God.* ▪ A man scatters *seed* on the ground. ▪ He goes to bed and gets up day after day. ▪ Through it *all* the seed *sprouts* and *grows* without his knowing how it *happens.* ▪ The soil produces of *itself* first the *blade,* then the *ear,* finally the ripe *wheat* in the ear. ▪ When the crop is *ready* he 'wields the *sickle,* ▪ for the time is ripe for *harvest.'"* ▪▪

A slightly different aspect of the "kingdom" is revealed here. It begins very small and becomes huge. Your voice can echo what the text says— beginning firmly but quietly and becoming more expansive.

Pause. This comment about Jesus' teaching technique is fascinating. With the disciples, he had to be more explicit, for they will soon take up his mission.

He went *on* to say: ▪ "What comparison shall we *use* for the reign of *God?* ▪ What image will help to *present* it? ▪ It is like a *mustard* seed which, when planted in the *soil,* is the smallest of all the earth's *seeds,* yet once it is *sown,* springs up to become the largest of *shrubs,* with branches big enough for the birds of the *sky* to build nests in its *shade."* ▪▪ By means of many such *parables* he taught them the message in a way they could *understand.* ▪ To them he spoke only by way of *parable,* while he kept *explaining* things privately to his *disciples.* ▪▪

TWELFTH SUNDAY IN ORDINARY TIME

LECTIONARY #96

READING I   Job 38:1, 8–11

A reading from the book of *Job* ▪ ▪

The NRSV begins thus: "The Lord answered Job out of the whirlwind: 'Who is this that darkens counsel by words without knowledge? I will question you, and you shall declare to me.'" It sets the scene, making this reading a bit easier to understand.

The Lord *addressed* Job out of the *storm* and said:
Who shut within doors the *sea,*
    when it burst forth from the *womb;*
When I made the clouds its *garment*
    and thick *darkness* its *swaddling* bands?
When I set *limits* for it
    and fastened the bar of its *door,*
And said: ▪ Thus *far* shall you come
        but no *farther,*
    and *here* shall your proud *waves* be *stilled!* ▪ ▪

READING II   2 Corinthians 5:14–17

A reading from the second letter of *Paul* to the *Corinthians* ▪ ▪

Try this phrasing: "The love of Christ—impels us who have reached the conviction that since one died for all—all died."

"But for him who for their sakes died and was raised up" is difficult to communicate clearly. The NRSV has: "but for him who died and was raised for them."

NRSV: "So if anyone is in Christ, there is a new creation: everything old has passed away; see, everything has become new!"

The love of *Christ* impels us who have reached the conviction that since *one* died for *all, all* died. ▪ He *died* for all so that those who *live* might live no longer for *themselves,* but for him who for their sakes *died* and was raised *up.* ▪ ▪

Because of this we no longer look on *anyone* in terms of mere *human* judgment. ▪ If at one time we so regarded *Christ,* we no longer *know* him by this standard. ▪ This means that if anyone is in *Christ,* he is a new *creation.* ▪ The *old* order has passed *away;* ▪ *now* all is *new!* ▪ ▪

READING I   God speaks from the midst of a sea storm; today's liturgy relates this reading to the gospel in which Jesus is revealed as the master of the elements. Job wants to know why he has to suffer, despite the fact that he is a just and upright man. God's reply is not the answer Job wanted, nor is it an answer we might find immediately helpful. The answer God gives is that the divine will is inscrutable and cannot be questioned. It may even sound sarcastic to us, for God seems to criticize Job even for asking the question. There is no denying, however, the truth of God's response. And there is no denying that we need to be reminded often that God is greater than our individual concerns. Our suffering will be seen in perspective only if we are able to remember that we are part of the vastness of creation. There is so much we cannot comprehend that faith in a God who is greater than all creation is our only comfort. Such faith enables us to look beyond ourselves.

None of this is to say that God is not provident. It certainly is not to say that God cares only for the "big picture" and ignores those he has created. We know, for instance, that at the end of Job's story, all that he lost is restored and he is rewarded bountifully for his humility and obedience.

READING II   The love of Christ is so convincing that it impels us to believe. The presumption here is that we have in some way experienced that love. If we can believe that Jesus loved the world enough to give his life for the ransom of every human being, we are forced to understand how all of us have been born anew in Jesus' death and resurrection. And we are compelled to live a life of love in response to such love. That means we *live* like people who have been born anew—or raised up with Christ to a new life.

In the second paragraph of this reading Paul is refuting a specific false belief that plagued his readers. There were those in Corinth who preached that Jesus was a great man, perhaps a divine man, but still only human, not God. Paul naturally had to argue against such an error of belief. Because of the resurrection, Paul says, it is impossible to believe that Jesus was only human. If at one time (before the resurrection) it was possible to think so, it is no longer. Further, all those who share the risen life of Christ through baptism can no longer be seen as merely human. They share in the divine life so intimately that they are a new creation. In fact, "all is new," and only God could have accomplished this.

GOSPEL The overall tone of this passage reveals again Mark's preoccupation with the "secret" of who Jesus is—a secret that is not fully revealed until after the resurrection. It is this "dramatic irony" in Mark that typifies his gospel.

One way of viewing this passage is to be aware of the question that concludes it even before we begin. The entire event is meant to prepare for the question, "Who can this be?" And it does so quite strikingly.

The idea of Jesus being master of the seas and weather is not an original one. The Hebrew scriptures are replete with instances in which prophets and "holy ones" are characterized this way. Indeed, that is part of Mark's purpose here—to show that Jesus comes from a long line of chosen prophets who manifested God in the world. The difference is that Jesus is the last and greatest of the prophets, the one in whom God dwells in an ultimate and perfect way.

Further, the context of this story in Mark makes it clear that Jesus' mastery over the storm is part of the slow revelation to his disciples of who he really is. Even the rhetorical question, "Why are you lacking in faith?", is designed to provoke the all-important question that must be asked again and again—and will be answered only slowly and in fragmented form until after the resurrection: "Who can this be?"

When we understand Mark's approach in this way, we realize at once that a reading of this gospel that reduces the text to a tempest and a wonderworker falls far short of Mark's larger purpose. The entire scene is carefully staged and choreographed to lead up to the all-important question. And even the question is no surprise. It is a ritual query, a formula that has weight and substance. Knowing the answer renders the question all the more meaningful for you, the reader, and for your hearers.

A reading from the holy *gospel* according to *Mark* ▪ ▪

This story has inspired many artists. Proclaim it with refreshing newness.

One day as *evening* drew on Jesus said to his disciples, ▪ "Let us cross over to the farther shore." ▪ Leaving the *crowd*, they took him away in the boat in which he was sitting, while the other boats accompanied him. ▪ It happened that a bad *squall* blew up. ▪

Pause. A new phase of the story begins here.

The *waves* were breaking over the *boat* and it began to ship *water badly.* ▪ Jesus was in the stern through it all, sound *asleep* on a cushion. ▪ They finally *woke* him and said to him, ▪ "Teacher, doesn't it *matter* to you that we are going to *drown?*" ▪ He awoke and

Pause again. The frantic question is answered with utter gravity.

rebuked the wind and said to the *sea:* ▪ "Quiet! ▪ Be *still!*" ▪ ▪ The wind fell off and everything grew *calm.* ▪ Then he said to them, ▪ "Why are you so *terrified?* ▪ Why are you lacking in *faith?*" ▪ ▪ A great *awe* overcame them at this. ▪ They kept saying to one

The voice rises at the end. The question hangs in the air for a moment. Only then do you say, "The gospel of the Lord."

another, ▪ "Who can this *be* that the *wind* and the *sea* obey him?" ▪ ▪

THIRTEENTH SUNDAY IN ORDINARY TIME

LECTIONARY #99

READING I   Wisdom 1:13–15; 2:23–24

This is poetry. A broad, expansive proclamation is best. You are dealing with cosmic truth here.

A reading from the book of *Wisdom* ··

God did not make *death*,
  nor does he rejoice in the destruction
    of the *living*. ·
For he fashioned all things that they might
    have *being*; ·
  and the creatures of the world are *wholesome*,
And there is not a destructive drug *among* them
    nor any domain of the *nether* world on *earth*, ·
For *justice* is *undying*. ··
For God formed man to be *imperishable*; ·
  the image of his own *nature* he made him. ·
But by the envy of the *devil*, *death* entered
    the world,
  and they who are in his *possession*
    experience it. ··

NRSV: "The generative forces of the world are wholesome, and there is no destructive poison in them." The use of "drug" is misleading.

Use second person plural: "For God formed us to be . . ." and "the image of his own nature he made us."

READING II   2 Corinthians 8:7, 9, 13–15

In other words, "You have everything required for doing good to others."

A reading from the second letter of *Paul* to the *Corinthians* ··

Just as you are rich in every *respect*, in *faith* and *discourse*, in *knowledge*, in total *concern*, and in our *love* for you, you may *also* abound in your work of *charity*. ··

You are well acquainted with the favor shown you by our Lord Jesus *Christ:* · how for your *sake* he made himself *poor* though he was *rich*, so that you might become *rich* by his *poverty*. · The relief of *others* ought not to *impoverish* you; · there should be a certain *equality*. · Your plenty at the *present* time should supply *their* need so that *their* surplus may *in turn* one day supply *your* need, with equality as the *result*. · It is written, · "He who gathered *much* had no *excess* and he who gathered *little* had no *lack*." ··

Irony and paradox are the literary devices at work here. The normal definitions of words are inverted. For example, what is true wealth; what is real poverty?

NRSV is much better: "The one who had much did not have too much, and the one who had little did not have too little."

READING I   The faithful Christian looks upon death as a passage through which we go to God. And such is our belief. But imagine what it would be like to look upon death as complete separation from God, as the end of participation in God and creation, and as the ultimate experience of aloneness. If we can imagine such a notion, we will begin to appreciate the view of death presented in this first reading. It is not attributed to God, of course, but rather to the devil and to sin. Those who are possessed by sin experience death. They do not live the "justice" spoken of here, which is obedience to the divine commands.

God is the author of life, and every created thing is good, even those things we do not understand well enough to see as good. Humankind was created for the kind of immortality that God has, for we are created in the divine image.

This reading complements beautifully the gospel narrative assigned to today's liturgy. Jesus reveals himself as the conqueror of death in all its aspects.

READING II   The burden of this passage from Paul is to show us the motivation behind our obligation to share our resources with those less fortunate. And Paul is not writing about almsgiving in the abstract. He is encouraging the Christians at Corinth to be generous in a specific collection of money for the Christian community in Jerusalem. Though we may not be accustomed to thinking of Paul's moral teaching as being so anchored in cold hard reality, here is an instance where it is.

There can be no denying the poverty we all experienced before the coming of the Messiah. We were enslaved in the human condition of sin when Jesus liberated us and made us rich in life and grace. And Jesus made himself the poorest of the poor in order to enrich us so. We are not instructed to make ourselves bereft of essentials in our almsgiving, but we are encouraged to be inspired by the example of Jesus, and to at least strive for equality.

Fortune is a fickle goddess. Though we may be poor at the moment and need the help of others, the day could well come when we will be able to reciprocate. There is much instruction for us in this reading—as individuals, as nations, as citizens of the world.

GOSPEL To take the shorter form of this gospel reading will weaken it, for the insertion of the healing story within the story of the raising from the dead has a purpose. The story of the woman cured of her hemorrhage and the story of the daughter of Jairus brought back to life complement one another and foretell the ultimate mission of Jesus: to cure the world of sickness (and the ultimate sickness, sin) and to conquer death once and for all. Assuming this to be Mark's larger purpose in the construction of his narrative, something is lost if the middle part of the reading is omitted.

In any case, the message underlying the narrative here is that Jesus is revealed as a descendant of a long line of prophets (Elijah, for instance) who cured the sick and raised the dead. The difference between Jesus and earlier prophets will not be revealed until after the resurrection. Then he will be recognized as the final prophet, the ultimate manifestation of God's saving love in the world.

In these two events we see further evidence of Mark's dramatic approach to the life of Jesus: His identity as Messiah is to be kept "secret" until the demonstration of his divinity and ultimate purpose are revealed in the resurrection. If we do not keep Mark's "secret" in mind, Jesus' admonition not to tell anyone about the little girl being raised seems ridiculous. But if we understand the "secret" as a dramatic device whereby Mark unveils the identity of Jesus slowly and systematically, then Jesus' admonition clearly makes sense, regardless of whether or not it was heeded.

GOSPEL Mark 5:21—43

This gospel selection is structured like a "play within a play." Your best story-telling skills must be applied.

Jairus = DZHAY-ruhs

Pause. Renew the energy level. The intervening event begins here.

Emphasize "heard" here. It implies a great deal about faith.

Jesus seems quite urgent about finding out who touched him. The words "immediately" and "wheeling about" have a sense of excitement.

There is more than calm assurance in Jesus' words here. There is also enthusiasm for the woman's exceptionally strong faith.

Emphasize the word "official's"—to get us back to the original story.

The people should sound sympathetic, not unfeeling, when they tell Jairus of his daughter's death.

A reading from the holy *gospel* according to *Mark* ▪ ▪

When Jesus had crossed back to the other side of the Sea of Galilee in the boat, a large *crowd* gathered around him and he stayed close to the *lake*. ▪ One of the officials of the *synagogue*, a man name *Jairus*, came near. ▪ Seeing *Jesus*, he fell at his feet and made this earnest *appeal*: ▪ "My little daughter is critically *ill*. ▪ Please come and lay your *hands* on her so that she may get *well* and *live*." ▪ The two went off *together* and a large crowd followed, *pushing* against Jesus. ▪ ▪

There was a *woman* in the area who had been afflicted with a *hemorrhage* for a dozen *years*. ▪ She had received treatment at the hands of doctors of every *sort* and exhausted her savings in the *process*, yet she got no *relief*; ▪ on the *contrary*, she only grew *worse*. ▪ She had *heard* about Jesus and came up behind him in the *crowd* and put her hand to his *cloak*. ▪ "If I just touch his *clothing*," she thought, ▪ "I shall get *well*." ▪ ▪ Immediately her flow of blood dried *up* and the feeling that she was *cured* of her affliction ran through her whole *body*. ▪ Jesus was *immediately* conscious that healing power had gone *out* from him. ▪ Wheeling about in the crowd, he began to ask, ▪ "Who touched my *clothing*?" ▪ His disciples said to him, ▪ "You can see how this crowd hems you *in*, yet you ask, ▪ 'Who *touched* me?'" ▪ Despite this, he kept looking around to see the woman who had done it. ▪ *Fearful* and beginning to tremble now as she realized what had *happened*, the woman came and fell in *front* of him and told him the whole *truth*. ▪ He said to her, ▪ "Daughter, it is your faith that has *cured* you. ▪ Go in *peace* and be *free* of this illness." ▪ ▪

He had not finished *speaking* when people from the *official's* house arrived saying, ▪ "Your daughter is *dead*. ▪ Why bother the Teacher *further*?" ▪ Jesus disregarded the report that had been brought and said to the official: ▪ "*Fear* is *useless*. ▪ What is *needed* is *trust*." ▪ He would not permit anyone to *follow* him except Peter, James, and James's brother John. ▪ As they approached the *house* of the synagogue leader, Jesus was struck by the noise of people wailing and crying loudly on all *sides*. ▪ He entered and said to them: ▪ "Why do you make this *din* with your

Significant pause. Change of tone: Jesus is in complete command of the situation.

wailing! ▪ The child is *not* dead. ▪ She is *asleep."* ▪ At this they began to *ridicule* him. ▪ Then he put them all out. ▪▪

Jesus took the child's father and mother and his own companions and entered the room where the child lay. ▪ Taking her hand he said to her, ▪ *'Talitha, koum,'* ▪ which means, ▪ "Little girl, get *up."* ▪▪ The *girl*, a child of *twelve*, stood up *immediately* and began to walk *around.* ▪ At *this* the family's astonishment was *complete.* ▪▪ He enjoined them strictly not to let anyone *know* about it, and told them to give her something to eat. ▪▪

[*Shorter: Mark 5:21–24, 35–43*]

"Give her something to eat" is quite anti-climactic! Be sure it doesn't sound trivial. The point: Things have been restored to normal.

The tone of total authority that characterizes everything Jesus says and does in this double event should come through clearly. Just as in last Sunday's gospel, when Mark showed Jesus to be master of the raging sea, so here he reveals him as master over sickness and death. Jesus' words here further demonstrate his confidence in his authority. So much so, in fact, that the people ridicule him when he makes statements such as, "The child is not dead. She is asleep." Likewise, his question, "Who touched me?" in the midst of a pressing crowd seems ludicrous to his disciples. But the point is, Jesus is master of the situation and Mark shows him to be in total command, thus emphasizing a purpose in the narrative much larger than the literal events described.

READING I In the plan of the lectionary, the first reading and the gospel reading are usually connected by an idea or theme or theological truth. This scheme is obvious in today's readings. The prophet Ezekiel is sent forth in the Spirit of God with a message for hardhearted and obstinate people. The parallel in the gospel passage is clear: Jesus is rejected in his own hometown, as though familiarity made it impossible for those who knew him to believe that he was endowed with a special mission.

Ezekiel's purpose, like that of Jesus, is larger than any resistance he encounters. Those who listen to the prophet's message will benefit greatly from it; those who refuse to listen will condemn themselves by their own blindness. But in either case, all will know that a prophet was in their midst.

God does not force us to listen to the prophets. Nor does God abandon us in our stubbornness. The prophets keep coming into our midst, sent by God as an opportunity for salvation. Whether or not we heed their words is our choice. It behooves us, in any case, to "seek the Lord where he may be found," and it may well be that those closest to us—the ones we might least suspect, are prophets.

READING II Paul has been called upon by the Corinthians to present evidence of his authority. He is criticized for not comparing favorably with other preachers who had appeared in Corinth with what Paul recognized as false doctrine. They also claimed to have had "extraordinary revelations" of one kind or another, which made them seem superior to Paul.

In his response to those who doubt his credentials, Paul has a two-pronged reply. No, I can claim no extraordinary revelations, he says, and thus I have been kept from becoming inflated with conceit. The implication, of course, is that those who claim such special gifts have obviously been deceiving themselves through vanity and a kind of competition quite foreign to genuine ministry.

But the reason Paul says he has been kept from conceit gives him the chance to make one of the most beautifully ironic observations in Christian literature. Some kind of physical malady has plagued Paul and kept him humble and realistic. And his earlier prayer to be rid of the malady has

FOURTEENTH SUNDAY IN ORDINARY TIME

LECTIONARY #102

READING I   Ezekiel 2:2–5

A reading from the book of the prophet _Ezekiel_ ▪▪

A dramatic scene. Urgency and intensity are required.

NRSV: "son of man" = "mortal."

NRSV: "fathers" = "ancestors."

"Thus says the Lord God!" is shorthand for "all that the Lord God has to say."

Spirit entered into me and set me on my *feet,* ▪ and I heard the one who was speaking *say* to me: ▪ Son of man, I am sending you to the *Israelites, rebels* who have *rebelled* against me; ▪ they and their fathers have *revolted* against me to this very *day.* ▪ Hard of *face* and obstinate of *heart* are they to whom I am *sending* you. ▪ But you shall *say* to them: ▪ Thus says the Lord *God!* ▪ And whether they heed or resist— for they are a *rebellious* house—they shall *know* that a *prophet* has been among them. ▪▪

READING II   2 Corinthians 12:7–10

A reading from the second letter of _Paul_ to the _Corinthians_ ▪▪

The feeling here is that "extraordinary" revelations are not the heart of Christian living.

The irony is thick here: "in weakness power reaches perfection" means that when our weakness makes us dependent on God, then we understand what God is all about.

As to the *extraordinary* revelations, in order that I might not become *conceited* I was given a thorn in the *flesh,* an angel of *Satan* to *beat* me and keep me from getting *proud.* ▪ *Three times* I begged the Lord that this might leave me. ▪ He said to me, ▪ "My *grace* is *enough* for you, for in *weakness* power reaches *perfection."* ▪ And so I willingly *boast* of my weaknesses *instead,* that the power of *Christ* may *rest* upon me. ▪▪

Therefore I am *content* with weakness, with mistreatment, with distress, with persecutions and difficulties for the sake of *Christ;* ▪ for when I am *powerless,* it is *then* that I am *strong.* ▪▪

A reading from the holy *gospel* according to *Mark* ▪ ▪

There is sadness in this story— but the point is the fulfillment of scripture.

These questions must be asked quite seriously.

Joses = DZHO-seez

"Too much for them" is too colloquial. NRSV has: "And they took offense at him." Also, NRSV has "Prophets are not without honor, except in their hometown, and among their own kin, and in their own house."

"Distress" is a questionable translation. NRSV has: "And Jesus was amazed at their unbelief." Notice that this event does not inhibit Jesus in his preaching.

Jesus went to his own part of the *country* followed by his disciples. ▪ When the *sabbath* came he began to teach in the *synagogue* in a way that kept his large audience *amazed.* ▪ They said: ▪ "Where did he *get* all this? ▪ What kind of wisdom is he *endowed* with? ▪ How is it such miraculous *deeds* are accomplished by his hands? ▪ Isn't this the *carpenter*, the son of Mary, a brother of James and Joses and Judas and Simon? ▪ Aren't his sisters our *neighbors* here?" ▪ They found him too *much* for them. ▪ ▪ Jesus' *response* to all this was: ▪ "No prophet is without *honor* except in his native *place*, among his own *kindred*, and in his own *house.*" ▪ ▪ He could work no *miracle* there, apart from curing a few who were sick by laying hands on them, so *much* did their lack of faith *distress* him. ▪ He made the rounds of the *neighboring* villages *instead*, and spent his time *teaching.* ▪ ▪

been transformed into gratitude for it. Through suffering he has learned the lesson of the cross: In weakness we are made strong. It was at the moment of Jesus' greatest helplessness—when he was on the cross—that he achieved the redemption of the world.

In our weakness we are compelled to rely on the one who can make us strong. It is our perceived strengths, not our weaknesses, that most threaten our relationship with Jesus.

GOSPEL When we are tempted, as we all are, to make of Jesus an all-powerful miracle worker in total command of every situation, we should read this gospel passage. It is evidence that, long before his suffering and death, he experienced rejection. Making the occasion even more poignant, but not surprising, was his rejection by his own relatives and friends. Mark is no doubt presenting us with a foreshadowing of the final rejection Jesus will experience. Perhaps, too, he is attempting to comfort those disciples who also experienced rejection as they went about the task of spreading the good news long after Jesus had completed his earthly mission.

Mark surrounds Jesus in mystery. There is no clear understanding of Jesus' work and mission in Mark until after the resurrection. This account of his rejection adds further to the mystery. And the question that appears again and again in Mark is asked here in a very different tone of voice: "Who is this man?" It is a question that appears elsewhere in the gospel as admiration, fear or respect. It is even a question Jesus asks about himself at the turning point of Mark's gospel: "Who do men [people] say that I am?" When Peter responds, "You are the Christ," Jesus knows progress has been made. Nevertheless, the question continues to be asked. It is part of Mark's method of revealing the nature of Jesus.

READING I There is clearly a conflict of interest here. Amos, against his personal wish, has been commissioned as a prophet by God. He apparently has a prophetic message that is not attractive to Amaziah, a professional priest in the king's court. The situation is reminiscent of a remark attributed to Queen Victoria, who was not particularly noted for her piety: "Religion is a fine thing, so long as it doesn't interfere with one's private life." Sadly, much of religion seems prone to becoming a social and civic duty rather than a transforming search for holiness.

In any case, Amos is driven away because his message is not a comfortable one. This reading complements the gospel account for today, in which Jesus sends the disciples out two by two, unencumbered with material possessions, and prepared to move on when they encounter rejection of their message. Notice the presumption here that rejection *will* be part of the disciples' experience. Jesus knows that the message he brings is not comfortable and that it will very often challenge those who hear it to change their ways. Not everyone can accept such a challenge. Amos doesn't seem too surprised either, although he is at some pains to point out that the choice to become a prophet was not his own. "This was not my idea," he says, "and I certainly never considered myself a member of the elite. So don't blame me for a message you can't accept. I've got a job to do, whether you approve or not."

There is something quite refreshing about Amos's straightforward honesty. It gives his prophetic role even greater credibility. There is a disinterestedness about Amos, or any "reluctant prophet," that is somehow reassuring; perhaps it is because there is less chance that the motives of such a prophet will be sullied by an interest in personal gain.

READING II This is the first of seven consecutive weeks during which we read from Paul's letter to the Ephesians. The beginning of the letter (after a salutation) is very likely a hymn of praise, centering on baptism.

Notice that we have a kind of summary of salvation history here. Beginning in the eternal mind of God where we were chosen and predestined before time began,

FIFTEENTH SUNDAY IN ORDINARY TIME

LECTIONARY #105

READING I   Amos 7:12–15

A reading from the book of the prophet *Amos* ▪▪

The tone here is disdain and annoyance. Amaziah = am-uh-ZAI-uh, Bethel = beth'l, Amos = AY-muhs.

Emphasize the word "there."

Don't confuse the words "prophesy" (verb) and "prophecy" (noun). The one used here is pronounced PRAH-fuh-sigh, with a secondary accent on the last syllable. "Prophecy" = PRAH-fuh-see (no secondary accent).

Amaziah (priest of *Bethel*) said to *Amos*, ▪ "*Off* with you, *visionary,* flee to the land of *Judah!* ▪ *There* earn your bread by prophesying, but never again prophesy in *Bethel*; ▪ for it is the *king's* sanctuary and a *royal* temple." ▪ Amos answered Amaziah, ▪ "I *was* no prophet, nor have I *belonged* to a *company* of prophets; ▪ I was a *shepherd* and a dresser of *sycamores.* ▪ The Lord took me from following the *flock,* and said to me, ▪ *Go,* prophesy to my people *Israel.*" ▪▪

READING II   Ephesians 1:3–14

A reading from the letter of *Paul* to the *Ephesians* ▪▪

This is a very challenging reading. The tone of exultation and triumph must be sustained throughout. It is a trumpeted summary of God's effort in our behalf.

Take lots of time and energy. NRSV: "sons" = "children."

The first section reaches its peak.
Pause. Renew the vigor.

The second section reaches a climax.

Pause. Begin quietly. "We" = the Jewish people. "You" = the Ephesians (Gentiles).

Praised be the God and Father of our Lord Jesus *Christ,* who has *bestowed* on us in Christ every spiritual blessing in the *heavens!* ▪ God chose us in him before the world *began,* to be holy and blameless in his *sight,* ▪ to be full of *love:* ▪ he likewise *predestined* us through Christ *Jesus* to be his adopted *sons*—such was his *will* and *pleasure*—that all might praise the divine favor he has *bestowed* on us in his *beloved.* ▪▪

It is *in* Christ and through his *blood* that we have been *redeemed* and our *sins* forgiven, so immeasurably generous is God's *favor* to us. ▪ God has given us the *wisdom* to understand *fully* the *mystery,* the plan he was pleased to decree in Christ, to be carried *out* in the fullness of *time:* ▪ namely, to bring *all* things in the *heavens* and on *earth* into *one* under Christ's *headship.* ▪▪

In *him* we were *chosen:* for in the decree of *God,* who administers everything according to his will and counsel, we were *predestined* to praise his *glory* by being the *first* to *hope* in Christ. ▪ In him you *too* were chosen; ▪ when you heard the glad tidings of *salvation,* the word of *truth,* and *believed* in it, you were sealed with the Holy *Spirit* who had been *promised.* ▪ He is the pledge of our *inheritance,* the first payment against the full redemption of a people God has made his *own* to praise his *glory.* ▪▪

[Shorter: Ephesians 1:3–10]

GOSPEL   Mark 6:7–13

Slower, but losing no energy.

A reading from the holy *gospel* according to *Mark* ▪▪

The commission of the Twelve is for all of us, for all time.

Each article renounced makes the point more dramatically.

Jesus summoned the Twelve and began to send them out two by two, giving them authority over unclean *spirits.* ▪ He instructed them to take *nothing* on the journey but a *walking* stick— ▪ no food, no traveling bag, not a coin in the purses in their belts. ▪ They *were,* however, to wear *sandals.* ▪ "Do not bring a second *tunic,*" he said, ▪ and added: ▪ "Whatever house you *find* yourself in, *stay* there until you leave the locality. ▪ If any place will not *receive* you or *hear* you, shake its dust from your *feet* in testimony against them as you leave." ▪ With *that* they went off, preaching the need of *repentance.* ▪ They expelled many *demons,* anointed the *sick* with *oil,* and worked many *cures.* ▪▪

There is no hint of arrogance here, simply a refusal to be discouraged by nonacceptance of the message.

There is great joy in the success of their mission.

we move through the incarnation event of Christ Jesus and the divine favor bestowed on us in him. The mighty sweep continues through the passion and death (the shedding of blood for forgiveness of sins), the resurrection and ascension, when Christ becomes head of creation. And finally, the text acknowledges the outpouring of the church's mission the world over—guided by the Holy Spirit—and the pledge of our future inheritance, an inheritance that enables us, God's chosen people, to praise his glory for all eternity. Let your proclamation echo the vastness of this powerful text.

GOSPEL   In this brief reading we hear the great commission that should guide any and all who profess to be called to ministry. Very simply it sets down the conditions under which genuine evangelization will be undertaken. There is no need to think that a literal implementation of these conditions in our own day is required, but there is every reason to preserve the spirit underlying them.

It is necessary to be unencumbered in the mission field, whether that field be in the farthest reaches of the globe or in one's own neighborhood. A heroic kind of faith is required—faith that presumes that the providence of God will sustain the dedicated worker. The virtue of detachment is being counseled here, for without detachment the preacher's attention cannot be centered on the good news.

Missionaries must be realistic; they cannot assume that they and their message will be universally welcomed and embraced. Far from it. They must prepare themselves for a cool reception, even rejection. And when they encounter rejection they must be able to move on. There is no restraining the word of God, but there can be no coercion either. "What we have been given we offer as a free gift," as scripture says elsewhere. Respect for the intended recipients includes the acknowledgement that they are free to refuse the gift. This is simply to recognize God's own respect for humankind: we are created in love, complete with the freedom to choose or not to choose.

The apparent success of the Twelve indicates that they took Jesus' counsel to heart.

READING I This first reading is concerned with bad shepherds. The gospel narrative shows us good shepherds. This is the parallel between the two readings. By hindsight and from a Christian viewpoint the "righteous shoot to David" who will govern wisely is Jesus. ("Shoot" is a metaphor meaning a branch from David's family tree.)

Jeremiah himself, however, is speaking with a different kind of hindsight. Because he can see that self-serving and evil kings have misled the Chosen People in the past, he reminds us of the Lord God's promise to raise up a good king who will put things right. Jeremiah is making a purely historical prediction by hindsight, and foretells an idyllic time when a righteous king will restore fidelity to the covenant.

It is always a mistake to read the Hebrew scriptures (the First Testament) simply as a preparation for (and a prediction of) the coming of Jesus. To do so misses the richness of our heritage and a long history of the Lord God's intervention on behalf of our ancestors in faith. The Christian tradition does see in the "Jesus event" a fulfillment of ancient promises, but this in no way reduces the Hebrew scriptures to "mere foreshadowing." Sadly, our lectionary sometimes lends itself to such a simplistic reading. Thus, the first reading sometimes seems to have been chosen merely as an opportunity to show how its content is brought to perfection in the gospel reading. Resist this tendency in yourself.

READING II This brief reading is a list of accomplishments. Not Paul's accomplishments, but the glorious results of God's movement toward the world through Jesus. Look at what has been achieved: the Gentiles (far off) have been brought (near) to the Jews in the unifying sacrifice (blood) of Christ. The barrier of hostility between them has been broken down by the transformation of the law of Moses into the one commandment of universal love. The mission of reconciliation that lay at the heart of Christ's earthly work has been successful. The end result is "peace" where hostility had reigned. The effect of peace is unity where division had reigned.

The final sentence sums it all up: Through him (Jesus) both Gentile and Jew have access to (can approach) the Father in the

---

SIXTEENTH SUNDAY IN ORDINARY TIME

LECTIONARY #108

READING I   Jeremiah 23:1–6

A reading from the book of the prophet *Jeremiah* ▪ ▪

Begin with strength.

"Thus says the Lord" always precedes a significant proclamation.

Notice the play on words: "You have not taken care of my people" but "I will take [extra] care in punishing you!"

Another play on a word: "shepherds" (noun) who will "shepherd" (verb).

Pause. More quietly, now, as the great promise unfolds.

Woe to the shepherds who *mislead* and *scatter* the flock of my pasture, says the Lord. ▪ Therefore, *thus* says the *Lord*, the God of *Israel*, against the shepherds who shepherd my people: ▪ You have *scattered* my sheep and driven them *away*. ▪ You have not *cared* for them, ▪ but *I* will take *care* to punish your evil *deeds*. ▪ I *myself* will gather the remnant of my *flock* from *all* the lands to which I have *driven* them and bring them back to their *meadow;* ▪ there they shall in*crease* and *multiply*. ▪ I will appoint shepherds for them who will shepherd them so that they need *no longer* fear and tremble; ▪ and *none* shall be *missing*, says the Lord. ▪ ▪

Behold, the days are *coming*, says the Lord,
     when I will raise up a righteous *shoot* to *David;* ▪
As *king* he shall reign and govern *wisely*,
     he shall do what is *just* and *right* in the land. ▪
In his days *Judah* shall be *saved*,
     Israel shall dwell in *security*. ▪

To give a name is to give an identity. If he is called "our justice," then he is justice personified.

This is the name they *give* him: ▪
     "The *Lord* our *justice*." ▪ ▪

READING II   Ephesians 2:13–18

A reading from the letter of *Paul* to the *Ephesians* ▪ ▪

"Far off" = exiled. "Near" = home, where you belong. "The two of us" is translated in the NRSV as "both Jews and Gentiles."

Jesus reconciles all differences. Emphasize all words that apply to him.

In Christ *Jesus* you who once were far *off* have been brought *near* through the *blood* of Christ. ▪ It is he who is our *peace*, and who made the *two* of us *one* by breaking *down* the barrier of *hostility* that kept us *apart*. ▪ In his own *flesh* he abolished the *law* with its *commands* and *precepts*, to *create* in himself one *new* man from us who had been *two*, and to make *peace*, reconciling *both* of us to God in one *body* through his *cross* which put that enmity to *death*. ▪ He came and "announced the good news of *peace* to you who were far *off*, and to those who were *near*"; ▪ through *him* we *both* have access in *one* Spirit to the *Father*. ▪ ▪

NRSV: "one new man" = "one new humanity."

The point is reiterated on different words. Make the ending quite strong.

GOSPEL Mark 6:30–34

A reading from the holy *gospel* according to *Mark* ▪ ▪

The reading is concerned with the demands of the apostolate, but the overall tone is "joy in accomplishment."

The apostles returned to Jesus and reported to him all that they had *done* and what they had *taught*. ▪ He said to them, ▪ "Come by *yourselves* to an out-of-the-way place and *rest* a little." ▪ People were coming and going in great *numbers*, making it impossible for them to so much as *eat*. ▪ So Jesus and the apostles went off in the *boat* by *themselves* to a *deserted* place. ▪ People *saw* them leaving, and many got to *know* about it. ▪ People from all the towns hastened on *foot* to the place, arriving *ahead* of them. ▪ ▪

There is a sense of "no matter what"—the people kept coming in throngs.

"He pitied them" echoes Jesus' concern for his exhausted apostles earlier.

"At great length" emphasizes the depth of Jesus' compassion.

Upon disembarking Jesus saw a vast *crowd*. ▪ ▪ He *pitied* them, for they were like *sheep* without a *shepherd*; ▪ and he began to *teach* them at great *length*. ▪ ▪

one Spirit. In every age there is division and hostility between and among peoples of different backgrounds and beliefs. This reading must remind us that to surrender to such division is to underestimate the power of the good news.

GOSPEL This brief passage is a conglomeration of story and commentary concerning the enthusiastic reception of the good news. Last Sunday we heard Jesus send the Twelve on mission; this week we see them returning to him and reporting on their achievement and on the content of their preaching.

The compassionate shepherd knows they need a rest after their labors, and he invites them to a secluded retreat. It is typical of Mark to record Jesus' secret sessions with his disciples, for one of his most effective dramatic techniques is to treat the "reign of God" as a deep secret to be revealed slowly. And Jesus' identity as Messiah is likewise a deep secret, revealed completely only after the resurrection. The attempt to steal away from the crowds is futile, however, for the people are so eager to hear more that they cannot be sent away or avoided. The demands placed upon the dedicated teacher are sometimes heavy.

The final paragraph of this passage recalls the first reading. Jeremiah laments the harm done by bad shepherds and foretells the coming of a king who will do "what is just and right." Jesus shows himself to be the good shepherd, for he has compassion on the abandoned flock and teaches them at length.

There is enormous poignancy in the pity Jesus feels for the crowds. "Sheep without a shepherd" is an expression that conjures empathy and compassion in all of us. There is great joy in the generous response of the Good Shepherd.

READING I In both the first reading and the gospel narrative, we see an apparently miraculous feeding of a multitude with very little food. The "man of God," Elisha, exhibits the faith of a prophet in knowing the boundless mercy and grace of the Lord God. Thus, with confidence, he directs that an obviously insufficient amount of food be set before a large crowd. It is no surprise to us that there is food left over—for we share Elisha's faith, and are accustomed to hearing (if not witnessing directly) events in which the prodigality of God overcomes the fear and doubt of mortals.

In the gospels there are several accounts of such miraculous feedings; this brief passage serves as the model for them. It is a straightforward assertion of the power of the Lord God and our need to trust in that power, despite what our powers of reason and logic may tell us is impossible. It is a difficult lesson to learn, and therefore bears repeating.

READING II Here Paul begins a discourse that leads to an undeniable conclusion. In fact, he begins with his conclusion: Live as one in peace. Then comes the argument. It demonstrates that we have no other choice if we accept the premises Paul places before us.

His argument could be sketched something like this:

"You must live in accord with what you have become."

"The hope given you is one."

"The Spirit is one and binds all together in one."

"The body is one."

"There is one Lord, one faith, one baptism, one God."

"All of these are yours, given by the God who is over all, works through all, and is in all."

"Therefore, I repeat, be what you are!"

"Be one, bound together in peace."

GOSPEL Beginning today, and for the next four Sundays, the gospel reading is taken from John, rather than from Mark (who is the evangelist of Year B). John's account of the feeding of the multitude parallels Mark's, but John then launches into a long section concerned with "the bread of life." We will be hearing this section for the next several weeks.

SEVENTEENTH SUNDAY IN ORDINARY TIME

LECTIONARY #111

READING I   2 Kings 4:42–44

A reading from the second book of *Kings* ▪▪

A brief and startling account of God's fidelity. Read it slowly. Baal-shalishah = BAY-uhl-shuh-LAI-shuh, Elisha = ee-LAI-shuh.

The exchange here is ritual. We know ahead of time how things will turn out. NRSV has "people" instead of "men."

No surprise here.

A man came from Baal-shalishah bringing to *Elisha*, the man of *God*, twenty *barley* loaves made from the *firstfruits*, and fresh *grain* in the *ear*. ▪ "Give it to the people to *eat*," Elisha said. ▪ But his servant *objected*, ▪ "How can I set this before a hundred *men?*" ▪ "Give it to the *people* to *eat*," Elisha insisted. ▪ "For thus says the Lord, ▪ 'They shall *eat* and there shall be some left *over*.'" ▪▪ And when they had *eaten*, there *was* some left *over*, as the Lord had *said*. ▪▪

READING II   Ephesians 4:1–6

A reading from the first letter of *Paul* to the *Ephesians* ▪▪

This reading has two directives and two assertions. The first directive: "live a life worthy of the calling."

Pause. The second directive: "make every effort . . ."

Pause. First assertion: "There is but one body. . . ."

Pause. Second assertion: "There is one Lord. . . ."

I *plead* with you as a prisoner for the *Lord*, to live a life worthy of the *calling* you have received, ▪ with perfect humility, meekness, and patience, ▪ bearing with one another *lovingly*. ▪ Make every effort to preserve the *unity* which has the *Spirit* as its *origin* and *peace* as its binding *force*. ▪ There is but one *body* and one *Spirit*, just as there is but one *hope* given *all* of you by your *call*. ▪ There is one *Lord*, one *faith*, one *baptism*; ▪ one God and Father of *all*, who is *over* all, and *works* through all, and is *in* all. ▪▪

A reading from the holy *gospel* according to *John* ▪ ▪

One of the best-known of all Jesus' signs: proclaim it lovingly. Tiberias = tai-BIHR-ih-uhs.

The scene is being set. Every detail is important.

Jesus crossed the Sea of Galilee [to the shore] of *Tiberias;* ▪ a vast *crowd* kept *following* him because they saw the *signs* he was performing for the *sick.* ▪ Jesus then went up the *mountain* and sat *down* there with his *disciples.* ▪ The Jewish feast of *Passover* was near; ▪ when Jesus looked *up* and caught sight of a vast *crowd* coming toward him, he said to Philip, ▪ "Where shall we buy *bread* for these people to eat?" ▪ (He knew *well* what he intended to do but he asked this to test Philip's *response*.) ▪ Philip replied, "Not even with two hundred days' *wages* could we buy loaves enough to give *each* of them a *mouthful!*" ▪ ▪

Philip's concern makes the ultimate outcome all the more wonderful.

Andrew's doubt enhances Jesus' confidence.

One of Jesus' disciples, *Andrew*, Simon Peter's *brother*, remarked to him, ▪ "There is a lad here who has five *barley* loaves and a couple of dried *fish*, but what good is *that* for so *many?*" ▪ Jesus said, ▪ "Get the people to *recline*." ▪ Even though the men numbered about five *thousand*, there was plenty of *grass* for them to find a place on the *ground.* ▪ Jesus then took the loaves of *bread*, gave *thanks*, and passed them *around* to those *reclining* there; ▪ he did the *same* with the dried *fish*, as much as they *wanted.* ▪ When they had had enough, he told his disciples, ▪ "Gather up the crusts that are left *over* so that nothing will go to *waste.*" ▪ At this, they gathered twelve *baskets* full of pieces left over by those who had been fed with the *five barley loaves.* ▪ ▪

Significant pause. What follows is a very effective anticlimax. Not only is there enough for everyone; there is an abundance left over.

This paragraph reminds us that Jesus will fulfill his calling in a way that will confound all expectations.

When the people saw the *sign* he had performed they began to say, ▪ "This is undoubtedly the *Prophet* who is to come into the world." ▪ At that, Jesus realized that they would come and carry him *off* to make him *king*, so he fled back to the *mountain alone.* ▪ ▪

William F. Barclay, author of the *Daily Study Bible,* offers an appealing explanation of this parable. He suggests that the real miracle in the feeding of the multitude was that an example of sharing on the part of Jesus prompted a generous sharing by all. Despite the fears of the crowd and their tendency toward selfishness, in a spirit of sharing they discovered there was more than enough for everyone. Clearly, such an interpretation understands "miracle" in a different sense. The laws of nature are not broken—but the grosser tendencies of human nature are overcome in love. Such an understanding of the multiplication story addresses quite effectively the inequity of resources existing among nations today.

Whatever happened at this crucial point in Jesus' ministry, it is clear that the feeding of the crowds has overtones of the banquet of heaven—where all will receive their fill. The eucharist is implied here as well: Jesus took the bread, gave thanks, and distributed it to all.

Finally, the effect of the miracle on the crowds is ominous. They are so overwhelmed with Jesus' power that they are in danger of mistaking the kind of messiah he will become. They may be expecting a conquering king, in line with their understanding of ancient prophecies. But their expectations must be thwarted, so Jesus must flee. His true mission as "suffering servant" (the opposite of conquering king) is yet to be revealed, and far from being understood. It must not be compromised at this point.

READING I

In today's liturgy, the manna story in Exodus ties the first reading and the gospel together. A long and rich tradition developed in the church that connected the manna in the desert, the multiplication of the loaves, Jesus' long "bread of life" discourse, and the eucharistic bread, the body of Christ. We see all of these elements brought together in today's readings.

In point of fact, the manna provided the grumbling Israelites was a secretion from desert insects. The quail were migratory birds which could not survive the trip across the desert and so fell from the sky. These natural occurrences were seen as a sign of the Lord God's providential care, so it was not a very big leap for the later Christian tradition to interpret the manna as a prefiguring of the "bread of life" which Jesus not only provides, but, indeed, is.

And because this bread "came down from heaven," and "those who ate had their fill," the fullness of the sign came to be seen in the banquet in heaven.

READING II

The consequences of baptism are dramatic. Genuine conversion is a basic expectation placed on all those who have been "buried with Christ" in baptism and have been "raised up" from the cleansing waters to a new mode of existence. It is unthinkable that baptism would have no effect on our behavior. After all, Jesus was very different after his descent into the grave.

Paul delights in the comparison of our baptism with Jesus' death and resurrection. According to his special kind of logic, we are totally new beings after baptism, so it is obvious that our old selves have been laid aside and we must take on a new way of thinking. Another image offered in this regard is the changing of clothes—the origin of our practice of using baptismal gowns. The old covering is "laid aside," and the newly baptized don a new and spotless garment.

The most dramatic change, however, takes place on the inside. The consequence of baptism is that we must "acquire a fresh, spiritual way of thinking." It is a daunting challenge, but there's no denying its validity—nor the joy that comes with having accepted the challenge.

EIGHTEENTH SUNDAY IN ORDINARY TIME

LECTIONARY #114

READING I   Exodus 16:2–4, 12–15

A reading from the book of *Exodus* ▪▪

Here is a short story with all the necessary dramatic elements of conflict and resolution. Use your best narrative technique, bringing out each element.

The whole Israelite *community* grumbled against *Moses* and *Aaron.* ▪ The Israelites said to them, ▪ "Would that we had died at the *Lord's* hand in the land of *Egypt,* as we sat by our *fleshpots* and ate our fill of *bread!* ▪ But *you* had to lead us into this *desert* to make the whole *community* die of *famine!*" ▪▪

Pause. The scene (problem) is set. Now for the solution.

Then the Lord said to Moses, ▪ "I will now rain down bread from *heaven* for you. ▪ Each *day* the people are to go out and gather their daily *portion;* ▪ thus will I *test* them, to see whether they follow my *instructions* or not. ▪▪

Pause. The transition is a bit awkward. Emphasize the word "flesh," to contrast with "bread," above.

"I have *heard* the grumbling of the Israelites. ▪ Tell them: ▪ In the evening twilight you shall eat *flesh,* and in the *morning* you shall have your fill of *bread,* so that you may know that *I,* the *Lord,* am your *God.*"

Another pause. Now it all happens in accord with God's pledge.

In the evening *quail* came up and covered the camp. ▪ In the morning a *dew* lay all about the camp, and when the dew *evaporated,* there on the surface of the *desert* were fine flakes like *hoarfrost* on the ground. ▪

"What is this?" could easily be unintentionally comical. The NRSV "What is it!" is not much better. You might want to say, instead, "What can this be?"

On seeing it, the Israelites asked one another, ▪ "What is *this?*" ▪ for they did not *know* what it was. ▪ But Moses told them, ▪ "This is the bread which the *Lord* has given you to eat." ▪▪

READING II   Ephesians 4:17, 20–24

A reading from the letter of *Paul* to the *Ephesians* ▪▪

Paul is very hard on the pagans—because they refused to "know" Christ.

I declare and solemnly attest in the *Lord* that you must no *longer* live as the *pagans* do—their minds empty. ▪ That is *not* what you learned when you learned *Christ!* ▪ I am supposing, of course, that he has been *preached* and *taught* to you in accord with the *truth* that is in *Jesus:* ▪ namely, that you must lay *aside* your *former* way of life and the *old* self which deteriorates through *illusion* and *desire,* ▪ and

A hint of understatement and irony here. Paul can probably do more than "suppose" that the Ephesians have been taught the truth about Jesus.

acquire a fresh, *spiritual* way of thinking. ▪ You must put on that *new* man created in *God's* image, whose justice and holiness are born of *truth*. ▪ ▪

Instead of "man," say, "You must put on that new self. . . ."

GOSPEL   John 6:24–35

A reading from the holy *gospel* according to *John* ▪ ▪

Begin by communicating how urgently the people are seeking Jesus. Capernaum = kuh-PER-nay-uhm

When the crowd saw that neither *Jesus* nor his *disci*-ples were at the place where they had eaten the *bread*, they *too* embarked in the boats and went to *Capernaum looking* for Jesus. ▪ ▪

The question is an honest one. State it simply.

When they found him on the other side of the *lake*, they said to him, ▪ "Rabbi, when did you come *here?*" ▪ Jesus answered them: ▪

"I assure you,
you are not looking for me because
    you have seen *signs*
but because you have eaten your fill
    of the *loaves*. ▪

There need be no hint that Jesus is scolding here. He is simply setting up a situation in which he can teach the crowd effectively.

You should not be working for *perishable* food
but for food that *remains* unto life *eternal*,
food which the Son of *Man* will give you; ▪
it is on *him* that God the Father has set
    his *seal*." ▪

The following dialogue is not a contest, and the people's questions are sincere. To ask for a sign is not necessarily to doubt; it could be to establish good reasons for believing.

At this they said to him, ▪ "What must we *do* to perform the works of God?" ▪ Jesus replied: ▪
"*This* is the work of God: ▪
have faith in the One he *sent*." ▪
"So that we *can* put faith in you," they asked him, ▪
"what *sign* are you going to perform for us to see? ▪
What is the '*work*' you do? ▪ Our ancestors had *manna* to eat in the *desert*; ▪ according to Scripture, ▪
'He gave them bread from the *heavens* to eat.'" ▪
Jesus said to them: ▪
"I solemnly assure you, ▪
it was not *Moses* who gave you bread
    from the heavens; ▪
it is my *Father* who gives you the *real*
    heavenly bread. ▪
God's bread comes down from heaven
and gives *life* to the world." ▪

The people believe in earnest now. Later they will have grave reservations.
A very bold assertion, indeed. It will drive some of his followers away.

"Sir, give us this bread *always*," they besought him. ▪
Jesus explained to them: ▪
"I *myself* am the bread of life. ▪
No one who comes to *me* shall *ever* be hungry,
no one who believes in *me* shall thirst
    again." ▪ ▪

GOSPEL   In this reading we see the beginning of Jesus' long discourse on the "bread of life." It is a classic instruction, touching on the many ways in which God reveals the divine will and plan for our salvation. Notice that the teaching is carefully structured. An assertion is made by the crowds, and then followed by an explanation by Jesus that corrects the mistaken or incomplete understanding of the assertion.

"When did you come here?" they ask. Jesus points out that their motivation is less than pure. They have been amazed by the miracle of the loaves, or perhaps simply feel they have found an inexhaustible food supply. It is necessary to instruct them on a different plane. Thus, he makes the distinction between perishable food and the imperishable food, the good news that leads to eternal life.

"How do we perform godly works?" they ask. And Jesus responds with the clarification that the only true work is to believe in the One God sent (himself).

"Can you prove that you are worthy of such belief?" they ask. And they cite history. For example, Moses earned credibility by providing manna to their ancestors. Jesus now has the opportunity to correct and clarify their thinking about him in some very striking words. "It was not Moses, but God who sent the bread from heaven; and that bread from heaven has now taken a new form [in me] to give life to the world."

"Give us this bread," they beg. Jesus now makes the dramatic assertion that he himself is the bread of life—a clear reference (for us, at least) to the eucharist, as well as to the giving of his body in death so that we might live. In a few weeks we will see that for some of the crowds, this assertion is too much. "How can he give us his flesh to eat?" they will scoff. Indeed, some of Jesus' own disciples will break away from him over this issue. "This sort of talk is hard to endure," they will say.

It is not difficult to see that Jesus' claims to be "the bread of life" resulted in a turning point in his ministry. The clouds begin to gather, the forces against him begin to conspire.

READING I Anyone who is devoted to a life of faith will experience some degree of Elijah's desperation. Times come when the struggle for religious values seems to hold out very little hope of victory. Elijah's belief in the Lord put his life in danger; armies pursued him. And he was discouraged in his attempts to persuade Israel to return to the one true God. Very few of us will encounter such dramatic challenges, though our feelings of despair can become just as strong.

But the point of this reading is not so much Elijah's feeling of hopelessness as it is the power of God's provident love. The last sentence of the story makes it clear: "Strengthened by that food, he walked forty days and forty nights." God will not abandon those who have been called to proclaim the good news. When hope seems most dim, God's promises shine through with greater brightness.

Christians see in this story a foreshadowing of Jesus' fast of forty days and forty nights, as well as the sacrament of the eucharist. In today's liturgy, the experience of Elijah parallels the experience of all who receive the "bread that comes down from heaven"—Jesus himself—which we hear about in the gospel. These parallels explain why the designers of the lectionary chose this first reading.

READING II We cannot remind ourselves too often that our motive for living the Golden Rule is that God first loved us. Sometimes we feel that we must obey the commandments in order to avoid punishment. Although this is true, it doesn't tell the whole story of what it means to be a Christian. Much more positive (and effective) is to love our neighbor in the realization that God first loved us.

Paul's logic doesn't specify propositions in any formal way (A+B=C), but it makes quite clear to us why we must heed his advice: The undeniable love we have been shown by Christ makes it undeniable that we must show love to our neighbor. Even more gratifying is the realization that such love goes far beyond "duty." Once we deeply believe in the overwhelming, unconditional love that God has for us, our love for each other becomes a spontaneous response. The greatest lovers are those who realize to the greatest degree how much they have been loved.

AUGUST 7, 1994

NINETEENTH SUNDAY IN ORDINARY TIME

LECTIONARY #117

READING I   1 Kings 19:4–8

A reading from the first book of *Kings* ▪▪

You are reading a short story, for which a brisk, alert tone is best. Use caution with "This is enough, O Lord," so it doesn't sound petulant or childish. NRSV: "ancestors" instead of "fathers."

Elijah went a day's journey into the desert, until he came to a *broom* tree and sat *beneath* it. ▪ He prayed for *death:* ▪ "This is *enough*, O Lord! ▪ *Take* my life, for I am no better than my *fathers*." ▪ He lay *down* and fell *asleep* under the broom tree, ▪ but then an *angel* touched him and ordered him to get up and *eat*. ▪ He looked and there at his head was a hearth cake and a jug of water. ▪ After he ate and drank, he lay *down* again, but the angel of the Lord came back a *second* time, touched him, and ordered, ▪ "Get up and *eat*, else the journey will be too *long* for you!" ▪ He got up, ▪ ate and drank; ▪ then *strengthened* by that food, he walked forty *days* and forty *nights* to the mountain of God, *Horeb*. ▪▪

Horeb = HAWR-ehb

READING II   Ephesians 4:30—5:2

A reading from the letter of *Paul* to the *Ephesians* ▪▪

"Do nothing to sadden . . ." is a strong beginning, but it is a plea, not a reprimand.

Here is a list; give each item equal time—but use a vocal variety to let each one stand out.

Do nothing to sadden the Holy *Spirit* with whom you were *sealed* against the day of *redemption*. ▪ Get rid of all bitterness, all passion and anger, harsh words, slander, and malice of every *kind*. ▪ In place of *these*, ▪ be *kind* to one another, compassionate, and mutually forgiving, ▪ just as God has forgiven you in Christ. ▪▪

What follows is the logical conclusion from what has gone before.

Be *imitators* of God as his dear *children*. ▪ Follow the way of *love*, even as *Christ* loved *you*. ▪ He gave *himself* for us as an offering to *God*, a gift of pleasing *fragrance*. ▪▪

A reading from the holy *gospel* according to *John* ▪ ▪

The Jews started to murmur in *protest* because Jesus claimed, ▪ "I am the bread that came down from *heaven*." ▪ They kept saying: ▪ "Is this not *Jesus*, the son of *Joseph?* ▪ Do we not know his *father* and *mother?* ▪ How can he claim to have come down from *heaven?*" ▪ ▪

"Stop your *murmuring*," Jesus told them. ▪
   "No one can come to me
unless the Father who *sent* me *draws* him; ▪
I will raise him *up* on the last day. ▪
It is written in the *prophets:* ▪
'They shall all be taught by *God.*' ▪
Everyone who has *heard* the Father
and *learned* from him
comes to *me.* ▪
Not that anyone has *seen* the Father—
only the one who is *from* God
has *seen* the Father. ▪
Let me firmly *assure* you, ▪
he who *believes* has eternal *life.* ▪
I am the bread of life. ▪
Your ancestors ate *manna* in the *desert,*
   but they *died.* ▪
This is the bread that comes down from *heaven,*
for a man to eat and *never* die. ▪
I *myself* am the *living* bread
come down from *heaven.* ▪
If anyone eats *this* bread
he shall live *forever;* ▪
the bread *I* will give
is my *flesh,* for the life of the *world.*" ▪ ▪

The word "murmur" is the key word in this passage. Give it special emphasis. It recalls the "murmuring" of the Israelites in the desert.

Jesus' command to "stop murmuring" should be less a strong reprimand and more an introduction to his explanation. NRSV: "unless drawn by the Father who sent me . . . I will raise that person. . . ."

A slight pause will indicate that a brief side comment begins here.

"Let me firmly assure you" always introduces a solemn pronouncement. Let your voice carry the weightiness of all that follows to the end of the reading. It is a startling revelation of who Jesus really is. NRSV: "whoever believes."

NRSV: "so that one may eat of it and not die."

NRSV: "Whoever eats of this bread will live forever."

GOSPEL The gospel writer here has constructed a comparison and contrast. His use of the word "murmur," the same word used in the Book of Exodus to describe the disgruntled Israelites exiled in the desert, is deliberate. John clearly intends for his readers to be reminded of the manna that came down from heaven in response to Israel's complaint. But he also wants his readers to see the difference between that manna and the "living bread" which is Jesus.

Those who hear Jesus describe himself as "bread from heaven" see the difference quite clearly indeed! They see the manna as a spectacular and miraculous occurrence in their history; Jesus, on the contrary, seems to them only a neighbor whose parents they know. There's nothing very spectacular about that. The point is, of course, that only the eyes of faith see Jesus for what he truly his. That's what Jesus means when he says, "Everyone who has heard the Father and learned from him comes to me." If we have opened ourselves to God's loving call, we will see in Jesus far more than a prophet from Galilee; we will see "the bread of life."

The difference between manna and Jesus, as John points out, is that those who ate the manna died, but those who eat "the bread of life" will live forever. We must remember the original audience for whom John is writing. He employs their familiar history in order to bring them into the present and future. It is not an easy task, for people have a tendency to cling to the familiar, to resist new insights.

READING I Wisdom's lovely, poetic invitation to the heavenly feast is a charming match to the invitation issued by Jesus in today's gospel reading. The final verses of this chapter of Proverbs contain the invitation of "Foolishness" to a far different feast. These lines serve partly as a backdrop to the second part of today's gospel, in which we see that refusing Wisdom's invitation has dire consequences.

The poet's description of the heavenly banquet is one of the loveliest passages in the Hebrew scriptures. The comparison of wisdom to life—and foolishness to death—is quite common in our tradition, and it deserves the kind of concentrated meditation and proclamation that will make it yield its richest insights. Wisdom, like faith, far exceeds any quantitative notions of knowledge or information. It embraces intuition, sensitivity, perspicacity—almost a "sixth sense" about the significance of life and events. Wisdom, like faith, brings peace—because it enables us to see things in perspective, to take the long view, to see beyond immediate situations into their lasting (or fading) significance. Wisdom, like faith, enables us to keep our priorities straight. Wisdom, like faith, brings "life"—more than mere existence. Wisdom opens us up to the fullness of life, making it possible for us to accept inevitable pain and suffering or to rejoice wholeheartedly in whatever life brings us.

Above all, the reward for those who seek wisdom, responding with love to her invitation, is the heavenly banquet of unending happiness.

READING II We have been reading from Ephesians in a more or less consecutive fashion for several weeks now. By happy circumstance, today's selection alludes to the contrast between wisdom and folly, which is dealt with directly in the first reading. Paul's special kind of logic makes the point that our behavior must be guided by our realization that salvation has been freely given to us.

It wouldn't make sense, Paul says, to continue in ignorance and foolhardiness now that God's loving will has been made clear to us. Few things are more unattractive than the ungrateful person who squanders opportunities. The Lord Jesus has opened the door to a new way of life for

TWENTIETH SUNDAY IN ORDINARY TIME

LECTIONARY #120

READING I   Proverbs 9:1–6

A reading from the book of *Proverbs* ··

Proverbs is a book of poetry. The poetic device employed here is personification: Wisdom is portrayed as a woman. An exalted (but not stuffy) tone is appropriate.

Wisdom has built her *house*,
    she has set up her seven *columns*; ·
She has dressed her *meat*, mixed her *wine*,
    yes, she has spread her *table*. ·
She has sent out her *maidens*; · she calls
    from the heights out over the city: ·

The second half begins here with an invitation. The delivery should be larger. NRSV: "To those without sense. . . ."

"Let whoever is simple turn in *here*; ·
    to him who lacks understanding, I say,
Come, eat of my *food*,
    and drink of the *wine* I have mixed! ·

The pace slows down to signal the ending.

Forsake foolishness that you may *live*; ·
    advance in the way of *understanding*. ··

READING II   Ephesians 5:15–20

A reading from the letter of *Paul* to the *Ephesians* ··

A direct and attention-grabbing opener. NRSV: "Be careful then how you live, not as unwise people but as wise, making the most of the time, because the days are evil."

A new section. The tone is not one of reprimand, but of the the enthusiasm of having a better option: Being intoxicated with the Spirit is better than being drunk on wine.

Keep careful *watch* over your *conduct*. · Do not act like *fools*, but like *thoughtful* men. · Make the most of the present *opportunity*, for these are evil *days*. · Do not continue in *ignorance*, but try to discern the will of the *Lord*. · Avoid getting drunk on *wine*; · that leads to *debauchery*. · Be filled with the *Spirit*, addressing one another in psalms and hymns and inspired *songs*. · Sing praise to the Lord with all your *hearts*. · Give thanks to God the *Father always* and for *everything* in the name of our Lord Jesus *Christ*. ··

A reading from the holy *gospel* according to *John* ▪ ▪

Let the beginning be fresh, a new bright introduction to the argument that follows. Jesus' words are a startling revelation. NRSV: "Whoever eats of this bread will live forever."

Jesus said to the crowds: ▪
"I *myself* am the living bread
come down from *heaven.* ▪
If anyone eats *this* bread
he shall live *forever*; ▪
the bread *I* will give
is my *flesh*, for the life of the *world.*" ▪ ▪

A darker tone is appropriate as the contest begins.

At this the Jews quarreled among themselves, saying, ▪
"How can he give us his *flesh* to eat?" ▪ Thereupon
Jesus said to them: ▪

"Let me solemnly assure you" always introduces a solemn pronouncement. Be sure your tone communicates this, not by exaggeration, but by strength and firmness.

"Let me solemnly *assure* you,
if you do not eat the *flesh* of the Son of *Man*
and drink his *blood,*
you have no *life* in you. ▪
He who feeds on my *flesh*
and drinks my *blood*
has life *eternal,* ▪
and I will raise him up on the last *day.* ▪

This lengthy exposition requires careful attention to each insight. The effect is a steady rise through ". . . will have life because of me." Then a pause, and a clear sense of conclusion in the summary statement. Use the plural to be inclusive: "Those who feed on me. . . ."

For *my* flesh is real *food*
and *my* blood real *drink.* ▪
The man who *feeds* on my flesh
and *drinks* my blood
remains in *me* and I in *him.* ▪
Just as the *Father* who has life sent me
and *I* have life because of the Father, ▪
so the man who feeds on *me*
will have *life* because of me. ▪
This is the bread that came down from heaven. ▪
Unlike your *ancestors* who ate and died
nonetheless, ▪
the man who feeds on *this* bread
shall live *forever.*" ▪ ▪

us—a way that makes foolishness and debauchery utterly unthinkable.

Paul's reasoning here is more compelling than a rule book or an arbitrary code of discipline. His admonitions are based on something entirely positive: We behave in a certain way because God has behaved in a certain way in our behalf. Our view of the world (with its good and evil) is shaped by God's view of the world, shown to us in the sacrificial love of Christ. In other words, the conversion we continually undergo as Christians is a spontaneous response to infinite love. Such a view of our faith takes us about as far away from "rule book religion" as you can possibly get. True wisdom makes it clear that the most appropriate expression of such faith is to "sing praise" and "give thanks."

GOSPEL   The gospel reading for the past few Sundays has been taken from the section of John referred to as the "Bread of Life" discourse. Today we come to its most direct and radical assertions. The effect of what Jesus says here is dire! It results in the loss of some of his followers, as we'll see in next Sunday's selection.

Those who ask, "How can he give us his flesh to eat?" are reacting quite naturally, though in the ancient world the notion of partaking in divine life by consuming the god in some way was common. Thus, there is room for argument among them regarding what Jesus really means. Is he speaking figuratively? Surely he is not speaking literally! What does it mean to "eat the flesh of the Son of Man and drink his blood?" Every Christian needs to ask the same question—and struggle toward an answer in faith.

Though the charge of "cannibalism" has appeared and reappeared throughout Christian history, Jesus clearly does not have literal cannibalism in mind. But he certainly shows us in dramatic language that intimate participation in him is the goal of his life, death and resurrection. And without that intimacy we have no life in us!

The final sentence of this passage brings back the manna theme from the last two Sundays. Jesus is like the manna: heaven-sent as food for our pilgrim journey. The difference, however, is profound. Those who eat this new "bread from heaven" live forever.

READING I   There is great solemnity and grandeur in the scene that describes Joshua as the head of all the tribes of Israel at Shechem. He places a weighty choice on the shoulders of the people, but retains his role as leader by making his own choice incontestably clear. It is a political statement, designed to affirm freedom of choice and at the same time encourage the assembly to follow his example.

The response of Israel is a precious formula, recounting the history of the Lord's mighty deeds in their behalf (deliverance from exile and slavery, provident care in all their journeys). And it clearly implies the rhetorical question, "How could we choose otherwise, seeing what the Lord God has done for us?" In other words, it is a model act of faith, based on a belief in God's all-powerful and provident care and the natural response to demonstrations of such overwhelming love.

READING II   *Editor's note: In June 1992, the Bishops' Committee on the Liturgy issued a statement that permits a shorter version of this text to be proclaimed. The shorter version is highly recommended (Ephesians 5:25–32).*

Paul is a product of his culture; we cannot expect that his writing will reflect twentieth-century American ideals of equality. We can, however, recognize that Paul's central theme here is the parallel between husband and wife and between Christ and his church. We must not be blinded to the beauty of this image (which asserts total mutuality and unqualified love) because we cannot see beyond cultural differences. In any case, Paul is rising far above his own cultural background when he describes a relationship that makes male domination relationship unthinkable in the relationship between husband and wife.

Paul has gathered a code of marital conduct from many preexisting sources and elevated it to the loftiest of ideals, based entirely on mutual love and respect, and modeled after divine life. Our response to his achievement should be admiration and encouragement, even as we recognize the differences between his culture and our own.

Proclaim this text with all the exaltation and joy the writer clearly wants to communicate. You can do no more than manifest complete conviction and peace, emphasiz-

TWENTY-FIRST SUNDAY IN ORDINARY TIME

LECTIONARY #123

READING 1   Joshua 24:1–2, 15–17, 18

A reading from the book of *Joshua* ▪

A solemn gathering, listing the various officers and leaders. Shechem = SHEE-khem

Joshua gathered together all the tribes of *Israel* at *Shechem*, summoning their elders, their leaders, their judges and their officers. When they stood in ranks before *God*, Joshua *addressed* all the people: "If it does not please you to serve the *Lord*, decide today whom you *will* serve, the gods your *fathers* served beyond the *River* or the gods of the *Amorites* in whose country you are *dwelling*. As for me and *my* household, *we* will serve the *Lord*." ▪

Joshua's address is formulaic, not conversational. He is presenting a ritual choice to a large crowd. NRSV: "ancestors."

But the people answered, "Far be it from us to forsake the *Lord* for the service of *other* gods. For it was the Lord, our God, who brought us and our fathers up out of the land of *Egypt*, out of a state of *slavery*. He performed those great *miracles* before our very *eyes* and protected us along our entire *journey* and among all the *peoples* through whom we *passed*. Therefore we also will serve the Lord, for he is our God." ▪

A new section begins here. Prepare for it with a pause. Then all the people respond, as if with one voice. It is a solemn ritual response.

NRSV: "ancestors."

The high energy level and fullness of your projection should not slacken. Keep the elevated tone right through to the end, slowing down for the final phrase to signal the end.

READING II   Ephesians 5:21–32

A reading from the letter of *Paul* to the Ephesians ▪

See the commentary: The first part of the passage may be omitted.

Defer to one *another* out of reverence for *Christ*. ▪ Wives should be submissive to their husbands as if to the *Lord* because the *husband* is head of his *wife* just as *Christ* is head of his *body*, the church, as well as its *savior*. As the church submits to *Christ*, so wives should submit to their *husbands* in everything. ▪

This is instruction.

Husbands, *love* your wives, as *Christ* loved the *church*. He gave himself *up* for her to make her *holy*, purifying her in the bath of *water* by the power of the *word*, to present to himself a *glorious* church, holy and immaculate, without stain or wrinkle or anything of that *sort*. Husbands should love their *wives* as they do their own *bodies*. He who loves his *wife* loves *himself*. Observe that no one ever hates his own *flesh*; no, he nourishes it and takes care of it as *Christ* cares for the *church*—for we are *members* of his body. ▪

Another facet of the instruction begins here.

"For this reason a man shall leave his *father* and *mother*,
and shall cling to his *wife*,
and the *two* shall be made into one."

The quotation from Genesis should be recognizable as a quotation. It can be vocally set apart from Paul's narrative.

This is a great *foreshadowing*; I mean that it refers to *Christ* and the *church*. ▪

Speak the final sentence with great reverence.

GOSPEL John 6:60–69

A reading from the holy *gospel* according to *John* ▪

The word "this," without a referent, makes it impossible for the assembly to know what you are talking about. See the commentary for a solution.

Many of the disciples of Jesus remarked, "This sort of talk is hard to *endure*. How can anyone take it *seriously?*" Jesus was *fully* aware that his disciples were murmuring in protest at what he had *said*. "Does it shake your *faith?*" he asked them. ▪

"What, then, if you were to see the Son of *Man*
ascend to where he was *before* . . . ?
It is the *spirit* that gives *life*;
the flesh is *useless*.
The *words* I spoke to you
are *spirit* and *life*.
Yet among you there *are* some who do not
believe."

Prepare for this new section with a pause and a fresh vocal intonation.

(Jesus knew from the *start*, of course, the ones who refused to *believe*, and the one who would hand him *over*.) He went *on* to say:

"This is *why* I have told you
that no *one* can come to me
unless it is granted him by the *Father*." ▪

NRSV: "unless it is granted by the Father."

From this time *on*, many of his disciples broke *away* and would not remain in his company any *longer*. Jesus then said to the Twelve, "Do *you* want to leave me *too?*" Simon Peter answered him, "Lord, to whom shall we *go?* You have the words of eternal *life*. We have come to *believe*; we are *convinced* that you are God's *holy* one." ▪

The narrative thus far has been rather sad. But a new tone of voice should predict the comforting vote of confidence which Simon Peter casts. The gospel story ends on a quiet note of conviction.

ing the warmth and intimacy that flow between Christ and the assembled church as the model for married love. Then you will have communicated the writer's fullest intention. The rest is up to the homilist.

GOSPEL This is one of those readings that begins right in the middle of things. It was a week ago that the congregation heard the message that the disciples find "hard to endure." We cannot expect them to recall it automatically. Take the liberty of establishing a context by beginning something like this:

"After the disciples heard Jesus proclaim that he is 'the bread from heaven,' they remarked, 'This sort of talk is hard to endure.'" And continue from there.

There are two reasons for altering the opening sentence: (1) so that the assembly will understand the context, and (2) so that it may become clearer to the assembly that it is Jesus' claim to be sent directly from the Father that the disciples find difficult to believe—not simply his command "eat my flesh and drink my blood." The evangelist John is eager to show us that the ultimate test of faith is believing in Jesus' divine origin, his credentials as the Son of God. The entire gospel of John is intent upon revealing (indeed, proving) that Jesus is heaven-sent, and pointing out that God is one who imbues us with the ability to believe. An assertion of Jesus' divinity is clearly implied in the parenthetical remark, "Jesus knew from the start, of course, the ones who refused to believe. . . ."

Now it becomes clearer why Jesus launches into apocalyptic imagery about his ascension, his return to the Father from whom he was sent. Now it becomes clearer why Jesus has to point out again that mere human experience or knowledge is insufficient for arriving at Christian faith. The spiritual part of us (that "inner eye") is what enables us to accept Jesus for what he truly is. And that spiritual part of us was instilled by God.

READING I Rules and regulations are negative things only when we fail to look behind them and see the ideals that gave them birth. If they seem like arbitrary restrictions, then we need to examine them carefully to discover their ultimate aim. The Law of the Lord God is presumed by Moses to make life for the Israelites a joyful and liberated experience.

"You shall not add to what I command you, nor subtract from it." In this sentence we see the parallel between this text and the gospel narrative for today. Something in human nature seems to want to elaborate on divinely revealed commandments — sometimes to the point of perverting the original. Well-intentioned or not, this tendency must be watched closely. The "spirit" and the "letter" of the law should coincide, but because the "letter of the law" seems easier to understand (or safer for the scrupulous), it is more subject to elaboration.

Moses clearly believes that one test of the quality of our observance is what others have to say about us. It is important to him that Israel "give evidence" of the goodness of God by observing the divine commandments. We cannot help being reminded of Jesus' words: "By this shall the world know you are my disciples — that you love one another."

READING II For the next five Sundays the second reading will be taken from James, a writer who is preoccupied with showing his readers how the precepts of Christ must be put into practice, not merely accepted in theory. His purpose is clear at the beginning of his letter: "Act on this word." By coincidence, this opening section of James fits nicely into the treatment of God's commandments that appears in the other two readings today.

You will notice that several verses have been eliminated in this selection, and that we have smatterings of verses between 17 and 27. From a literary point of view, this is a shame. James develops the metaphor of the word as a plant in a lovely way, even mentioning the necessity of removing weeds and preparing the soil to receive the word. All this precedes "welcome the word that has taken root in you," and makes the image complete. Later, "acting on the word" is prepared for by use of a wonderful "mirror" image. As a listening experience, this reading is more effective

TWENTY-SECOND SUNDAY IN ORDINARY TIME

LECTIONARY #126

READING I Deuteronomy 4:1–2, 6–8

The whole Israelite people stands on the threshold of the promised land and receives final instructions. Let the solemnity of the occasion be reflected in a large and solemn voice. The first instruction is "Hear!" NRSV: "ancestors."

The second instruction is "You should not add or subtract from it."
The third instruction.

The rhetorical question is powerful and full of pride and encouragement. Rhetorical questions do not necessarily end on a vocal upswing, like other questions. They do not expect an answer, so the voice falls naturally, as at the end of a declarative sentence.

A reading from the book of *Deuteronomy* ▪▪

Moses told the people: ▪ "Now, Israel, *hear* the statutes and decrees which I am teaching you to *observe*, that you may *live*, and may enter in and take possession of the *land* which the Lord, the God of your fathers, is *giving* you. ▪ In your observance of the commandments of the Lord, your God, which I enjoin upon you, you shall *not add* to what I command you *nor subtract* from it. ▪ Observe them *carefully*, for thus will you give evidence of your *wisdom* and *intelligence* to the *nations*, who will hear of all these statutes and say, ▪ "This great nation is *truly* a wise and intelligent people. ▪ For what great nation *is* there that has gods so *close* to it as the Lord, our God, is to *us* whenever we *call* upon him? ▪ Or what great nation has statutes and decrees that are as *just* as this whole *law* which I am setting before you today?" ▪▪

READING II James 1:17–18, 21–22, 27

The feeling of this opening sentence is that of a hymn or a poem, which, indeed, it may well be. It requires an exalted tone.

The second sentence is a piece of straightforward instruction.

The next two sentences are commandments — not harsh, by any means, but urgent and encouraging.

The final sentence is a definition of healthy religion. Proclaim it with utter conviction and strength.

A reading from the letter of *James* ▪▪

Every worthwhile *gift*, every genuine *benefit* comes from *above*, descending from the Father of the heavenly *luminaries*, who *cannot* change and who is *never* shadowed over. ▪ He wills to bring us to birth with a *word* spoken in *truth* so that we may be a kind of *firstfruits* of his creatures. ▪▪

Humbly welcome the word that has taken *root* in you, with its power to *save* you. ▪ *Act* on this word. ▪ If all you do is *listen* to it, you are *deceiving* yourselves. ▪▪

Looking after orphans and widows in their *distress* and keeping oneself unspotted by the *world* make for *pure* worship without stain before our God and Father. ▪▪

A reading from the holy *gospel* according to *Mark* ▪ ▪

Here we have a little drama containing the essential elements of conflict, climax and resolution. Set the scene with careful attention to the details that lead to the confrontation between Jesus and the Pharisees.

The Pharisees and some of the experts in the law who had come from Jerusalem *gathered* around Jesus. ▪ They had observed a few of his disciples eating meals without having purified —that is to say, washed— their *hands.* ▪ The Pharisees, and in fact all Jews, cling to the custom of their ancestors and never *eat* without scrupulously washing their *hands.* ▪ Moreover, they never eat anything from the *market* without first *sprinkling* it. ▪ There are many *other* traditions they observe —for example, the washing of cups and jugs and kettles. ▪ So the Pharisees and

After the necessary background information has been supplied, the narrative continues here.

the scribes *questioned* him: ▪ "Why do your disciples not follow the tradition of our *ancestors,* but instead take *food* without purifying their *hands!*" ▪ He said to them: ▪ "How accurately *Isaiah* prophesied about

Here is the climax of the drama. Jesus rebukes strongly, but not angrily. The truth of what he says weighs more heavily than the emotion with which he says it.

you hypocrites when he wrote, ▪

'This people pays me *lip* service
   but their *heart* is *far* from me. ▪
Empty is the reverence *they* do me
   because they teach as *dogmas* mere
      human *precepts.*' ▪

You disregard *God's* commandment and cling to what is *human* tradition." ▪ ▪

NRSV: "There is nothing outside a person that by going in can defile, but the things that come out are what defile. Let anyone with ears to hear listen."

He summoned the crowd again and said to them: ▪ *"Hear* me, *all* of you, and try to understand. ▪ Nothing that enters a man from *outside* can make him impure; ▪ that which comes *out* of him, and *only* that, constitutes *impurity.* ▪ Let everyone *heed* what he *hears!*" ▪ ▪

The list of ugly vices cannot be rattled off. Each item on the list receives emphasis. Take your time. Resist the temptation to "get it over with." If the list is read with extreme care, the final sentence will be all the more compelling. NRSV: "a person."

"Wicked designs come from the deep recesses of the *heart:* ▪ acts of fornication, theft, murder, adulterous conduct, greed, maliciousness, deceit, sensuality, envy, blasphemy, arrogance, an obtuse spirit. ▪ *All* these evils come from *within* and render a man impure." ▪ ▪

in an unedited version. Feel free to pick up a Bible and proclaim the text in its fullness (verses 17 through 27).

The reading ends with specific examples of faith that is put into practice. These examples constitute a definition of true religion and the purest form of worship.

GOSPEL   Some people hear this passage with inordinate glee. They interpret it as justification for trivializing or jettisoning rituals and rubrics, sometimes coming dangerously close to reducing the liturgical expression of faith to whatever one feels like doing, and the social implications of religion to a version of our welfare system. Nothing could be further from the mind of Jesus. The point is that the heart is the seat of faith, and unless exterior observance of religion proceeds from there, it is bound to become dry and barren. Ritual observance is never empty; but sometimes those who engage in it are.

The narrative here is punctuated with parenthetical remarks and clearly covers more than one event. It is not "of a piece." The writer finds it necessary to describe some of the ritual practices of the Pharisees, and all Jews, because he is writing for a wider audience, including us. When he has Jesus quote Isaiah, Mark again digresses a bit from the specific encounter with the Pharisees, because the "lip service" mentioned is not particularly relevant to the situation at hand. And finally, the narrative covers more than one occasion, moving to another setting in the second to last paragraph, and apparently yet another in the final sentences. Nevertheless, the unity of the passage is maintained, centering as it does on the distinction between genuine and insincere (or misguided) faith. Effective proclamation depends on effective pauses between clearly distinct passages.

The striking metaphor that describes the difference between what "goes into us" and and what "comes out of us" is a treasured one. It serves as an excellent examination of conscience. Fasting is of no avail unless it is accompanied by good works. "Prayers without thoughts never to heaven go," says King Claudius in *Hamlet.*

READING I You are privileged to read a portion of one of the loveliest passages in the Bible. Isaiah's visions of the world to come—a world of wholeness and freshness—are unsurpassed in scripture. Clearly, the text is poetry and must be proclaimed with the exalted style that comes naturally to verse. If you are familiar with Handel's *Messiah,* you cannot help but hear the composer's energetic treatment of these words.

The predictions Isaiah sings about here become real in the gospel narrative today. Jesus makes the prophecy come true: "the tongue of the dumb will sing." The obvious parallel explains the choice of this first reading for today's liturgy.

Isaiah was extolling the wonders of Israel's historical deliverance from exile, of course, and proclaims his message of hope to a people oppressed and discouraged. It was a proclamation of hope in the midst of much suffering—and no less relevant for us today. Passages such as this one should renew our sense of connection with the entirety of our Christian heritage—a heritage that extends back to the very beginnings of Hebrew history. As Pope John XXIII loved to remind us in his efforts to reestablish our oneness with the Jewish people, "Spiritually we are all Semites."

READING II This is the second of five consecutive readings from the Letter of James we hear this summer. We see again the major theme that permeates this pastoral letter: Faith in Jesus must be expressed in good works, deeds that proclaim a faith alive with purpose. No heady theology or speculative fine distinctions for James! His ethical code is firmly grounded in specific examples. If you treat the rich better than you treat the poor, you have not yet grasped the heart of Jesus' life and words.

What is so compelling in James' approach is his constant reminder that we behave in a certain way because God has loved us in a certain way. Only when we forget that we ourselves have been rescued from dire spiritual poverty will we treat the poor with disdain, or be taken in by the material wealth of others.

This reading reminds us again of the most fundamental motive for Christian love: God has first loved us; therefore, the

SEPTEMBER 4, 1994

TWENTY-THIRD SUNDAY IN ORDINARY TIME

LECTIONARY #129

READING I   Isaiah 35:4–7

A reading from the book of the prophet *Isaiah* ▪▪

The poetry of Isaiah appears in the lectionary with delightful regularity. It is some of the most beautiful literature in the Bible. Recognize it as poetry and proclaim it with appropriate exaltation. The comforting joy of the first six lines is unsurpassed in scripture.

Say to those whose hearts are *frightened:* ▪
    Be strong, fear *not!* ▪
Here is your *God,*
    he comes with *vindication;* ▪
With divine *recompense*
    he comes to *save* you. ▪
Then will the eyes of the *blind* be *opened,*
    the ears of the *deaf* be *cleared;* ▪
Then will the *lame* leap like a *stag,*
    then the tongue of the *dumb* will *sing.* ▪

The prediction of this joyful time deserves a joyful and energetic voice.

Streams will burst forth in the *desert,*
    and *rivers* in the *steppe.* ▪
The burning *sands* will become *pools,*
    and the thirsty *ground,* springs of *water.* ▪▪

The end comes quickly. Be sure to let the assembly know we are reaching the conclusion, by slowing down and reading the final line with a sense of closure.

READING II   James 2:1–5

A reading from the letter of *James* ▪▪

The tone is warm because of the word "my" in the salutation. (Say "My brothers and sisters" to be inclusive.)

James is pointing out a scandalous hypothetical situation here. The rhetorical question at the end of it is an indictment of such behavior.

Another rhetorical question to end the reading. It has the effect of saying, "Isn't it obvious how we should conduct ourselves?"

My brothers, your faith in our Lord Jesus Christ glorified must *not* allow of favoritism. ▪ Suppose there should come into your *assembly* a man fashionably *dressed,* with gold *rings* on his fingers, ▪ and at the same time a *poor* man dressed in *shabby* clothes. ▪ Suppose further you were to take *notice* of the *well-dressed* man and say, ▪ "Sit right *here,* please;" ▪ whereas you were to say to the *poor* man, ▪ "You can *stand!*" ▪ or "Sit over *there* by my *footrest.*" ▪ Have you not in a case like this discriminated in your *hearts*? ▪ Have you not set *yourselves* up as *judges* who hand down corrupt *decisions*? ▪▪

Listen, dear brothers. ▪ Did not God choose those who are poor in the eyes of the *world* to be rich in faith and heirs of the *kingdom* he promised to those who *love* him? ▪ ▪

GOSPEL Mark 7:31–37

A reading from the holy *gospel* according to *Mark* ▪ ▪

Tyrian = TEER-ee-uhn
Sidon = SAI-duhn

This story is filled with visual and tactile details that make it especially vivid. Give special attention to the ritual of the healing.

Ephphatha = EHF-uh-thuh

The commentary on the healing event is a new section. Pause first, then proceed more briskly. The final sentence is full of amazement, which you can only suggest by your tone of voice.

Jesus left Tyrian territory and returned by way of Sidon to the Sea of Galilee, ▪ into the district of the Ten Cities. ▪ Some people brought him a *deaf* man who had a *speech* impediment and begged him to lay his *hand* on him. ▪ Jesus took him off by himself *away* from the *crowd*. ▪ He put his fingers into the man's *ears* and spitting, touched his *tongue;* ▪ then he looked up to heaven and emitted a *groan.* ▪ He said to him, ▪ *"Ephphatha!"* (that is, *"Be opened!")* ▪ At once the man's ears were *opened;* ▪ he was *freed* from the impediment, and began to speak *plainly.* ▪ Then he enjoined them *strictly* not to tell *anyone;* ▪ but the more he ordered them *not* to, the more they *proclaimed* it. ▪ Their amazement went beyond all *bounds:* ▪ "He has done everything *well!* ▪ He makes the deaf *hear* and the mute *speak!"* ▪ ▪

---

good we do and the evil we avoid is simply the natural response to having been loved beyond measure. Our sins are simply the result of not fully realizing (yet!) how much we are loved. We are still grasping and clutching after faith, and have not yet come to see that faith rushes in when we relax, open our hearts, and allow God to love us.

GOSPEL The early Christian community delighted in seeing the ministry of Jesus as a fulfillment of ancient prophecies in Israel's history. In today's miracle story, there is specific reference to Isaiah's prophecy in the first reading. *Mogilalos,* the Greek word chosen to describe the deaf man with the speech impediment, is precisely the same word used by Isaiah in the prediction, "the tongue of the dumb will sing." The word is very rare, indicating the likelihood that Mark chose it with great care to show that Jesus was fulfilling Isaiah's prophecy. The crowd's joyful exclamation hints at their recognition of the fulfillment.

The miracle recounted here appears only in Mark's gospel and not in the other three. It has some features that are particular to Mark, most notably the physical actions that accompany the healing (putting his fingers in the deaf man's ears, spitting, touching his tongue). The other gospel writers prefer to emphasize the divine power of Jesus by having him heal with the simple utterance of a word. Mark's gospel creates a feeling of suspense, seeing Jesus now as a mysterious wonder-worker whose true identity will become clear only with the resurrection.

The "secrecy" of Jesus' mission in Mark's approach is made very clear in the strict command not to tell anyone about the miracle. And the writer's intended irony is asserted in the crowd's complete disregard for the command: "The more he ordered them not to, the more they proclaimed it." The message is cleverly and clearly made: there's no stopping the inexorable growth of the kingdom of God!

TWENTY-FOURTH SUNDAY IN ORDINARY TIME

READING I Who is speaking in this first-person passage? Christians see Jesus in the role described. But the voice also belongs to the God of heaven and earth, now revealed to be a God of compassion, intimately involved with creation. It is also the voice of those who spoke on God's behalf throughout history: Jeremiah (a prophet appointed to live out in his person the suffering of his people), the whole people of Israel, and, indeed, men and women of every age who have borne the pain of the suffering poor and carried the burden of straying sinners.

You speak for all these as you proclaim this text. The ideal response of the assembly will be that they hear themselves speaking these words—and experience a renewal of their oneness with (and responsibility for) a pain-ridden world.

The last two verses, which deal with those who would oppose God's chosen one, are echoed strongly in the altercation between Peter and Jesus in the gospel story. The Messiah cannot be hindered in his mission, even by those who are well-intentioned but not in step with the providential and mysterious plan of the Lord God. That ultimate salvation (healing) should come out of suffering (sickness), is one of those striking ironies that abound in our spiritual history.

READING II For the third Sunday in a row, we read from the Letter of James. The writer is concerned with the distinction between "profession" and "practice." Anyone can utter a formula that includes articles of faith. We do that every Sunday in the profession of faith (the Creed). Anyone in any age can go through the motions of being a follower of Christ. For the twentieth-century American Catholic, the accepted behavior is regular attendance at Mass on Sundays and holydays and a contribution to the collection plate. If that's all that issues from our profession of faith, then our faith is fairly lifeless. The proof of faith is good works.

Is that what James is telling us here? Well, not quite. More specifically (and more interestingly), he is teaching us that good works *automatically* proceed from *genuine* faith. There's more than a subtle distinction involved. It's not as though we are being urged to do good works so much as we are being urged to embrace true

LECTIONARY #132

READING I   Isaiah 50:4–9

A reading from the book of the prophet *Isaiah* ▪▪

The suffering servant speaks in the first person. And in poetic form. Let your tone be exalted.

The Lord God opens my *ear* that I may *hear*
And I have not *rebelled*,
   have not turned *back*. ▪
I gave my *back* to those who *beat* me,
   my *cheeks* to those who plucked my *beard*; ▪
My *face* I did not *shield*
   from buffets and spitting. ▪▪

A new section begins here. It explains why the servant can endure suffering.

The Lord *God* is my help,
   therefore I am *not* disgraced; ▪
I have set my *face* like *flint*,
   knowing that I shall *not* be put to *shame*. ▪
He is near who upholds my *right*; ▪
   if anyone wishes to *oppose* me,
   let us appear *together*. ▪

Pause before this rhetorical question. Then ask it boldly. NRSV: "Who are my adversaries? Let them confront me."

Who disputes my *right?* ▪
   Let him *confront* me. ▪
See, the Lord *God* is my help; ▪
   who will prove me *wrong?* ▪▪

READING II   James 2:14–18

A reading from the letter of *James* ▪▪

"My brothers and sisters" is more inclusive. A series of rhetorical questions extracts from the hearers an inner response. Ask the questions with conviction.

My brothers, what good is it to *profess* faith without *practicing* it? ▪ Such faith has no power to *save* one, has it? ▪ If a brother or sister has nothing to *wear* and no *food* for the day, and you say to them, ▪ "Good-bye and good luck! ▪ Keep warm and well fed," but do not meet their bodily *needs*, ▪ what good is *that?* ▪ So it is with the *faith* that does nothing in *practice*. ▪

Pause after "what good is that?" Let it sink in. Then continue.

It is thoroughly *lifeless*. ▪▪

This final section is difficult. You may find the NRSV translation clearer: "But someone will say, 'You have faith and I have works.' Show me your faith apart from your works, and I by my works will show you my faith."

To such a person one might say, ▪ *"You have faith* and I have *works*—is *that* it?" ▪ Show me your faith without *works*, and I will show you the faith that underlies my works! ▪▪

GOSPEL   Mark 8:27–35

A reading from the holy *gospel* according to *Mark* ▪▪▪

This passage is the turning point of Mark's gospel. Proclaim it energetically. Caesarea Philippi = seh-zuh-REE-uh fih-LIH-pai, Elijah = ee-LAI-dzhuh.

"And you" is a thunderclap followed by silence.

Jesus and his disciples set out for the villages around Caesarea Philippi. ▪ On the way he asked his disciples this question: ▪ "Who do people say that I *am*?" ▪ They replied, ▪ "Some, John the Baptizer, ▪ others, Elijah, ▪ still others, *one* of the prophets." ▪ "And *you*," he went on to ask, ▪ "who do *you* say that I am?" ▪▪ Peter answered him, ▪ "You are the *Messiah*!" ▪▪ Then he strictly ordered them not to *tell* anyone about him. ▪▪

A new section. Pause.

He then began to teach them that the Son of Man had to *suffer* much, be *rejected* by the elders, the chief priests, and the scribes, be put to *death*, and rise three days *later*. ▪ He said this quite openly. ▪ Peter then took him aside and began to *remonstrate* with him. ▪ At this he turned around and, eyeing the disciples, *reprimanded Peter* in turn: ▪ "Get out of my sight, you *satan!* ▪ You are not judging by *God's* standards but by *man's!*" ▪▪

These strong words are perhaps most effective when said softly. NRSV: "You are setting your mind not on divine things but on human things."

Another new section. Pause. NRSV: "If any want to become my followers, let them deny themselves and take up their cross and follow me. For those who want to save their life will lose it, and those who lose their life for my sake, and for the sake of the gospel, will save it."

He summoned the *crowd* with his disciples and said to them: ▪ "If a man wishes to come after *me*, he must deny his very *self*, take up his *cross*, and follow in my *steps*. ▪ Whoever would *save* his life will *lose* it, but whoever *loses* his life for *my* sake and the *gospel's* will *save* it." ▪▪

faith. Once we have done the latter, the former will come naturally. Once we have opened ourselves to a full and vibrant belief in what the Lord has done for us, our good deeds will spring from us as naturally as fruit springs from a healthy, fertile fruit tree.

In our religious culture there is far too much emphasis on duties and obligations. Perhaps if we were to place more emphasis on the the kinds of religious experience and knowledge that lead to fuller love of God and neighbor, the duties and obligations would take care of themselves.

GOSPEL   With today's gospel narrative we find ourselves at the exact middle of Mark's account of Jesus' ministry. Mark is a dramatist. He has constructed his gospel like a play. The climax occurs today in the profession of faith placed on the lips of Peter. Everything leading up to this moment has been preparation; all that follows is resolution, the playing out of Jesus' role as Messiah.

The overriding question that guides Mark's gospel is, "Who is this man?" And the events of Jesus' ministry are hints at an answer to this question. Mark keeps the secret of Jesus' true identity until the very end. Only the resurrection can answer the question adequately. Thus, even after Peter has proclaimed that Jesus is the Messiah, the apostles are admonished not to tell anyone. The secrecy motif must be played out to the end, even as the revelation of Jesus' nature becomes more and more inevitable.

Clearly, Jesus is a Messiah who differs markedly from the conquering hero whom many were expecting. This Messiah is one who will conquer sin by taking it upon his own shoulders. He will become all the ugliness of our sin in order to restore us to the beauty of his own innocence. Peter finds this quite impossible to imagine, and his outburst in protest is perfectly understandable. It is not, however, acceptable.

Finally, this Messiah tells us that those who follow in his footsteps will also have to embrace suffering. We have to do what he did: lose our lives in order to save them. Not an easy task. Impossible, in fact, except that genuine love has shown us otherwise.

READING I The poetry of Wisdom is best understood in its original historical application: It was written for devout Jews under persecution by the godless. The "just one" also could represent the entire Chosen People in their struggle to maintain their relationship to God in the face of wicked influences from the outside. One of the most lamentable quirks of human nature seems to be intolerance of those whose lives put our own to shame. Instead of recognizing the good and imitating it, we sometimes manufacture reasons for hating it, and thereby justify ourselves.

The Wisdom writer is looking at the struggle from the point of view of the innocent and just, and the scene is painted in black and white, not the subtle shades that characterize human behavior. Nevertheless, the poetry has captured one of the most tortured of human tendencies, and will strike a resonant chord in the hearts of all who are honest enough to detect within themselves the frightening ability to be mean and small.

READING II In this fourth of five consecutive readings from James, the writer poetically describes the contrast between human and heavenly wisdom.

The jealousy and strife we saw at work in the first reading (the wicked envy the good) are described by James in terms of their consequences: "inconstancy" (translated by others as "disorder") and "all kinds of vile behavior" (an exaggerated way of saying "untold evil"). The point, of course, is that terrible things can proceed from human wisdom that does not have unity and peace as its goal. Sadly, we must admit that there is always an element of such misguided wisdom at work in every Christian community. Very often it masquerades as zeal for God's will.

James tells us that there is a litmus test for wisdom. If we find certain qualities resulting from the work of the zealous, then we can judge the source of their wisdom. The NRSV translation of these qualities is clearer: "pure, peaceable, gentle, willing to yield, full of mercy and good fruits, without a trace of partiality or hypocrisy." Look for these qualities the next time the zealots in your midst proclaim their dedication to whatever cause. If you find them, rejoice. If you find something more like "jealousy" and "disorder," flee!

SEPTEMBER 18, 1994

TWENTY-FIFTH SUNDAY IN ORDINARY TIME

LECTIONARY #135

READING I Wisdom 2:12, 17–20

The entire reading is in poetic form, and in the subjunctive mood: "Let us beset. . . . Let us see. . . . Let us condemn." The tone is arrogant, but don't overdo it.

Keep building the list. A bit louder.

The most brutal of all. At the end of this reading, the assembly may be stunned into silence.

A reading from the book of *Wisdom* ▪▪

[The *wicked* say:] ▪
Let us beset the *just* one, because he is
      obnoxious to us; ▪
   he sets himself against our *doings*,
Reproaches us for transgressions of the *law*
      and charges us with violations of our *training*. ▪
Let us see whether his words be *true*; ▪
   let us find out what will *happen* to him. ▪
For if the *just* one be the son of *God*, he will
      defend him
   and deliver him from the hand of his *foes*. ▪
With revilement and torture let us put him
      to the *test*
   that we may have *proof* of his gentleness
   and try his *patience*. ▪
Let us condemn him to a shameful *death*; ▪
   for according to his own *words*, God will
      take *care* of him. ▪▪

READING II James 3:16—4:3

Let the first sentence echo the first reading.

The contrast is striking and comforting. Read each item on the list with care, isolating it from the others.

This sentence is a "dictum," a proverb, a nugget of truth.

New energy. Rhetorical questions arouse an inner response.

A reading from the letter of *James* ▪▪

Where there are jealousy and *strife*, there also are *inconstancy* and all kinds of vile *behavior*. ▪ Wisdom from *above*, by contrast, is first of all *innocent*. ▪ It is also peaceable, lenient, docile, rich in sympathy and the kindly *deeds* that are its fruit, impartial and sincere. ▪ The harvest of *justice* is sown in *peace* for those who *cultivate* peace. ▪▪

Where do the conflicts and disputes among you *originate?* ▪ Is it not your inner *cravings* that make war within your *members?* ▪ What you *desire* you do not *obtain*, and so you resort to *murder*. ▪ You *envy*

PLAN AHEAD FOR 1995

By Labor Day of 1994, the 1995 volumes will be ready.

Use the card below anytime in 1994 to place your order and ensure that your books will be on hand in plenty of time for distribution and use.

1995 Manual para proclamadores de la palabra is the Spanish version of the *Workbook for Lectors and Gospel Readers*. It has been written especially for Hispanics in the United States.

1995 Sourcebook for Sundays and Seasons will take the Sundays of Year C season by season and Sunday by Sunday to discuss the factors that are constants each year and those that may vary.

At Home with the Word will have the three readings for each Sunday of 1995 (Year C), together with brief reflections to help an individual or a group bring together scripture and life. Prayers for the home and the prayers of Mass are included. It's inexpensive enough to buy one for every parish household.

The *1995 Year of Grace Liturgical Calendar* will have the same general format as earlier years with the seasons and feasts clearly marked. Two sizes are available, each in paper or laminated editions.

Orders will be filled on a first-come, first-served basis.

USE THIS CARD TO ORDER 1995 (YEAR C) BOOKS AND CALENDARS ONLY!

Place postage here

Advance Order Department
Liturgy Training Publications
1800 North Hermitage Avenue
Chicago IL 60622-1101

PRICES FOR THE 1995 (YEAR C) BOOKS

Advance orders honored at these pre-publication prices for the 1995 books until June 1, 1994.

1995 Workbook for Lectors and Gospel Readers

1995 Manual para proclamadores de la palabra

Single copies: **$10** each
2 – 49 copies: **$7.50** each
50 or more copies: **$6.50** each

1995 Sourcebook for Sundays and Seasons

Single copies: **$10** each
2 or more copies: **$7.50** each

1995 At Home with the Word

Single copies: **$6** each
2 – 99 copies: **$4** each
100 or more copies: **$2.50** each

1995 Year of Grace Liturgical Calendar

Poster size (26 x 26 inches, paper)
Single copies: **$7** each
2 – 24 copies: **$4** each
25 or more copies: **$3** each

Poster Size (26 x 26 inches, laminated)
$15

Notebook Size (17 x 11 inches, paper)
Pack of 25: **$10** per pack
(Sorry, we cannot ship less than a full pack.)

Notebook Size (17 x 11 inches, laminated)
$3 each

Prices subject to change without notice.

TEAM UP WITH OTHERS TO ORDER IN BULK AND SAVE!

ORDER EARLY FOR 1995 (YEAR C)

THREE CONVENIENT WAYS TO ORDER:

PHONE
1•800•933•1800
(7:30 am to 7:00 pm CST)

FAX
1•800•933•7094
(anytime day or night)

MAIL
◀ *Send this card*
(To inquire about orders or payments call 1•800•933•4779.)

USE THIS CARD TO ORDER 1995 (YEAR C) BOOKS ONLY!

1995 ADVANCE ORDER CARD

Please send the following:

_____ 1995 *At Home with the Word*

_____ 1995 *Workbook for Lectors and Gospel Readers*

_____ 1995 *Manual para proclamadores de la palabra*

_____ 1995 *Sourcebook for Sundays and Seasons*

1995 *Liturgical Calendars*
_____ Poster Size, *paper*
_____ Poster Size, *laminated*
_____ Notebook Size (*Pack of 25*)
_____ Notebook Size, *laminated*

LTP

Thank you for ordering early!

SEND NO MONEY NOW!

You will be sent an invoice with the books when they are shipped. The usual 10% for shipping and handling to destinations in the United States will be added to the invoice. **Minimum $3.00.**

Bill to_____

Account #_____

Address_____

City, State, ZIP_____

Phone _____ / _____

Send to/Attention_____

Street address_____
(We ship UPS. Give only street address please. No PO Boxes.)

City, State, ZIP_____

Date ordered: ___/___/___ . To avoid duplication of orders, please keep a copy for your records.

and you cannot *acquire,* so you quarrel and *fight.* ▪ You do not *obtain* because you do not *ask.* ▪ You ask and you do not *receive* because you ask *wrongly,* with a view to squandering what you receive on your *pleasures.* ▪▪

Make full use of the wordplay here: "obtain . . . ask; ask . . . receive." The ending of this reading leaves us with an unpleasant recognition of our selfishness.

GOSPEL   Mark 9:30–37

A reading from the holy *gospel* according to *Mark* ▪▪

Edit the opening sentence: "Jesus and his disciples came down the mountain [of Transfiguration] and began. . . ." This makes it clear what Jesus did not want anyone to know about.

Jesus and his disciples came down the mountain and began to go through Galilee, but he did not want anyone to *know* about it. ▪ He was teaching his disciples in *this* vein: ▪ "The Son of Man is going to be delivered into the hands of men who will put him to *death,* ▪ three days *after* his death he will *rise."* ▪ Though they failed to *understand* his words, they were afraid to *question* him. ▪▪

NRSV: "The Son of Man is to be betrayed into human hands, and they will kill him, and three days after being killed, he will rise again."

They returned to Capernaum and Jesus, once inside the house, began to ask them, ▪ "What were you *discussing* on the way home?" ▪ At this they fell *silent,* for on the way they had been arguing about who was the most *important.* ▪ So he sat down and called the Twelve around him and said, ▪ "If anyone wishes to rank *first,* he must remain the last one of *all* and the *servant* of all." ▪ Then he took a little *child,* stood him in their midst, and putting his arms around him, said to them, ▪ "Whoever welcomes a *child* such as this for *my* sake welcomes *me.* ▪ And whoever welcomes *me* welcomes, not *me,* but him who *sent* me." ▪▪▪

"So he sat down . . ." signals an important teaching.

NRSV: "Whoever wants to be first must be last of all and servant of all."

The final sentence is a bit complex. Proclaim it slowly. It is a memorable teaching.

Finally, James reminds us that the worst side of our nature resides in our wants. Without the wisdom that comes from above, we are unable to resist the call of our desires (meaning far more than sexual lust), and we pursue them relentlessly, even convincing ourselves that they have priority over the wants of others. Only the wisdom that comes from God enables us to see our better side, not governed by what we want, but liberated from want and converted to peace.

GOSPEL We must remind ourselves again and again that Mark wrote his gospel in part to contest those who would see in Jesus only a worker of wonders, and not the Son of God sent to redeem the world from sin. Thus, we hear several prophecies of his suffering and death from the lips of Jesus himself. And we hear Jesus foretell his resurrection as well, though it is beyond his disciples to understand fully what he is saying. They are afraid to ask him to explain further, as though they have an inkling of the terrible (yet wonderful) truth, and are reluctant to hear the details. We certainly can identify with such fear.

In the second part of the passage, we find more bad news for those who would make of Jesus a mighty ruler in the earthly realm. And it is revealed to us in a little human drama. Though they should have known otherwise, the disciples seem to have held out hope for some sort of earthly kingdom with Jesus as ruler. Thus, as his followers, they needed to begin choosing important positions for themselves—as Jesus' cabinet ministers, perhaps.

Clearly, they knew they were discussing something inconsistent with what Jesus had been telling them. So, in shame, they fall silent when asked. It is important here to notice how seriously Jesus deals with their misconceptions. The formula Mark uses to introduce the instruction tells us a great deal: "So he sat down and called the Twelve around him." Solemnly he tells them a fundamental Christian truth: To rank first, one must be the last of all. To serve is to reign. If only we could learn this simplest and most basic of Jesus' sayings—the one most dramatically exemplified in his life and death.

READING I We should not be too hard on the young man who tattled on Eldad and Medad. No doubt he was reared to believe that God works in a special way through special people, that there is a hierarchy of "access" to the truth and that those who are not ordained for divine ministry should not assume functions and privileges reserved for the "chosen ones." But we certainly should thank Moses for putting the boy straight. And we probably need to examine our own perceptions about how God's will and love are revealed.

This brief story teaches us about God and about ourselves. First, it teaches us that God will not (cannot!) be hemmed in by any human institutions, no matter how old or how venerable they may be. It teaches us that God is not to be claimed as anybody's exclusive right. Though we may speak of "the God of the Christians" or "the God of the Hebrews" or "the God of the Upanishads," there is only one God. Those who stake an exclusive claim on God have no idea who God is!

The story also teaches us about ourselves. There is something inherent in ecclesiastical institutions that makes them prone to exclusiveness. We invest so much time, energy, and money in our religion that it is difficult for us to believe in the rights of other religions. The spirit of God moves where it will, certainly not unaware of my devotion, but in no sense defined by it.

READING II James's position on material possessions is made horrifically clear in this brief passage. I always think of Charles Dickens's *A Christmas Carol* and Ebenezer Scrooge when I read this text. The ghost of Christmas Yet to Come reveals to Scrooge the misery of those who have died in their wealth, taunted by the cries of the poor they have systematically robbed of basic necessities. It is a horrible scene. Here, in James, the very wages withheld from the poor cry out to condemn the selfish wealthy.

James covers the gamut of possessions and reveals how insubstantial they are. He mentions "wealth" first. This does not mean money (which is mentioned later). It refers to food, bread, the harvest, wealth in agricultural terms. And it has rotted.

Second, he mentions wardrobe. There are many references throughout the Bible

TWENTY-SIXTH SUNDAY IN ORDINARY TIME

LECTIONARY #138

READING I   Numbers 11:25–29

A reading from the book of *Numbers* ··

The intimacy Moses has with God makes this passage awe-inspiring. God bestows the prophetic spirit on others to lessen Moses' burden of responsibility.

A little story of conflict and resolution. Eldad = EHL-dad, Medad = MEE-dad.

The Lord came down in the cloud and spoke to Moses. ▪ Taking some of the spirit that was on *him*, he bestowed it on the seventy *elders*; ▪ and as the spirit came to *rest* on them, they *prophesied*. ··

Now two men, one named Eldad and the other Medad, were not *in* the *gathering* but had been left in the *camp*. ▪ They *too* had been on the list, but had not gone out to the *tent*; yet the spirit came to rest on *them* also, and they prophesied in the camp. ▪ So, when a young man quickly told Moses, ▪ "Eldad and Medad are prophesying in the camp," *Joshua*, son of Nun, who from his youth had been Moses' *aide*, said, ▪ "Moses, my lord, *stop* them." ▪ But Moses answered him, ▪ "Are you jealous for *my* sake? ▪ Would that *all* the people of the Lord were prophets!" ▪ Would that the Lord might bestow his spirit on them *all!*" ▪▪

"So . . ." begins a rather involved sentence. The simple sentence is: "So Joshua said 'stop them.'" Joshua = DZHAH-shoo-uh, Nun = nuhn.

READING II   James 5:1–6

A reading from the letter of *James* ··

This is a strong condemnation, proclaimed in an exalted tone.

"See!" Renew the energy level.

"You lived . . ." Continue the build until the end. The final sentence carries a sense of horror. NRSV: "You have condemned and murdered the righteous one, who does not resist you."

You *rich*, weep and wail over your impending miseries. ▪ Your wealth has *rotted*, your fine wardrobe has grown *moth-eaten*, your gold and silver have *corroded*, and their corrosion shall be a *testimony* against you; ▪ it will devour your flesh like a *fire*. ▪ See what you have stored up for yourselves against the last days. ▪ *Here*, crying aloud, are the *wages* you withheld from the *farmhands* who harvested your *fields*. ▪ The shouts of the harvesters have reached the ears of the *Lord of hosts*. ▪ You lived in wanton *luxury* on the earth; ▪ you fattened yourselves for the day of *slaughter*. ▪ You condemned, even *killed*, the *just* man; ▪ he does not *resist* you. ▪▪

A reading from the holy *gospel* according to *Mark* ▪▪

John means well. Jesus must teach him that the spirit of God cannot be rationed.

The meaning is clearer in the NRSV: "No one who does a deed of power in my name will be able soon afterward to speak evil of me."

NRSV: "Whoever gives you a cup of water . . . will by no means lose the reward."

NRSV: "If any of you put a stumbling block before one of these little ones who believe in me, it would be better for you if a great millstone were hung around your neck and you were thrown into the sea."

Pause before "If your hand. . . ." A new teaching begins here. Gehenna = geh-HEHN-uh.

John said to Jesus, ▪ "Teacher, we saw a man using your name to expel demons and we tried to stop him because he is not of our company." ▪ Jesus said in reply: ▪ "Do *not* try to stop him. ▪ No man who performs a miracle using my *name* can at once speak *ill* of me. ▪ Anyone who is not *against* us is *with* us. ▪ Any man who gives you a drink of water because you belong to *Christ* will not, I assure you, go without his *reward.* ▪ But it would be better if anyone who leads *astray* one of these *simple believers* were to be plunged in the *sea* with a great *millstone* fastened around his neck. ▪▪

"If your *hand* is your difficulty, cut it *off!* ▪ Better for you to enter life *maimed* than to keep *both* hands and enter *Gehenna,* with its unquenchable *fire.* ▪ If your *foot* is your undoing, cut it off! ▪ Better for you to enter life *crippled* than to be thrown into Gehenna with both *feet.* ▪ If your *eye* is your downfall, tear it *out!* ▪ Better for you to enter the kingdom of God with *one* eye than to be thrown with both *eyes* into *Gehenna,* where 'the worm dies *not* and the fire is never *extinguished.*'" ▪▪

that show us how precious clothing (especially fine clothing) was in a culture that did not have mass production. Though difficult for us to appreciate, perhaps, garments in the ancient world were prized possessions. And they have grown motheaten.

Third, he refers to gold and silver, treasures both in James's culture and in our own. But notice: The gold and silver are corroded. Gold and silver do not rust or corrode. James is making the point quite strongly that even those possessions that seem most certain to last will desert us in the end.

GOSPEL   There are actually three separate messages in this brief passage, though the first and the second seem to be related, as Mark tells them. John has the same problem Joshua had in the first reading: He presumes that those who are not in the inner circle of Jesus' company should not invoke his name in ministry. Jesus teaches us a great deal in his reply to John, namely, that no one can lay exclusive claim to the reign of God as revealed in Christ. It is there for the taking, and sincere men and women in every time and culture are welcome to it. Even the simplest expression of Christian concern will have its reward.

On the other hand, even the simplest disciple shares the inestimable dignity of divine life; those who would lead such innocents astray are in for the harshest kind of judgment.

In the final section of this gospel text we hear some of the most dramatic language of the scriptures, language that reminds us once again of the difference between East and West. We know that some readers have taken these words literally, maiming their bodies in the hope of alleviating temptation. Nothing could be further from the mind of Jesus. The point of the hyperbole here is to emphasize beyond any doubt how important it is to enter the reign of God, no matter what the cost. We are being taught in a very striking way what our hierarchy of values must be. *Nothing,* absolutely *nothing,* is more important than belonging to the kingdom. Anything that jeopardizes our participation in the kingdom must be expunged from our lives. Christians have to make tough choices.

READING I It is almost impossible for us to conceive of human nature as the writer of Genesis did. We have an ingrained dualist point of view (flesh and spirit, or even flesh versus spirit); by contrast, the Hebrews saw one, whole, integral being. Thus, when man and woman "become one body" in this reading, the union is total, implying that man is incomplete without woman and vice versa. In other words, the teaching about the complementary nature of man and woman in Genesis is much stronger and more radical than we might think.

The notion that woman was taken from man's side has supported views of male domination in some cultures throughout their history. Such a view is hardly central to this text—which emphasizes the complementary oneness of man and woman. "Bone of my bone and flesh of my flesh" is a proclamation of equality and unity.

Further, though the man is to be ruler of the animal kingdom—by naming the animals—none of them proved to be a suitable partner. It was only from the flesh of the man that a match could be created. The implication is clear: Human nature as perceived by the author of Genesis presumes that wholeness is found in the union of man and woman, each fulfilling the other.

READING II There is a special kind of logic at work in this brief section: Jesus is high priest not because of what he is, but because of what he has done, namely, shared completely in our weakness and suffering and thereby become a perfect leader in the work of salvation. It is Jesus' identity with us that makes him the perfect high priest. There is no implication that Jesus lost anything by being made "for a little while lower than the angels." Indeed, in becoming identified with us he gained something: the ability to taste suffering and death, the means by which he consecrated both himself and us to "one and the same Father."

This passage might also tell us something about effective priesthood in the church today: identification with the people's suffering rather than any exalted position over them. This would apply both to priests who are ordained and all who are priests by baptism. For priests to be good leaders in the work of salvation, their

---

TWENTY-SEVENTH SUNDAY IN ORDINARY TIME

LECTIONARY #141

READING I   Genesis 2:18–24

A reading from the book of *Genesis* ▪ ▪

Your finest storytelling ability is needed here. We are in the world of legend and myth— accounting for the relationship between man and woman.

The Lord God said: ▪ "It is not *good* for the man to be *alone.* ▪ I will make a suitable *partner* for him." ▪ So the Lord God formed out of the ground various wild *animals* and various birds of the *air,* and he brought them to the man to see what he would *call* them; ▪ whatever the man *called* each of them would be its *name.* ▪ The man gave names to all the cattle, all the birds of the air, and all wild animals; ▪ but *none* proved to be the suitable *partner* for the man. ▪

"The man gave names . . . :" Notice the pattern: God wills / the man does.

Another pattern explains why things are the way they are: the man was alone / so God formed animals; none was suitable / so God made the woman.

So the Lord God cast a deep *sleep* on the man, and while he was asleep, he took out one of his *ribs* and closed up its place with *flesh.* ▪ The Lord God then built up into a *woman* the *rib* that he had taken from the *man.* ▪ When he *brought* her to the man, the man said: ▪

The NRSV is clearer: "This at last is bone of my bones and flesh of my flesh; this one shall be called Woman, for out of Man this one was taken."

   "*This* one, at last, is *bone* of my *bones*
       and *flesh* of my *flesh;* ▪
   This one shall be called '*woman,*'
       for out of 'her *man*' this one has been
       taken." ▪ ▪

The intimacy of matrimony is explained.

That is why a man *leaves* his father and mother and clings to his *wife,* and the two of them become one *body.* ▪ ▪

READING II   Hebrews 2:9–11

A reading from the letter to the *Hebrews* ▪ ▪

The language of Hebrews is always exalted, teaching and explaining in the noblest of terminology. NRSV: "taste death for everyone" and "bringing many children to glory."

Jesus was made for a little while lower than the *angels,* that through God's gracious will he might taste *death* for the sake of *all* men. ▪ Indeed, it was fitting that, when bringing many sons to *glory,* God, for whom and through whom all things *exist,* should make their *leader* in the work of salvation *perfect*

---

through *suffering.* ▪ ▪ He who *consecrates* and those who are *consecrated* have one and the same *Father.* ▪ Therefore, he is not *ashamed* to call them brothers. ▪ ▪

ministry must be made perfect through experience of the full range of human need and suffering. Then they are able to complete the work for which they, like Jesus, are appointed.

GOSPEL   Mark 10:2–16

A reading from the holy *gospel* according to *Mark* ▪ ▪

Some Pharisees came up and as a *test* began to ask Jesus whether it was permissible for a *husband* to *divorce* his *wife.* ▪ In reply he said, ▪ "What command did *Moses* give you?" ▪ They answered, ▪ "Moses *permitted* divorce and the writing of a *decree* of divorce." ▪ But *Jesus* told them: ▪ "He wrote that commandment for you because of your *stubbornness.* ▪ At the beginning of *creation* God made them *male* and *female;* ▪ for this reason a man shall leave his father and mother and the two shall become as *one.* ▪ They are no longer *two* but *one* flesh. ▪ Therefore let no man *separate* what *God* has *joined.*" ▪ Back in the *house* again, the disciples began to *question* him about this. ▪ He told them, ▪ "Whoever divorces his *wife* and marries *another* commits *adultery* against her; ▪ and the woman who divorces her *husband* and marries *another* commits adultery." ▪ ▪

People were bringing their little *children* to him to have him *touch* them, but the disciples were *scolding* them for this. ▪ Jesus became *indignant* when he noticed it and said to them: ▪ "Let the children *come* to me and do not *hinder* them. ▪ It is to just such as *these* that the kingdom of *God* belongs. ▪ I assure you that whoever does not accept the kingdom of God like a little *child* shall not enter *into* it." ▪ Then he *embraced* them and *blessed* them, placing his *hands* on them. ▪ ▪

[Shorter: Mark 10:2–12]

GOSPEL   The laws governing marriage and divorce are not as absolute or simple as many Christians believe. They reflect the reality of human weakness as well as the validity of the highest ideals. In the Bible itself, we find certain exceptions to the indissolubility of marriage alongside black-and-white formulations. Even here in Mark, the mention of "the woman who divorces her husband" is startling, admitting a possibility which did not exist in Jewish law, but signals Mark's awareness of Roman law. Mark's purpose, of course, is to forbid divorce.

In this passage, the belief regarding the indissolubility of marriage is plainly based on the teaching of Genesis, which Jesus quotes: "They are no longer two but one flesh." It is *impossible* to separate "one flesh." If you divide "one" you end up with something not whole, but fractional.

Nevertheless, Moses had permitted divorce. How could this be? Jesus says this was necessary because of "stubbornness" (NRSV = "hardness of heart"), a concession to human weakness and sin. With the coming of Jesus, sin has no power in the world, and a return to the earlier ideal is possible. It is understandable that Mark would have Jesus reiterate the ideal, convinced as he was that a whole new order of life has arrived with the reign of God established by Jesus.

Elsewhere in the Bible we see exceptions to this ideal. Matthew, for example, permits divorce on grounds of a wife's infidelity. And there are other concessions. The upshot is that the indissoluble nature of marriage is written in the very nature of men and women as described in our earliest tradition and teaching. But throughout Christian history, the ideal is experienced in the context of human weakness and sin (conquered by Christ, but not yet fully realized). Thus, the Christian community experiences the tension of living the ideal and living the reality of the human condition at the same moment. And the true function of this community is compassionate ministry to real human beings.

READING I The predominant mood of this lovely piece of poetry is confidence. The poetic device is parallelism, a favorite in Hebrew verse, in which the thought in each line is echoed or expressed in a slightly different way in the following line. Thus we have "I prayed" and "I pleaded," and "gold is a little sand" and "silver is to be accounted mire."

The literary device is comparison and contrast. Wisdom (knowledge of God and perceptive insight into human life) is greater than power, riches, health, beauty. Wisdom is brighter than light itself, and never yields to darkness.

The final twist is delightful: Even though Wisdom is greater than all these good things, all these things come to those who are truly wise. The reading is nicely packaged, drawing to a close with gentle irony.

This poetic meditation on an enlightened hierarchy of values serves as excellent preparation for Jesus' words to the young man in the gospel story who is blinded by material possessions.

READING II Though there is a note of warning in this text—"we must render an account"—the overall mood is one of exhilaration and delight. Like a lightning bolt, the word of God lights up our world with a blinding flash, showing things exactly as they are and in sharp outline. And yet, in our experience, it does not shine steadily. It gives us only a quick glimpse of reality; then we must call upon our mind and heart to apply the fleeting truth we saw.

Though nothing is concealed from the word of God, we know well that much is concealed from us. The ups and downs of daily living leave us with questions and quandaries. Like the Hebrews who first received this message, we are subject to the stupor and malaise that life's concerns can bring. We therefore need to return often to the word of God, where we can depend on another flash of insight to help us along the dark journey.

GOSPEL Here we have a neatly packaged story. It comes complete with a situation ripe for controversy, a startling revelation, a sad ending, but an application (the moral) that raises our spirits again and throws the whole event into clearer light.

The impetuous nature of the man who approaches Jesus explains a lot. He "comes

TWENTY-EIGHTH SUNDAY IN ORDINARY TIME

LECTIONARY #144

READING I   Wisdom 7:7–11

A reading from the book of *Wisdom* ▪ ▪

The poetic structure here is parallelism: "I prayed / I pleaded." The text is almost sung—but, of course, not singsong. Lift your voice and proclaim!

I *prayed*, and *prudence* was given me; ▪
  I *pleaded*, and the spirit of *Wisdom* came
    to me. ▪ ▪
I preferred her to *scepter* and *throne*,
And deemed *riches nothing* in comparison
    with her, ▪
  nor did I liken any priceless *gem* to her; ▪

"Gold is sand," "silver is mire": another parallelism.

Because all *gold* in view of *her*, is a little
    sand,
  and before *her*, *silver* is to be accounted
    mire. ▪
Beyond *health* and *comeliness* I *loved* her,
And I chose to have *her* rather than the *light*,
  because the *splendor* of her never yields
    to *sleep*. ▪

The intensity descends to a calm and peaceful level to conclude.

Yet all good things *together* came to me in *her*
    company,
  and countless *riches* at her *hands*. ▪ ▪

READING II   Hebrews 4:12–13

A reading from the letter to the *Hebrews* ▪ ▪

Brevity here calls for high intensity.

In the second half, the subject is not God's word, but God's very nature! There is no hint of threat here—just a fact.

God's word is *living* and *effective*, sharper than any two-edged *sword*. ▪ It penetrates and divides *soul* and *spirit*, *joints* and *marrow*; ▪ it judges the reflections and thoughts of the *heart*. ▪ *Nothing* is concealed from him; ▪ *all* lies bare and exposed to the *eyes* of him to whom we must render an *account*. ▪ ▪

A reading from the holy *gospel* according to *Mark* ▪ ▪

An energetic opening will communicate something of the young man's impulsiveness.

As Jesus was setting out on a journey a man came *running* up, *knelt down* before him and asked ▪ "Good *Teacher*, what must I do to share in everlasting *life?*" ▪ Jesus answered, ▪ "Why do you call *me* good? ▪ No one is *good* but God *alone.* ▪ *You* know the commandments: ▪

Take time with these. Don't rattle them off.

'You shall not kill; ▪
You shall not commit adultery; ▪
You shall not steal; ▪
You shall not bear false witness; ▪
You shall not defraud; ▪
Honor your father and your mother.'"

The young man is almost hurt that Jesus would remind him of what he knows so well. Is this why Jesus "looked at him with love"?

The impulsive love is not equal to the challenge.

He replied, ▪ "Teacher, I have kept all *these* since my *childhood."* ▪ Then Jesus looked at him with *love* and told him, ▪ "There is one thing *more* you must do. ▪ Go and sell what you *have* and give to the *poor;* ▪ you will *then* have treasure in *heaven.* ▪ After *that* come and follow *me."* ▪ At these words the man's face fell. ▪ He went away sad, for he had many *possessions.* ▪ Jesus looked around and said to his disciples, ▪ "How *hard* it is for the rich to enter the kingdom of *God!"* ▪ The disciples could only marvel at his words. ▪ So Jesus *repeated* what he had said: ▪ "My sons, how *hard* it is to enter the kingdom of *God!* ▪ It is easier for a *camel* to pass through a needle's *eye* than for a *rich* man to enter the kingdom of *God."* ▪ ▪

A well-known saying here. Make it fresh. NRSV: "Children, how hard it is" and "than for someone who is rich to enter the kingdom of God."

The disciples are perplexed because material wealth was seen as a sign of God's blessings. NRSV: "For mortals it is impossible. . . ."

They were completely overwhelmed at this, and exclaimed to one another, ▪ "Then who *can* be saved?" ▪ Jesus fixed his gaze on them and said, ▪ "For *man* it is *impossible* but not for *God.* ▪ ▪ With *God* all things are possible." ▪ ▪

A very long sentence. Read it slowly, building through to the end. The closure should be upbeat.

Peter was moved to say to him: ▪ "We have put aside *everything* to follow you!" ▪ Jesus answered: ▪ "I give you my *word,* there is *no one* who has given up home, brothers or sisters, mother or father, children or property, for *me* and for the *gospel* who will not receive in this *present* age a hundred *times* as many homes, brothers and sisters, mothers, children and property— ▪ and *persecution besides*—and in the age to *come,* everlasting *life."* ▪ ▪

[Shorter: Mark 10:17–27]

running up," he kneels, he flatters, he is young. We have all seen this man. He is rather like the go-getter, the entrepreneur, the climber who has managed to do very well for himself. There is no reason to dislike him. He is following the advice of his seniors and is making a name for himself. He wants to be sure he doesn't miss out on anything. He covers all the bases. An attractive rabbi with a following may well afford an opportunity for taking care of the spiritual side of this young man's effort to build the perfect life.

Jesus calms him down first by dismissing the irrelevant flattery. There is more of a "There, there . . ." tone than a rebuke, though it is clear that Jesus' response to the question will not be softened by the young man's deference. The list of commandments is fundamental and the young man no doubt was faithful to them. Thus, Jesus "looked at him with love." There can be no doubt that Jesus was attracted to the youthful eagerness, the bright-eyed naivete, even the excessive enthusiasm— which could not yet know what discipleship really involved.

The young man turns away sadly, unable to detach himself from all that had gone into his success. Jesus, too, is sad, appreciating the difficulty of radical discipleship. Only one who knows the genuine beauty of this world's material things could know how hard it is to give them up. Jesus reveals himself here again as one who has profound understanding of human nature.

And the disciples are sad. They wonder, too, how Jesus can expect anyone to follow him if the demands are so great. The reassurance they get may seem meager, but it must suffice: God alone can make it possible for you. And the reassurance is effective. Peter points out that, indeed, the Twelve have renounced everything, so it must be possible. Jesus responds with comforting and inspiring words, not because he promises that "delayed gratification" will be great, but because he shows them that discipleship has its own immediate reward. We are reminded of the first reading and its concluding irony.

READING I This text is from one of the five "songs" in Isaiah that describe the "suffering servant" of God, whose afflictions have a redeeming effect. Redemption and salvation through suffering is an idea that existed long before the Christian era. Who is this servant? Is it an individual person, or is it the remnant of those who remain faithful to God? Or is it the entire people of Israel? Probably the latter, according to the teaching of Jewish history.

The problem of suffering and pain in a world created by a provident and loving God has been an issue for every believer in every religion since the beginning of time. Almost universally, it is the redemptive value of suffering that emerges as the answer to the problem. Isaiah sees the matter rather clearly here: "It is the Lord's will that the servant give his life as an offering for sin, and thereby justify the world." It is the age-old image of the scapegoat, the one chosen to bear the sins of all. The long, painful history of persecution in the life of the Jewish people gives Isaiah's suffering servant songs a wrenching poignancy—but adds a note of hope as well. God's Chosen People "shall see the light in fullness of days."

READING II This is the third consecutive reading in a series of seven from Hebrews. You may wish to consult earlier and later commentaries on the selections from Hebrews.

The writer is intent on pointing out the superiority of Jesus' priesthood over that of any that came before him. This is by virtue of the great work of salvation accomplished by him, and the fact (hinted at here, but boldly expressed elsewhere) that Jesus existed in heaven before his earthly ministry began. Thus, he has "passed through the heavens," effected the salvation of the world, and returned to the realm of God—that "throne of grace" that we are so confidently to approach in time of need.

It is difficult to believe in a leader whose experience is totally different from our own. The patrician presidential candidate who claims to champion the cause of the poor, but who has never known a life other than wealth and power, will have a difficult time securing the vote of simpler folk. We like to think that those who govern us are able to understand our situation.

TWENTY-NINTH SUNDAY IN ORDINARY TIME

LECTIONARY #147

READING I   Isaiah 53:10–11

A reading from the book of the prophet *Isaiah* ▪ ▪

The Canadian lectionary, which uses the NRSV, precedes this reading with an earlier verse, creating the context for the hearers: "We like sheep have gone astray; we have all turned to our own way, and the Lord has laid on his servant the iniquity of us all." Then continue with "The Lord was pleased."

Don't forget that you're reading poetry. The tone of voice communicates an exalted theology and overwhelming love.

[But the Lord was pleased
    to *crush* him in *infirmity*.] ▪
If he gives his *life* as an offering for *sin*,
    he shall see his *descendants* in a *long* life,
        and the will of the *Lord* shall be *accomplished*
            through him. ▪ ▪

Because of his *affliction*
    he shall see the *light* in fullness of *days*; ▪
Through his *suffering*, my servant shall justify
        many,
    and their *guilt* he shall *bear*. ▪ ▪

READING II   Hebrews 4:14–16

A reading from the letter to the *Hebrews* ▪ ▪

There is great pride and comfort in the author's tone.

Using the negative "we do not have a high priest who is unable" is what makes the teaching even more impressive.

The ultimate promise of peace.

We have a great *high* priest who has passed through the *heavens*, *Jesus*, the Son of *God*; ▪ let us hold fast to our profession of *faith*. ▪ For we do not have a high priest who is unable to *sympathize* with our *weakness*, but one who was tempted in every way that *we* are, yet never *sinned*. ▪ So let us *confidently* approach the throne of grace to receive mercy and favor and to find *help* in time of *need*. ▪ ▪

A reading from the holy *gospel* according to *Mark* ▪ ▪

Is the boldness of James and John a little annoying? Jesus doesn't seem to think so. The NRSV translation "Grant us" is gentler than "See to it." Zebedee = ZEH-beh-dee.

The tone here is not argumentative. Jesus responds to their request with equanimity and love.

The conflict arises out of envy. All the disciples want to have a special place with Jesus.

Jesus' tone is not one of rebuke. He reminds the disciples of what they already know about tyrants, and shows them himself as model for a very different kind of greatness.

Zebedee's sons, James and John, approached Jesus. ▪ "Teacher," they said, ▪ "we want you to grant our request." ▪ "What is it?" he asked. ▪ They replied, ▪ "See to it that we sit, one at your right and the other at your left, when you come into your *glory*." ▪ Jesus told them, ▪ "You do not know what you are *asking*. ▪ ▪ Can you drink the *cup* I shall drink or be baptized in the same *bath of pain* as I?" ▪ "We *can*," they told him. ▪ Jesus said in response, ▪ "From the cup *I* drink of you *shall* drink; ▪ the bath *I* am immersed in *you* shall *share*. ▪ But sitting at my right or my left is not mine to *give*; *that* is for those for whom it has been *reserved*." ▪ ▪ The other *ten*, on hearing this, became *indignant* at James and John. ▪ Jesus called them together and said to them: ▪ "You know how among the *Gentiles* those who seem to exercise authority *lord* it *over* them; ▪ *their* great ones make their *importance* felt. ▪ It cannot be like that with *you*. ▪ Anyone among *you* who aspires to greatness must *serve* the rest; ▪ whoever wants to rank first among *you* must serve the needs of *all*. ▪ The Son of Man has not come to be *served* but to *serve*—to give his *life* in ransom for the *many*." ▪ ▪

[Shorter: Mark 10:42–45]

Jesus shared completely in our weakness. He was tested in every way we are, which is not to say that we have detailed accounts of Jesus' encounters with temptation. We do know, however, from his confrontations with Satan in the desert, that he was tempted in several ways to be unfaithful to God. He did not submit. All our temptations are meant in some way to compromise our fidelity to God. But we do not submit—because we know that temptation can be resisted. Our great high priest has shown us that.

GOSPEL   The request made by James and John reveals their complete lack of understanding about Jesus' mission. They are still hanging onto notions of Jesus as a conquering hero with earthly power and glory. Though he has told them more than once that his ultimate ministry and mission is to die, they cannot rid themselves of older notions.

But they do give Jesus another opportunity to describe his passion and death. Further, they provide the context in which Jesus can predict the suffering and death of *all* who would follow him in radical discipleship. All will, in some way, give their lives in ransom for the many—like the suffering servant in Isaiah.

In the second part of this passage another theme is undertaken: the quality and nature of Christian ministry. The other ten, in becoming indignant with James and John, reveal their own lack of understanding of true discipleship. If they are indignant, then they are envious that James and John got ahead of them in making special requests for personal honor. In short, these Twelve are very ordinary men, by nature prone to be worried about their "station in life."

Jesus sets them straight. It will be very different in this company, he says. Those who want to rank first must serve the rest. It is "serving," not "being served" that tells you who rates in this group. In other words, human expectations about rank and privilege are turned upside down. Will Christians ever be able to take such a revolution seriously?

READING I Jeremiah has a reputation (and it is justified) of being a prophet of doom. Our language has even adopted his name as a tag for a message that is unrelieved bleakness and tragedy. Such a message we call a "jeremiad." But this selection is not typical of the genre, and it should remind us that for all Jeremiah's dark words, he was nonetheless God's intermediary in heralding the ultimate restoration of Israel, the end of exile, and the return to the land of promise.

Jeremiah here envisions a triumphant procession of God's chosen people, returning from bitter exile and reentering the fertile and peaceful land that was their birthright. It is quite a scene, reminding Flannery O'Connor readers of one of her best stories, "Revelation." The immense throng includes more than the strong and hearty. Indeed, such are not singled out for mention. That honor is reserved for the blind and the lame, mothers and pregnant women. A God of compassion leads them, a God who is partial to the weak and so provides them with a level road. It is a God who is "father," exhibiting the special love he has for his first-born.

There is a similar scene in today's gospel narrative, complete with those most in need of God's merciful healing. For the blind man whose sight is restored, this prophecy of Jeremiah comes true in the most wonderful way imaginable.

READING II For four Sundays now we have been hearing from the letter to the Hebrews, and we will continue to do so for three more. The writer's purpose is to explain the nature and quality of Jesus' priesthood to the Jewish-Christian community in Rome. He calls upon the knowledge and experience these people already have of priesthood, and then explains how all the finest qualities of priestly ministry are summed up in Jesus.

The most compelling aspect of Jesus is his total identity with the people for whom he functions as priest. He has shared their weakness; the ultimate offering of his body on the cross was a sin offering for himself as well as for the people. Now enthroned at God's right hand, this priest is patient in dealing with others in their sins, for he knows full well the struggles they face.

A new point is raised as the writer discusses Jesus' credentials. Those who

THIRTIETH SUNDAY IN ORDINARY TIME

LECTIONARY #150

READING I   Jeremiah 31:7–9

A reading from the book of the prophet *Jeremiah* ▪ ▪

"Thus says the Lord" indicates that something big is coming! In poetry, Jeremiah records the joyous news of Israel's return from exile. Your tone must be strong and joyful. Jeremiah = dzhehr-eh-MAI-uh.

Thus says the Lord; ▪
Shout with *joy* for *Jacob*,
　exult at the head of the *nations*; ▪
　Proclaim your praise and say: ▪
The Lord has *delivered* his people,
　the remnant of *Israel*. ▪
Behold, I will bring them *back*
　from the land of the *north*; ▪
I will *gather* them from the ends of the *world*,
　with the *blind* and the *lame* in their midst,
The *mothers* and those with *child*; ▪
　they shall return as an immense *throng*. ▪

Renew the energy. Don't slack off.

A little quieter for these four lines, but no less intense.

They *departed* in *tears*,
　but *I* will *console* them and *guide* them; ▪
I will lead them to brooks of *water*,
　on a level *road*, so that none shall *stumble*. ▪
For *I* am a *father* to Israel,
　Ephraim is my *first*-born. ▪ ▪

The last two lines give us the reason for the promises. God is doing what any loving and forgiving parent would do. Ephraim = EE-fray-ihm.

READING II   Hebrews 5:1–6

A reading from the letter to the *Hebrews* ▪ ▪

You are explaining the vocation of priesthood. NRSV: "from among mortals." "He is able . . . for he himself is beset by weakness." Don't miss the paradox. The word "erring" is pronounced ER-ing, not AIR-ing.

Every *high* priest is taken from among men and made their *representative* before *God*, to offer gifts and sacrifices for *sins*. ▪ He is able to deal *patiently* with erring sinners, for he is *himself* beset by weakness, and so must make sin offerings for *himself* as well as for the *people*. ▪ One does not take this honor on his own *initiative*, but only when called by *God* as Aaron was. ▪ Even *Christ* did not glorify *himself*

"Even Christ" introduces the ultimate example of obedience.

with the office of high priest; ▪ he *received* it from the One who said to him, ▪

> "You are my *son*; ▪
>> today I have *begotten* you"; ▪

just as he says in *another* place, ▪

> "You are a *priest forever*, ▪
>> according to the order of *Melchizedek*." ▪▪

The two quotations are from the Psalms. Make them sound like quotations. Melchizedek = mehl-KIHZ-eh-dehk.

GOSPEL   Mark 10:46–52

A reading from the holy *gospel* according to *Mark* ▪▪

The energy level in this story is high.
Jericho = DZHEHR-ih-ko,
Bartimaeus = bar-tih-MEE-uhs,
Timaeus = tai-MEE-uhs

Do not shout Bartimaeus's plea. You are telling the story, not reenacting it.

As Jesus was leaving Jericho with his disciples and a sizable *crowd*, there was a blind *beggar* Bartimaeus ("son of Timaeus") sitting by the roadside. ▪ On hearing that it was Jesus of *Nazareth*, he began to call *out*, ▪ "Jesus, Son of David, have *pity* on me!" ▪ Many people were *scolding* him to make him keep *quiet*, but he shouted all the *louder*, ▪ "Son of David, have *pity* on me!" ▪▪ Then Jesus stopped and said, ▪ "Call him *over*." ▪ So they called the blind man over, telling him as they *did* so, ▪ "You have nothing whatever to fear from *him*! ▪ Get *up*! He is *calling* you!" ▪▪ He threw aside his cloak, *jumped* up and came to Jesus. ▪ Jesus asked him, ▪ "What do you want me to *do* for you?" ▪ "Rabboni," the blind man said, ▪ "I want to *see*." ▪ Jesus said in reply, ▪ "Be on your *way*! ▪ Your *faith* has healed you." ▪ Immediately he received his *sight* and started to follow him up the *road*. ▪▪

Notice how the people change their attitude when Jesus acknowledges the beggar.

The beggar's request is simple: "I want to see."
Rabboni = ra-BO-nai

Don't miss the fact that, although Jesus says, "Be on your way," the healed beggar "started to follow him up the road."

have received the honor of priestly ministry have not taken it upon themselves. They accept a call that is initiated by God. Not even Jesus took it upon himself, but like Aaron, received the summons from God. The quotations are from the Psalms and refer to David the king; the writer of Hebrews applies them now to Jesus, whom we hear called "Son of David" in today's gospel story.

GOSPEL   One of the most endearing and comforting features of this gospel story is its revelation of the predilection Jesus had for the poor, the abandoned and the neglected. Surrounded by a crowd of disciples and followers who were at least curious if not enthusiastic, Jesus' attention is captured by an insistent beggar.

The crowd is annoyed at the interruption and, typically, tries to keep the nuisance quiet. It is amazing how prone we are to ignore or wish away the very kind of people Jesus singles out for special blessings. When caught in such behavior, we try to cover our tracks just like this crowd does. Their scolding quickly turns to encouragement once they become aware that Jesus' attention is focused on the beggar and not on themselves.

Bartimaeus teaches us a great deal about "seizing the moment." The vigor and volume of his cry caught the ear of Jesus. In his haste to respond, he throws aside his cloak and *jumps* up to approach Jesus. When asked what his request is, he states it with a simplicity that is heart wrenching: "I want to see."

In questioning this admirable beggar, Jesus extracts an act of faith from him, as he so often does in these healing events. And that act of faith is confirmed and rewarded: "Your faith has healed you."

The delightful twist at the end should not be missed. Although Jesus directs Bartimaeus to be on his way, the grateful beggar follows Jesus up the road instead. In other words, he does not go on *his* way, he goes on *Jesus'* way.

READING I "Hear, O Israel! The Lord is our God, the Lord alone!" These few words contain one of the most ancient and treasured prayers of our heritage. It is still the daily prayer of the devout Jew. It could be the daily prayer of every Christian, for as Pope John XXIII said so wisely, "Spiritually we are all Semites." The treasured text is called the *Shema* (which is simply the first word: "hear!"). There is no mistaking in the words that follow the radical nature of our devotion to the one God. To love with heart, soul and strength is not to love in three different ways or with three different parts of ourselves. The people to whom Moses is speaking here would be incapable of thinking of themselves as body and soul, or flesh and spirit, which is so familiar to us. Human nature was an entity, an integral reality. Flesh and spirit were one. To love with heart, soul and strength is, quite simply, to love totally and without reserve, excluding all that would compete with unqualified devotion.

This revered text appears in Deuteronomy as the Israelites stand on the threshold of the promised land. In a long series of exhortations and instructions, Moses clarifies for them the conditions under which they must live in this new land. They are reassured of God's promises in their behalf and are reminded of their response— their side of the mutual covenant of love and fidelity.

When Jesus quotes this greatest commandment in today's gospel story, we may be sure it came quite naturally to his lips.

READING II In this fifth of seven consecutive readings from Hebrews, the author is concerned primarily with pointing out the differences between Christ our high priest and the high priests who preceded him. The text is part of a lengthy development of the theology of Christ's function as priest. Consult earlier commentaries for more background.

In contrast to the many priests of the "old covenant," there is now only one: Jesus. The reason for this is obvious. When death claimed the lives of the priests of old, they were succeeded by others; Jesus, who conquered death in his resurrection, has no need of successors. The intercession Jesus makes for those who approach God is unending, not subject to death or the passage of time.

THIRTY-FIRST SUNDAY IN ORDINARY TIME

LECTIONARY #153

READING I   Deuteronomy 6:2–6

This reading contains one of the most precious texts we have. Proclaim it with great conviction.

"Hear then, Israel!" A call to fidelity.

NRSV: "fathers" = "ancestors."

"Hear, O Israel!" The great prayer that sums up our relationship with God. Lift your voice and sustain a tone of solemn proclamation through to the end.

A reading from the book of *Deuteronomy* ••

Moses told the people: • Fear the Lord, your *God*, and keep, throughout the days of your *lives*, all his *statutes* and *commandments* which I *enjoin* on you, • and thus have long *life*. • *Hear* then, Israel, and be careful to *observe* them, that you may *grow* and prosper the more, in keeping with the promise of the *Lord*, the God of your fathers, to give you a land flowing with *milk* and *honey*. •• "*Hear*, O Israel! • The *Lord* is our *God*, the Lord *alone*! • Therefore, you shall *love* the Lord, your God, with *all* your heart, and with *all* your soul, and with *all* your strength. • Take to *heart* these words which I *enjoin* on you today." ••

READING II   Hebrews 7:23–28

The second covenant is born from the first. The writer to the Hebrews makes the development clear.

"Always" and "forever" are the crucial words here.

Pause. After the definition of Jesus' priesthood comes a description of it.

The emphasis is on contrast here: "law . . . weak," "oath . . . perfect."

A reading from the letter to the *Hebrews* ••

Under the *old* covenant there were *many* priests because they were prevented by death from remaining in *office*; • but *Jesus*, because he remains *forever*, has a priesthood which does *not* pass away. • Therefore he is always able to *save* those who approach God through him, since he forever lives to make *intercession* for them. ••

It was *fitting* that we should have such a high priest: • holy, innocent, undefiled, separated from sinners, higher than the heavens. • Unlike the *other* high priests, he has no *need* to offer sacrifice *day* after *day*, first for his *own* sins and then for those of the *people*; • he did that *once* for *all* when he offered *himself*. • For the law sets up as *high* priests men who are *weak*, • but the word of the oath which came *after* the law appoints as priest the *Son*, made perfect *forever*. ••

A reading from the holy *gospel* according to *Mark* ▪ ▪

The dialog in this reading has a cumulative effect. Jesus and the scribe build off each other's responses.

It should be obvious to the assembly that Jesus is quoting from the book of Deuteronomy (the first reading).

One of the scribes came up to Jesus, and asked him, ▪ "Which is the *first* of all the *commandments?*" ▪ Jesus replied: ▪ "This is the first: ▪ ▪

'*Hear*, O Israel! ▪ The Lord our God is *Lord* alone! ▪

Therefore you shall *love* the Lord your *God* with *all* your heart, with *all* your soul, with *all* your mind, and with *all* your strength.' ▪ ▪

This is the *second*, ▪

'You shall love your *neighbor* as *yourself*.' ▪ There is no other commandment greater than these." ▪ The scribe said to him: ▪ "*Excellent*, Teacher! ▪ You are *right* in saying, ▪ 'He is the One, there is no *other* than he.' ▪ Yes, 'to love him with *all* our heart, with *all* our thoughts and with *all* our strength, and to love our *neighbor* as our*selves*' is worth more than any burnt *offering* or *sacrifice*." ▪ Jesus approved the *insight* of this answer and told him, ▪ "You are not *far* from the reign of *God*." ▪ ▪ And no one had the courage to ask him any more *questions*. ▪ ▪

Jesus announces the second greatest commandment. No surprise to his hearers, but an insightful addition.

The scribe joyously paraphrases the greatest commandment, then puts religious observances into proper perspective when he says that love is more important than sacrifices and burnt offerings.

"You are not far. . . ." Words we all want to hear.

Unlike the old priesthood that offered sacrifice day after day, the sacrifice of Jesus was a once-and-for-all act. That is, in Jesus' sacrifice of himself, all the sin of the world — past, present, yet to come — is atoned for and there is no further need of reparation.

Why is it, then, that we celebrate the sacrifice of the Mass over and over, day after day? The answer is simple. Each celebration of the eucharist is not a separate sacrifice; rather it is a re-presentation and remembering of the one sacrifice offered by Christ. The people who offer the eucharist offer the same sacrifice offered by Christ, who "forever lives to make intercession for them."

Finally, the writer makes the distinction between those who were priests by virtue of the law ("men who are weak"), and Jesus the Son, appointed by the "word of the oath which came after the law," in other words, appointed by the promise of God.

GOSPEL   The context of this story is a prolonged discussion between Jesus and the Sadducees on life after death. The Sadducees were questioning Jesus with the intent of tricking him. Into this rather tacky scene comes an expert in the law, a scribe, with an honest question. In the Judaism of Jesus' time, the tendency to reduce the written and oral law to "one great commandment" was always present. So was the tendency to multiply the laws and commandments beyond all human reason in an effort to cover every aspect of daily life. So the scribe asks a legitimate question.

Jesus' answer seems immediate, confident and knowledgeable. He quotes the great text from Deuteronomy (6:4ff, the *Shema*), which to this day may be found on the doorway and in the heart of every devout Jew. But then Jesus does something new. He adds another quote from the Hebrew scriptures (Leviticus 19:18), which would not have startled his audience except for the implication that the two "commandments" are inseparable, in effect two sides of the same coin.

The first and the second commandment then are seen as one. Love of God is demonstrated by love of neighbor. Love of neighbor proves our love of God.

READING I The wonderful majesty of John's revelation was written to comfort a church under persecution. It can serve that same purpose today. Since the church is, by definition, a "pilgrim," we are on the way to glory, and the way is difficult. Nevertheless, a great many have completed the journey successfully, and that is what we celebrate today.

The kind of literature you are proclaiming here is called "apocalyptic," which means that it is concerned with the end of time and what lies beyond human experience. It is visionary and imaginative and powerful. Nevertheless, it is not pure fancy.

An effective proclamation of texts such as this will surrender to the splendor, so to speak, and revel in the poetic majesty of it all. Clearly, John is eager to paint a picture of supreme joy in showing us that the triumph to come is more than adequate recompense for present sufferings.

Concentrate on the feeling and the beauty of this reading, and you will succeed in giving the members of the assembly a message of comfort and joy.

NOVEMBER 1, 1994
ALL SAINTS

LECTIONARY #667

READING I Revelation 7:2–4, 9–14

A reading from the book of *Revelation* ▪▪

Literature such as this must ring out. Any proclamation that sounds literal or "heady" is out of the question.

I, *John*, saw *another angel* come up from the *east* holding the seal of the living *God*. ▪ He cried out at the top of his *voice* to the four angels who were given power to ravage the *land* and the *sea*, ▪ "Do no harm to the *land* or the *sea* or the *trees* until we imprint this *seal* on the foreheads of the servants of our *God.*" ▪ I heard the *number* of those who were so marked— ▪ one hundred and forty-four *thousand* from every tribe of *Israel*. ▪▪

144,000 = 12,000 from each of the 12 tribes of Israel. The missing verses here list each tribe. The hypnotic effect of the ritual listing is quite effective. The verses could be restored.

After this I saw before me a huge *crowd* which *no one* could *count* from every *nation, race, people,* and *tongue*. ▪ They stood before the throne and the Lamb, dressed in long white *robes* and holding *palm* branches in their hands. ▪ They cried out in a loud *voice,* ▪ "Salvation is from our *God,* who is seated on the *throne,* and from the *Lamb!*" ▪ All the angels who were standing around the throne and the elders and the four living creatures fell down before the throne to worship *God.* ▪ They said: ▪ "*Amen!* Praise and *glory,* wisdom, *thanksgiving,* and honor, power and *might* to our God forever and *ever.* ▪ Amen!" ▪▪

These acclamations are perhaps more effective in a quieter tone. The speakers are prostrate before the throne.

Then one of the elders *asked* me, ▪ "Who do you think these *are,* all dressed in *white?* ▪ And where have they *come* from?" ▪ I said to him, ▪ "Sir, *you* should know better than *I.*" ▪ He then *told* me, "*These* are the ones who have survived the great period of *trial;* ▪ they have washed their *robes* and made them *white* in the blood of the *Lamb.*" ▪▪

Here they are: the saints, among whom we are destined to find ourselves!

A reading from the first letter of *John* ▪ ▪

A strong and lovely beginning. Be sure it is heard by the assembly. You may have to pause until things quiet down.

See what love the Father has *bestowed* on us
in letting us be *called* children of *God!* ▪
Yet that in fact is what we *are.* ▪
The reason the world does not *recognize us*
is that it never recognized the *Son.* ▪

A tender reassurance to those who are concerned about the future.

Dearly beloved,
we are God's children *now;* ▪
what we shall *later be* has not yet come to
   light. ▪
We know that *when* it comes to light
we shall be like *him,*
for we shall *see* him as he *is.* ▪

NRSV: "And all who have this hope in him purify themselves, just as he is pure."

Everyone who has this *hope* based on him
keeps himself *pure,* as he is pure. ▪ ▪

A reading from the holy *gospel* according to *Matthew* ▪ ▪

Like Moses, Jesus teaches on the mountain. Like all teachers with recognized authority, he sits down to proclaim his doctrine.

When Jesus saw the crowds he went up on the mountainside. ▪ After he had sat *down* his disciples gathered *around* him, and he began to *teach* them: ▪
   "How *blest* are the *poor in spirit:* the reign of
      God is theirs. ▪

Each of the beatitudes deserves its own special tone and emphasis. Great vocal variety is required!

   Blest too are the *sorrowing;* they shall be
      consoled. ▪
   [Blest are the *lowly;* they shall inherit the
      land.] ▪
   Blest are they who hunger and thirst for
      holiness;
   they shall have their *fill.* ▪
   Blest are they who show *mercy;* ▪ mercy shall
      be *theirs.* ▪
   Blest are the *single-hearted,* for they shall
      see God. ▪

So far, the list has been concerned with personal attributes. Now we shift to situations in which others are involved.

   Blest too the *peacemakers;* they shall be
      called *sons* of God. ▪

"Children of God."

   Blest are those persecuted for *holiness'* sake;
      the reign of *God* is *theirs.* ▪
   Blest are *you* when they *insult* you and
      persecute you and utter every kind of
      slander against you because of *me.* ▪

The final statement is most encouraging. Suffering is seen in its true light. The saints are our proof.

   Be *glad* and *rejoice,* for your reward in heaven
      is *great.*" ▪ ▪

READING II   John reminds us here that we *are* children of God. It is something that has *happened* to us because of the immense love God has for us. Christians so often concentrate on their duty and fail to recognize sufficiently their dignity. John is eager to convince us that, although we do not know exactly what life in total union with God will be like, we do know what we are now: children of God—all evidence to the contrary notwithstanding!

The effect of realizing our dignity is that we are thereby inspired to behave accordingly. The effect of realizing only our duty is that we feel only obligation and burden—a far cry from what the love of God intends for us. The destiny in store for us is glorious. Believing in that glory will enable us, as it did the saints, to live now in accord with that future destiny.

GOSPEL   Matthew conceives of Jesus as "the new Moses." Thus the "new commandments" are proclaimed from a mountaintop, just as the "old commandments" were proclaimed on Mount Sinai. Only the formulation and the lawgiver are new; every one of the so-called "beatitudes" can be found in the scriptures that Jesus knew so well.

The list of "blests" is perhaps most revealing when we apply it to Jesus himself and see that his life is an incarnation of each one. He was poor in spirit, lowly, hungry for holiness, merciful, single-hearted, a peacemaker, persecuted, insulted, slandered and sorrowful. And yet he was the most joyful man who ever lived. It is the life of Jesus that gives such power to his teaching.

And it is the life of Jesus that gives us the ability to follow his teaching. The saints prove this to us, and we celebrate that proof in today's feast. Indeed, we prove the power of Jesus' teaching in our own lives. And this need not surprise us, because we ourselves are among those who are called "the saints," made so by the love and election of God.

Proclaiming the beatitudes is not easy. Your objective must be to enable the assembly to hear each one in its uniqueness. It is not a list of "blests" after all. It is a series of acclamations, a song of praise, a declaration of freedom and a portrait of Jesus the Christ.

READING I Elijah is one of the more colorful prophets in the Hebrew scriptures. He speaks confidently and sounds almost arrogant to us, and yet we are attracted to him. Elijah spent most of his ministry prophesying in the name of the one true God of Israel, and against Baal, the false god of the lands beyond Israel. In today's reading, we find him in Zarephath—which lies within the boundaries of Baal country.

Several important points are made: The Lord works through Elijah even among the foreigners who worship false gods; those whom the God of Israel favors (e.g., the generous poor widow) will receive good things regardless of where they are; and the Lord's power cannot be hindered (the drought decreed by Elijah extends past Israel to Zarephath). The subject of the story is the word of the Lord as spoken through the prophet. This word achieves whatever it is sent for, completely victorious over all other forces, including life and death. The word of God is faithful, and promises of blessing will not go unfulfilled. The widow and her son were provided for as promised: the jar did not go empty, nor the jug run dry.

There is no chaining the word of God!

READING II This is the sixth consecutive reading from the letter to the Hebrews. You may wish to consult earlier commentaries. The author continues to instruct the Jewish Christians in Rome about the nature and effect of the high priesthood of Jesus, contrasting Jesus' ministry with that of the priests of the old covenant.

The contrast continues as the writer compares the earthly sanctuary, where the priests of the old covenant entered to offer sacrifice, with the prototype of all sanctuaries, the ultimate Holy of Holies, heaven itself. This is where Jesus entered and appears before God to intercede for us.

Further, Christ enters the heavenly sanctuary only once to accomplish the work of our salvation, offering the sacrificial blood of his own death. There is no need to enter over and over again—as the priests of old had to do, offering the blood of animals. The thought of Christ dying over and over again from the creation of the world is unthinkable. Notice however, that it presumes the preexistence of Christ before he became flesh and dwelt among us. This is a cardinal point of the letter to the Hebrews.

THIRTY-SECOND SUNDAY IN ORDINARY TIME

LECTIONARY #156

READING I 1 Kings 17:10–16

A reading from the first book of *Kings* ▪ ▪

The promises of God will not go unfulfilled, whether they be promises of provident love for the lowly or wrath upon those who abuse their power. Try to communicate the full strength of Elijah's faith in God's promises. Elijah = ee-LAI-dzhuh, Zarephath = ZEHR-ee-fath.

Elijah [the prophet] went to Zarephath. ▪ As he arrived at the entrance of the city, a *widow* was gathering *sticks* there; ▪ he called *out* to her, "*Please* bring me a small cupful of *water* to drink." She left to get it, and he called out *after* her, ▪ "Please bring me a bit of *bread*." ▪ "As the Lord, your God, lives," she answered, ▪ "I have nothing *baked*; there is only a handful of *flour* in my jar and a little oil in my *jug*. ▪ Just now I was collecting a couple of sticks, to go in and prepare something for myself and my *son*; ▪ when we have *eaten* it, we shall *die*." ▪ ▪

Elijah's seemingly unreasonable demands reveal the depth of his trust in God.

"Do *not* be afraid," Elijah said to her. ▪ "Go and do as you *propose*. ▪ But first make me a little *cake* and *bring* it to me. ▪ *Then* you can prepare something for yourself and your *son*. ▪ For the Lord, the God of Israel, says, ▪ 'The jar of *flour* shall not go *empty*, nor the jug of *oil* run *dry*, until the day when the Lord sends *rain* upon the earth.'" ▪ She left and did as Elijah had said. ▪ ▪ She was able to eat for a *year*, and he and her *son* as *well*; ▪ the jar of flour did *not* go empty, nor the jug of oil run *dry*, as the Lord had *foretold* through *Elijah*. ▪ ▪

We have moved from total deprivation to complete fulfillment. There is enormous satisfaction in the final lines.

READING II Hebrews 9:24–28

A reading from the letter to the *Hebrews* ▪ ▪

Careful placement of emphasis is required here to show the contrast between Christ's priesthood and its inadequate earthly counterpart.

"Not that . . ." introduces an involved construction. Your voice must sustain an upward (suspended) tone through "not his own." Then the resolution: "were that so. . . ."

Christ did not enter into a sanctuary made by *hands*, a mere *copy* of the *true* one; ▪ he entered heaven *itself* that he might appear before God *now* on our behalf. ▪ Not that he might offer himself there *again* and *again*, as the high priest enters year after year into the *sanctuary* with blood that is not his own; ▪ were *that* so, he would have had to suffer death *over* and *over* from the creation of the *world*. ▪ But *now* he has

"But now he has appeared" is bursting with the joy of long-awaited fulfillment. NRSV: "it is appointed for mortals to die once."

appeared, at the end of the *ages* to take away sins *once for all* by his *sacrifice*. ▪ Just as it is appointed that men die *once*, and after *death* be judged, ▪ so *Christ* was offered up *once* to take away the sins of *many*; ▪ he will appear a *second* time not to take away *sin* but to bring *salvation* to those who eagerly await him. ▪ ▪

Jesus' sojourn on earth was preparation for the ultimate priestly act of his reentry into heaven following his resurrection.

Unlike human beings, who die and then are judged, Jesus died and then rose and will come to earth again to judge and convict the world of sin in order to save it. For those who eagerly await his return, that day will be wonderful beyond imagination. Those who refuse to acknowledge Jesus can only anticipate that day with terror in their hearts.

GOSPEL Mark 12:38–44

Jesus' teaching here is uncompromising.

A reading from the holy *gospel* according to *Mark* ▪ ▪

In the course of his teaching Jesus said: ▪ "Be on guard against the *scribes*, who like to parade around in their *robes* and accept marks of *respect* in *public*, front *seats* in the synagogues, and places of *honor* at *banquets*. ▪ These men devour the savings of *widows* and recite long *prayers* for *appearance'* sake; ▪ it is they who will receive the *severest* sentence." ▪ ▪

Taking a seat opposite the *treasury*, he observed the crowd putting money into the *collection* box. ▪ Many of the *wealthy* put in sizable *amounts*; ▪ but one poor *widow* came and put in two small copper *coins* worth about a *cent*. ▪ He called his disciples over and told them: ▪ "I want you to observe that this poor *widow* contributed more than *all* the *others* who donated to the treasury. ▪ *They* gave from their surplus *wealth*, but *she* gave from her *want*, all that she had to *live* on." ▪ ▪

[Shorter: Mark 12:41–44]

"It is they. . . ." The condemnation is shocking, but just.

This story of "the widow's mite" is one of the most popular in Christian tradition. The lesson it teaches is simple. Communicate Jesus' admiration for the widow—to contrast with his wrath toward the hypocritical scribes. (The contrast will be lost, of course, if the short form of the gospel is chosen. Choose the longer form.)

GOSPEL Today's narrative is composed of two parts (if the longer form is read). The first is a condemnation of religious leaders who make a business of their ministry and pursue the external trappings of religion for selfish reasons. The language Jesus uses here gives a clear picture of the depth of his contempt for such people. "They will receive the severest sentence."

It seems that rip-off artists find easy prey in just about any branch of institutionalized religion. Perhaps that is because devout people naturally want to believe that those in ministry can be trusted. Though some today feel that the credibility of the clergy is at an all time low, it was worse in earlier centuries.

Jesus' warnings about misusing positions of public trust are quite clear. They provide us with a thorough examination of conscience. The condemnation of those who abuse public trust is a lesson in the difference between sincere service and the worst kind of hypocrisy.

When Jesus observes that the poor widow gave more than all the rest, he points out the quality of her gift, not the amount of her donation. This can be a consolation and a challenge to us. Whether we are giving our lives or our money, we need to examine the gift for its quality. Are we holding so much back that no real sacrifice is involved? Is our gift given in the abandonment of genuine faith or are we playing it safe, giving just enough for appearance's sake? The widow gave all she had; the fact that the amount was very small is irrelevant. It is the quality of the act of giving, not the gift itself, that will be judged.

THIRTY-THIRD SUNDAY IN ORDINARY TIME

READING I The liturgical year is coming to a close. All the readings today speak of the "end time" when the universe will be transformed in some cataclysmic way. In the first reading we have a classic example of the kind of biblical literature called "apocalyptic." It is an attempt to describe the indescribable, to speak the ineffable, to give form and order to what ultimately is perceived as chaotic. Notice, of course, that the reading is in poetic form. It is the language of poetry that serves us best when we struggle to voice the extraordinary.

There is no question regarding the *purpose* of the "end time" as described here. It is a time of judgment, of seeing clearly what could not be seen before, of discerning the ultimate truth about ourselves and each other, of reward and punishment. This section of Daniel is the earliest text in the Hebrew scriptures that refers clearly to resurrection from the dead: "those who sleep in the dust of earth shall wake."

And there is no question regarding the fate of the just and faithful when the end comes. Their names are written in the book of life and they will live forever.

READING II This is the last of seven consecutive readings from the letter to the Hebrews. The author concludes here a long comparison of the priestly work of Christ and the ministry of the priests of the old covenant. Again the writer makes the point that the old sacrifices had to be repeated over and over, and even then, they did not take away sin. But the sacrifice that Jesus offered need never be repeated, because it was a perfect sacrifice that took away all sin for all time.

The sacrifice that Jesus offered was, of course, himself, a sacrifice chosen by God at the scene of the baptism in the Jordan: "This is my Son, my Chosen One." The sacrifice was completed in his return to the God who sent him into the world to redeem it. Thus, he now takes his seat forever at the right hand of God. The cycle is completed, the redemption is won, the sacrifice is ended, though its effect will continue until the end of time.

Now Jesus waits until his enemies are subdued. There is no need to presume that those enemies will be slain or punished. It is altogether more in character with Jesus'

LECTIONARY #159

READING I   Daniel 12:1–3

A reading from the book of the prophet *Daniel* ▪ ▪

A cosmic proclamation in poetic form. Anything less than your most exalted tone will be inadequate for this text.

At *that* time there shall arise
　Michael, the great *prince,*
　guardian of your *people;* ▪
It shall be a time unsurpassed in *distress*
　since nations *began* until that *time.* ▪
At *that* time your people shall *escape,*
　everyone who is found written in the *book.* ▪

Shift down a notch for this explanatory section. There is great sadness in the loss of those who will not live forever.

Many of those who sleep
　in the dust of the earth shall *awake;* ▪
Some shall live *forever,*
　others shall be an everlasting *horror* and
　　disgrace. ▪

Finally, return to exaltation—and unbounded joy.

But the *wise* shall shine *brightly*
　like the splendor of the *firmament.* ▪
And those who lead the many to *justice*
　shall be like the *stars forever.* ▪ ▪

READING II   Hebrews 10:11–14, 18

A reading from the letter to the *Hebrews* ▪ ▪

This is the last of seven consecutive readings from Hebrews. The contrast between Jesus' priesthood and its earthly counterpart is complete.

Every *other* priest stands ministering *day* by *day,* and offering *again* and *again* those *same* sacrifices which can *never* take away *sins.* ▪ But *Jesus* offered *one* sacrifice for sins and took his seat forever at the right hand of *God;* ▪ *now* he waits until his enemies are placed beneath his *feet.* ▪ ▪ By *one* offering he has forever perfected those who are being *sanctified.* ▪

There is an enormous sense of "resolution" and "mission accomplished" at the conclusion.

Once sins have been *forgiven,* there is no further *offering* for sin. ▪ ▪

A reading from the holy *gospel* according to *Mark* ▪ ▪

The language of Jesus here is "apocalyptic"—dealing with the events that signal the end of the world. Your proclamation must be big!

NRSV: "Then they will see 'the Son of Man coming in clouds' with great power and glory." With proper inflection you can set off the quotation within the quotation.
Now the tone switches to an explanation by means of example.

Jesus said to his disciples: ▪ "During that period after trials of every *sort* the sun will be *darkened,* the moon will not shed its *light, stars* will fall out of the *skies,* and the heavenly *hosts* will be shaken. ▪ Then men will see the Son of *Man* coming in the clouds with great power and glory. ▪ He will dispatch his *messengers* and *assemble* his chosen from the four winds, from the farthest bounds of earth and sky. ▪ ▪ Learn a lesson from the *fig* tree. ▪ Once the *sap* of its *branches* runs high and it begins to sprout *leaves,* you know that *summer* is near. ▪ In the same *way,* when you see *these* things happening, you will know that he is *near,* even at the *door.* ▪ I *assure* you, this generation will not pass away until all these things take *place.* ▪ The *heavens* and the *earth* will pass away, but my *words* will *not.* ▪ ▪

This popular saying deserves to be heard in its most familiar form, which the NRSV retains: "Heaven and earth will pass away, but my words will not pass away."

"As to the exact *day* or *hour,* no one *knows* it, neither the angels in *heaven* nor even the *Son,* but only the *Father.*" ▪ ▪

priestly mission that those enemies will be subdued by love, and thereby join those whose names are written in the book of life.

GOSPEL   The thirteenth chapter of Mark's gospel is filled with Jesus' teaching about the end of the world, the consummation of time, and the coming of the Son of Man. All the images here come from the Hebrew scriptures. The body of literature having to do with the end of the world is called "apocalyptic"—a word that means "revelation" or "unveiling." The very name of this kind of writing connotes that its subject is shrouded in mystery.

Apocalyptic literature exists because of the Jewish belief that God would one day intervene in history in a cataclysmic way to destroy evil and restore Israel to fullness of life, abundance and peace. Jesus employs this complex tradition in speaking of the end of time because it was familiar to his hearers.

Certain features of this specialized literature are constant, and they are repeated here in Jesus' discourse. Cosmic upheaval is characteristic. Thus the "sun will be darkened . . . stars will fall out of the skies." Great signs will appear. Thus the world "will see the Son of Man coming in the clouds." Judgment of the earth and all its inhabitants will precede the restoration of the just. "He will dispatch his messengers and assemble his chosen ones."

Though we do not know *when* these things will happen, we can be certain that they *will* happen. We will even be able to recognize signs that the end time is near, just as we can predict spring when the sap rises in the trees, and plants sprout from the ground. Here too we see a feature typical of apocalyptic literature.

How should we understand such sayings? The best way is probably the simplest way. Taken together, these predictions in Mark's gospel seem most useful to us as a poetic and dramatic assertion that God will, in the end, become "all in all," that is, the kingdom of God inaugurated by Christ will be fully realized, and the promise of eternal reunion with the Creator of all things will be fulfilled.

READING I The book of Daniel is filled with apocalyptic imagery: scenes of the end of time and the beginning of eternity. This brief passage depicts the ultimate exaltation of the chosen people (personified in the "son of man" image). It is the final restoration and vindication of a people who were predestined to be God's elect, a people who had known bitter struggle, persecution and exile. Daniel records the tradition that developed to give them hope of final victory over the ups and downs of life.

In the firm conviction that Israel would one day be gathered from among the nations and presented to God whole and entire, a literature describing the longed-for "day of the Lord" was inevitable. And the longing continues.

Later developments saw "the son of man" as the promised messiah, the messianic king, symbol of the perfect ruler who would bring justice, peace and prosperity to Israel. He would receive homage from all the nations of the world, and his reign would know no end. This would be God's perfect spokesperson in Israel, reflecting in his rule the perfect observance of God's law.

In the Christian experience, Jesus becomes the son of man by applying the title to himself. From this viewpoint, the reading is interpreted as the final fulfillment of the kingdom of God that Jesus inaugurated during his earthly ministry.

READING II Notice the titles that make up the first sentence. John is writing to the Christian communities about the revelations he received concerning Jesus, so he must first define his topic. Jesus is faithful witness. The import of this title is that he can safely be believed. He is a witness to all he has taught us about God, for he came from God, and fulfilled God's instructions perfectly. He was faithful (obedient) in all that he did on our behalf.

Jesus is firstborn from the dead. The implication here is broader than "the first one to rise from the dead," though it includes that. Jesus is firstborn from the dead in the sense that he is Lord and Master over death, as he is over life. Our comfort is that death no longer has dominion over us because it has no dominion over our champion.

Jesus is ruler of the kings of the earth. This title is relevant for today's feast, of

LAST SUNDAY IN ORDINARY TIME, CHRIST THE KING

LECTIONARY #162

READING I   Daniel 7:13–14

A reading from the book of the prophet *Daniel* ⸱⸱

The language is that of a visionary, poetic in form, awe-inspiring and mysterious in its purpose.

As the visions during the night *continued,* ⸱
  I saw
One like a son of *man* coming,
  on the clouds of *heaven;* ⸱
When he reached the *Ancient* One
  and was presented *before* him,
He received dominion, glory, and kingship; ⸱
  nations and peoples of every *language* serve
    him. ⸱

There is more than one way to conclude, depending on the "feel" of the text. Try ending at the "top" of your voice, rather than descending gradually. Only the last word, "destroyed," should fall.

His dominion is an *everlasting* dominion
  that shall not be taken *away,*
  his kingship shall not be *destroyed.* ⸱⸱

READING II   Revelation 1:5–8

A reading from the book of *Revelation* ⸱⸱

A paean of exultant praise. Your proclamation should be bright.

Jesus Christ is the faithful *witness,* the firstborn from the *dead* and ruler of the kings of *earth.* ⸱ To him who *loves* us and *freed* us from our sins by his own *blood,* who has made us a *royal* nation of *priests* in the service of his *God* and *Father*—to him be *glory* and *power forever* and *ever.* ⸱ Amen. ⸱⸱

Pause. Then launch into the mixed joy and pain of this poem.

See, he comes amid the *clouds!* ⸱
  Every eye shall *see* him,
  even of those who *pierced* him. ⸱
All the peoples of the earth
  shall *lament* him *bitterly.* ⸱
  so it is to *be.* ⸱ Amen! ⸱

Pause. The final sentence is wonderful. Assurance should be the feeling you communicate. Try for a calm (but strong) ending, rather than a triumphant one.

The Lord God says, ⸱ "I am the *Alpha* and the *Omega,* the One who *is* and who *was* and who is to *come,* ⸱ the *Almighty!*" ⸱⸱

A reading from the holy *gospel* according to *John* ▪▪

Pilate said to Jesus: ▪ "Are you the king of the *Jews?*" ▪ Jesus answered, ▪ "Are you saying this on your *own*, or have others been *telling* you about me?" ▪ *"I* am no Jew!" Pilate retorted. ▪ "It is your own *people* and the chief *priests* who have handed you *over* to me. ▪ What have you *done?*" ▪ Jesus answered: ▪

"*My* kingdom does not *belong* to this world. ▪
If my kingdom *were* of this world,
my subjects would be fighting
    to *save* me from being handed over to the
        Jews. ▪
    As it *is*, *my* kingdom is not *here.*" ▪▪
At this Pilate said to him, ▪ "*So*, then, you *are* a king?" ▪ Jesus replied: ▪
"It is you who *say* I am a king. ▪
The *reason* I was born,
the reason why I came into the world,
is to testify to the *truth*. ▪
Anyone committed to the *truth* hears my
    voice." ▪▪

Pilate's question is an honest one. He wants to know. The whole text, however, is concerned with the difference between Pilate's definition of "king" and the kind of "kingdom" over which Jesus reigns.

The important word is "my."

Pilate's second question makes it clear that he and Jesus have irreconcilable notions about kingship.

Jesus' response renders Pilate's question irrelevant. The point is this: Anyone who sincerely seeks the truth will understand the unique nature of Jesus' "kingship."

course. But it surpasses any notions we have about earthly kings. It simply means that Jesus is the promised Messiah, the one whom peoples of every language and nation will serve (as we saw in the first reading from Daniel).

A paean of praise follows the titles; it recounts what Jesus has accomplished for us in love. He has freed us from sin and given us direct access to God.

GOSPEL   It is difficult to imagine Jesus as king except in the context of heaven, seated on a throne, judging the world at the end of time and reigning at God's right hand for all eternity. And yet, these images are tempered by the gospel passage chosen for today. What kind of a king is Jesus?

The answer may be found in Jesus' responses to Pilate. He does not avoid the first question ("Are you the King of the Jews?"), although he does not answer it directly. The point of Jesus' counter-question is to find out whether the charges against him are the point at issue, or whether the nature of his mission is being asked of him. He decided to answer in terms of his mission.

When Jesus says his kingdom is not of this world, we need to know what "of this world" meant to the author, John. What it meant was the unbelieving or unenlightened world, the world that had not accepted Jesus. Obviously, his kingdom is not of that world; if it were, he would have armies at his disposal.

But Jesus does claim kingship, and Pilate is quick to pick up on that claim. Again, however, Jesus qualifies his royal nature. Indeed, he is the messianic king, but not the conquering hero come to restore the political well-being of Israel. Rather, he is the Messiah sent from heaven to reveal the truth about God. For this he will be crucified.

Our liturgical celebration of Christ the King reveals the tension between a "king of shreds and patches" and a king of eternal glory. It is precisely the kind of tension most appropriate as we stand on the threshold of a new liturgical year and look back upon the old one. In the contradictory images of this strange king, we see the personification of a kingdom that has come but is not yet fully revealed. It is the realm of "already . . . but not yet."

PRONUNCIATION GUIDE

Aaron	àr"-*n	Caesarea	sez-a-re"-a	Ezra	ez"-ra
Abba	ab"-a, a-ba"	Caiaphas	ki"-ya-fas, ka"-a-fas		
Abel Meholah	a"-b*l mi-ho"-la	Cana	ka"-na	Gabbatha	ga"-ba-tha
Abiathar	a-bi"-a-thêr	Canaan	ka"-nan	Galatia	ga-la"-sha
Abijah	a-bi"-ja	Canaanite	ka"-na-nit	Galatians	ga-la"-shanz
Abilene	a-bi-le"-ne	Capernaum	k*-pêr"-na-um	Galilean(s)	ga-li-le"-an(z)
Abishai	a-bi"-shi, a-bi"-sha-i	Cappadocia	ka-pa-do"-sha	Galilee	ga"-li-le
Abiud	a-bi"-*d	Carmel	kâr-mel"	Gehazi	ge-ha"-ze, ge-ha"-zi
Abner	ab"-nêr	Cephas	se"-fas	Gennesaret	ge-nes"-a-ret
Abraham	a"-bra-ham	Chaldaeans	kal-de"-anz	Gethsemane	geth-sem"-a-ne
Abram	a"-bram	Chloe	klo"-e	Gibeon	gi"-be-an
Achaia	a-ki"-ya, a-ka"-ya	Chronicles	kron"-i-k*lz	Gilgal	gil"-gal
Achim	a"-kim	Chuza	ku"-za	Golgotha	gol"-ga-tha
Advocate	ad"-vo-kat	Cilicia	si-lis"-ya, si-lish"-a	Gomorrah	ge-môr"-a
Ahaz	a"-haz	Cleopas	kle"-o-pas		
aloes	a"-loz	Clopas	klo"-pas	Habakkuk	hab"-a-kuk,
Alpha	al"-fa	Colossians	ko-losh"-anz		ha-bak"-uk
Alphaeus	al-fe"-us	Corinth	kôr"-inth	Hadad-rimmon	ha"-dad-rim"-on
Amalek	am"-a-lek	Corinthians	kôr-in"-the-anz	Hades	ha"-dez
Amalekites	a-mal"-e-kitz	Cornelius	kôr-nel"-yus	Hebron	he"-bron
Amaziah	a-ma-zi"-a	Cretans	kre"-tans	Hellenists	hel"-*n-ists
Amminadab	a-min"-a-dab	Cushite	k*sh"-it	Herodians	he-ro"-de-anz
Ammonites	a"-mo-nitz	Cyrene	si-re"-ne	Hezekiah	he-ze-ki"-a
Amon	a"-mon	Cyrus	si"-rus	Hezron	hez"-ron
Amorites	a"-môr-itz			Hilkiah	hil-ki"-a
Amos	a"-mos	darnel	dâr"-nel	Hittite	hit"-it
Amoz	a"-moz	Damascus	da-mas"-kus	Horeb	ho"-reb
Anna	a"-na	Decapolis	di-ca"-po-lis	Hosea	ho-za"-a, ho-ze"-a
Annas	a"-nas	denarius, -rii	de-nâr"-e-us,	Hur	hûr
Antioch	an"-te-ok		de-nâr"-e-e		
Apollos	a-pol"-os	Deuteronomy	dyu-têr-on"-o-me	Iconium	i-ko"-ne-um
Arabah	âr"-a-ba	drachmas	drak"-maz	Immanuel	i-man"-yu-el
Aramaean	âr-a-me"-an			Isaac	i"-zak
Archelaus	âr-ke-la"-us	Ebed-melech	e-bed-mel"-ek	Isaiah	i-za"-a
Arimathaea	âr-i-ma-the"-a	Ecclesiastes	e-kle-ze-as"-tez	Iscariot	is-kàr"-e-ot
Asa	a"-sa	Elamites	el"-a-mitz	Israel	iz"-ra-el, iz"-re-el
Asher	a"-shêr	Eldad	el"-dad	Israelites	iz"-re-*l-itz
Attalia	a-ta-li"-a	Eleazar	el-e-a"-zèr	Ituraea	i-tu-re"-a
Azariah	a-za-ri"-a	Eli	e"-li		
Azor	a"-zôr	Eli, Eli, lama	a"-le, a"-le, la"-ma	Jairus	ji"-rus
		sabachthani	sa-bak-ta"-ne	Javan	ja"-van
Baal-shalishah	ba"-al-sha"-li-sha,	Eliab	e-li"-ab	Jechoniah	jek-o-ni"-a
	bal" ...	Eliakim	e-li"-a-kim	Jehoshaphat	je-hosh"-a-fat,
Babel	ba"-b*l	Elijah	e-li"-ja		je-hos"-a-fat
Babylon	ba"-bi-lon	Elisha	e-li"-sha	Jeremiah	jàr-a-mi"-a
Barabbas	bâr-ab"-as	Eliud	e-li"-ud	Jericho	jàr"-i-ko
Barnabas	bâr"-na-bas	Eloi, Eloi, lama	a"-loy, a"-loy, la"-ma	Jerusalem	je-ru"-sa-lem
Barsabbas	bâr-sa"-bas	sabachthani	sa-bak-ta"-ne	Jesse	jes"-e
Bartholomew	bâr-thol"-om-yu	Emmanuel	e-man"-yu-el	Jethro	jeth"-ro
Bartimaeus	bâr-ti-me"-us	Emmaus	e-ma"-us	Joanna	jo-an"-a
Baruch	bàr"-uk	Ephah	e"-fa	Job	job
Beelzebul	be-el"-za-b*l	Ephesians	e-fe"-zhanz	Joel	jo"-*l
Bethany	beth"-a-ne	Ephphatha	ef"-a-tha	Jonah	jo"-na
Bethel	beth"-el	Ephraim	e"-fra-im, ef"-r*m	jonquil	jon"-kwil
Bethlehem	beth"-le-hem	Ephrata	e"-fra-ta	Joram	jôr"-am
Bethphage	beth"-fa-je	Ephrathah	e"-fra-tha,-ta	Joses	jo"-ses
Bethsaida	beth-sa"-i-da	Euphrates	yu-fra"-tez	Joset	jo"-set
Boaz	bo"-az	Ezekiel	e-zek"-e-el	Joshua	josh"-yu-a
				Josiah	jo-si"-a

Jotham	jo"-th*a*m
Judah	ju"-d*a*
Judaism	ju"-d*e*-izm
Judas (Iscariot)	ju"-d*a*s (is-kàr"-**e**-ot)
Judea, Judaea	ju-de"-*a*
Justus	jus"-tus
Kedron	k**e**d"-ron
Lazarus	la"-z*a*-rus
Lebanon	leb"-*a*-non
Levi	l**e**"-vi
Levite(s)	l**e**"-v**i**t(z)
Leviticus	le-vit"-i-cus
Libya	lib"-**e**-*a*
Lud	lud
Lysanius	li-s**a**"-n**e**-us
Lystra	lis"-tr*a*
Maccabees	mac"-*a*-b**e**z
Macedonia	ma-s*a*-do"-n**e**-*a*
Magdala	mag"-d*a*-la
Magdalene	mag"-d*a*-l*I**n
Malachi	mal"-*a*-k**i**
Malchiah	mal-ki"-*a*
Malchus	mal"-kus
Mamre	mam"-r**e**
Manasseh	m*a*-nas"-e
manna	ma"-n*a*
Massah	mas"-*a*
Matthat	math"-at
Matthew	math"-y**u**
Matthias	ma-thi"-*a*s
Medad	m**e**"-dad
Medes	m**e**dz
Megiddo	me-gid"-**o**
Melchizedek	mel-kiz"-e-dek
Meribah	mêr"-i-b*a*
Mesopotamia	m**e**"-s**o**-p**o**-ta"-m**e**-*a*
Micah	m**i**"-k*a*
Midian	mid"-**e**-an
Moriah	m**o**-r**i**"-*a*
Moshech	m**o**"-shek
myrrh	mûr
Naaman	na"-*a*-man
Nahshon	na"-shon
Nain	na"-in
Naphtali	naf"-t*a*-l**i**
Nathan	na"-th*a*n
Nathanael	na-than"-y*l
Nazara	na"-z*a*-ra
Nazarene	na"-z*a*-r**e**n
Nazareth	na"-z*a*-reth
Nebuchadnezzar	neb"-y**u**-k*a*d-nez"-êr
Nehemiah	n**e**-he-m**i**"-*a*
Nicanor	ni-k**a**"-nôr
Nicodemus	ni-ko-d**e**"-mus
Nicolaus	ni-ko-l**a**"-us
Nineveh	ni"-ne-v*

Nun	nun
Obed	**o**"-bed
Omega	**o**"-me-g*a*, **o**-me"-g*a*
Onesimus	o-nes"-i-mus
Ophir	**o**"-fer
Pamphylia	pam-fi"-l**e**-*a*
Parmenas	pâr"-me-n*a*s
Parthians	pâr"-the-*a*nz
Patmos	pat"-mos, pat"-m**o**s
Perez	pêr"-ez
Perga	pêr"-g*a*
Persia	pêr"-zh*a*
Phanuel	fan"-y**u**-el
Pharaoh	fàr"-**o**
Pharisees	fàr"-i-s**e**z
Philemon	fi"-li-mon
Philippi	fi-lip"-**i**
Philippians	fi-lip"-**e**-anz
Phrygia	fri"-j**e**-*a*
phylacteries	fi-lak"-t*-r**e**z
Pisidia	pi-si"-d**e**-*a*
Pontius Pilate	pon"-shus pi"-l*t
Pontus	pon"-tus
Portico	pôr"-ti-k**o**
Praetorium	pre-tôr"-**e**-um
Prochorus	pr**o**-kôr"-us, pr**o**"-ko-rus
proselytes	pro"-s*a*-l**i**tz
Put	p**u**t
Qoheleth	ko-hel"-eth
Quirinius	kwi-rin"-**e**-us
Rabbuni	ra-b**u**"-n**e**
Rehab	r**a**"-hab
Ram	ram
Rehoboam	re-o-b**o**"-am
Rephidim	ref"-i-dim
Rosh	r**o**sh, rosh
Rufus	r**u**"-fus
Sabaoth	s*a*"-b*a*-**o**t, s*a*"-b*a*-**o**th
Sadduccees	sad"-j**u**-s**e**z
Salem	s**a**"-lem
Salmon	sal"-mon
Salome	s*a*-l**o**"-m**e**
Samaria	s*a*-màr"-**e**-*a*
Samaritan(s)	s*a*-màr"-i-t*a*n(z)
Sanhedrin	san"-hi-drin, san-he"-drin
Saul	sol
Scythian	sith"-**e**-*a*n
Seba	s**e**"-ba
Shaphat	sha"-f*a*t
Sharon	shàr"-*n
Shealtiel	she-al"-t**e**-el
Sheba	she"-b*a*
Shebna	sheb"-n*a*

Shechem	she"-kem, shek"-*a*m
Sheol	she"-**o**l
Shinar	shi"-nar
Shunem	shu"-nem
Shunammitess	shu"-n*a*-mi"-tes
Sidon	si"-d*n
Sidonian	si-d**o**"-ne-*a*n
Silas	si"-l*a*s
Siloam	si-l**o**"-*a*m, si-l**o**"-*a*m
Silvanus	sil-va"-nus
Simeon	sim"-**e**-*n
Sinai	s**i**"-n**i**
Sion	s**i**"-*n, z**i**"-*n
Sirach	s**i**"-rak
Sodom	sod"-*m
Solomon	sol"-o-m*n
Sosthenes	sos"-the-nez
Sovereignty, -ties	sov"-rin-te(z)
Susanna	s**u**-za"-n*a*
Sychar	si"-kâr
Syria	se"-r**e***a*
Syrian	se"-re-*a*n
Talitha kum	ta-li"-th*a* k**u**m
Tamar	t**a**"-mâr
Tarshish	târ"-shish
Tarsus	târ"-sus
tetrarch	tet"-rârk
Thaddaeus	tha"-d**e**-us, tha-d**e**"-us
Theophilus	the-of"-i-lus
Thessalonians	thes"-*a*-l**o**"-ne-anz
Thessalonika	thes"-*a*-lo"-ne-k*a*
Tiberias	ti-be"-r**e**-*a*s
Tiberius Caesar	ti-be"-r**e**-us se"-zêr
Timaeus	ti-me"-us
Timon	ti"mon
Titus	ti"-tus
Trachonitis	tra"-k**o**-ni"-tus
Tubal	t**u**"-b*a*l
Tyre	t**i**r
Ur	ûr
Uriah	y**u**-r**i**"-*a*
Uzziah	*-z**i**"-*a*
wadi	w*a*"-d**e**
Zacchaeus	za-ke"-us
Zadok	za"-dok
Zarephath	zàr"-*a*-fat
Zealot	zel"-*t
Zebedee	zeb"-i-d**e**
Zebulon, Zebulun	zeb"-y**u**-lon
Zechariah	zek"-*a*-r**i**"-*a*
Zedekiah	zed"-*a*-k**i**"-*a*
Zephaniah	zef"-*a*-n**i**"-*a*
Zerah	ze"-r*a*
Zerubbabel	ze-r**u**"-b*a*-bel
Zion	z**i**"-*n
Ziph	zif

Key:

Accented syllable is marked by "

f**a**te	**e**vil	b**i**te	h**o**pe	j**u**te
fat	bet	bit	hop	but
târ	hêr	fîr	ôr	tûrn
alas	wanted	easily	book	pull
*las	want*d	eas*ly	b*k	p*ll
sh**à**re			cow	
extr*a*			boy	

NOTES

NOTES

NOTES

NOTES

NOTES

NOTES

NOTES

NOTES

NOTES